ALSO BY RICHARD KREITNER

Break It Up: Secession, Division,
and the Secret History of America's Imperfect Union

Booked: A Traveler's Guide to
Literary Locations Around the World

FEAR NO PHARAOH

FEAR NO PHARAOH

AMERICAN JEWS,

THE CIVIL WAR,

and the

FIGHT TO END SLAVERY

RICHARD KREITNER

Farrar, Straus and Giroux
New York

Farrar, Straus and Giroux
120 Broadway, New York 10271

Printed in the United States of America
First edition, 2025

Library of Congress Control Number: 2024035532
ISBN: 978-0-374-60845-3

Designed by Patrice Sheridan

Our books may be purchased in bulk for promotional, educational, or business
use. Please contact your local bookseller or the Macmillan Corporate and
Premium Sales Department at 1-800-221-7945, extension 5442, or by email at
MacmillanSpecialMarkets@macmillan.com.

www.fsgbooks.com
Follow us on social media at @fsgbooks

1 3 5 7 9 10 8 6 4 2

For my grandparents—

Muriel and Gerald Lesonsky,
Elaine and Horace Kreitner

For Zion's sake I will not keep silent
And for Jerusalem's sake I will not rest,
Until her righteousness goes forth as brightness,
And her salvation as a burning torch.

—ISAIAH 62:1

Contents

FEAR NO PHARAOH

Introduction

JUDAISM IS AN OLD TRADITION. SLAVERY IS EVEN older. Modeled on the domestication of animals, it appeared early in the world's first civilizations, its legitimacy—and its limits—laid out in codes of law carved into stone. Ancient slavery looked different from the version that later took hold in the Americas—different, too, from its murkier present-day form. Yet the goal, typically, was the same: to reduce human beings to a state of submission, to make them into bodies wholly subject to the will of others. A stalwart defender of the practice, Aristotle held that slaves, by definition, were subhuman.

Having once been enslaved was nothing to brag about, then, either for an individual or a community. It denoted weakness, subjugation, vulnerability. Had they not made it the basis of one of the most influential narratives in human history, it might seem strange for a people to have put the memory of imprisonment in a foreign land at the center of the epic tale of their own origins and destiny. And yet there it is, at the beating heart of the Jewish tradition—a rebellion of slaves against their masters. A charismatic leader, summoned by a deity in the desert, guides them out of bondage.

The enslaver's army, tricked into pursuing the runaways, meets its just, violent end. Passover, a central holiday in the Jewish tradition, marks the successful exodus.

This narrative, however familiar today, offered something truly new in the ancient world: By commemorating the experience of slavery rather than obscuring it, the story placed freedom from bondage at the core of the people's nationhood and their religion. Why tell such a story? Why cherish and memorialize it? Whatever its roots in reality, however contrived, the Exodus story relates not only the birth of a people but the origin of their essential ideas. The liberation from Egypt is to be remembered and reenacted, year after year, with each participant in the Passover seder encouraged to imagine that they, too, were personally delivered from bondage.

It is striking, in the biblical tale, that as soon as the Hebrews escape enslavement they devote their attention to coming up with laws governing the same oppressive institution they just fled. As the Book of Exodus has it, one of the first items of business after the desert wanderers receive the Ten Commandments is lessening the burden of their own slaves.

The law code of the Torah, the Hebrew Bible, like the even older Code of Hammurabi, establishes rules about slavery to limit its cruelty. Slaves have rights. There are limits to how long one can hold them. Fellow Israelites who have fallen into slavery (usually to pay off a debt) must be freed after six years and given sheep and wine as parting gifts. Slaves are not permitted to work on the Sabbath. "Thou shalt not deliver unto his master the servant which is escaped from his master unto thee," one provision demands—an obligation to shelter runaways rather than turn them in.

The practice, however, was not banned—an ambiguity that left open to interpretation the ancient scripture's fundamental position on the rightness or wrongness of bondage.

Throughout the Bible, and especially in the Haggadah text read and recited at every Passover seder, Jews are urged to "remember that you were a slave in Egypt, and that the Lord your God redeemed you from there." But what does that mean in the modern world? Is the point that Jews should remember their years of bondage so as to avoid being persecuted ever again, or is it that slavery, like all subjugation, is inherently wrong and unjust and that Jews should seek to end oppression for everyone?

The United States appeared to be disintegrating. Abraham Lincoln had carried every state in the North and none in the South. South Carolina was about to secede from the Union, and other states were likely to follow. The outgoing president, James Buchanan, opposed disunion but believed the federal government had no power to stop it. Instead of acting to crush the rebellion, he issued a proclamation, "in view of the present distracted and dangerous condition of our country," naming January 4, 1861, a national day of prayer.

When the day came, Morris Jacob Raphall addressed his congregation, B'nai Jeshurun, one of the most prominent synagogues in New York. A leading traditionalist rabbi, Raphall was a favorite of well-heeled business and civic leaders who maintained close commercial ties with the South. The Union fracturing even as he spoke, Raphall gave a sermon arguing that the Southerners were right: the Bible endorsed the practice of human slavery. Addressing abolitionists who claimed the opposite, Raphall asked, "Does it not strike you that you are guilty of something very little short of blasphemy?"

Raphall's sermon brought to an abrupt end the efforts of many American Jews to avoid the subject dividing the nation. Some praised his interpretation. Others agreed with his arguments but opposed any political intervention from the pulpit. Only a few condemned him outright. To David Einhorn, Raphall had effectively taken the side of the Jews' historical oppressors. The rabbi of a Baltimore synagogue, Einhorn represented the leading edge of a new religious movement: Reform Judaism, which criticized established rabbinic authorities and questioned long-accepted traditions. Not all Reform Jews opposed slavery, and not all traditional Jews supported it. But Einhorn's belief that the Bible should be interpreted not as timeless, divine revelation but as a relatively progressive document from a primitive time informed his opinion that defending slavery in the name of the Torah amounted to a betrayal of Jewish ideals—and even a threat to Jewish interests. Claiming that God condoned the oppression of an entire people would "prove the greatest triumph of our adversaries and our own *destruction*," Einhorn warned in a response to Raphall, "and would be paying too dearly for the fleeting, wavering favor of this moment."

Einhorn was far from representative of most Jews in America. Some affirmed Raphall's defense of the South, while others argued for Jews not to get involved. They thought nothing good could come from an already vulnerable group getting embroiled in a bitter political debate, especially one likely to lead to civil war. Another rabbi in Baltimore, an Orthodox critic of Einhorn, merely wished that "the whole thing should pass peacefully for the Jews." Isaac Mayer Wise, an influential Cincinnati rabbi, published an editorial whose title, "Silence, Our Policy," announced what he believed should be the official Jewish position. Silence seemed the best way to protect American Jews from both external hostility and internal schism.

For David Einhorn, by contrast, a Jewish community preserved at the cost of its commitment to equality and justice would be worse than no community at all. Within days of the outbreak of the Civil War, his fiery denunciations of human bondage led to a proslavery mob threatening his life. Even then, Einhorn refused to be silent. "Jews for thousands of years consciously or unconsciously were fighting for freedom of conscience," he argued. They were fighting not only for themselves but "for the whole world."

This book is about how American Jews shaped and participated in the most wrenching conflict of our national history—the fight over slavery that culminated in the Civil War—and how that conflict, in turn, shaped the lives of American Jews even long after the war.

As the country broke apart, Jews in both the North and the South and across political and religious divides wrestled with common questions: Did assimilation require complicity with America's worst practices, or could a long-oppressed people achieve lasting security only by urging the nation to live up to its supposed ideals? Was the temptation to place self-preservation above all else a retreat from Judaism's deepest ethical principles, or a pragmatic lesson to draw from the Jews' sorrowful history of exiles and inquisitions? Should American Jews stick together no matter what, or should each individual do whatever seemed necessary—toss aside musty old laws and rituals, work on the Sabbath, even convert to another faith—to survive and succeed in the promising but cutthroat world of nineteenth-century America?

While surveying the varied experiences of the country's small but growing Jewish community, a population that rose from just 15,000 in 1840 to 50,000 in 1850, then soared to 150,000 on the eve of the war, we will follow six individuals whose experiences help illuminate these larger tendencies and themes. Three are the rabbis who debated the Jewish view of slavery in 1861: Morris J. Raphall, the slavery-defending traditionalist; Isaac Mayer Wise, who wanted Jews to stay out of the controversy so as not to draw unwanted attention; and David Einhorn, the bold dissident who denounced both Raphall's proslavery position and Wise's quietism as a betrayal of what it meant to be a Jew.

The other three with whom we will navigate the perilous waters of the 1850s and 1860s were not rabbis—nor, for the most part, religiously observant at all—but political actors and activists. Out on the western plains, amid an outbreak of bitter political violence that foreshadowed the deadlier cataclysm to come, we will follow the transatlantic freedom fighter August Bondi, a veteran of the failed 1848 revolutions in Europe who, once in the United States, took up arms with the abolitionist John Brown and later joined the Union Army. Devoted to the cause of liberty, appalled by the mistreatment of enslaved people that he witnessed on his travels through the antebellum South, Bondi embodies the ideals that many Jewish immigrants brought to the United States—and the limits to how far they were willing to go to put those ideals into effect.

We will also follow Ernestine Rose, the daughter of a Polish rabbi, who began traveling around the United States within months of her 1836 arrival in New York, condemning women's subjugation, economic inequality, organized religion, and chattel slavery. A close friend of reformers like Susan B. Anthony, Rose often stood alone—the rare Jew among abolitionists, and atheist among feminists. Disavowing biblical inspiration for her antislavery activism, it was only amid the unprecedented surge of anti-Jewish bigotry during the Civil War that Rose finally decided to speak up for her fellow Jews and identify herself with the people she had once spurned.

Our sixth and final character is at once the best-known and perhaps the most elusive: Judah P. Benjamin. A former slave-owning sugar planter from Louisiana who served as a US senator and then the most powerful member of the Confederate cabinet, Benjamin, like Rose, wanted nothing to do with the Judaism in which he had been raised. And yet, also like Rose, Benjamin could never completely escape identification as a Jew. A close confidant of Confederate president Jefferson Davis, yet conspicuously absent from the Lost Cause pantheon, a mystery to his friends and, later, to his biographers (one called him "one of the most secretive men who ever lived"), Benjamin offers a revealing example of the choices and compromises many American Jews of the time made in order to succeed in a country that had not yet proved it was willing to accept them. Eager to downplay (but not deny) his Jewish identity and show himself a loyal American, Benjamin embraced the cause of slavery—even to the point of committing treason against the United States.

When the stories of Jewish slave owners and abolitionists, rabbis and atheists, city dwellers and frontiersmen, are put into conflict and conversation with each other, certain suggestive coincidences and correspondences become legible. Only then is it possible to begin to answer questions that could hardly be more historically significant or relevant today. How did Jews in America, from the profoundly devout to the avowedly nonreligious, confront the practice of slavery and the racism that upheld it? How did they make sense of the systems of oppression and discrimination they found as immigrants in a new land? Did they see themselves as allies of the victims of those systems, or did they aspire to be the beneficiaries? This book shows how two histories often told separately—the story of slavery and white supremacy in America and the story of the Jews in America—have in fact, from the very beginning, been thoroughly intertwined.

The subject of American Jews and American slavery has been discussed in a few academic papers and in a handful of books and biographies—and in irresponsible and inflammatory works of propagandistic pseudo-scholarship trafficking in outright lies that, despite numerous and thorough debunkings, still circulate to this day. Strangely, the topic has never been given its proper due, foregrounding the rich lives and consequential careers of the major players against the well-known events of a crucial period in American history, when a succession of rapid changes and political crises forced all Americans to navigate moral conflicts and weigh the competing imperatives of collective unity and local loyalties. In that sense, Jews were just like everyone else—perhaps only more so. The experience of one small and scattered community at a time of intense turmoil reveals deeper, more universal truths about the immigrant encounter with American politics, the contest over slavery, and the continuing battle over its legacy.

This story also represents the little-known first chapter of a more familiar saga: how successive generations of Jews have engaged in American politics and assimilated, fitfully and never quite fully, into the mainstream of American society. Usually, that tale begins with the massive wave of east European immigration in the 1880s, when my own ancestors came over, and follows a clean, linear arc from outcasts to insiders, Yiddish-speaking socialists to suburb-dwelling liberal stalwarts. Winding the clock back just a few decades shows a more complicated trajectory and highlights aspects of the American Jewish experience that have not been adequately acknowledged or addressed—perhaps in part because of fear of playing into conspiracy-minded distortions. But that silence, a continuation of the strategy adopted by many American Jews during the period in question, has only ceded the field to hateful exaggerations of Jewish iniquity on the one hand, and comforting, self-congratulatory delusions on the other.

It is a story that resists easy answers or generalizations. It may be clear to us that the only defensible position on slavery was to be opposed to it, and, as this book will show, there were indeed American Jews who, like David Einhorn, saw slavery for the evil it was and called for its abolition. But many more were either silent or complicit. It would be simple enough to dismiss them. Yet careful consideration of the challenges American Jews faced in the period shows how difficult it was for both leaders and ordinary men and women to figure out where they fit in American society and what they thought should be done about the most divisive political issue of the day. For those in the South, outright criticism of the slave system would have been dangerous. In the North, Jews gravitated toward the immigrant-friendly Democratic Party and adopted its generally proslavery views. Speaking out against slavery would mean criticizing an institution protected by the country's hallowed Constitution, a document that Jewish immigrants—many of them refugees from persecution, deeply grateful to have been taken in—all but worshipped for its unparalleled guarantee of religious freedom. Declaring oneself an abolitionist would have meant standing out in the crowd, an armed and dangerous one at that.

Nor was it obvious—not that it ever is—what the properly *Jewish* position truly was. This was an era when the meaning and purpose of both the United States and of Judaism had been thrown wildly in flux. How the slavery struggle would turn out, what opinions and actions would seem centuries later to have been vindicated by history, was hardly clear to everyone at the time. Appreciating this atmosphere of chaos and uncertainty, trying to understand why people in the past made the choices and compromises they did, is crucial for understanding not only that period of Jewish and American divisions but our own.

PART I

"When Israel Was in Egypt Land . . ."

1

"Emancipation of All Kinds"

FOR AS LONG AS HE COULD REMEMBER, AUGUST BONDI enjoyed freshly laundered clothes and well-polished shoes brought to him by a servant every morning. His father, Herz Emanuel, heir to a successful clothing business in Prague, had moved to Vienna with his new wife, Martha, shortly after their marriage in 1832. The following year, Martha gave birth to their first child, a boy. A proud Mason, Herz raised August to admire the secret order, as well as the immortal Napoleon, whom he had once glimpsed on a bridge during the Battle of Dresden. The great emperor, for all his faults, had brought the French Revolution's emancipation of the Jews to every land he had conquered. Decades later, Jews across Europe, groaning under their reimposed yoke, continued to lament his downfall.

For a Jewish boy in central Europe in the mid-nineteenth century, August received an unusually rigorous education, learning not only German and Hungarian but Hebrew, French, and Latin. His parents observed Jewish customs and laws but also exposed him to other traditions. They had him read the New Testament by the time he was eight years old. The young scholar often embarked on long walks around the Austrian capital with his tutor—"an enthusiastic

Jew," Bondi later remembered, but one who looked at religion from "a liberal standpoint." Though his religious observance would wax and wane through his long and eventful life, August remained committed to what the tutor taught him to revere as the core ethical teaching of Judaism: "Thou must love the Eternal, thy God and thy neighbor as thyself." He would never keep a kosher home, but he did consider himself, too, an "enthusiastic Jew," and a "lover of humanity."

Around the time of August's bar mitzvah, the Bondi family ran into trouble. In 1846, following the devastating potato blight in Ireland, European economies crashed. Herz's business failed, and he soon landed in debtors' prison. Martha, a strong-willed and resourceful woman, arranged the necessary bribes to get her husband released. But the corrupt imperial system had grown insupportable, triggering an eruption that August would always remember with fondness and awe: "those glorious days of March, 1848," when young revolutionaries sought to "kindle the light of freedom of 'Liberty' in priest-ridden, despotism-cursed Austria."

What began as a small, disorganized student uprising against censorship turned into a general revolution after soldiers fired on a crowd of protesters, fourteen-year-old Bondi among them. Friends fell dead all around him. As he crawled out from the pile of bodies, a soldier pummeled him in the head with a musket. Another punctured his overcoat with a bayonet. He escaped through Vienna's narrow streets, blood soaking through his hat and trickling down his back.

That night, the emperor gave in to the protesters' demands. Klemens von Metternich, the ironfisted Austrian chancellor for nearly a third of a century, stepped down. The insurgents formed a people's militia to keep order in the city. Students organized an Academic Legion, split into five corps based on scholarly disciplines. Borrowing a gun from his neighbor, August joined the Battalion of the Faculty of Philosophy. One of its youngest members, he later claimed to have been the first in Vienna to suggest using a pick and crowbar to lift the granite blocks of the city's streets to build barricades. Within hours, hundreds had gone up around the city.

The revolution seemed like a success. The emperor left town on a curiously timed vacation. The people controlled the city. For young August, the atmosphere was intoxicating. He loved listening to the older revolutionaries denounce tyranny and debate the most pressing reforms. "We boys were fairly fanaticized with sympathy for the downtrodden of the globe," Bondi would remember. "All our aspirations centered in the longing for a government in which thrones did not exist."

Yet it soon became clear that the emperor had no intention of following through on his promises. A massacre of protesters in Prague seemed to augur a similar crackdown in Vienna. The Bondis decided it was time to leave. The family boarded an evening train out of Vienna. As it wound through the city, fifteen-year-old August watched the cross on top of St. Stephen's Cathedral, "gilded by the setting sun," fade into the distance. He buried his face in his hands and cried himself to sleep.

Tens of thousands of central European Jews like the Bondis, along with many more non-Jews, crossed the Atlantic in the wake of the crackdown that followed the 1848 uprisings in Vienna and Prague, Paris and Berlin, Budapest and Milan. Some sought political liberty or freedom from religious discrimination, but most came looking for economic opportunity. Reports had circulated for more than a century of the undreamt-of prosperity, as well as the relative freedom and equality, to be found in America. Unlike in most of Europe, Jews in the United States could own property, homes, and businesses without having to seek permission from the state. They could marry whomever they wished, live and work how and where they wanted, and they would not be pressed into military service. Jews served in high public office and edited some of the nation's most popular newspapers. They lived in bustling seaboard towns and cities and in newly cleared settlements on the frontier. Though far from universally accepted socially, legally they belonged: According to the Naturalization Act of 1790, white immigrants could apply for citizenship after residing in the United States for only five years. Crucially, European Jews, however little English they spoke, however foreign their manners, were always and immediately considered, under the law, as white.

America offered unparalleled promise to those Jews facing a new wave of backlash following the failed revolutions in Europe. The new arrivals scattered across the United States. Some achieved prominence in journalism, others in chemistry or medicine. A few became successful merchants and manufacturers. Many struggled to make ends meet as roving peddlers, hawking goods in their packs as they hoofed it across the land.

To that point, most American Jews had tried their best to stay aloof from politics and contentious public issues. Jews in the early United States still faced bigotry and exclusion, both official and otherwise: they could not hold public office in Maryland until 1826, in North Carolina until 1868, in New Hampshire until 1877. Everywhere they had to reckon with the taunts of Christian neighbors and the condescending solicitations of evangelizing missionaries and societies promoting the conversion of the Jews. The hostility that new Jewish residents (and their native-born coreligionists) met with in America hardly matched what they had faced in Europe, yet the typical struggles of all new immigrants—making rent, finding a job, building a life—were compounded for Jews by a centuries-old prejudice that often kept them from easily blending in.

In that sometimes hostile atmosphere, it was best to simply keep one's head down and not draw attention. But after 1848, the new arrivals brought a vigorous and sometimes radical energy that transformed the small Jewish communities they joined. Their hopes disappointed but their ideals intact, many of the émigrés looked for a worthy substitute for the struggles that had been tragically lost at the barricades in Europe. In America, those ideals could have another chance.

The immigrants did not have to look far for a cause worthy of their efforts. After leaving Vienna, the Bondis stopped in Prague to say goodbye to relatives, then traveled by stagecoach, steamship, and railroad to the German port town of Bremen, where they boarded a large three-mast ship, the *Rebecca*, bound for America. Unlike the 180 other passengers who braved the voyage in steerage, the Bondis, despite their financial setbacks, could afford one of the ship's three well-appointed cabins. After six weeks at sea, the *Rebecca* dropped anchor at La Balize, an old French town at the mouth of the Mississippi, battered by hurricanes and soon to disappear beneath the waves. From there they switched to a tugboat headed upstream to New Orleans. The next day, the boat stopped for wood at a sugar plantation along the riverbank, and it was there that August caught his first glimpse of American slaves. They were wearing coffee sacks tied around their waists and seemed, to his mind, to have only recently arrived from Africa. Bondi did not record the name of the plantation, but it is possible, given his description of its location, that both the plantation and its sack-clad workers were owned by a fellow Jew—though hardly, in this case, an enthusiastic one.

———

Around the time that August Bondi and his family fled revolution-wracked Vienna, a Jewish lawyer in New Orleans, nearly blinded through overwork, began overhauling his vast sugar plantation on a bend in the Mississippi just downstream from the lively, polyglot city. Brilliant, audacious, and endlessly curious, the lawyer threw himself into the project, corresponding with leading scientists and studying up on the latest advances in sugar refinement. Aspiring gentleman that he was, however, he would not be doing the work himself. He purchased no fewer than 140 slaves to manage his plantation and execute his experiments. That made him the largest Jewish slave owner of his time.

Caribbean-born, Charleston-raised Judah Benjamin would later serve as attorney general, secretary of war, and secretary of state for the Confederate States of America, the closest adviser to President Jefferson Davis. He profited from slavery and gave every appearance of being a true believer. Yet a few years earlier, in 1842, litigating a high-profile case over a slave revolt at sea, Benjamin had made a startling concession to antislavery arguments. He acknowledged that holding people in bondage deprived the enslaved of their humanity. "What is a slave?" Benjamin asked the Louisiana Supreme Court. "He is a human being. He has feeling and passion and intellect. His heart, like the heart of the white man, swells with love, burns with jealousy, aches with sorrow, pines under restraint and discomfort, boils with revenge and ever cherishes the desire for liberty."

Echoing Shylock's famous speech in *The Merchant of Venice*— "Hath not a Jew eyes? . . . If you prick us, do we not bleed?"— Benjamin was making a canny legal argument on behalf of a deep-pocketed client, an insurance company that did not want to pay for human cargo lost in the mutiny: Because slavery violated the natural rights of its victims, the risk of insurrection was built into the system, and the insurance company should not be held liable when an uprising occurred.

Benjamin never again said anything of the kind and was embarrassed when abolitionists used his words to buttress their own arguments. He was not about to condemn the very social and economic system in which he was eagerly seeking to gain a foothold. Indeed, Benjamin may have purchased his own plantation and the slaves to work it in part because he feared that as a Jew, and therefore an outsider from the Southern political elite, he would be deemed a potential threat to the slave system unless he presented himself as both its direct beneficiary and stalwart defender.

Judaism and slavery had been intertwined in Benjamin's life

from the beginning. Born on the British territorial island of St. Croix in 1811, the son of Sephardic parents who had moved from London, Benjamin spent his formative years learning to find his way as an outsider. When he was two years old, the family left St. Croix for North Carolina, before finally settling in Charleston, South Carolina, in 1822. The commercial capital of the Deep South, Charleston was also home to the largest community of Jews in the United States. The Benjamins lived in a neighborhood with many Jews as well as with other German-speaking immigrants, just blocks from the largest slave market in the South. Judah's parents owned a fruit stand on King Street, at the heart of the city's main shopping district. It was largely run by Judah's hardworking mother, Rebecca, who came from a more respectable family than her husband. Of her eight children—four boys and four girls—Rebecca placed her greatest hopes in Judah, who often helped out at the shop.

Judah's bookish, somewhat hapless father, Philip, was a member of Charleston's Congregation Beth Elohim, founded in 1749 by Spanish and Portuguese Jews. In 1824, however, he helped lead a rebellion of reformists who wanted briefer, English-language services, as well as other innovations. Eventually, Philip would be kicked out of the reformers' society, too, for refusing to close the family's shop on the Sabbath. At a time when many cities banned trading on Sundays—the traditional Christian day of rest—Jewish merchants faced a difficult choice: ignore their own Sabbath laws or lose out to gentile competitors. Like many Jews in the new republic, the elder Benjamin opted to toss tradition aside and work on Saturday, even after the synagogue officially censured him for doing so. Whether or not they meant to teach him the lesson, Judah learned from his parents to do whatever it took to succeed, even at the cost of sundering his ties to the Jewish community.

The Benjamins were by no means wealthy, but even they owned slaves. Back in St. Croix, when Judah was born, the family had three enslaved house servants. When they first arrived in America, in 1817, they lived with Rebecca's uncle, Jacob Levy, in Fayetteville, North Carolina. Jacob owned a woman named Margaret, who cared for Judah from the age of five to eleven years old. Jacob also purchased a twenty-six-year-old man named Isaac to help raise Judah and his brother. As he grew older, Judah was attended by a house slave named Hannibal, who became his personal servant and playmate. They would often fish together in the waters off the Carolina coast.

Only weeks after the Benjamins arrived in Charleston, rumors of insurrection swept through the city. Denmark Vesey, a free Black preacher whom a fellow conspirator later testified had "read to us from the Bible, how the children of Israel were delivered out of Egyptian bondage," had allegedly plotted to murder whites en masse. A cache of weapons was found not far from the Beth Elohim synagogue. Authorities hanged some thirty-five Black people in response, including a slave owned by a wealthy Jewish plantation owner and worshipper at Beth Elohim. Some of the bodies were left swaying in the air for more than a week, the gallows visible from the top floor of the Benjamins' house.

Judah was recognized at an early age as a brilliant student, skilled at memorizing passages from Shakespeare, which he would recite while playing marbles with other boys. Impressed, a prominent Jewish merchant in Charleston offered to pay for Judah's education. At age fourteen he set off for Yale College, a book of the psalms in Hebrew in his luggage.

Benjamin stood out at Yale; the first and last Jewish student had departed nearly twenty years earlier. A former classmate later recalled Judah as "a small, bright-eyed boy, of a dark and swarthy complexion [who] passed his time in sauntering around the college grounds or dropping in at the students' room . . . Without any attention to his studies, and following out this desultory and vagrant existence, he easily and without dispute, took at once the highest stand in his class and was acknowledged to be a riddle and prodigy of intellectual power." Benjamin modeled himself after the aristocratic students around him, adopting their manner of speaking and steeping himself in the classics and natural sciences. He became an active member of the debate society, but when the election of a Northern president led the Southerners to secede and form their own club, Judah went with them.

Two years after arriving, however, Benjamin was expelled from Yale. His departure would be attributed by various sources to theft, gambling, or some other form of "ungentlemanly conduct." Whatever the cause, he returned to Charleston, still only sixteen years old, but it was clear that the city was a dead end for him, its commercial importance superseded by the westward expansion of the slave economy. There were few opportunities for an ambitious young man not already accepted by the city's gentile elite. He had disappointed his mother's high hopes; his relationship with his father never recovered. Within months, Benjamin took off for New Orleans, where he hoped to try his luck as a lawyer.

Arriving in the city with only five dollars in his pocket, he found a rambunctious, remarkably diverse port town full of peddlers, planters, sailors, prostitutes, gamblers, and businessmen, as well as a flourishing market for slaves and land, cotton from the Southern states, grain from the Midwest, spices from Asia, whale oil from the Atlantic, and indigo, sugar, and rum from the Caribbean. In just the first decade of Benjamin's residence, the town's population doubled to one hundred thousand. By 1861, some eight thousand Jews—one-third of those in the entire South—lived there. Shaped by centuries of racial and cultural mixing and without Charleston's insular planter elite, New Orleans offered an ideal venue for Benjamin's prodigious talents and boundless ambitions.

Moving to New Orleans also meant moving deeper into slave country. The entrepôt of the institution's rapid southwestern expansion, the city was defined by the presence of human bondage, no less for Jews than for others. Slave auctions were a daily occurrence, a noisy affair that drew tourists eager to gape at the misery of those bought and sold like chairs or cattle. As their fortunes rose with those of the booming city, Jewish immigrants joined the slaveholding class. Nathan Hart, the owner of a New Orleans cotton press, claimed one slave in 1820 but fifteen by 1830. Edward Gottschalk, the Jewish father of the Civil War–era composer Louis Moreau Gottschalk, owned one of the largest commission brokerages in New Orleans in the 1820s, through which he sold land, liquor, furniture, rope, and people. The famous philanthropist Judah Touro, who left huge sums on his death in 1854 to Jewish charities and synagogues around the world, largely avoided the trade in human beings. Yet even Touro profited from the 1809 sale of fifteen people owned by a firm indebted to him that had gone bankrupt, and later offered rewards for the capture of seven fugitives from a plantation owned by a client.

Studying law on the side, Benjamin worked odd jobs—in a merchant's business, as a schoolteacher, as apprentice to a notary. To master the Napoleonic Code, which still shaped the Louisiana legal system decades after France had sold the colony to the United States, Benjamin needed to learn French. A neat solution appeared in the handsome form of Natalie St. Martin. Her father, an insurance businessman who had fled the Haitian Revolution, hired the twenty-one-year-old Benjamin to teach English to his sixteen-year-old daughter. Judah accepted the offer, but only if she, in turn, taught him French. He began courting Natalie, and in 1833, just a few months after he was admitted to the bar, they were married. She brought to the union a dowry of $3,000—and two slaves.

Marrying a gentile was fairly common for Jewish men in New Orleans at the time, even for those who remained affiliated with Judaism and attended synagogue. Congregation Shaarei Chesed, founded in 1828, even permitted the non-Jewish spouses of its members to be buried in its graveyard. But Natalie's father wanted his new son-in-law to convert to Catholicism. Though he avoided identification with the rapidly growing Jewish population of New

Orleans, never joined a synagogue, and reportedly knew little of the Hebrew Bible or the religious tenets of Judaism, Benjamin refused. Jewishness represented little more than a burden, but one he knew he could never hope to completely escape. His name alone made concealment impossible. "You might well have written Jew across my forehead," he was once heard complaining to his mother. Though he would not convert, Benjamin agreed that the couple's children could be raised as Catholics rather than Jews.

In a city flourishing with shipping and trading of all kinds, as well as related businesses like insurance and railroads, Benjamin became a go-to legal expert. In 1834, he and a friend, Tom Slidell, published a digest of Louisiana case law that became indispensable for lawyers in the state. Slidell's brother John, a successful maritime lawyer and the wily leader of the local political machine, would later take Benjamin on as an understudy, propelling him into the highest echelons of the New Orleans elite.

In 1847, a New Orleans judge observed that Benjamin was "remarkable for the vivacity of his features, his sparkling and intelligent eyes, the perfect neatness and elegance of his costume, and the finished courtesy of his manners." His voice rang with "a silvery, mellifluous sweetness." Throughout his life, observers could not help commenting on Benjamin's voice. Varina Davis, first lady of the Confederacy and a close friend of Benjamin during the Civil War, recalled it as "low, full and soft, yet the timbre of it penetrated every ear like a silver trumpet."

In 1844, two years after he described slavery in court as a violation of man's natural rights, Benjamin partnered with an acquaintance to purchase Bellechasse, a sprawling old mansion south of New Orleans. Joining agriculture with industrial production, employing the most modern techniques of assembly-line work, sugar cultivation and refinement ruined human bodies so fast that the enslaved population of Louisiana actually decreased around this time, despite the influx of fresh bodies from the soil-exhausted states of the Upper South. Benjamin's labor force—some of whom young August Bondi may have glimpsed from his tugboat that day in the fall of 1848—would have required constant replenishment, and Benjamin was personally involved in the plantation's management. He could not have avoided witnessing firsthand the merciless brutalities of the system. He was directly responsible for them.

Because of his penchant for burning his correspondence and other papers, we know little about Benjamin's thoughts regarding slavery and his life as a slaveholder. It has been tempting for biographers to fill in the gaps with their own biases and flights of wishful thinking. Pierce Butler, in his 1907 study, assured his readers that Benjamin's former slaves, some of whom were still alive, related "none but kindly memories and romantic legends of the days of glory on the old place." Eighty years later, another scholar, the late Eli Evans, citing Butler, contended that Benjamin "took care to have a plantation noted for its humaneness." There is no evidence for such claims and plenty of reason to doubt the supposed "kindly memories" of formerly enslaved people, still ensnared in the web of racial domination, being interviewed by a white historian in the segregated South—one who would refer in his text to the enslaved as "hordes of half-tamed savages."

Though he bought the property to make money and to ingratiate himself with the state's planter class, Benjamin may also have hoped to satisfy his wife's desire to host lavish soirees. But his career was taking off just as his marriage was coming to an end. The union had served to smooth his social, economic, and political rise, yet rumors constantly circulated about Natalie's affairs. The year after Benjamin purchased Bellechasse—a decade into their marriage—Natalie finally gave birth to a daughter, Ninette, then fell into depression. Months later, Natalie announced that she and the baby were moving to Paris. Benjamin remained in New Orleans. He regularly sent money and even visited Paris almost every year. By all accounts, Benjamin seems to have remained faithful to a marriage that for all the world, and certainly for Natalie, had ceased to exist. He invited his mother, long separated from her shiftless husband, to move to New Orleans and live with him at Bellechasse. Benjamin stayed silent for the rest of his life about any sense of embarrassment over his wife's departure.

Salving his wounds, Benjamin threw himself into his work on the plantation. He designed innovative drainage and fertilization techniques and was the first planter in the state to try boiling the juice from sugarcane in a vacuum rather than in open pans, to increase production and efficiency. His sugar won state prizes, and the equipment he installed at his plantation continued to function for a half-century. He demolished the old house and replaced it with a larger one—with upper and lower balconies around the perimeter, soaring ceilings, a grand staircase, massive columns hewn from cypress trunks. Bellechasse became a social center for the local planter elite and the base for Benjamin's bid for public office.

In a city well-known for its mixture of cultures and ethnicities, Benjamin's Jewishness was not held against him. His rigorous preparation, brilliant speechmaking, and ingenious arguments had spread his fame outside Louisiana, and in 1848 he was admitted to practice before the United States Supreme Court. The federal government appointed him to help sort out thorny questions related to the absorption of California into the Union. Benjamin also found work as a lawyer for corporations trying to build a railroad across Central America. As befit a member of the urban elite, he gravitated to the Whig Party, which supported government subsidies for railroads, canals, and other infrastructure projects that would be good for business.

As a young representative in the Louisiana legislature, Benjamin recognized sooner than most the direction in which national politics was headed. The existing divisions between Democrats and Whigs would soon matter little, he predicted as early as 1845. A more serious division loomed over the country. "That man must be indeed blind not to perceive from whence the danger comes," he said, referring to the rise of abolitionism in the North. Recent fights over the admission of new slave states had revealed that "we must rely upon ourselves and our Southern confederates to maintain our rights and cause them to be respected, and not upon the stipulations in the Federal compact."

By the age of forty, Benjamin had already experienced a series of reversals in fortune: his expulsion from Yale, his breach with his father, his abandonment by Natalie. Many more were to come. In 1852, a crack in the Mississippi River levee flooded Bellechasse and ruined Benjamin's sugar crop. Then a friend defaulted on a $60,000 loan that Benjamin had guaranteed. It could have been a devastating setback, but the plantation had already served at least one purpose for which Benjamin had purchased it: admission into the state's political elite. Months earlier, thanks to his friend John Slidell's skillful maneuvering, Benjamin had been appointed by the Louisiana legislature to serve in the United States Senate. He was elected because, as a slave owner, he understood the interests of the planter aristocracy. "The country members rather preferred a gentleman . . . [who] was a sugar planter, and had, therefore, a common interest and sympathy with them," one paper observed. His object attained, short on cash, Benjamin sold his share in Bellechasse to his business partner for the equivalent of around $5 million today, then set off to make his mark in Washington as one of the most eloquent defenders of Southern slavery the federal legislature had ever seen.

In the spring of 1853, a few months after Judah Benjamin took his seat in the Senate, a New York–based organization called the American and Foreign Anti-Slavery Society published its annual report on the state of the movement to abolish human bondage. After surveying the opinions of various Protestant sects on the all-consuming issue, the report noted that American Jews held no communal view on the matter. Their newspapers avoided it. Even those who opposed slavery kept silent. There was no chief rabbi in America, and no central forum to debate the crisis of the Union, much less to enunciate a coherent Jewish vision about what, if anything, should be done. The report ended with a stern appeal for more Jewish support for abolition: "The objects of so much mean prejudice and unrighteous oppression as the Jews have been for ages, surely they, it would seem, more than any other denomination ought to be the enemies of CASTE, and the friends of UNIVERSAL FREEDOM."

It was true that few Jews had publicly condemned slavery. That likely had much to do with the overwhelmingly Christian nature of most antislavery organizations, including the American and Foreign Anti-Slavery Society, founded by the evangelical brothers Arthur and Lewis Tappan, conscientious businessmen whose shared lifelong goal was to "enlarge the kingdom of our Lord and Savior Jesus Christ." The Second Great Awakening, peaking between 1820 and 1840, brought new religious fervor to American life just as both abolitionism and Jewish immigration to the United States were on the rise. As the historian Maxwell Whiteman once noted, "Frequently a preacher would cite Genesis and Exodus to uphold an antislavery argument and in the following passage of a sermon, if not in the same breath, speak of Jews as 'now a corrupt people and guilty of hypocrisy, deceit, and craftiness.'" As the struggle over slavery escalated, some abolitionists even called for altering the Constitution to make America an officially Christian nation.

Turned off by such rhetoric, many Jews had only distaste for the activism it was meant to encourage. Jewish skepticism of reform movements like temperance and abolitionism was based in part on the understanding that their leaders were also involved in efforts to convert the Jews.

For all his commitment to racial equality, William Lloyd Garrison, leader of the radical wing of the antislavery movement, embodied the anti-Jewish tendencies of some abolitionist leaders. While he frequently cited the prophets of the Old Testament, Garrison rarely had a kind word to say about modern-day Jews, and he considered himself to be a more faithful interpreter of Hebrew scripture than the Jews themselves. To him, both Judaism and Catholicism were backwards cults that aided and abetted evil. The worst he could think of to say about a more theologically conventional Christian critic was that he was "groping in Jewish darkness."

When an opponent was Jewish, Garrison made sure to take note of it, and Mordecai Manuel Noah, the most prominent Jew in the United States in the second quarter of the nineteenth century, offered the perfect target for Garrison's scorn. A bombastic journalist and playwright, Noah had briefly served as consul to the Kingdom of Tunis until he was fired because, as the then secretary of state James Monroe told him, "the religion which you profess" served as an "obstacle to the exercise of your Consular functions." Noah protested the termination as an act of bigotry and, on returning home, appointed himself chief defender and spokesperson for American Jews. In 1825, alarmed by a wave of anti-Jewish riots and pogroms in Europe, Noah promoted a scheme to resettle world Jewry on an island in the Niagara River in western New York State. Wrapping himself in a gaudy Richard III costume borrowed from a Shakespearean troupe, the self-proclaimed "Judge of Israel" told a largely gentile crowd packed into a Buffalo church that his "Ararat" colony—named for the mountain where the biblical Noah's ark came to rest—would serve as a temporary "asylum for the oppressed," a proving ground where Jews could ready themselves for an eventual return to Palestine. But after widespread ridicule from Jews and Christians alike in both Europe and America—the chief rabbi of Paris dismissed Ararat as "the chimerical consulate of a pseudo-restorer," while a New York paper suggested the promoter find himself "a convenient apartment in the lunatic asylum"—Noah lost interest in the scheme. He never even set foot on the island.

Noah began his public career as a critic of slavery. "How can

Americans be engaged in this traffic," he once asked, "men whose birthright is *liberty*, whose eminent peculiarity is *freedom*?" But with age and his own shifting political fortunes, Noah allied with proslavery politicians like John C. Calhoun and became an outspoken opponent of emancipation. Like Calhoun, Noah embraced slavery as not merely an unfortunate necessity but a "positive good." In the South, Noah argued, "there is liberty under the name of slavery. A field negro has his cottage, his wife, and children, his easy task, his little patch of corn and potatoes, his garden and fruit, which are *his* revenue and property. The house servant has handsome clothing, his luxurious meals, his admitted privileges, a kind master, and an indulgent and frequently fond mistress." Noah argued that it was "perfectly ridiculous to give [free people of color] the right of suffrage—a right which they cannot value." Black people, he believed, were simply an "inferior species" to whites.

As the editor and publisher of some of New York's leading newspapers, Noah's racism was influential. The first Black-owned periodical in America, *Freedom's Journal*, was founded in part to respond to Noah, whom its editors called the "bitterest enemy" of Black Americans. Should not a Jew well acquainted with his people's history of oppression, the editors asked, "sympathize with the oppressed of every hue"?

Noah was not interested in drawing such connections. He accused abolitionists—that "set of knaves whose sole object is to prey upon the credulous and unwary"—of trying to split the North from the Union. "To emancipate slaves," he warned, "would be to jeopardize the safety of the whole country." In 1842, when an abolitionist convention met in New York, Noah, then serving as a city judge, charged a grand jury to indict any attendees who endorsed "a dissolution of our happy form of government." William Lloyd Garrison, who attended the meeting, vehemently denounced Noah and even suggested that Noah's proslavery impulses reflected the evil nature of his religion. He described Noah as a "Jewish unbeliever, the enemy of Christ and Liberty," "the miscreant Jew . . . that lineal descendant of the monsters who nailed Jesus to the cross between two thieves." Theodore Parker, a prominent abolitionist minister, alleged that Jewish minds were "sadly pinched in those narrow foreheads" and claimed that Jews "did sometimes kill a Christian baby at the Passover." Another writer in Garrison's *Liberator*, Edmund Quincy, the scion of a prominent Boston family, wrote that if Noah was "a fair specimen of the race, it is no wonder they have been an insulted and despised people."

Nor should it have been any wonder that so few Jews opted to join the abolitionists' often openly anti-Jewish crusade.

————

There was at least one Jewish abolitionist well-known to Garrison and his fellow activists. In 1847, as Judah Benjamin began overhauling his slave plantation and just before August Bondi joined the revolutionary uprising in Vienna, Ernestine Rose, a Jewish immigrant from Poland, embarked on a trip to Charleston, the belly of the proslavery beast. An outspoken atheist, feminist, and abolitionist, Rose did something unthinkable in the Charleston of that time, especially for a woman: she gave a public lecture denouncing slavery. A friend remarked that it was "due partly to her sex, and partly to the paralysis caused by her audacity, that she was not torn to pieces."

Born in 1810 in Piotrkow, a small town in central Poland thirty miles southeast of Łódź, the daughter of an Orthodox rabbi, Ernestine had always been an unusual girl. "I was a rebel at the age of five," she would recall. Most Jewish girls received little formal education at the time, but Ernestine's father accepted her request to teach her to read the Torah in Hebrew, and they often discussed what they read. Yet her probing mind and endless questions about the importance of tradition, the existence of God, and the sanctity of the Sabbath made her father fear that Ernestine was pushing the proper bounds of a girl's place in society, probing too deeply into religious mysteries that ought not be subjected to reason.

Rose would labor through her long life to obscure certain facts about her origins. She never published a memoir and, like Judah Benjamin, burned many of her papers before she died. The story she told to inquiring journalists over the years was the story she wanted recorded. It has been repeated and elaborated by biographers ever since. The truth, or part of it, has come to light only in recent years, thanks to some startling archival discoveries.

What Ernestine said was that after her mother died, leaving fifteen-year-old Ernestine a sizable inheritance, her father worked out an arranged marriage to an older man. Ernestine refused, telling her father that she intended someday to marry someone she loved, not someone who would control her. She asked her fiancé for release from the arrangement, but he refused, noting that according to his contract with her father, if Ernestine broke the engagement, her mother's inheritance would be his. Traveling to a distant town by sleigh in deep winter, Ernestine sued to be released from the engagement and won. Arriving home to find her father had remarried a woman nearly her own age, she took off for Berlin, leaving behind everything she had known.

When she arrived in the Prussian capital, Ernestine found that Jews were forbidden from moving to the city unless they posted bonds ensuring good behavior. Ernestine said she asked a police chief to make an exception for her and that he took her to a royal minister, who finally secured her an audience with the Prussian king, Frederick William III. The king suggested that Ernestine would be allowed in only if she converted to Christianity, but she refused, retorting, "I have not abandoned the trunk in order to attach myself to the branches. If my reason prevents me from being Jewish, it cannot allow me to become Christian." Impressed by the young woman's bravery and bravado, the king relented, and granted her a permit, or so she claimed.

Ernestine lived in Berlin for nearly two years, making ends meet by inventing and selling a type of perfumed paper to counter the foul odors in the crowded tenements of the city. She lived "alone, in a modest, little room," supported by the remainder of the inheritance money she had brought with her from Poland. Immersing herself in the city's literary community, she began studying "not dead books"—like the Torah her father had schooled her in—"but living ones," consuming them "with great curiosity."

Decades later, in recalling her time in Berlin to an interviewer, Ernestine would refer vaguely to having endured "public and private misfortunes" in the city. Thanks to records unearthed by the researcher Susan Higginbotham, we now know what those misfortunes were. Contrary to the story Rose liked to tell about her brave refusal to convert to Christianity in order to settle in Prussia, it turns out that that is exactly what she did, along with a young man named Marcus Kaufmann, a Jewish shopkeeper whom Ernestine subsequently married. She was pregnant, and the couple's conversion may have been necessary for Marcus to find suitable work to support the family. Shortly after the wedding, they left Berlin. Eventually the couple likely divorced. Their daughter, born in early 1829, was probably one of the two children whom Ernestine later told an interviewer she had lost at an early age. Rose never spoke of her first marriage, nor of her conversion. Her exchange with the Prussian monarch almost certainly did not occur as represented by Rose, yet her account of it suggests at least some lingering pride in her Jewish origins, as well as regret, even anger, that she had been compelled to betray them.

Ernestine spent the subsequent years traveling through Western Europe. In Paris, she witnessed a key moment in the July Revolution of 1830, when the aged revolutionary hero, the Marquis de Lafayette, presented the "citizen king" Louis Philippe as a compromise solution to the political crisis following Charles X's abdication. Ernestine tried to return to Poland to join a growing insurrection against Russian rule, but she was stopped by Austrian troops who forced her to turn back or face certain death in a Hapsburg prison. Bitterly disappointed, Ernestine would continue to identify herself with Poland, "my poor unhappy country," as she called it, "which has been prostrated, but I hope not lost."

Eventually, she found her way to London. When she was not tutoring a duke's daughters in German and Hebrew, as she later told a journalist, she attended lectures and reform meetings, soon embracing a form of socialism propagated by the utopian industrialist Robert Owen, drawn both by his embrace of religious freedom, including the freedom to have no religion at all, and by his belief that marriage should be based only on mutual love. At his company town in Scotland, Owen had banned child labor, limited work hours, and abolished physical abuse. The operation supported a generally happy and stable workforce and reaped impressive profits. Ernestine began volunteering to speak at Owenite gatherings, then organized them herself, doing everything from spreading the word beforehand to doing the dishes afterward. She later praised Owen for working "to infuse the benign spirit of charity and kindness into every heart." He taught "mankind that the law of kindness is the most effective law in the well training of man; that if we want to have man rational, consistent, virtuous, and happy, we must remove the causes that have a tendency to make him irrational, inconsistent, vicious, and consequently miserable." Owen served as a substitute father figure for Ernestine—she referred to him as "my dear and respected Father" and called herself his "Daughter"—while Owen, who lost two daughters and his wife during Ernestine's time in London, embraced the ardent Polish reformer almost as a member of his family.

It was through Owenite socialism that Ernestine met her second husband and beloved lifelong partner, William Rose, a non-Jewish English silversmith three years her junior. By all accounts theirs was a partnership of mutual respect, shared political commitments, and love for dancing. Ernestine's close friend and fellow activist, Susan

B. Anthony, would later tell a colleague that William "idolized" his wife, whose zest for liberty he never sought to control.

In 1836, William and Ernestine, then twenty-six, set sail for the United States, part of a passel of Owenites seeking to set up a new commune. But the Roses feared their comrades were not up to the task, so they broke off from the group and settled in New York City. William opened a silversmith shop—he specialized in hardware for canes and walking sticks—while Ernestine lost no time finding a cause to champion. Within months, she began gathering signatures for a petition to the New York legislature demanding that women be allowed to hold their own property rights in marriage, precisely the kind of law that would have prevented her from being held hostage to an unwanted betrothal back in Poland. Then she set out on the first of countless speaking tours to build support. She took trains when she could but mostly endured the inconveniences of public stagecoaches. Often she simply had to walk.

After five months' toil and "a good deal of trouble," Rose remembered, "I obtained five signatures." Many women simply laughed at her, while "the men said the women had too many rights already." A New York legislator who opposed the bill noted that it raised "the whole question of woman's proper place in society, in the family and everywhere." That was precisely the point for Rose. She was patient and determined. The law finally passed in early 1848, three months before the Seneca Falls convention inaugurated the women's rights movement (and just as revolution was breaking out in Europe). Rose had already been at it for more than a decade and had notched a significant victory.

Over the coming years, Rose traveled through nearly every state in the Union. With fierce eyes and curly brown hair flowing over her shoulders—she refused to cover her hair as married women were expected to do—Rose punctuated her words with emphatic hand gestures, ridiculed hecklers, and used caustic humor as well as finely honed arguments to make her points. Daringly, given that she had just arrived in the country, Rose focused on how far short America fell from its promises. Invoking the slogan "No taxation without representation," she argued that women should not be subject to laws they had not been permitted to help craft.

Just as Rose's campaign for women's rights sought to prevent others from having to depend, as she once had, on fathers and husbands for protection, her crusade against organized religion may have been a way to get back at both traditions that had sought to limit her freedom and constrict her life: Judaism when she was a girl in Poland and Christianity when she was a young woman in Berlin. A self-described "Infidel" (the term of abuse often hurled at nonbelievers), Rose eschewed religion as the source of ethical and political commitments and implored her audience to rely only on their own reasoning. She saw all religions, including Judaism, as imposing an all-encompassing darkness and obscurity on the human mind, and she compared emancipation from its constraints to the ancient Hebrews' liberation from Egyptian slavery. Rose spoke annually at celebrations to mark Thomas Paine's birthday, an attempt to restore the *Common Sense* author's reputation after it had faltered due to his more radical views on politics and religion. Yet whereas Paine simply disavowed religious belief and identification, Rose and her generation of freethinkers actively opposed them. She ridiculed one advocate at a national women's rights convention—Antoinette Brown, the first woman in the United States to be ordained as a minister—for seeking to claim biblical justification for gender equality. "We need no such authority," Rose said. "Our claims are on the broad basis of human rights, irrespective of what Moses, Paul or Peter may say." The Bible could be used to justify anything, good or evil, and "inculcates war, slavery, incest, rapine, murder, and all the vices and crimes that blind selfishness and corruption could suggest." Religion oppressed women in particular, Rose argued: "The Bible has enslaved you, the churches have been built upon your subjugated necks; do you wish to be free? Then you must trample the Bible, the church, and the priests under your feet."

Even as she compared organized religion to mental slavery, Rose also condemned "that great incomprehensible inconsistency, that slavery should exist in a country that calls itself a Republic." She became one of the most prominent abolitionist orators in the country, appearing alongside Frederick Douglass, Sojourner Truth, and William Lloyd Garrison at conventions and meetings where she was often the only woman on the speakers' platform (and was not shy pointing it out). She encouraged audiences to imagine themselves in chains: "I would that, instead of speaking and listening today, we could all sit down in perfect silence, and each and every one of us ask ourselves what is it to be a slave? . . . Slavery is not to belong to yourself—to be robbed of yourself. There is nothing that I so much abhor as that single thing—to be robbed of one's self."

Douglass later recalled how Ernestine and William Rose "met me as a brother, and by their kind consideration did much to make endurable the rebuffs I encountered elsewhere." William Lloyd Garrison praised Ernestine—possibly the first Jewish person he ever actually met—in the pages of the *Liberator*, marking her "great vigor of appeal, powers of reasoning, and masterly ability," and adding that "for one born and educated in Poland, [she] speaks our language with astonishing precision and accuracy." Rose in turn called Garrison "the great and noble voice of humanity . . . for emancipation." Yet Garrison never suggested that Rose's abolitionist activities somehow reflected positively on Jews, as Mordecai Manuel Noah's proslavery writings did negatively.

Rose frequently compared the plight of women to that of the enslaved, noting that neither was master of their own destiny. "Woman is a slave, from the cradle to the grave," she declared. "Father, guardian, husband—master still. One conveys her, like a piece of property, over to the other." While the comparison is exaggerated in many respects—white women were not treated nearly as badly as Black chattel slaves—women did effectively become the property of their husbands upon marriage, a status that the law Rose had advocated for in New York only partly alleviated. As horrific as the 1850 Fugitive Slave Law was, Rose argued one month after it passed, it was "no more unjust than some of the laws are towards women. If a woman is compelled by the tyranny and ill treatment of her husband to leave him and seek a refuge among her friends, the law will deliver her up into his hands. He may compel her return."

Rose seems to have identified with runaways from oppression. She, too, had been robbed of herself, trapped between the stultifying Orthodox Judaism of her father and the oppressive state-backed Christianity of imperial Prussia. Though a proud atheist who professed no affection for the faith of her father, in speaking publicly about her flight from Poland she at once emphasized her escape from religious despotism and her grounding in the Jewish saga of suffering and subjugation. When the chair of a women's rights convention introduced her as "a Polish lady of the Jewish faith," Rose objected that she relied on reason rather than faith as the basis for her ideals. Yet she went on to acknowledge her own background as evidence of "the universality of our claims," identifying herself as "a daughter of poor, crushed Poland, and the down-trodden and persecuted people called the Jews, 'a child of Israel.'"

Whether fighting for women's rights, economic equality, freedom from religious domination, or the abolition of slavery, Rose conceived all her causes as linked, seeing in each an extension and reflection of the others. "I go for emancipation of all kinds," Rose said, "white and black, man and woman. Humanity's children are, in my estimation, all one and the same family, inheriting the same earth; therefore there should be no slaves of any kind among them."

———

The 1848 uprisings in Europe commanded attention across the Atlantic. Watching from New York, Ernestine Rose called it "a year full of the most interesting, startling, and important events—events which . . . will become the causes of an entire change in the political and social affairs of Europe, perhaps the world."

But when the uprisings failed, the revolutionaries needed somewhere to go. Rose urged Americans to adopt a generous attitude toward them. "Every sympathy, encouragement, and means of help ought to be extended towards . . . [those who] seek shelter in this land of Liberty," Rose insisted. Perhaps she hoped that once they arrived in the United States and saw, as she did, how far short it fell from its ideals, some of the exiles would opt to keep up the fight.

August Bondi would be one of the most committed among them. Leaving behind the sack-clad slaves at the sugar plantation below New Orleans, the Bondi family disembarked in the city, then found their way by steamer to lively St. Louis, a raw, fast-expanding frontier town where thousands of German-speaking immigrants had settled in recent years. Bondi's father began working as a peddler before opening his own store, while his mother and sister ran a private school for girls. His family joined a new congregation, which, in line with the tendencies of the new arrivals, had a more relaxed approach to tradition than the older synagogue in town.

Still, the teenage Bondi grew restless and bored. His first job, as a shop clerk, did not go well. "When first ordered to sweep the store I broke out in tears," he would recall. "A late member of the Vienna Legion, to do such menial work." He tried teaching in a backwoods schoolhouse but hated to discipline the unruly students. He thought of California and finding fortune in the gold hills—as many Jews did, not so much as diggers themselves but as sellers of supplies—but his mother refused to let him go. He tried to enlist in Commodore Matthew Perry's expedition to Japan, but he arrived at the recruiting office in New Orleans just after it closed.

Along with other "political fugitives," as he described the idealistic 1848 exiles, Bondi was drawn to public debate and attended meetings whenever he could: "We youngsters from the barricades and struggles of the revolutionary movements of Germany, Austria and Hungary . . . were eager to grasp the opportunity which would prove our important political influence in our new home."

Most German speakers in the United States supported the Democratic Party, which tended to have a more welcoming view of immigration than the rival Whigs. That was an important consideration at a time when nativism was on the rise. In 1852, angry mobs attacked German immigrants in St. Louis and hurled rocks through the windows of the community's newspaper. Bondi and other Jewish immigrants would have to contend with this nativist upsurge for years.

Though largely friendly to immigrants, the Democrats were increasingly split, in Missouri and throughout the nation, between a more aggressive proslavery faction and a more skeptical splinter group. Bondi and his fellow "political fugitives" lined up behind Missouri's long-serving senator, Thomas Hart Benton, who had begun pushing back against slavery's domination of the party and the Union. Benton was far from an abolitionist. Like many opponents of "the slave power," he wanted to ensure that western expansion served white farmers and workers, not wealthy slave masters. Bondi once saw the powerful Benton, his voice "like the roaring of a lion," address a St. Louis crowd twenty thousand strong. To support Benton, Bondi helped form a group called the Freie Manner Verein, or Society of Free Men, which organized German American political influence in Missouri politics.

Yet Bondi was no radical. Had he met Ernestine Rose, he would have scorned her as a crank. He later remembered encountering a band of utopian reformers who tried to start a commune in southern Illinois, just across the Mississippi River from St. Louis. The settlers, even after their experimental village broke up, "made themselves contemptible in my eyes with their continued mouth-slobbering, upholding communism, atheism and other isms." While his antislavery activities in the United States were an outgrowth of the liberal ideas he had imbibed on the streets of revolutionary

Vienna, there was also a degree of self-interest involved. What motivated the Germans in St. Louis to line up behind Thomas Hart Benton and his antislavery politics "was not sympathy for the negro slave," Bondi would later recall, "it was antipathy against the degradation of labor." Slavery weakened the bargaining position of white workers, including new immigrants. Bondi quickly understood how identification with the white majority offered distinct advantages in nineteenth-century America.

Looking for work, Bondi ventured down to Texas, where he tended bar aboard a steamboat in the Gulf of Mexico. Sleeping on sacks of grain, he earned his keep by interpreting for the German-speaking immigrants arriving in droves. It was in Texas that Bondi first encountered up close the brutal realities of the labor system he had only dimly perceived that day at the sugar plantation below New Orleans. In Galveston, a thriving port town, Bondi woke at four o'clock in the morning to "the howlings of the slaves receiving their morning ration of cowhiding." Another time he was on a vessel that passed close to a rowboat from which the son of a local luminary was duck hunting with his manservant. When the slave accidentally let an oar drop into the water, scaring the ducks away, the angry master fired bird shot into the slave's shoulder. Bondi "loudly condemned such cruelty," as he later wrote, with "all the vinegar of an 18 years [old] smart aleck." An older man on Bondi's ship—a Methodist minister—admonished him to keep his mouth shut: "We have no use for northern abolitionists, and only your age protects you from deserved punishment."

Had he learned to keep silent, Bondi might even have become a slave owner himself. "Every good-looking young man from the north could have his pick of southern young ladies of first families," he recalled. "I disliked to marry a woman with slaves. . . . While really I did not have much sympathy for the Negroes, I felt that my father's son was not to be a slave driver."

Bondi's claim not to have had much sympathy for the enslaved might have more to do with the conservative politics he adopted in the decades after the Civil War, when he was writing his memoirs, than his actual feelings during his Southern sojourn in the early 1850s. Once, when a ship captain told him to make the enslaved workers hurry up with their loading of a boat, Bondi used a piece of wood to prod them into working faster. One of the slaves, a man named Ike, turned to him and said, "Massa, I didn't think dat of you." The captain had promised Bondi he could find him a job as a plantation overseer, but that same day Bondi decided to ask for his pay and return home to Missouri.

Back in St. Louis, helping out around a clothing shop, he felt his life wasting away. "I was tired of the humdrum life of a clerk," he later wrote. "Any struggle, any hard work would be welcome to me. I thirsted for it, for adventure."

That he would find. An editorial by Horace Greeley in the *New York Tribune* pointed Bondi in a fateful direction: Greeley implored freedom-loving citizens to move to the Kansas territory, newly opened to white settlement, and "save it from the curse of slavery." The controversial Kansas-Nebraska Act of 1854, overturning the decades-old Missouri Compromise, left it up to settlers on the ground to choose whether slavery would spread to the new prairie states. Antislavery idealists from New England and elsewhere were flocking to the new territories. Bondi decided to join them. Packing a pair of four-inch Colt pistols, he boarded a ship headed up the Missouri River to Kansas City. From there he traveled by foot into Kansas, arriving in Lawrence, the headquarters of the anti-slavery settlers, with sore feet and an empty belly, exhausted but exhilarated, ready for action.

2

Of Hebrew Bondage

FOR HUNDREDS OF YEARS, JEWS IN THE NEW WORLD participated in slavery and the slave trade. They were investors and creditors, importers and exporters, agents and auctioneers, masters and mistresses. Thousands of men, women, and children were bought on the coast of Africa and shipped in miserable, deadly conditions across the Atlantic on vessels owned by Jews, some even bearing biblical names: the *King Solomon*, the *David*, the *Hannah*, the *Abraham and Sarah*.

While most Jewish slave traders, like their non-Jewish counterparts, were based in the sugar islands of the Caribbean, many others lived in seaboard towns and cities that later became part of the United States. They were some of the most prominent members of the earliest American Jewish communities.

The extent of Jewish involvement in the Atlantic slave trade has been wildly exaggerated by antisemites of all stripes. Each group, for its own warped reasons, has blamed the slave trade solely on the Jews. In the 1960s, an essay in a neo-Nazi magazine argued that Jews were largely responsible for the colonial-era commerce in Africans and concluded that it would have been better for everyone had they never been allowed to settle in America. In 1991, *The Secret Relationship Between Blacks and Jews*, a publication by the Nation of Islam's "Research Department," focused exclusively on Jewish slave traders without any mention of others who played a far bigger role in the trade. Nation of Islam leader Louis Farrakhan even claimed that Jews owned 75 percent of Black slaves in the American South, a ridiculous exaggeration. The text has been thoroughly discredited and debunked by numerous historians, most notably Winthrop Jordan, David Brion Davis, Saul S. Friedman, and Eli Faber, all of whom have shown that Jewish participation in the slave trade was in no sense disproportionate to that of the overall white population. The absence of any Jews from the slave trade would hardly have made a difference. The same is true of Jewish slave ownership. Free Black people in the antebellum South owned many more slaves than Jews did.

Yet even if Jewish traders were responsible, as one estimate has it, for a fraction of 1 percent of the roughly twelve million people seized from Africa and transported to the Americas while the trade was active, that still amounts to tens of thousands of individuals. We can grant that Jewish traders played a minuscule role in the overall system while still wanting to know more about those who were involved. These are stories worth knowing. The scholarly focus on mere quantification—even to the noble end of dispelling prejudicial myths—can miss deeper racial, social, and economic dynamics that shaped the experience of Jews in America, even long after slavery's abolition.

The truth, inconvenient both for reflexive defenders of the faith and for its hate-filled foes, is that Jews were neither disproportionately invested in slavery nor consistently opposed to the institution. Those who participated in the practice and profited from its perpetuation were not always reluctantly complicit. Conflicted and divided, implicated and appalled, Jews were pretty much like everyone else. Yet their peculiar history and position gave them a distinct relationship to slavery and to the struggle over its future. American Jews' experience of American slavery—as, later, of the Civil War—was in many respects a Jewish one.

The earliest Jews who settled in the New World brought with them the memory of an exodus much more recent than the one in the Bible: the expulsions that accompanied the Spanish Inquisition, a centuries-long reign of torture and terror, property confiscation, and public executions. The banishment of all Jews from Spain in 1492, and from Portugal five years later, dramatically shaped the settlement of the Americas and the development of the Atlantic world.

For centuries, Jews in the Iberian Peninsula had been relatively safe and prosperous. That all ended when "the Lord," as one Jewish writer put it at the time, "visited the remnant of his people . . . and exiled them." Forced to convert to Catholicism or leave, many Spanish and Portuguese Jews adopted the faith of their persecutors and became so-called *conversos*, or New Christians. Some were sincere in their conversion and gave up all practice of Jewish rituals, even in private, while others, the famous "crypto-Jews," continued to secretly identify with the ancient faith, taking extreme precautions not to get caught and suffering elaborate punishments whenever they were. In 1506, as plague spread through Portugal and economic disasters immiserated the population, the *conversos* were blamed for the calamities. A mob in Lisbon "fell upon the wretched Jews," one chronicler wrote, and "killed great numbers, and threw many half alive into the flames." Some two thousand people were murdered in that killing spree, and countless more in the years to come.

Hundreds of families who could afford to flee settled in the Netherlands, drawn by its atmosphere of religious tolerance. Though not accepted as full citizens, the Jews in Amsterdam prospered from the city's growing involvement in trade and colonization. Their business skills helped turn the country into a powerful empire. The complex financial instruments that Jews had devised to get around onerous commercial restrictions in the Middle Ages and keep their assets fluid became building blocks of modern capitalism. A few Jews invested in the Dutch West India Company, which established outposts in distant North America and played a crucial role in expanding the Atlantic slave trade. As did their Christian competitors and associates, Jewish merchants in Amsterdam commissioned ships to seize captives in Africa. Nearly all the Jews of Dutch Curaçao, the largest Jewish settlement in the Americas by the end of the seventeenth century, owned at least a few slaves, while one, in 1754, owned more than four hundred.

Most Jews who ventured to the Americas between 1500 and 1800 settled in the Caribbean, where they built up affluent, tight-knit communities. In some Jamaican towns, Jews owned as much as 20 percent of the land, possibly the highest rate of Jewish land ownership anywhere in the world at the time. Few Caribbean Jews became plantation owners themselves, since Jewish life in medieval Europe, concentrated in towns and cities, had poorly outfitted them with the skills and know-how needed for large-scale agricultural success. They were mostly aspiring merchants, small-time shopkeepers, and real-estate investors. When they did get involved in the slave trade, it was generally as investors, shipowners, and resale agents. Alexander Lindo, one of the most successful Jewish businessmen in Jamaica, imported and sold many thousands of slaves. By the 1790s, Lindo owned his own wharf and the largest house in Kingston.

Marginalized from official centers of power, Jewish merchants in the Atlantic world had at least one advantage over the competition. Access to extensive kinship ties connecting Europe, Africa, and the Caribbean offered a ready-made supply chain for sourcing materials and a built-in network for long-distance trade, including the burgeoning slave trade. Thanks to their meandering travels and convoluted family histories, many colonial-era Jews were fluent in several languages—Spanish, Portuguese, English, Dutch, French, and Hebrew—which also helped smooth commerce. Given the unprecedentedly globe-spanning trade networks of the time, being able to trust the people one did business with offered a crucial edge.

In 1760, a slave rebellion broke out on the island of Jamaica. Tacky, a charismatic former African chieftain, led hundreds of followers to storm plantations and murder their white masters. The initial revolt was quickly suppressed and Tacky was killed, but it inspired unrest and uprisings across the rugged island. When they, too, fizzled out, captured rebels faced beheading, hanging, or starvation. According to the Jamaican-born judge and politician Edward Long's 1774 history of Jamaica, late one night, a Jewish guard stood watch over an imprisoned rebel. The inmate sidled up to the sentry and begged for mercy. "You Jews . . . and our nation . . . ought to consider ourselves as one people," the prisoner pleaded. "You differ from the rest of the Whites, and they hate you. Surely then it is best for us to join in one common interest, drive them out of the country, and hold possession of it to ourselves." The Jewish lookout refused to help the inmate and reported the conversation to his superiors.

Their exclusion from white Christian society gave enslaved Blacks and exiled Jews in the colonial Americas something in common. Yet the enmeshment of some Jews in both the slave trade and slavery itself would prove an obstacle to forming an alliance of the kind the prisoner proposed. Expelled from their homes at just the moment that seagoing exploration and colonization provided new opportunities, Jews were desperate enough to travel to the farthest reaches of the known world to escape violence and uncertainty. Colonial outposts were hardly free of bigotry; agents of the Inquisition followed Jews to the New World and held occasional burnings at the stake. Yet the Americas nevertheless offered havens of relative tolerance. In a dismal historical irony, it was precisely those far-flung relocations and do-or-die adaptations that put Jewish exiles from European oppression in a position to profit from the oppression and enslavement of others. The security and prosperity made possible by the slave trade offered an escape hatch, an exit from their restricted lives in Europe and the chance to amass some capital so their children would not start out with nothing.

No person exemplifies the entwinement of those two world-historical catastrophes, the Inquisition and Atlantic slavery, better than the most prolific Jewish slave trader in the colonial period, indeed one of the most successful North American businessmen of the time. Born to a *converso* family in Portugal, Duarte Lopez followed a brother to Newport, Rhode Island, in 1752, changed his name to Aaron, and submitted to circumcision at the age of twenty-one. Here, finally, he could live freely as a Jew. Rhode Island's charter, granted in 1663 by King Charles II, stated that all residents were to enjoy "a full libertie in religious concernements."

Working with another Portuguese exile, Jacob Rodrigues Rivera, whose daughter he soon married, Lopez rose quickly in Newport, moving from candlemaking to whaling to shipping and trading of all kinds. Lopez's business interests ranged around the world. He was constantly sending ships not only to New York, Philadelphia, and Quebec, but to Jamaica, Barbados, Suriname, London, Amsterdam, Lisbon, and Gibraltar. He bought and sold everything he could get his hands on: axes, chocolate, textiles, molasses, whale oil, sugar, cocoa, ginger, cotton, tea, coffee, rum, pewter, silk, furniture, hay, fruit, butter, indigo, shoes, corn, onions, horses, cheese, turpentine, mustard, oats, saddles, chairs, lumber, wool, peas, kettles, hides, jackets, Bibles, beer, mirrors, violins, beef, sheep, geese, fish— and pork.

By 1775, Lopez was the largest contributor on Newport's tax rolls, a gentleman of influence. He had a hand in almost every part of the colonial economy, even the construction of prefabricated bungalow-style houses. By all accounts, Lopez was intelligent, ambitious, and generous. He contributed lumber for the construction of Brown University. Devoutly religious, he refused to let his ships leave port on the Sabbath and closed shop for Jewish holidays. Despite selling pork, he shipped "coushier" meat to Jewish communities throughout North America and the Caribbean. After Lopez's death, Ezra Stiles, the president of Yale College, lauded his friend as an "eminent Jew merchant" who "bore a most respectable, unblemished character and was universally esteemed."

None of that, however, stopped him from getting rich off the trade in human beings. Every spring, Lopez commemorated the Hebrews' emancipation from Egyptian slavery—his account books list several large orders of matzah and haroset for Passover—even as he financed and oversaw the abduction of hundreds of men, women, and children from the African coast and their shipment in horrific conditions to a distant continent. With its deep, well-protected harbor, Newport was a center of the Atlantic slave trade, controlling some three-quarters of all imports into North America. Jews were responsible for perhaps 2 percent of those voyages—hardly dominant, but not quite negligible either. Lopez sent fourteen ships to the western coast of Africa between 1761 and 1774. One entry in Lopez's account book describes the contents of a ship headed for Africa: a few hogsheads of rum, flour, beef, wine, molasses, and salt, as well as iron hoops, chains, and "40 pair sheckells"—shackles for fresh captives. The trade in humans, Lopez wrote, was "a very gainful and advantageous commerce." By the outbreak of the American Revolution, he personally owned twenty-seven slaves.

Neither Aaron Lopez nor any other Jewish slave trader in eighteenth-century Newport left a word of regret or discomfort about slavery. They simply do not seem to have recognized it as a moral question, like most others of the time, though one Rhode

Island contemporary did condemn "that unrighteous traffic." When Lopez's congregation offered prayers on Yom Kippur to "all our brethren . . . who are captives," it was a reference not to enslaved Africans but to Jewish victims of the Inquisition.

In the early 1760s, Lopez and other Newport Jews plowed the profits they reaped from the slave trade and other ventures into the construction of a synagogue. Designed by an accomplished English architect and built by slaves owned by the congregation's members, the Palladian-style structure was completed in 1763. The synagogue still stands prominently in the oldest part of town, both a functioning synagogue and a popular tourist attraction, a standing monument to the deep roots of the American Jewish experience.

After the Revolution, Newport's role in the slave trade declined. Its Jewish community declined as well. Aaron Lopez died in 1782 in a drowning accident in full view of his horrified family. Today, Newport's eighteenth-century Jewish community is best remembered for an oft-quoted letter that George Washington wrote to its leaders in 1790, thanking them for the good wishes they had offered the new president on his recent visit to the city. Echoing the Newport Jews' own address to him, Washington agreed that the Constitution "gives to bigotry no sanction, to persecution no assistance," even while pointedly advising the ever-pesky Hebrews to be sure to "continue to merit and enjoy the good will of the other Inhabitants."

Heralded as an unimpeachable statement of Jewish belonging in the United States, Washington's letter reads somewhat differently when one considers that the Newport Jewish community's leaders had, like him, profited from the enslavement of others. That much these once lowly refugees from oppression had in common with the father of the republic. In the coming decades, American Jews would often behave as if they got the message: continuing to enjoy the goodwill of the other inhabitants required assisting in, or at least keeping silent about, the persecution of others.

On any given Saturday morning in 1730s New York, amblers out for a stroll on Mill Street in lower Manhattan could behold a striking sight: Luis Moses Gomez, a wealthy merchant, marching off to synagogue, followed by the usual train of family members and enslaved servants, the latter bearing in their arms the Gomez family's prayer books and shawls. When the procession reached the synagogue steps, the slaves scurried into the sanctuary and deposited the holy items on the Gomezes' seats, then left as the family settled in for Sabbath services.

In the North, slavery was concentrated among successful merchants like Gomez who kept a few people to help out with the business or toil around the house. The first Jews in the remote Dutch outpost then known as New Amsterdam owned slaves within a decade of their 1654 arrival. Asser Levy, one of the earliest Jewish residents of Dutch Manhattan, owned at least one person, a man named Cressie, set free, according to Levy's wish, after the master's death. Haym Salomon, the Philadelphia merchant celebrated by posterity as the "financier of the Revolution"—his contributions, in fact, were exaggerated by his son—placed an advertisement in 1783 offering "a couple of very likely Negro boys." Michael Gratz, who had started out selling imported goods from his shop off Philadelphia's Market Street before turning to the western fur trade and land speculation, tasked one of his slaves with keeping his kitchen kosher. One of Michael's sons, Hyman Gratz, took over his father's claim to Mammoth Cave in Kentucky and bought seventy slaves to mine it for bat droppings to turn into gunpowder. His other son, Benjamin, a founder of the city of Lexington and a close friend of the statesman Henry Clay, owned seventy-five enslaved workers who ran his rope and hemp factory. Traders and businessmen were not the only ones who found slave ownership useful. Even the respected religious leader Emanuel Nunes Carvalho, who moved from

Barbados to New York and then to Philadelphia, was recorded in the 1810 census as the owner of three enslaved people.

In the South, Jewish ownership of slaves was more widespread, and the number of slaves owned, on average, was higher. Most Southern Jews who could afford to own slaves and had a use for them did so. Roughly one-fourth of Southern Jews owned at least one slave, about even with the overall Southern population. Slave owners included prominent members of their communities: rabbis and community leaders, public office holders, founders of Jewish philanthropies. The historian Bertram Korn observed that, in the colonial period, "engaging in business transactions in Negro flesh was not regarded as incompatible with being a good Jew."

Like Aaron Lopez's Rhode Island, South Carolina had a history of religious toleration. The original constitution for the colony, drafted by the philosopher John Locke, welcomed "Heathens, Jues and other Disenters." With between three and six thousand Jews by the Revolution, the city hosted the largest Jewish community in the United States. It also featured the highest concentration of Jewish slave owners. Abraham Mendes Seixas, born to a prominent Jewish family in New York, arrived in Charleston in 1774, just before the Revolution. He fought for the rebels and became captain of a militia company, the only Jewish officer in the South Carolina forces. In 1777, Seixas married the daughter of another Jewish Charlestonian, "a young lady of the most amiable qualifications," to whom Abraham promised 3,500 pounds, pieces of furniture and silver, and two slaves. In 1784, he published in the *South Carolina State Gazette* a few lines of verse trumpeting the qualities of the individuals available for purchase from his store:

> *He has for sale*
> *Some Negroes, male,*
> *Will suit full well grooms,*
> *He has likewise*

Some of their wives
Can make clean, dirty rooms.

For planting, too,
He has a few
To sell, all for the cash,
Of various price,
To work the rice
Or bring them to the lash.

For many years Seixas managed the Charleston workhouse, where refractory slaves were sent to be tortured into submission. Before his death in 1799, he served as city magistrate and president of Congregation Beth Elohim.

Slavery was particularly essential to the success of the small but thriving Jewish community in early Georgia, a haven for debtors and other outcasts. The Prussian-born Benjamin Sheftall, one of the first Jewish arrivals in Savannah, found success as a farmer, merchant, and shipper. He eventually became an officer of the militia and founded both the Masonic lodge in Savannah and Congregation Mikveh Israel, the third-oldest synagogue in North America. He owned three slaves by the time of his death in 1765, a mother and two sons. When he died, Sheftall's will split them all apart.

Benjamin's sons outpaced their father in both business success and slave ownership. The eldest son, Mordecai, came to own thousands of acres, as well as a thriving warehouse, sawmill, and stocks of cattle, then rose to the highest rank of any Jew in the Continental Army, as deputy commissary general. When Savannah fell in 1780, he and his son, Sheftall Sheftall, were captured by the British and held on a prison ship, apparently considered leaders among the rebels. After the war, Mordecai returned to Savannah accompanied, his travel permit stated, by "two Negro servants." He resumed his business activities, helped secure rented quarters for Mikveh Israel, and donated the land for Savannah's first Jewish burial ground. He and another Jewish Savannahian, Moses Nunez, were among the five men appointed by the state of Georgia to regulate the leasing out of slaves.

Judaism and slavery were inextricably linked in the life of the Sheftalls. In a 1792 letter to his son and fellow captive, Mordecai asked Sheftall Sheftall, who had moved to New York, to send him some Hebrew-language prayer books for the Savannah synagogue's library—and to help track down a few slaves who had run away from the family plantation. Mordecai's brother, Levi Sheftall, the owner of a rice plantation and some forty-four people, as president of Mikveh Israel in the early 1790s, hired one of his slaves to serve as "Shammas," or sexton, responsible for keeping ritual objects and the sanctuary in order. The man was to be paid the symbolic sum of $18, "due the 1st day of Roshashona." When Levi died in 1808, his son, also named Mordecai, remembered his father as a "kind, indulgent & benevalent . . . master." Weeks earlier, an enslaved woman named Polly, one of the ostensible recipients of that benevolence, had seized the opportunity offered by her master's illness to flee. From his deathbed, Levi sold Polly while she was still out hiding in the woods.

The separation of enslaved families and loved ones was not merely an unfortunate byproduct of the slave system but a tool to enforce control. Mordecai Cohen was a Polish-born immigrant who arrived in the United States in 1788. Like many Jewish merchants, he started out as a peddler, hauling goods through the Southern backcountry, before rising to the heights of economic success. One of the richest men in South Carolina, Cohen provided the silver used at the banquet to honor the Marquis de Lafayette's visit to Charleston in 1825. Cohen owned thousands of acres as well as dozens of people to work the fields, tend his house, and raise his children. Between 1795 and 1838, Cohen bought or sold human beings more than fifty times. In 1809, he sent an enslaved woman named Mary-Ann more than a hundred miles outside the city to labor on a plantation owned by a fellow Jewish planter named Michael Lazarus. Cohen told Lazarus to "keep her at as hard labor as you possibly can." Mary-Ann's crime? Consorting with an enslaved man, a "rascally fellow" of whom Cohen disapproved. Distance, he hoped, would "cure" her of the infatuation. During her absence, Cohen took pity not on heartsick, hard-worked Mary-Ann, but on himself, for being deprived of "the most valuable wench I have."

Like Benjamin Sheftall of Savannah, Cohen passed the tradition of slave ownership down to his two sons, Marx and David. Marx Cohen kept meticulous records of the work at his plantation, Clear Springs, where some twenty slaves cleared the land, chopped lumber, manufactured bricks, planted potatoes, cut the hay, and ground the corn. David Cohen took over Soldier's Retreat, his father's other plantation. A memoir published anonymously by a fugitive slave in Boston in 1838 describes how the narrator suffered a severe beating after his master, David Cohen, accused him of theft. He decided to flee to the woods, but Cohen, with his powerful father's help, tracked his property down and had the runaway sent to Charleston's notorious workhouse, whose overseers (including, decades earlier, the slave-trading doggerel writer, Abraham Mendes Seixas) were experts in refining the perfect techniques to "correct" troublesome bondsmen. The former slave reports having "heard a great deal said about hell, and wicked places, but I don't think there is any worse hell" than what he found at the workhouse. The torture came directly at David Cohen's direction: "He told them to whip me twice a week till they had given me two hundred lashes. My back, when they went to whip me, would be full of scabs, and they whipped them off till I bled so that my clothes were all wet." Lashings were interspersed with trips to the dreaded treadmill, which forced prisoners to hold a bar and climb for hours at a time. Laggards were beaten. The runaway's condition worsened so rapidly that Cohen was forced to sell him at a loss.

Violence was inherent in the practice of human bondage, no

more or less so when practiced by Jews than by others. One form such violence took was sexual assault. An especially disturbing document, preserved in the public records of Northampton County, Pennsylvania, concerns a German-born Jewish man named Michael Hart. By the outbreak of the Revolution, Hart had become one of the wealthiest traders in Easton, on the Delaware River. On court days and around election time, villagers gathered on the steps of Hart's shop to talk politics. Remembered by his daughter as "pious . . . reverencing and strictly observant of the Sabbath and festivals," Michael Hart slaughtered his own kosher meat. Legend has it that George Washington stopped for lunch at Hart's home in 1778. Some versions even say that it was the sixth night of Hanukkah, that Hart's wife, Leah, prepared latkes, and that Washington said he was already familiar with the holiday because he had witnessed a Jewish soldier lighting a menorah at Valley Forge.

There is no evidence that any of that happened. Here is what did. In 1780, Pennsylvania passed the first abolition law in the United States. It freed those born after the act's passage, but only once they reached twenty-eight years old. The law also required all masters to register their bondsmen. Michael Hart claimed an eighteen-year-old named Phillis. Three years later, the Harts' housekeeper discovered that Phillis was pregnant. She informed Hart's wife, Leah, who, on confronting Phillis, learned that Michael was the father. It is not known what Leah Hart did with that information, but somehow Phillis found her way to Robert Levers, justice of the peace for Northampton County. Levers recorded Phillis's deposition, dated November 6, 1783:

[H]e, the said Michael Hart, used to call the said Negro Phillis
to light him in the stable, he used to promise her ribbons and
blow out the candle and make her stay with him in the stable,
and then made her lay down in the stable, he used to pull up her
clothes, and put into her his ██████ and had carnal knowledge of

her body. And at other times whilst the said Michael Hart lived in the same house, he would get up in the night whilst Mrs. Hart was in bed, and go down stairs as if he wanted a drink of water, and then call her, the said Phillis, from up stairs out of her bed to get water for him, and then he would lay the said Negro Phillis down on the kitchen floor and have carnal knowledge of her body in the same manner as before. And whilst the said Michael Hart lived in the same house in this manner he had carnal knowledge of her a great many times, sometimes but seldom, and sometimes very often. That after said Michael Hart had moved out of the said house into the new house where he now lives, about two or three weeks after, he used, when Mrs. Hart was gone out, to send her [Phillis] upstairs, and then follow her, and sometimes to throw her on the bed and sometimes on the floor, and have carnal knowledge of her as before. And in the same manner frequently afterward whilst Mrs. Hart was gone abroad in Easton, as well as when she went to Philadelphia, sometimes in the daytime and sometimes in the nighttime. That she at last found herself with child, and Mrs. Brills, the housekeeper, first discovering her the said Phillis to be with child, she told it to Mrs. Hart who called said Negro Phillis, up stairs alone and asked her if she was with child. That she answered her mistress she was; that Mrs. Hart asked her who was the father, that she, the said Phillis, told her that her master was the father of the child then in her body. And the said Phillis solemnly declares that the said Michael Hart was the only person who ever had carnal knowledge of her, the said Phillis, since he the said Michael Hart first laid her down in the stable as aforesaid and knew her carnally. And that the said Michael Hart, whilst she was with child, wanted to have again carnal knowledge of her but that she absolutely refused him. And further this deponent saith not.

Phillis signed at the bottom with a simple X.

It is not known how this remarkable document, an anguished scream from the archives, came to exist. The deposition offers rare direct testimony from a victim of the sexual violence endemic to Black slavery. Did Leah Hart, fifteen years her husband's junior, wish to enter evidence into the legal record in anticipation of a divorce suit that never materialized, perhaps because she died a few years later? Did Robert Levers, the English-born county official who took the deposition and who seven years earlier, as a prominent local patriot, had read the newly published Declaration of Independence on the town green, making Easton only the second town outside Philadelphia to hear the news of America's separation from Britain, harbor antislavery sympathies? Did Michael Hart know about the document and fear exposure? We have no answers to these questions and likely never will. It is also not known if Phillis carried her pregnancy to term. If she did, the child would have been born the right and lawful property of the said Michael Hart.

Assimilation in early America, to a large extent, meant assimilation into a slave society. Challenging its social and legal norms would have brought severe costs, particularly for vulnerable, often isolated immigrants. For Jews in the South, not owning slaves "carried with it social and business disadvantages," the historian Max Kohler once observed, while in the North support for abolition was discouraged by "business and trade policy," which "rendered such avowals inexpedient." It is hardly surprising that when a people chased over the millennia from one end of the earth to another finally found a refuge, they placed a high value on expediency.

American Jews were as divided as their neighbors over slavery and its future. Any Jews who decided to speak—or act—against slavery had to do so as individuals, without communal protection or encouragement of any kind.

What they did have, at least in their own minds, was a tradition of antislavery Judaism reaching all the way back to the Torah itself. Even if the Mosaic law code did not abolish slavery, measures intended to ameliorate the condition of slaves suggested to some Jews that the Bible did not approve of the practice. Maltreatment and gratuitous abuse are forbidden. Undue injury to a slave justifies their emancipation. Murder of a slave merits vengeance. Hebrew slaves were to go free after six years of bondage. The Torah's restrictions on slave ownership were indeed relatively enlightened for the time, one of the first examples in history, as the scholar Isaac Mendelsohn once observed, of "an open denial of the right of man to own man in perpetuity."

In reality, however, those biblical laws were likely seldom followed. Samaritan papyri show that ancient Hebrews held both their own countrymen and foreigners in permanent slavery, in contravention of the biblical injunctions. To take the Bible's legal stipulations at face value, the historian David Brion Davis once noted, would be like reading the Declaration of Independence's promise that "all men are created equal" as an accurate description of American society in the era of the Revolution. Slavery was widely accepted as an uncontroversial aspect of everyday life in ancient Israel. It had always existed and always would.

Even so, a rich strain in ancient Jewish thought criticized the failure of the Israelites to adhere to the biblical restrictions. The Prophets regularly invoked the Exodus experience—and even compared rich Israelites to Pharaoh—to call the people back to God and his laws. Jeremiah, the prophet who witnessed the fall of Jerusalem to the Babylonians in 587 BCE, insisted that the Israelites' refusal to emancipate their slaves was the cause of their exile. "On the day that I brought your ancestors out of Egypt," Jeremiah reports God telling him (34:12–15), "I made an agreement with them that they would let their slaves go free after six years. And your ancestors did not listen to me." Nehemiah, who oversaw the rebuilding of Jerusalem's walls, suggested that the re-enslavement of the Israelites under foreign empires was retribution for their refusal to release their own bondsmen (9:34–36).

Two offshoot sects of ancient Jews went even further by banning slavery from their communities. The Essenes were an ascetic group of some four thousand men scattered in towns throughout first-century CE Palestine, especially in an isolated settlement near the Dead Sea, leading some to hypothesize that they were the keepers of the mysterious scrolls discovered by a Bedouin shepherd in 1947. They deplored war and animal sacrifice, shared property in common, and refrained from contact with women. They also refused to own slaves. "Not a single slave is to be found among them," wrote Philo, a Jewish philosopher in Alexandria, "but all are free, exchanging services with each other, and they denounce the owners of slaves, not merely for their injustice in outraging the law of equality, but also for their impiety in annulling the statute of Nature, who mother-like has borne and reared all men alike, and created them genuine brothers."

The other Jewish sect that rejected slavery were the Therapeutae, a group of men and women near Alexandria, devoted to mystical contemplation of the divine. They rejected slavery, Philo wrote, because, like the Essenes, they deemed it contrary to nature: "For nature has borne all men to be free, but the wrongful and covetous acts of some who pursued that source of evil, inequality, have imposed their yoke and invested the stronger with power over the weaker."

The Essenes and the Therapeutae, utterly atypical of ancient Jewish society (and the ancient world more generally), appear to have been the first groups in history to reject slavery because of moral objections to holding humans in bondage. Though permitted by religious law, they saw slavery as a backward and wicked institution incompatible with their utopian ideals. Centuries later, in a place and a context unimaginable to either sect, a handful of similarly visionary Jewish abolitionists would argue much the same thing.

———————

Though there was no overarching Jewish organization in early America to take the lead in criticizing slavery, there were Jews in the early republic who freed their own slaves, protested the institution of bondage, or even devised comprehensive—if far-fetched—plans for its abolition.

Jewish veterans of the Revolutionary War were among the earliest members of the country's first antislavery organization, the Quaker-dominated Pennsylvania Society for Promoting the Abolition of Slavery, the Relief of Free Negroes Unlawfully Held in Bondage, and for Improving the Condition of the African Race. Solomon Bush, a prominent Mason and former lieutenant colonel in the Continental Army, badly wounded in the Battle of Brandywine, contributed funds to the construction of the first synagogue building for Philadelphia's Congregation Mikveh Israel and joined the antislavery society. When he died in 1795, Bush opted to be buried in the city's Quaker cemetery, alongside fellow members of the antislavery group.

Another early Jewish member of the abolition society was Benjamin Nones, who in 1777, at twenty years old, journeyed from his native Bordeaux to aid the American rebellion. After the Revolution, Nones settled in Philadelphia and took an active hand in the city's affairs. His fortunes rose and fell in the turmoil of the economically depressed postwar years, but Nones managed to accrue enough capital to buy enslaved and indentured servants. When some ran away, Nones posted rewards for their return. But after befriending a liberal-minded Philadelphia alderman, he decided to free at least one of his bondsmen. Nones later served as a witness to ten manumissions by other Philadelphians, including a family of French Jews who fled Haiti after the 1791 slave uprising. A member of Mikveh Israel, Nones staked his political views on a firmly Jewish foundation. "I am a Jew," he wrote in 1800, explaining his support for Thomas Jefferson's presidential bid, "and if for no other reason, for that reason I am a republican."

In New York, too, Jews belonged to an early abolition group, the Society for Promoting the Manumission of Slaves, which also counted Alexander Hamilton and John Jay as members. Mordecai Myers, a veteran of the War of 1812, the first Jewish representative in the New York legislature, and the great-great-grandfather of the poet Robert Lowell, was an active member of both Congregation Shearith Israel and the Manumission Society. Moses Judah, an active Mason and the owner of a hardware store, was admitted to the society's membership in 1799, the same year the New York legislature passed a law gradually easing slavery out of existence in the state. While serving on the society's governing committee, Judah provided legal assistance to enslaved New Yorkers seeking to sue for their freedom, including a Black man named Jack Moore who, like Judah, had fought in the Revolution and believed he had thereby earned his emancipation. During Judah's years on the committee, the society helped liberate some fifty people, but Jack Moore was not among them.

Antislavery activities among Jews declined as the larger movement faded in the early nineteenth century. The momentum of relatively easy victories after the Revolution was halted by the intransigence of the increasingly cotton-dependent South. But in the 1830s, as a new wave of abolitionism rose in the Northern states, Jews again participated in the push. In 1838, the then Pennsylvania senator James Buchanan introduced a petition from twenty-four Philadelphia Jews calling for the abolition of slavery in the District of Columbia, part of a broader citywide initiative. In the 1840s,

Rebecca Hart of Philadelphia joined the Female Anti-Slavery Society and served as an officer for several years. Hart worked with William Still, the leader of Philadelphia's Underground Railroad network, and Thomas Garrett, an abolitionist based in Wilmington, Delaware, a slave state, to aid runaways from bondage.

Perhaps the most curious case of an antislavery Jew in the early republic was that of the eccentric merchant and philanthropist Moses Levy, who in 1828 promoted a comprehensive program for slavery's abolition even while he owned and oversaw a Florida sugar plantation worked by dozens of enslaved people. Born to a wealthy Sephardic family in Morocco, Levy was a religious utopian, a successful transatlantic businessman (he once partnered in a lumber business with Judah Benjamin's father), and a proto-Zionist who believed Jewish political action should be directed toward resettlement in the Holy Land. Dismissing assimilation as a mirage, Levy believed strongly in Jewish separation and autonomy. Like many adherents of the Enlightenment, Levy believed in modernizing Judaism—but unlike them, he opposed integrating its adherents with the society around them. He embraced conventional piety but dismissed the rabbinical establishment, "which by ignorance and superstition is erecting barriers and fences." Agricultural communities offered the best chance for Jews to escape their "degraded state" and flourish, Levy thought, much like his contemporary Mordecai Manuel Noah, whose own "Ararat" scheme Levy's plans may have inspired. He first tried to establish a refuge for European Jews in Illinois, where cheap land was available in abundance. When that scheme fell prey to the Panic of 1819, he turned his attention to northern Florida, where, with funding from a member of the Warburg banking family in Europe, he bought up nearly 100,000 acres and set some aside to establish an experimental community known as Pilgrimage. On scrubby land amid arching, aged oak trees, he built a plantation house surrounded by a garden, a sugar mill, a blacksmith shop, and a handful of "negro houses." Attempting to reintroduce sugar planting in Florida, Levy innovated by using alligator dung as fertilizer.

The experiment lasted thirteen years. At its height, Pilgrimage was home to some thirty-one slaves. But Levy held idiosyncratic views about the practice of human bondage. Inspired by the Hebrew Bible, he believed bondsmen should be freed at twenty-one years old and provided the training and resources needed to succeed as freedmen. Levy did not support immediate abolition, which he thought would throw the formerly enslaved into a state of helplessness and desperation; their bondage had made them "indolent, deceitful, and vicious . . . unaccustomed to think for themselves." But he thought the suffering of slavery's victims could be alleviated. Running a plantation in which he treated his workers decently and kept families together would help bring about the institution's demise.

In the rough-and-tumble world of antebellum Florida, surrounded by already suspicious Christian planters, Levy had to keep his antislavery views to himself. Yet while visiting London in the late 1820s to raise funds for his Florida colony, Levy anonymously published a pamphlet advocating for the end of slavery. Reflecting what his biographer Christopher Monaco calls "a unique blend of Utopianism, biblicism, business-like pragmatism, agrarian and educational reform, and travelogue," the pamphlet called for the establishment of beneficial ventures like his Florida plantation, which could experiment with ways to make free labor profitable. The children of the enslaved would be educated in agriculture, the arts and sciences, and the Old and New Testaments, which would in time "introduce such a state of society as will be a blessing . . . to the world at large." Levy also suggested sending British convicts to the Americas to mate with enslaved women—such racial mixing would "counteract [the] insurmountable prejudices" that might ruin the prospects for newly freed Black people after emancipation—as well as arming a naval fleet of African-crewed sailing vessels empowered to eradicate the illegal slave trade once and for all.

To Levy's frustration, American Jewish leaders never encouraged emigration to his Florida colony, and the Jewish families that did arrive proved ill-equipped to eke out a living in the tropical swamps. Florida, only recently acquired from Spain, infested by venomous snakes, alligators, and disease-bearing mosquitoes, rife with hostile Seminoles and runaway slaves, proved a poor choice for such a communal experiment. "It is not easy," Levy complained, "to transform old clothes men or stock brokers into practical farmers." The venture suffered what Monaco calls an "unrelenting volley of misfortunes," culminating in the burning of Levy's sugar mill in the Seminole Wars of the 1830s. Levy mortgaged his slaves for cash and eventually sold them in exchange for shares in an insurance company that soon went bankrupt, leaving Levy penniless at the age of sixty-one. The old man found himself "without family, friends, or society in a land I perfectly detest." Yet fortune smiled on him again when a court ruled in his favor in a dispute concerning his title to thousands of acres of prime Florida real estate.

Levy was devastated when his son David, who spent his formative years living on the Florida plantation while his father traveled abroad, not only embraced slavery but changed his last name to Yulee in order to conceal his Jewish origins (it came from a Moroccan ancestor). He married a devout Kentucky Christian and bought a Gulf Coast plantation worked by some eighty slaves. Father and son went years without speaking. Levy disparaged his son as "a Presbyterian," while Yulee blamed his father's "peculiar views and condition of mind" for alienating him from his family. A stalwart follower of Andrew Jackson, Yulee pushed for the forced removal of the Seminoles and Florida's admission to the Union as a slave state. Elected to the Senate in 1845—eight years before his equally alienated coreligionist, Judah Benjamin—Yulee would emerge as a fiery spokesman for slave-state interests, a fierce advocate of states' rights, and an early proponent of forming a Southern Confederacy.

———————

Whether someone was Jewish had little impact on whether they embraced slavery. For all their unique history of oppression and much-lauded ethical teachings, Jews were unexceptional when it came to antebellum bondage. It is possible that some were only complicit with slavery because they were afraid to make themselves conspicuous in a slavery-dominated society. In general, however, they did not merely acclimate to the opinions and practices of their neighbors. They shared them.

While Jews did not contribute much to American slavery, American slavery contributed greatly to the success of early American Jews. Slavery and the bigotry that supported it deflected much of the hostility that Jews had faced in the Old World. I. J. Benjamin, a Romanian Jewish traveler who spent three years in America before the Civil War and wrote a book about what he saw, observed that Jews in the United States benefited from the direction of racial hostility toward enslaved Black people. "Since the Israelites there did not do the humbler kinds of work which the Negro did, he was quickly received among the upper classes, and early rose to high political rank," Benjamin wrote.

The relative success of Jews in America had to some extent been predicated from the beginning on the oppression of a group even more hated and feared than they were. Jewish immigrants would have been less welcome in the United States had the presence of racial slavery not put them on the right side of a starkly drawn color line. In their newly adopted homeland, race mattered more than religion. A gut-level awareness of this dynamic may have discouraged

American Jews from speaking out against slavery. They perceived their interests lay with the perpetuation not only of slavery as an institution but of the ideas that supported it.

As with Jewish participation in the Atlantic slave trade, the extent of Jewish slave ownership in the early republic was roughly on par with that of the white population overall. Jews were neither uniquely guilty nor a morally enlightened exception. They went along with the practices of those among whom they lived. "The law of the land is the law," the Talmud has it. In all the American colonies and, after the Revolution, in much of the new nation, the law said the enslavement of human beings was perfectly fine. Just as suggesting that Jews were more responsible than others for the slave trade amounts to inexcusable, ahistorical bigotry, it is wishful thinking to assume they somehow avoided complicity with the crimes of their times. Only a few denounced slavery for the evil it was. Even fewer acted to bring it down.

3

"First Truth and Then Peace"

BORN IN A SMALL BOHEMIAN VILLAGE, ISAAC MAYER Wise considered himself an American from birth. The eldest son of a poor schoolteacher, he studied at a yeshiva outside Prague, then at the university in Vienna, before landing a job as rabbi in a tiny rural outpost. But Europe was a dead end. Autocratic governments ruled everywhere. Even among Jews, a smothering religious conservatism reigned supreme. "Everything was commonplace, ordinary, and exceedingly dull," Wise would recall. He was entranced by a collection of eighteenth-century American journals he purchased in a bookstore, enthralled by the frontier novels of James Fenimore Cooper. Obscure and penniless, twenty-five years old, he fled, along with his wife and young child, and crossed the border from the Hapsburg empire into Saxony. As they crested the final ridge, Wise waved one last teary goodbye, not to a towering city steeple, as August Bondi would on his way out of Vienna two years later, but to a majestic river valley. Soon he would find another.

First he had to find his way out of New York City. He hated the place. It was cramped and crowded and depressing, full of "small, insignificant-looking people" whose only purpose in life, apparently, was to buy and sell, cheat or be cheated. As soon as he disembarked, his ears were assaulted by rumbling wagons and the cries of fishmongers, milkmen, and newsboys. The city barely extended above Fourteenth Street. "Everything seemed so pitifully small and paltry," Wise wrote in his autobiography. New York offered a bitter disappointment to his earlier "exalted" ideas about America.

Only a few weeks later, however, Wise felt sure that in America he had found himself—and his people—a new home. A congregation in Syracuse, far out in the wilds, had not seen a religious leader visit in years. They asked a more established Manhattan rabbi, Max Lilienthal, to come and deliver a sermon for them. Lilienthal, busy occupying the pulpits of three different synagogues, asked his brash new acquaintance to take his place. Wise was thrilled to leave the noisy, confusing city behind him. "An inexplicable force directed my attention to the interior of America," he would recall.

The impressions of that first day's steam up the Hudson were among the richest of his life: the towering Palisades north of Manhattan that "seemed to shut off the Old World," then the imposing peaks of the Highlands, those lofty green hills ringing West Point—made famous, only a few years earlier, by artists like Thomas Cole and Asher Durand—leading, finally, to a steep, windswept gap between the mountains, a "giant gate opening into the New World." As the boat lurched onto a broad bay surrounded by rolling vistas of sun-speckled farmland, Wise succumbed to vivid, dreamlike visions of promise and possibility: "I could have embraced every mountain, every rock." Taking in the splendors of the Hudson Valley, glimpsing the same mystic sublime so many painters and poets of his day likewise beheld on their riverine voyages, the rabbi realized America offered a more than adequate replacement for the benighted old continent he had left behind. Judaism "develops far more swiftly and splendidly in the sunlight of freedom," he wrote to a Jewish newspaper in Germany the following year. Wise's vision of America as he sailed up the great river inspired him to set out a new mission not merely for his own life but for Judaism itself, and for all his fellow Jews.

———

The idea of reforming Judaism to better suit the modern age had deep roots in Europe, going back to Moses Mendelssohn, the late eighteenth-century German Jewish philosopher who believed that all human beings would eventually unite around a rational form of universal religion, one fully compatible with the essential tenets of traditional Judaism. Mendelssohn favored secular studies for Jewish children and social mixing with gentiles. He engaged in vigorous debates with Christian thinkers of his day. Yet while he thought Jews should adapt their cultural tastes to the European civilization around them, Mendelssohn rejected significant religious change. Judaism in its essence could never change. It was what it always had been, and it was the obligation of modern-day Jews to adapt themselves to it, not for the millennia-old faith to adapt itself for them.

But after the master's death in 1786, Mendelssohn's followers explored more extensive alterations of religious ceremonies and even theological dogmas. Modernization would ease the way toward the broader social integration their mentor had envisioned. Prayer services should be conducted in the vernacular language of the congregation, they thought, rather than the ancient Hebrew few understood. They also wanted shorter services, the inclusion of soul-stirring choirs or even organs, and sermons explaining the meaning of the weekly Torah portion and emphasizing the ethical lessons it entailed. Rituals were only a means of instilling a greater sense of devotion. It might be necessary to adjust or even abandon some to better satisfy the spiritual needs of both the community and the individual.

History itself showed the legitimacy of adapting to changing circumstances. Reinventing Judaism was just what the postbiblical rabbis had done in interpreting scripture and applying its often thorny, tangled, contradictory dictates to the business of daily life. The Talmud, composed in the centuries after the 70 CE destruction of the Second Temple and the subsequent Jewish dispersal across Europe and the Near East, was the record of these debates and interpretations. For nearly two millennia, it had strictly governed Jewish life. But increasingly those old rabbinic teachings and rules were seen as latter-day adornments, arbitrary and inessential. Channeling the spirit of scripture, rather than adhering rigidly to its precise letter, was what mattered. As one early German reformer contended, "The Talmud speaks out of the consciousness of its age and for that it was right; I speak out of the higher consciousness of my age and for this age I am right."

The new spirit of reform was also a response to new circumstances. Around the turn of the nineteenth century, after the French Revolution and Napoleon's rise to power, states and empires began to loosen constraints that had governed their Jewish subjects for centuries. As political emancipation or even equality beckoned, the impulse to shear away ancient impediments to full participation in European life grew stronger. Inspired by the Enlightenment's suspicion of superstitious beliefs and unexamined traditions, as well as Protestantism's emphasis on the need for spiritual rituals to nourish the worshipper's soul, Jewish reformers sought to stake a more universalist claim for their faith. To survive, it had to be devoted to reason, progress, justice, and equality, rather than obscurantist texts, irrelevant rituals, and exclusivist claims.

One of the first age-old tenets that came under scrutiny was faith in the arrival of the Messiah—not Jesus of Nazareth, that pretender, but a genuine, heaven-sent, world-redeeming savior who would liberate the chosen people from their centuries-long exile and restore them to political sovereignty in the promised land. Jews had prayed for such a deliverance for millennia. But perhaps a literal savior was no longer necessary, nor a return to the Holy Land, the longing for which could be perceived as disloyal to secular authorities increasingly tolerant of their Jewish subjects. As one reformer put it, "Wherever you are treated humanely, wherever you prosper, there also is your Palestine, your fatherland, which in accordance with your laws you must love and defend."

For all the hopes raised by the Enlightenment and the push for political equality, the defeat of Napoleon in 1815 proved the high-water mark of Jewish emancipation, at least for a while. Four years later, a wave of anti-Jewish riots and pogroms swept across Germany, dashing the optimism of Mendelssohn's successors. Restored conservative governments saw proposals for religious reform as harbingers of political unrest. Responding to pleas by traditionalist Jewish leaders, Christian authorities shut down radical-leaning congregations. In 1823, the Prussian government closed a reformist temple in Berlin, claiming its ideas had rendered Jews "even more dangerous to civil society than they were before." The opposition of both Jewish traditionalists and reactionary state authorities proved too stultifying an environment for this new, more modern form of Judaism to take root and thrive. It sorely needed another.

───────

Even before the Reform movement reached its apogee in Europe, a parallel effort was underway in the United States. In the early 1820s, a group of young, educated, socially aspiring worshippers at Charleston's Congregation Beth Elohim broke off and decided to form their own society of religious dissenters. Among them was Judah Benjamin's father, Philip, a man of proud Jewish heritage but unorthodox practices and beliefs who had clashed with synagogue officials over his insistence on keeping his fruit shop open on the Saturday sabbath. Like their Enlightenment-inspired counterparts in the Old World, Charleston's reformers wanted the prayer service shortened and at least partly translated into English. They also wanted to end the unseemly practice of selling off to the highest bidders such honors as the recitation of important blessings before and after the reading of the weekly Torah portion. "We wish not to *overthrow*, but to rebuild," the group's manifesto insisted. "We wish not to *abandon* the Institutions of Moses, but to *understand and observe* them." To blindly follow tradition, they contended, would make them "*slaves of bigotry and priestcraft.*"

It is an interesting choice of phrase. It may not have been a coincidence that the first Reform congregation in the New World sprung up in the de facto capital of American slavery. Jews in Charleston had long been accepted as more-or-less equal members of society, fully enfranchised citizens who not only voted for their own political representatives but served in office themselves. Many had grown rich and flaunted their wealth and public benevolence. Charleston's Jews enjoyed a degree of comfort and confidence, a sense of newfound security that encouraged them to blend in with those around them. In 1824, the same year the Reformed Society of Israelites broke off from Beth Elohim, Isaac Harby, a dramatist and journalist who served as the splinter group's most eloquent leader, published an essay defending the states' rights doctrine of South Carolina's planter class. Denouncing "the abolitionist society and its secret branches," Harby, himself the owner of seven Black bondsmen, objected to those "new-fangled doctrines" of antislavery, which, if put into effect, would "jeopardize the well-being of the Planting States."

After a few years, however, the Reformed Society foundered, done in by personal conflicts, Harby's death, and the defection of other leaders. Its members returned to Beth Elohim, where they soon managed to wrest control of the congregation and force the traditionalist members, in turn, to leave. The final break came in 1841, when a new leader of the synagogue, a Polish native named Gustav Poznanski, pushed for an organ to be included in the congregation's new building, after the old temple had been destroyed in a fire. (The building was constructed, as nearly every building in Charleston would have been at the time, by enslaved laborers; one was specifically tasked with painting the Ten Commandments on the eastern wall.) Jewish law prohibited playing musical instruments on the Sabbath, but in Europe some reformers were introducing the organ into the synagogue, arguing that it was acceptable if used as part of worship. The organ became a dramatic symbol of the conflict between tradition and innovation, the embodiment of a congregation's embrace of Reform. Poznanski and his followers won a lengthy legal battle when the Supreme Court refused to intervene on the side of the traditionalists, a landmark ruling that confirmed the separate space reserved for religion in American public life.

That separate space was just what Reform Judaism needed. The United States proved in many ways the perfect environment for its message, strengthened by the influx of liberal-minded rabbis and others who arrived in the late 1840s and 1850s. The new thinking appealed to those already in the process of altering so much about themselves and their lives. Reformers cut from prayer services all references to the return of Jews to the Holy Land, rebuilding the Temple in Jerusalem, and the coming of the Messiah. Instead, they professed to have found a stable and permanent home in America. Inaugurating the new Beth Elohim building in Charleston in 1841, Gustav Poznanski boldly declared, "This synagogue is *our* temple, this city *our* Jerusalem, this happy land *our* Palestine, and as our fathers defended with their lives *that* temple, *that* city, and *that* land, so will their sons defend this temple, this city, and this land."

And so they would, from Fort Sumter to Appomattox.

———

The American reformers needed a leader, however, and it did not take long after his 1846 sail up the Hudson River for Isaac Mayer Wise to offer his own not-so-humble self for the role. Accepting a job as rabbi for Congregation Beth El of Albany, a boomtown thanks to the opening of the Erie Canal, Wise began to institute his idiosyncratic vision for an authentically American form of Judaism, inspired by the efforts in Europe but free from the restrictiveness of the Old World. It was up to each individual to determine how much he or she owed to the rituals and dogmas of the past. In America, "anyone can do what he wants," one Jewish immigrant wrote home to her parents in Hamburg in 1791. "There is no rabbi in all of America to excommunicate anyone."

Before 1840, when the first credentialed rabbi arrived in America, synagogue services were led by ill-trained laypersons, an arrangement conducive to the democratic, congregation-centered bent of American religious culture. The influx of German-educated rabbis triggered conflicts within Jewish communities. Many resented the imposition of top-down leadership where none had previously existed. New arrivals from Europe, especially after the revolutions of 1848, were already familiar with Reform principles. They had grown used to quieter, shorter, more organized services. The first American rabbi, Abraham Rice, hired to lead the Baltimore Hebrew Congregation, promptly split his congregation by opposing Jewish participation in Freemasonry and demanding strict observance to Jewish law. "I dwell in complete darkness," Rice complained to his mentor in Germany. "I wonder whether it is even permissible for a Jew to live in this land."

By 1845, Orthodoxy, formerly an uncommon word, came into broader use to describe the traditional Judaism that the reformers were trying to replace. It had not previously needed a name, because it was the only kind of Judaism around.

In Albany, Wise did not want to err in the other direction of pushing his members too far toward Reform, so he introduced only basic changes at first: a mixed-gender choir, German and English hymns, a ban on the sale of synagogue honors. He also encouraged the congregation to remain seated during the reading of the

Torah. Traditionalist members of his congregation tried to push back against such changes—one was even fined four shillings for refusing to sit—but Wise, a masterful organizer, succeeded in marshaling votes to defeat them.

The absence of institutional pillars inevitably fostered a communal disunity that Wise feared would threaten not only his program to reform American Judaism but the survival of the Jewish people in America. "Each congregation pursues its own way," he complained, "has its own customs, and mode of worship, its own way of thinking about religious questions . . . [O]ne Jew is a stranger in the Synagogue of the other Jew." In a vast and conflict-ridden country like the United States, Jews would inevitably break into competing camps and dissolve into the broader culture. In 1848, a poet in Charleston, South Carolina, offered a pithy survey of the American Jewish scene: "Some are reformed and wisdom boast / Some orthodox, indifferent most."

To combat this fractiousness and apathy, Wise hoped to institute new forms of organization to replace those left behind in Europe. A tireless proponent of his cause, Wise traveled far and wide inaugurating new synagogues, presiding over Sabbath services, battling with opponents, and eventually, after decades of struggle, founding the first national Jewish institutions. In the 1850s alone, he would open the first-ever college for American Jews; edit two newspapers, one in English (*The Israelite*) and one in German (*Die Deborah*), that not only served but helped shape the evolving American Jewish community; and publish *Minhag America*, a prayer book designed to embody his distinctly American style of Reform Judaism.

Though prone to depression, hypochondria, and self-doubt, Wise maintained an intense work ethic and a stubborn faith in his own good intentions. For Wise, the crucial fact was that in America, the land of pluralism and free expression, no religion had an official monopoly. Here the Jews could finally "work out a new peculiar destiny" for themselves. The point was not to establish a separate denomination so much as to see Judaism itself "reformed and re-constructed, by the beneficent influence of political liberty and pro-gressive enlightenment," Wise insisted. "It is the American phase of Judaism."

———

The circle of rabbis in America in the 1840s was small and scattered, self-obsessed and gossipy, constantly reshaped by jealous rivalries and shifting alliances. Morris Jacob Raphall immediately rubbed almost everyone the wrong way.

Born in Stockholm in 1798, Raphall was the son of a wealthy banker who had worked for the king of Sweden. When he and a brother fell ill as children, their father promised that if they survived, he would consecrate their lives to God. After graduating from a Copenhagen seminary, Raphall studied philosophy at universities in Germany. He then moved to England, where he would live for a quarter-century and pick up a crisp, posh accent. He worked as secre-tary to England's chief rabbi before securing a post at a synagogue in sooty, industrial Birmingham, where factories turned cotton picked by enslaved people in the Americas into finished cloth.

Raphall would never waver from his Orthodox convictions, but his secular education set him apart from the most hidebound tradi-tionalists. He thought it was vital to educate Jews about their rich cultural legacy, especially the Hebrew language and its literature. While he held the Talmud as sacred and binding, Raphall objected to rabbinical efforts to keep Jews uninformed about intellectual developments in the wider world. Raphall blamed "the mystics of Poland," a shorthand for some of the most closed-off religious authorities, for spreading "the opinion that it was sinful to read any books other than Hebrew or Rabbinical." The Reform move-ment had gone too far—but so had the Orthodox establishment's reaction. He was not "hostile to reform," Raphall said. He only hoped to raise all Jews to the "standard of a heaven born religion," rather than lower the religion to the "base level of the people's convenience."

Widely respected for his learning, Raphall proved a popular orator on subjects like biblical poetry and relations between Christians and Jews. One Jewish paper called the rabbi "the most eloquent preacher that has recently appeared on the scene." Some Jews in Birmingham criticized him for neglecting his rabbinic responsibilities, but Raphall believed his activities served an important function in explaining Jews to gentiles. Christians packed into his Birmingham synagogue to hear him preach on Passover. John Mills, a Methodist intent on converting Jews, grudgingly acknowledged Raphall as "one of the finest minds of the age."

In sermons and lectures, Raphall constantly praised his adopted country, toasting "the land we live in," referring to himself and his Anglo-Jewish listeners as "us Britons" and likening the rugged climate of the isles to the character of the nation. Yet England proved too small a home for someone of Raphall's ambition, too rigid for a thinker of idiosyncratic views. Frustrated by the low pay of his Birmingham position, Raphall decided to undertake a lecture tour in the United States. He knew before he left England that he likely would not be returning.

Carrying the banner for Orthodoxy to an increasingly Reform-minded America, Raphall, unlike Isaac Mayer Wise, felt right at home in New York and comfortable among the higher classes. Raphall contracted with the oldest Ashkenazi synagogue in the city, B'nai Jeshurun, founded in 1825, to serve as rabbi at the annual salary of $2,000, the highest rate ever given to a Jewish leader in America. Within a year, the congregation put up another $50,000 to build a soaring English-style neo-Gothic synagogue near Manhattan's fashionable Washington Square, more than twice the cost of a typical church at the time. The congregation rolls swelled with new and wealthier names. Speaking shortly after his arrival at a banquet for the Hebrew Benevolent Society, Raphall toasted the liberty he had found in America and lauded the country's recent triumph in the war with Mexico. He heralded the fast-approaching day when the American republic would assume "a leading rank among the nations of the earth," leaving revolution-torn Europe far behind.

Within weeks of landing in New York, Raphall was traveling through his new country, trying to rebuild the career he had left behind in England. American audiences found his lectures as graceful and eloquent as the British had, and Raphall was feted by editors up and down the East Coast. A Southern newspaper praised Raphall's ability to bring together "Jew and gentile, clergy and laity, manly intelligence and womanly beauty" for "an intellectual feast . . . rich in literary gratification and moral instruction."

The acclaim was not universal, however. Isaac Mayer Wise took an intense dislike to the newly arrived Orthodox leader, "a rotund little man with a black velvet skullcap," not only because they disagreed on doctrinal questions but because Raphall struck Wise as pompous and arrogant. When Raphall visited Wise's friend Max Lilienthal at his home on the Lower East Side, Lilienthal asked the younger rabbi why he had come to America. Raphall responded by quoting an ancient sage: "Where there are no men, strive thou to be a man." Recounting the episode in his memoir, Wise scoffed at those who came to America from Europe "with the idea . . . that they need only come, and they will conquer at once." Of course, Wise himself often fell prey to such delusions.

A year after arriving in America, Raphall decided to travel to Charleston, to lecture on Hebrew poetry and to debate Gustav Poznanski, leader of the city's Reform faction. Appalled by the increasing dominance of Jewish modernizers in the United States, Raphall wanted to challenge them on their home turf.

Hearing about the coming confrontation, Isaac Mayer Wise decided to follow Raphall to Charleston. Never one to shirk from confronting a rival, Wise also had his own reasons for traveling to

Charleston: He was interviewing for the aged Poznanski's job as rabbi of Beth Elohim. Decades later, in his memoir, Wise would claim he had traveled south on doctor's orders, to recuperate from his latest bout of illness and depression. Tired of the constant strife with traditionalist holdouts in his Albany congregation, he was in fact interested in moving to Charleston to lead the Jewish reformers.

The Charlestonians, many of them descendants of eighteenth-century Sephardic immigrants, had an upper-crust bearing, and Wise was intimidated at first. But his hosts went out of their way to put their visitor at ease. "I was domiciled in splendid rooms," Wise would remember. "A negro was placed at my disposal. I was the guest of American aristocrats for the first time in my life." Wise expressed no discomfort, in his recollection of the Charleston visit, with having had an enslaved servant made to wait on him. He instead remembered basking in the luxury.

Despite his trepidation and feelings of inadequacy, Wise's trial run at Beth Elohim went well. Across town, at the breakaway Orthodox synagogue, Raphall bitterly countered Wise's lecture, and the two traded barbs for the better part of a week. One night, at a Purim party in the house of a community leader, the two spoke alone. Raphall encouraged Wise to give up his misguided efforts to overhaul the ancient tradition. Wise, of course, declined the invitation. Within ten or twenty years, he told Raphall, Orthodoxy would die out entirely in America.

The culmination of the showdown came at the planned debate between Poznanski and Raphall. Wise sat in the audience, ostensibly a mere observer, but in fact, as everyone knew, an even more vigorous leader of the Reform forces than Poznanski himself. Wise was impressed by both debaters but, unsurprisingly, thought Poznanski the victor. He had kept his cool, Wise remembered, while Raphall "grew excited, and declaimed violently." Raphall particularly took issue with the Reform movement's willingness to give up the belief in the coming of the Messiah, a faith born of centuries of displacement and wandering that, the reformers held, had now come to an end with the comfortable home the Jews had found in America. Raphall had assured an earlier Charleston audience that the savior would indeed come "without fail." Now his anger got the best of him. Raphall's elegance and surface-level congeniality concealed a contentious, hardheaded streak. Singling out Wise in the audience, Raphall asked pointed questions meant to clarify the extent of the reformers' tradition-shredding radicalism. Did Wise still believe that the Messiah would come? Did he believe that the body would be resurrected after death? To both, Wise shouted, "No!" At that, the Orthodox leader furiously gathered up his books and fled the stage, his entourage following behind him.

Never before, at least in America, had the battle lines between Reform Judaism and Orthodoxy been so clearly drawn. It had been a triumphant trip for Wise. By the time he returned to Albany he learned that the aristocratic Charlestonians had elected him rabbi. He had done nothing to offend them and much to win their favor. Perhaps lending him a slave for the week had been a kind of test; if so, he passed. Wise was inclined to accept the offer, but leading members of his Albany congregation begged him to stay. Convincing his wife that the humid Southern climate would be bad for her husband's health, they succeeded. Wise signed on for another three years. But the surprisingly radical stance he took in his responses to Raphall in Charleston accelerated the deterioration of his already precarious relationship with the Albany congregation. When word of Wise's defiant stance against the two tenets of Orthodoxy got out, denunciations came in from all sides. Mordecai Manuel Noah, the self-proclaimed "Judge of Israel," mere months from the grave, argued that a rabbi rejecting faith in the Messiah "played the hypocrite as to his own beliefs." Abraham Rice, the Orthodox leader in Baltimore, said that neither Wise nor any other endorser of the Charlestonians' Reform program had "a right or a voice to talk about Judaism."

Wise's Albany opponents seized on the controversy as the

chance they had long sought to get rid of him. After a monthslong power struggle, Louis Spanier, the synagogue's wealthy, tradition-minded president, suspended Wise's pay and eventually fired him. Spanier cited a petition from some congregants denouncing Wise's "hellish plans for Judaism" and accusing him of being "impertinent and presumptuous" and having been seen writing on the Sabbath. But the rabbi refused to go down without a fight. The next day, on the morning of Rosh Hashanah, Wise rose in the sanctuary, as he had countless times before, to remove the Torah scroll from the sacred ark. Spanier leapt up and, in what Wise later called "a rage of madness," tried to keep him from taking hold of the scroll. Spanier punched the rabbi in the head, knocking his yarmulke to the ground. The whole synagogue fell into a brawl—a "general melee," as one local paper put it—during which "several severe assaults were committed." The fighting only ceased when the sheriff arrived with a posse, cleared the building, and locked the doors. Arriving home "bowed with pain and irrepressible grief," as he would recall, Wise was taken into custody by a local constable. The charges were later dropped. Wise sued Spanier over the assault and won. The whole episode felt to Wise like "agonizing, hellish torture."

Following the melee, Wise and his progressive followers split off from Beth El and formed their own congregation, Anshe Emeth ("People of Truth"). They bought a former church. Instead of bothering to renovate the chamber, they kept the family pews, thereby introducing mixed-gender seating in an American synagogue for the first time. Wise traveled up and down the East Coast raising funds for the new congregation. He tried to make his breakaway Reform group in Albany a success, but he was desperate for new and wider horizons. That first glimpse of the vast continental interior as his steamboat chugged up the Hudson River in the summer of 1846 had never left him. Wise imagined the American West as a place where "the people are young and aspiring and not yet cast into a fixed mold."

He soon found a new home in Cincinnati, a growing industrial city known as "Porkopolis" for its dense concentration of pig-processing plants. Despite its nonkosher epithet, by 1850, the city offered a comfortable refuge for some three thousand Jews. One nineteenth-century historian may only have been slightly exaggerating when he called Cincinnati "a sort of paradise for the Hebrews."

Offered a lifetime contract to serve as Congregation B'nai Jeshurun's rabbi, Wise was thrilled to move to what he described as the "center of the country." The city was poised on the tenuous border between the free state of Ohio and the slave state of Kentucky. Many of Wise's followers had close family and economic ties to slavery, making it difficult for a community leader to speak out against the institution even if one had been so inclined.

Wise was not. For him, America offered the long-wandering Jewish people their best chance at finding a secure and stable home. Drawing attention by adding their own voices to the already cacophonous debate over slavery seemed counterproductive, even, for a scattered and still-vulnerable group, potentially catastrophic.

In 1855, just as August Bondi was traveling to Kansas to fight the spread of slavery, a new rabbi arrived in the tumultuous port town of Baltimore. Born in a Bavarian village in 1819, David Einhorn had been raised by his mother, a widow intent on giving her children the best possible education. From an early age, he had shown an eagerness for learning. Outpacing the village teacher, he enrolled at a yeshiva in nearby Fuerth, a bastion of ultratraditional rabbis who feared any departure from centuries-old laws and practices. Even at nine years old, much younger than the other pupils, Einhorn stood out. The yeshiva only taught religious subjects, especially Talmud. Students caught possessing books in German or Latin faced punishment, possibly even expulsion. Soon after Einhorn

graduated—he received his rabbinical diploma at just seventeen—
the yeshiva would close rather than comply with a government order
to also teach secular subjects like literature, history, and the natural
sciences.

Yet the already rebellious Einhorn was intent on rounding out
his education. In his first break from Orthodoxy, Einhorn enrolled
in philosophy classes at one German university after another. A
signal influence was the work of Friedrich Schelling, who argued
that all world religions were simply different versions of an original, prebiblical revelation. Everything other than the primordial
core of religion had been added later and therefore was not truly
essential. Einhorn came to see the ancient rites and rituals of Judaism as merely representations of a single higher power ordering
the universe. It was not particularly important which survived and
which disappeared, so long as the underlying truth remained. Indeed, those trappings and fashions of bygone centuries inhibited
rather than abetted worship of the divine. Einhorn often called his
religion not Judaism but Mosaism, after the prophet and political
leader who received the Ten Commandments from God at Mount
Sinai, an event that marked, as Einhorn put it, "the first momentous
step toward the moral uplifting of mankind."

But only the first step: revelation was not a onetime encounter
at Sinai, Einhorn believed, but an ongoing phenomenon, accessible
for every person, without priestly assistance or scriptural interpretation. Judaism, to Einhorn, was not a fixed and inalterable system
of laws but rather a set of humanistic beliefs about the purpose
of human beings in a God-created universe, a systematic way of
grasping those "axioms of the human spirit" embedded in man by
God. "Judaism in its essence is older than the Israelites," Einhorn
argued, channeling what he had picked up from Schelling. "As pure
humanity, as the emanation of the inborn divine spirit, it is as old
as the human race."

Einhorn wanted to shear away the elements of traditional Juda-

ism he found outdated or useless in modern times. It was vital to ensure that Jewish traditions were modified to suit "the urgent needs
of the present day." Rituals should be preserved or abandoned based
on how well they fit with the unfolding progress of history. The
long-dead rabbis who had interpreted the biblical text and crafted
laws had no authority to dictate what Judaism looked like hundreds or even thousands of years into the future. Judaism had always
changed with the times. To reject the necessity of updating it now,
Einhorn contended, "would be like exhaling the breath of life, and
inhaling the stale breath which was exhaled by older generations."

By the time he left university, Einhorn had turned decisively
against the Orthodoxy in which he had been trained. Eager to help
shape the growing movement to reform the ancient religion, he
sought a rabbinical post, but his former teachers in Fuerth, fearing
the heretical ends to which their brilliant former pupil might devote
his talents, conspired to block an appointment. Finally, in 1842,
a liberal-minded Jewish community invited him to become their
rabbi, and Einhorn accepted. It was a satisfying if limited post for a
man of Einhorn's ambition. He soon found a more prominent one
as the chief rabbi of the Grand Duchy of Mecklenburg-Schwerin, a
role previously filled by Samuel Holdheim, one of the most prominent leaders of the radical wing of Reform Judaism. Again, Einhorn's former teachers tried to prevent his appointment, even going
so far as to denounce him as an "insolent and wicked infidel" to
the secular authorities whose approval was necessary for Einhorn to
win the job. But Einhorn outmaneuvered them and won the post.

Relentlessly attacked by the Orthodox, he lasted four years before moving on to another Reform synagogue, this time in Pest,
Hungary, where the revolutionary fervor of the 1848 uprisings had
been brutally suppressed. Now the liberal spirit of the young insurgents, stymied in politics, turned toward the religious sphere. Ditching yarmulkes, abolishing circumcision, disregarding dietary laws,
its members had gone further than almost any other Jews in doing

away with ancient customs—further, perhaps, than even Einhorn supported. He had to remind them that the purpose of Reform was not to "unscrupulously cast aside" every tradition but to "further develop Judaism into an ever more vigorous life." It was not enough to tear down the old; something new had to be built in its place. "We wish to know what Judaism is," Einhorn said, "not what it is not." But he never had a chance to guide the Pest congregation toward this new Judaism. The imperial authorities had grown wary of ties between the liberal-minded Jewish reformers and the insurrectionary movement to overthrow the monarchy. In late 1851, the emperor shuttered Einhorn's synagogue. As Wise and Raphall had discovered in turn, Einhorn realized that the conflict-ridden Old World was not a place to build something new. Like those outdated rituals he wanted to discard, Europe itself had outlived its purpose. He had to leave it behind.

For three years, Einhorn busied himself writing *The Principles of Mosaism*, an exposition of his religious philosophy. In early 1855, he received an invitation to lead a small Reform congregation in Baltimore, Maryland. More than a decade earlier, the Har Sinai congregation had broken away from Rabbi Abraham Rice's Orthodox synagogue to protest what its members saw as the "establishment of a Jewish hierarchy." Like their counterparts in Charleston, the Baltimore reformers used an organ in their prayer services. After a few years the group managed to build an impressive new worship space complete with a Star of David in the window, a rare symbol in synagogue architecture of the time. Isaac Mayer Wise visited Baltimore on his way to Charleston in 1850 and stopped by to visit. Har Sinai was "small and hated," he wrote, "but firm and persevering," full of "intelligent people."

In the summer of 1855, the forty-six-year-old Einhorn and his family took a ship across the Atlantic. His reputation had preceded him. The Einhorns were met at the dock by an honorary delegation of Reform-minded Jews from New York who wished the new rabbi well. In a rousing first sermon, Einhorn defended the principles of the Reform movement and encouraged his followers to brace themselves for the battles to come. He was hopeful that in America, freedom and reason would replace superstition and the blind worship of authority. In a land where "we fear no Pharaoh on this sacred soil of religious liberty," a newly reinvigorated Judaism would finally have room to grow. It was time to shear away the external forms of traditional Judaism to reveal "the religious and moral truth" of the teachings handed down at Sinai. Einhorn criticized those who favored mere ceremonial updates intended to make Jewish services more attractive and orderly. Such superficial changes "merely hide the inner decay," Einhorn sneered. A more extensive renovation was required.

Pining for a return to Zion was only the most obvious example of confusing the temporal and the eternal, of sacrificing the spirit for the form. Einhorn believed that America offered the most hospitable environment for his vision of Judaism to flourish, and for the messianic age to take root and spread throughout the world.

Yet he was not unaware that others in America did have pharaohs to fear. For all its promise, America continued to support an institution that, by its nature, denied the equality of all human beings, the presence in every person of the divine breath. In his inaugural Baltimore sermon, Einhorn professed his abiding belief "in one humanity, all of whose members, being of the same heavenly and earthly origin, possess a like nobility of birth and a claim to equal rights, equal laws, and an equal share of happiness." A year later, in his new monthly periodical *Sinai*, Einhorn explained what he meant. The time would soon arrive "in which God's teaching will be unfolded." Kingship would be abolished. "Slavery is eliminated as well," he added. "God's spirit will rule everywhere . . . The blood-drenched lies which persisted for thousands of years will go up in smoke."

It was a risky thing to say in a city and state where slavery was legal. But Einhorn was unafraid. In time, he would pay a high price for that courage.

In 1850, while traveling from Albany to Charleston to attend the debate between Raphall and Poznanski, Isaac Mayer Wise had stopped for a few days in the national capital. Congress was considering the package of bills that would later be known as the Compromise of 1850, a desperate, last-ditch attempt to stave off a national collapse into secession and civil war. Months of acrimonious debate revolved around the question of whether slavery would be allowed to spread into lands recently seized from Mexico. The great statesmen of American politics—John C. Calhoun, Daniel Webster, and Henry Clay—gave soaring addresses outlining their own views of the issue. Wise sat in the Senate gallery every day to watch the riveting debates. "The Great Sanhedrin made a deep impression on me," Wise wrote, comparing the senators to the assemblies of ancient Israelite leaders; "the earnest, serious, prominent men of national fame sat there in council, wrapped in a dignity that commanded respect." He even visited Calhoun on his deathbed. An aspiring orator, Wise immersed himself in the "powerful and eloquent words of these aged, gray-headed intellectual giants." He had been sick; now he felt magically healed. "I lived a new life," he later recalled, "or, rather, I dreamed a new dream, and my imagination soared to other heights."

Like his first sail up the Hudson four years earlier, Wise's week in Washington "exerted an Americanizing influence," he remembered. His mission, he now saw, was to take the style of politics he had witnessed in Congress that stormy, crisis-ridden winter and apply it to American Jewish life. Indeed, Wise once referred to the congregations scattered across America as so many "little republics."

Like the squabbling states, they needed a formal union to bring them together. Through uplifting oratory, crafty statesmanship, and his own labors, he would bridge the gap between opposite factions and philosophies. No differences were so important they could not be melded into some kind of workable compromise.

An energetic organizer, Wise desperately wanted to create a single overarching religious organization to act as a unifying force in American Jewish life. Five years after his visit to Washington, he convinced eight other rabbis, from moderate reformers to relatively open-minded traditionalists, to cosign his appeal for a conclave in Cleveland. David Einhorn declined to attend. Most Orthodox leaders like Morris Jacob Raphall also stayed away, refusing to meet with those they held as heretics and apostates. But other tradition-minded leaders did go, hoping that by engaging with the Reform movement they might be able to control it.

At the 1855 conference, held in Cleveland's Masonic Hall, the Orthodox and the Reform leaders sat on opposite sides of the room, scowling at one another. What accommodation could be reached between those who felt that Judaism could never change and those who believed it must? Yet both sides wanted to strike some kind of bargain. Wise wanted to exclude more radical reformers like the recently arrived Einhorn from whatever organization took shape to guide the development of a new American form of Judaism. Under the slogan Shalom Al Yisrael—"Peace be unto Israel"—the group hammered out a tenuous compromise between tradition and innovation, Orthodoxy and Reform. The rabbis adopted a joint statement declaring that not only the Torah but the Talmud, too, was a divine document, binding on future generations.

In a blistering open letter, David Einhorn denounced the Cleveland statement. The Talmud was a human document, reflecting the practices and prejudices of its time. Building a modern Judaism based on the outdated dictates of long-dead rabbis would condemn the faith to "perpetual stagnation," he wrote. Peace in Israel, unity among Jews, was important, "but a peace which necessarily degrades Judaism . . . appears to us too dearly bought." Unity was not worth the price Wise was asking the Reform movement to pay. "May the free American Israel keep a strict watch on hierarchical movements which would again forge its chains though under the most charming lullabies of peace," Einhorn warned, suggesting that Wise's proposed compromise with tradition would impose on Jews a fealty to the past that was tantamount to a form of spiritual bondage.

Einhorn saw no room for compromise in the moral and political implications of his progress-oriented religious philosophy. To his rival's slogan of "Peace be unto Israel," Einhorn countered with his own: "First Truth and Then Peace." Truth meant "peace with God," which "must stand higher than peace with humans."

For Einhorn, working for the coming of the messianic age was not an empty slogan but a fierce and urgent command. In moving to Baltimore, he had arrived in a place where it was perfectly legal for one human being to claim dominion over another. The intense scholar from a tiny Bavarian village, the new rabbi in town, decided that he would not stay silent.

4

Kansas Meshugas

IT WAS THE SPRING OF 1856, AND THE PLAINS OF KAN-
sas were ablaze with violence. Decades of rhetorical sparring between Northerners and Southerners had finally devolved into
combat. John Brown, a devout Christian visionary and sworn foe of
slavery, had gathered a band of hardy amateurs to attack an enemy
camp. Bullets, not ballots, would determine whether slavery or freedom prevailed in the West, and therefore, all agreed, in the country
at large. Bullets like those that flew one fine morning over the heads
of two Jewish immigrants crouching in the tall prairie grass.

August Bondi cherished the memory of that morning at Black
Jack Creek. He was twenty-two at the time. The man beside him,
Theodore Wiener, an acquaintance from St. Louis, a fellow fighter
in Brown's ragtag frontier army, was twelve years his senior and, at
250 pounds, not quite fit for active duty. Wiener lugged a double-
barreled shotgun, Bondi a rickety old musket left over from the War
of 1812, as they crawled up a small rise. Bondi remembered how
Wiener "puffed like a steamboat."

"Nu, was meinen Sie jetzt?" Bondi called out. *Now, what do you
think of this?*

Wiener replied, "Was soll ich meinen?" Then, invoking a Hebrew phrase: "Sof odom muves." *What shall I think of it? The end of man is death.*

As bullets whistled around them, Wiener added, "Machen wir den alten Mann sonst broges." *Look out, or we'll make the old man angry.*

Bondi laughed as they joined Brown behind a stump.

With the passage of the Kansas-Nebraska Act two years earlier, Congress had opened the territories west of the Missouri River to white settlement. The law left it up to settlers on the ground to decide whether slavery would become legal. Southerners and Northerners alike saw the future of the Union at stake in the contest over Kansas. Antislavery stalwarts known as "free-staters," mainly from New England and the upper Midwest, competed with proslavery "Border Ruffians" from the South, especially rural areas of neighboring Missouri. Only eight hundred white settlers had lived in Kansas at the time of the act's passage; nine months later that figure had grown tenfold. The free-staters had the advantage in numbers, but Southerners vowed not to let the territory slip from their grasp.

Weeks before Bondi's arrival, in the spring of 1855, thousands of rough-looking Border Ruffians, guns hoisted on their shoulders and knives sticking out from their boots, had disrupted the first territorial election by invading the territory and casting thousands of illegal votes. One antislavery lawyer was seized, stripped, shaved, tarred and feathered, then ridden out on a rail and sold for a dollar at a mock slave auction. Judges were told to approve the election results within five minutes or be shot. Crossing into the territory that first spring after the act's passage, Bondi encountered hordes of drunk Missourians streaming back toward their farms.

Citizens in the free states were horrified by Southerners' willingness to resort to force and fraud to obstruct free elections. Abolitionism, once a fringe movement, moved closer to the mainstream. Prominent figures in the North like the journalist Frederick Law Olmsted and the minister Henry Ward Beecher raised funds for Kansas settlers to buy rifles and cannons. "Shall Kanzas be governed by Missouri, or by her own people?" one paper asked. For Ernestine Rose, the freethinking socialist, feminist, and abolitionist, the issue was simple: whether "the yet virgin soil, the broad acres stretched in the far West," would be "consecrated to freedom or polluted by the unhallowed touch of slavery."

When Bondi first arrived in Kansas, he found an atmosphere suffused with paranoia, fear, and hatred. The first thing every settler asked a stranger was his position on slavery. White farmers in the area, Bondi recalled, were "very suspicious of 'Yankee Negro thieves.'" Not long earlier, another outspoken free-soiler in Kansas had been dragged from his cabin, whipped, and hanged from a tree, then cut down and told to leave the territory.

Bondi decided not to hide his antislavery views, and that put him in danger. When they first met, one neighbor, "Dutch Henry" Sherman, a fellow German speaker but rabidly proslavery, asked Bondi about his politics. Bondi acknowledged he was a free-stater. Sherman started to curse the "abolishtenists" and promised that Kansas would become a slave state "by fair means, if we can; by foul means, if we must." Another settler spent the days after he met Bondi and Jacob Benjamin, a Jewish friend from St. Louis who had joined him in Kansas, riding around the district trying to raise a mob to "drive the two Dutch abolitionists out of the county."

That first year on the frontier could hardly have been more difficult. Between clearing his land, chopping wood, setting fences, and building a cabin, while dealing with rattlesnakes, torrential downpours, and unfordable rivers, even as he bandaged a few fingers shortened to nubs by a sharp axe and nursed himself back from a fever—at one point he felt so weak he picked out a spot on the hill behind his cabin to serve as his grave—Bondi had reason to fear that his own neighbors would seize the first opportunity to kill him.

Fortunately, the idealistic Jewish frontiersmen would not have to face the threat alone. One afternoon, a few months after he and Jacob Benjamin had settled along Pottawatomie Creek, a herd of cows strayed onto Bondi's land. Their owners, Jason and Owen Brown, emigrants from Ohio and ardent opponents of slavery, soon came to retrieve them. They had suffered through the harsh winter in a three-sided lean-to, nourished only by beans and cornmeal pancakes washed down with an occasional glass of milk from their cattle. The brothers stayed to chat about the struggles of frontier living and the brewing conflict in the land. When Bondi told them of Dutch Henry's threat, the Browns promised to come to his aid if he needed them.

The Brown family patriarch, yet to arrive in Kansas, had instilled the principles of abolitionism in his sons from a young age. Free-staters in Kansas, like the German immigrants in St. Louis, tended not to oppose slavery on moral grounds so much as on economic and political ones. They wanted to preserve the western territories for white farmers and workers like themselves and to deny the South supremacy over national affairs.

John Brown was an exception. The descendant of a *Mayflower* passenger, Brown derived his radical views from a reading of the Old Testament that saw God's deliverance of the Hebrews from Egyptian bondage as containing a broader message. Slavery, to Brown, was a sin in the deepest sense, a moral stain on the nation, and God had appointed him personally to act decisively, as nobody else would, to get rid of it. Brown consciously modeled himself after the biblical patriarchs Abraham and Jacob and what he saw as their absolute belief in the mission of spreading justice and righteousness through the world. After following his sons to Kansas, Brown rejected the free-state leadership as too passive—"broken-down politicians" who "would rather pass resolutions than act." Brown wanted to act, and he wanted others to act with him.

Bondi first met John Brown on the morning of a crucial territorial election in the fall of 1855, when the free-staters in Kansas gathered to elect their own representatives to draw up a constitution that would ban slavery from the future state. When he arrived, Bondi saw the Brown boys and an older man riding in a wagon. The man wore a plush cap with a cavalry saber and a huge revolver hanging from his belt. Leaning down to shake hands with Bondi, Brown explained he and his sons had come to keep armed watch at the polls.

Bondi would later recall that before Brown got involved, the free-state cause appeared lost. The "bogus legislature" elected in the fraudulent spring elections passed a law sentencing anyone who criticized slavery to two years of hard labor. Death was the punishment for helping a slave escape from bondage. The president, Franklin Pierce, condemned the antislavery Kansans as "treasonable" and ordered federal troops to put down the supposed insurrection.

Late in 1855, Bondi returned to St. Louis for supplies and to recuperate from his illness. While he was gone, a fight over land claims led to the killing of a free-state settler. As tensions escalated, Border Ruffians seized arms from federal arsenals in Missouri and marched on the free-state headquarters of Lawrence, Kansas—"that nasty Abolition town," one Southerner called it. In the muddy streets between rough-board cabins, free-staters dug trenches and built fortifications to stave off the expected assault. At the last minute, the territorial governor negotiated a truce. Both sides hunkered down for the cold, wind-swept Kansan winter.

It was only a lull. New migrants were arriving every day. The free-staters refused to recognize the legislature and defied its orders. Rival governments demanded allegiance and forced the residents to choose sides. Come spring, the proslavery side called for action. "Let us purge ourselves of all abolition emissaries," one paper declared, "and give distinct notice that all who do not leave immediately for the East, *will leave for eternity!*"

In late May 1856, the proslavery forces again laid siege to Lawrence. They fired their cannons, then pillaged the town. Hearing the news, John Brown and a handful of men—Theodore Wiener, Bondi's heavy-breathed friend, among them—set off across the prairie, bent on revenge.

The brewing turmoil forced all Jews, and all Americans, to choose sides. Ernestine Rose had long ago chosen hers. Soon after her 1836 arrival in New York, she attended a raucous Fourth of July celebration in Manhattan and thought about how Southern bondage made a mockery of the republic. The Declaration of Independence had "sent forth to the world a great and glorious truth . . . the equality of men," she said. That truth "wafted like a bright vision of hope on the breezes of heaven to the remotest parts of the earth, to whisper freedom and equality to the downtrodden millions of men." Rose herself had caught a whiff of that breeze in far-off Poland and in Berlin, as had August Bondi and countless other new arrivals. Yet all that time, while the great and glorious truth wafted abroad, back in America, "under its shadow, the children that had been born and brought up here are subjected to dark and bitter bondage."

For more than a decade, Rose's other causes—her campaign for women's rights, the crusade against religion—had taken precedence. But as the conflict over slavery grew more heated, abolitionism captured more of Rose's attention. Remembering—and likely embellishing—her 1847 visit to Charleston, Rose described an argument about slavery she fell into with a young Southern lawyer. The enslaved were the only civilized people in the South, Rose said she observed, since they were the only ones who did any work. When he told her to be grateful she was a woman, since a man saying such things was liable to be tarred and feathered, Rose replied that at least it would give the lazy Southern whites something to do.

Even in the Northern states, Rose faced the constant threat of violence. In 1850, she tried to address an abolition convention in

New York, only to be interrupted by a mob that had invaded the hall with implicit approval from the city's Tammany-aligned mayor and chief of police. At one point, after Rose left the stage, men in the crowd shouted, "Rose! Where's that sweet Rose?"

Though committed to atheism, Rose at times seemed to draw on her own complicated, long-buried past, and the Jews' centuries of oppression, in denouncing the evils of American slavery. She compared American slavery with Russian serfdom, but argued that Russia's oppressive labor system was more forgivable because the tsarist government made no pretense of a belief in democracy or human rights, "while here, with all the glorious professions of republicanism and freedom, the whole land is cursed with the odious system of slavery."

The mid-1850s marked the frenzied height of Rose's activism, a time of ferment in both the antislavery and women's rights movements. By 1856, Rose had traveled through more than two-thirds of the states. She was "always on the go," a contemporary noted, "leaving the train to speak two or three hours from a stage, getting back on a rail car only to do the same in other places." In 1855, Rose began the year by attending nearly a dozen women's rights meetings in upstate New York, then lectured in Massachusetts and testified before a legislative committee in Albany. In March, she delivered antislavery speeches in New York, and later in the spring traveled to Boston before attending an "Anti-Slavery Excursion and Pic-Nic" on Long Island. That was followed by a women's rights convention in Saratoga, and, in the fall, a swing through Michigan, Ohio, and Indiana, before closing out the year with some lectures in Maine.

These travels required intricate planning and immense personal sacrifice. An English acquaintance marveled at the extent of Rose's tireless journeying across the land: "She has traveled alone, for months together, along rivers and lakes, through the towns and cities, the woods and swamps of that vast continent, under a burning sun, amid winter storms, exposed to the deadly vapors of unhealthy regions, lecturing in Legislative halls and rude log huts, to the highest and the lowest, the richest and the poorest, to the most refined and learned, and to the rudest and most neglected of her species."

Rose was likely the best-known woman orator of the time. The *New York Times* felt compelled to note, in its dismissive coverage of one freethought convention, that Rose, a "scoffing Infidel," spoke "broken English." Yet others marveled that Rose did not have a discernible accent. Even those who vehemently disagreed with her politics often praised her talents. An Ohio newspaper noted her "offhand, able, and spirited speech . . . the equal of which few men are competent to make." An observer at a women's rights convention noticed that she felt "infinitely relieved" when Rose began speaking: "A good delivery, a forcible voice, the most uncommon good sense, a delightful terseness of style, and a rare talent for humor" had inspired the two-thousand-person audience with "a spirit of interest," while other speakers left them in "a comatose state." Despite a fierce streak of self-righteousness, Rose could be sarcastic and self-deprecating, once joking that if she died and found herself in heaven, she would have no choice but to say, "How very stupid I was!" "Her eloquence is irresistible," another admirer wrote. "It shakes, it awes, it thrills, it melts—it fills you with horror, it drowns you with tears." "She is far before any woman speaker I ever heard," an antislavery comrade noted. "She is splendidly clear and logical. But oh! I cannot give any idea of the power and beauty of her speech. I can only stammer about it a little."

Despite her travels, Ernestine and William maintained a deep partnership, likely solidified in the 1840s by the bonds of shared tragedy. Rose spoke only once on the record about the pain of seeing her two children die in infancy. Like Judah Benjamin when his wife and daughter left him, she threw herself into her work. William's business making canes and silver pitchers, as well as real estate investments the couple made in Boston and Chicago, supported

Rose's activism. Unlike most in the women's and antislavery movements, she refused payment for her lectures and even declined
reimbursement for her travel expenses. William took care of the
housework while his wife was away. They saved money by not hiring a servant. One journalist who interviewed Ernestine observed
that "aside from the obligations imposed by her mission, [she] sees
few people, and does not make social calls." Avoiding the loose-
fitting "bloomer" costume popular among younger members of the
women's movement, she dressed plainly and conventionally, usually
in long dresses accented with lace collars and cuffs. Rose "tactfully
avoids any appearance of eccentricity," one reporter observed.

Little can be known for sure of Rose's private life. She left
no diaries and had many acquaintances but few intimate friends.
Her union with William appears to have been of the kind that
Rose praised in lectures: "a true and natural marriage," with "no
jarring . . . of mine and thine, all is ours . . . no more and no less
but perfect equality." William helped organize the annual Thomas
Paine dinners in New York, though he rarely spoke at them except
to toast his wife as "the faithful and devoted advocate of universal
mental freedom." For nearly fifty years, he faithfully saved newspaper articles that mentioned her.

One person Ernestine Rose did see socially was the journalist
and poet Walt Whitman, who first listed Rose in his address book
in 1855, the same year a pair of Scottish-born printers published
the first edition of Whitman's *Leaves of Grass*. As a young journalist, Whitman had visited a Manhattan synagogue and admired
how the congregants, a "remnant of the mighty nation," though
"scoffed, scouted, and scorned," still "came to worship their God
after the manner of their ancestors." A decade later, Whitman and
Rose traveled in the same downtown circles. On one memorable
occasion, the poet and the activist started talking about the French
Revolution—"one of the very few things which [could] ruffle her

beautiful placidity," the aged Whitman remembered. Rose exclaimed to him, "What!—to be trod down and not turn! Were the people mere playthings? blocks of wood or boulders of stone?" Struck by Rose's passionate phrasing, Whitman wrote the words down in his notebook, and in 1890 said he had "kept them all these years. . . . And today it applies as then."

Whitman remembered Rose, "a first rate lady friend," as "a splendid woman; big, richly gifted, brave, expansive." While "in body a poor sickly thing a strong breath would blow away," she had "a head full of brains—the amplitude of a [Daniel] Webster . . . I can see the flash in her eye now—the noble, containing eye!"

———

Rose's foreign birth, Jewishness, and atheism set her apart from the predominantly Protestant speakers at antislavery and women's rights gatherings. Perhaps because of their overtly Christian attitudes, she did not belong to any of the official antislavery societies. That gave her the freedom to go about her advocacy in her own way. "I stand before the world as I am, unprotected and unsupported by sect or party," she once wrote. "In principle I know no compromise, I expect no reward, I fear no opposition." Rose once urged women to think, speak, and act for themselves, "though you find yourself in a minority of one."

Sometimes that independent attitude—and especially her Jewish origins—brought scorn or outright discrimination. Hostile newspapers often noted her Jewish and Polish background. In 1854, the *Albany Register* condemned the "ringleted, glove-handed exotic, Ernestine L. Rose" as a "foreign propagandist." Rose's efforts, the editor insinuated, were meant "to obliterate from the world the religion of the Cross." "We know of no object more deserving of contempt, loathing, and abhorrence than a *female* Atheist," an editor in

Bangor, Maine, wrote in an unsuccessful effort to stop Rose from speaking in his town. "We hold the vilest strumpet from the stews to be by comparison respectable."

Even Rose's fellow reformers, including some of her colleagues in the women's rights movement, derided her foreign birth, her Judaism, and her atheism. Rose refused to use religious language or biblical passages to justify her beliefs. Unlike even her closest allies, Rose's activism was not based on Christian principles, or any religious principles at all, but on Enlightenment rationalism and the Owenite socialists' commitment to human rights and universal emancipation. While Rose saw all her causes as linked to a greater struggle for human freedom, others saw conflicts between abolitionism and atheism, or between securing rights for native-born women and offering a welcoming attitude toward European immigrants.

Her advocacy for the latter made Rose feel most keenly that she stood alone. A nasty streak of nativism coursed through both the antislavery and women's movements. With the rise of the anti-immigrant Know-Nothing Party in the mid-1850s, some reformers wanted to appeal to its members by adopting their crowd-pleasing invective. At one women's rights convention, the abolitionist Wendell Phillips framed the struggle at hand as between "the Saxon race," which had long "led the van" for equality of the sexes, and "the Jewish—yes, the Jewish—ridicule which laughs at such a Convention as this." Judaism represented the backward ways of old, a stubborn unwillingness to entertain new revelations or progressive ideas.

Though Rose saw herself as a nonbeliever and a citizen of the world, others still saw her as Jewish and foreign-born. Lucy Stone, an active abolitionist and women's rights leader, had once within Rose's hearing condemned "the foreigner, who can't speak his mother tongue correctly." A devout Christian, Stone believed American-born women more deserving of civil and political rights than foreigners were. In 1855, she wrote to Susan B. Anthony that while Rose "spoke well" at a recent convention, "there are so many mean Jews . . . and her *face* is so essentially Jewish, that the people remarked the likeness and feared her." Stone alleged that Rose had complained about the cost of travel and clothing and went on "a tirade about the low fee, said it was shameful." She added that Rose was a poor organizer. "My advice to you," Stone told Anthony, "is not to let Mrs. Rose do anything."

Some of her fellow activists took pity on Rose. "There are so few who dare to be friendly to her," Martha Wright told her sister, Lucretia Mott, who agreed: "It is too bad for such a woman to have to feel neglected."

Rose felt worse than neglected, as became clear in a tense exchange with Anthony, her closest friend in the movement. Early in the spring of 1854, the two hit the road. Rose was the star attraction. Anthony served as tour organizer. They first headed for the upper South and immediately encountered obstacles. In the federal capital, Rose was denied the use of a room in a Capitol Hill hotel on account of her atheism. The Smithsonian also refused to give her a platform. Instead the pair rented a large room attached to a saloon, where her audience swelled from one hundred the first night to some five hundred by the third, including sitting members of Congress in the midst of intensely debating the Kansas-Nebraska Act.

Rose had previously rejected William Lloyd Garrison's call for the dissolution of the Union between the free and slave states. But as she spoke in the Washington saloon, Rose realized she could not summon a convincing argument to show that slavery might ever be abolished without the Union first breaking apart. Desperate attempts to appease the South only made the problem worse. Now she held that the separation of the North from the South—the destruction of "that false, corrupt Union, where there is no liberty and no humanity"—was the crucial first step toward the abolition of slavery. "Whatever the Union might have been before [the Kansas-Nebraska] Bill was passed," she observed a year later, "the slender thread which held it together is now snapped asunder." Three years before Abraham Lincoln's famous "House Divided" speech, Rose insisted that "freedom and slavery could no more exist together than truth and falsehood. It is all true or all false; all free or all slave, and as we are not all free, we are all slaves and we are all slaveholders to some extent."

The only path forward was "to break that unholy Union—of wickedness, of crime, of sin, and of shame. A Union of freedom and slavery cannot exist any more than fire and water."

Leaving Washington, Rose and Anthony visited Mount Vernon. In her diary from the trip, Anthony marveled "that it was here, that he whose name is the pride of this nation was the *Slave Master.*" She was astonished to find slaves still laboring on the grounds. But she was even more startled to find herself growing accustomed to being waited on by them. After being in the South for only a few weeks, Anthony wrote, she had "ceased continually to be made to feel its blighting, cursing influence, so much so that I can sit down and eat from the hand of the bondsman, without being once mindful of the fact that he is such." Rose did not record her own impressions of the trip. Whether she felt similarly hardened against the horrors she so often denounced cannot be known. It seems unlikely.

Days later, in Baltimore—a year before David Einhorn's arrival in the city—the pair lodged in a boardinghouse where the workers were enslaved. Anthony was disappointed to find the enslaved woman serving her not so visibly abject as she had expected. "Oh how I long to probe her soul in search of that Divine spark that scorns to be a slave," Anthony wrote. "But then would it be right for me by so doing to add to the burden of her wretched life?"

In their Baltimore lodgings one evening, the women fell into conversation about Rose's sense of isolation within the movement.

She blamed leaders like Wendell Phillips and Lucy Stone, whom Rose thought guilty of unwarranted bigotry against the foreign-born, and Jews in particular. Anthony countered that Rose had a habit of holding her friends and comrades to impossibly high standards. She could be condescending toward allies who agreed with her on every issue but one. The exchange grew heated. Rose replied that Anthony was too keen to protect fellow activists from criticism, even when it was accurate. "No one can tell the hours of anguish I have suffered, as one after another I have seen those whom I had trusted betray falsity of motive," Rose sighed. Anthony asked if Rose considered her, too, guilty. Rose said she would tell Anthony if she ever thought her "untrue." Silence engulfed the room. Anthony asked Rose if she had hurt her feelings. No, Rose answered, "but I expect never to be understood while I live."

Anthony came away from the exchange with sympathy for Rose's position as a victim of her own uncompromising radicalism. "She is too much in advance of the extreme ultraists even, to be understood by them," Anthony wrote. "It filled my soul with anguish to see one so noble, so true . . . so bowed down, so overcome with deep swelling emotions." After their Southern tour, Rose took a few months off from the lecture circuit to recover her health. But the years of endless travel had taken their toll.

Forty-six years old, Rose felt isolated and exhausted. Years earlier, in a letter to her old mentor, the utopian socialist Robert Owen, Rose had reported having endured "several quite severe attacks of depression of mind." Now those attacks had returned. In May 1856, just as August Bondi got ready to go to war with Border Ruffians, the Roses left for Europe in an effort to, as Ernestine put it, "renovate a once exceedingly strong and enduring constitution, so as to enable me to perform my part in the great drama of life a few years longer." Before setting sail—nearly twenty years to the day after her arrival in the United States—Ernestine wrote in an open letter, published in a freethought paper, that she considered herself "a volunteer soldier in the cause of Truth." A brief "furlough" would let her "gather fresh strength for the glorious battle of freedom."

The position of an outspoken American Jew in the antebellum period was hardly less lonely on the opposite side of the political spectrum. Judah P. Benjamin was elected in 1852 as a United States senator from Louisiana, only the second Jew to serve in the upper chamber of the legislature. Through nearly a decade in Washington representing Louisiana in the Senate, he, like Ernestine Rose, struggled with the feeling of not quite belonging. He remained silent during congressional debates about issues of interest to the Jewish community. Benjamin likely felt that speaking up might be seen as special pleading and would do more harm than good. Despite his best efforts to avoid identification as a Jew, he often faced pointed comments from both enemies and admirers. Once, after Benjamin presented an argument before the Supreme Court, a justice told the opposing counsel that he had better step up his effort, for "that little Jew from New Orleans has stated your case out of court."

It did not help his attempts to blend in that Benjamin looked so markedly Jewish: short and swarthy, full-cheeked, with a short beard and a large forehead crowned by a mess of curly black hair. "A Hebrew of Hebrews," one acquaintance later remembered, "the map of the Holy City was traced all over his small, refined face."

In 1850, Benjamin had an intense conversation about religion with the Massachusetts senator Daniel Webster and a rabbi passing through Washington en route to some kind of theological showdown in Charleston, South Carolina. It was, of course, Isaac Mayer Wise, who recorded the exchange in his memoir decades later, confusing some of the details along the way. (Benjamin was not yet in the Senate; he may have been there on legal business.) When Webster suggested that whatever their superficial differences, they were all "coreligionists," since they were all monotheists, Benjamin disagreed, insisting, as Wise recalled, that "in his opinion Judaism and Christianity were entirely different." As Wise remembered, Benjamin possessed "a confused notion of orthodox Portuguese Judaism." He had, after all, been raised by a heterodox dissenter and had little to do with religion as an adult. Still, the rabbi was disappointed that while Webster knew the Bible thoroughly, Benjamin "could not cite one Jewish source."

Benjamin's Jewishness may have hindered his legal and political success, but not much. He rose to unprecedented heights for a Jewish politician at the time. Franklin Pierce offered him a seat on the Supreme Court, and James Buchanan sought to appoint him ambassador to Spain, the country his Sephardic ancestors had been forced to flee centuries earlier. Benjamin turned down both positions in favor of staying in the Senate and continuing to pursue his lucrative legal career. He traveled widely through the Americas, investigating conflicts over silver mines in California, surveying a possible route for a railroad across Mexico, even looking into reports of rich guano deposits—a valuable source of fertilizer for Southern plantations—in the Galápagos Islands. During senatorial recesses, Benjamin would often hasten back to Louisiana to represent the state's leading corporations and businessmen. His private interests as an attorney had a convenient way of aligning with his public actions as a senator.

For the first two years after he entered the Senate in 1853, Benjamin mostly kept quiet. With his Whig Party in the minority and struggling to survive, there was not much to do. Benjamin was rare among Southern senators in enjoying the admiration of Northern colleagues even at a time of bitter division. John Hale of New Hampshire, one of the leading antislavery senators, praised Benjamin's "acknowledged ability, his great eloquence, his very persuasive

powers, his mellifluous voice, his winning and graceful manner"—
all of which, Hale sighed, "only makes me regret that he is in a
wrong position."

An eager gossip, a gifted socialite, a habitual card player, Benjamin gathered opponents around his dinner table in an effort "to
bridge the river of bitterness which flowed wide and brimming
over between the North and South," as Jefferson Davis's wife,
Varina, an intimate friend of Benjamin's, later put it. She first met
the Louisianan at a White House dinner hosted by Pierce, under
whom Davis served as secretary of war. Varina was twenty-six, well
educated in literature and philosophy, and initially unimpressed
with Benjamin, who "had rather the air of a witty bon vivant than
that of a great Senator." His looks she described as "decidedly
Hebrew . . . boyish in the extreme," with thick curls ringing his
fleshy face.

The passage of the Kansas-Nebraska Act in May 1854, even
as it sent August Bondi into a brewing civil war on the plains and
convinced Ernestine Rose it was time for disunion, cleaved the national capital and scrambled political alliances. Popular outrage at
the measure forced Northern politicians to take a more radical stand
against slavery, while the rise of abolitionism led Southern politicians to insist on the rights of the slave states. Benjamin saw the
country beginning to crack. But he still preferred that the South
remain in the Union so that slavery received the protection of the
national government. A member of the federal bar, Benjamin suggested submitting the Kansas dispute to the Supreme Court. He
criticized antislavery Northerners for instead opting to battle it
out—as August Bondi was doing at that very moment—through
"appeals to Sharpe's rifles instead of courts of justice."

Amid the turmoil, Benjamin left the splintering Whig Party
for the more aggressively proslavery Democrats. He was wounded
by those Northern Whigs who, as he put it, "again and again refused
to stand by the rights guaranteed to the South in the Constitution

and now assailed by the Abolitionists." The Democrats offered a more congenial political home for Benjamin, not least because they had taken control of the Louisiana legislature, which would decide whether to reappoint him to the Senate.

The only other option would have been the anti-immigrant Know-Nothing Party, which many of Benjamin's fellow Whigs were now joining. It would not have been inconceivable for a Jew to join the increasingly powerful anti-immigrant coalition. The founder of the party's 1840s forerunner, the Native American Party, was Lewis Charles Levin, a son, like Benjamin, of Jewish Charleston. Eager to blend in, both had distanced themselves from the religion of their birth, though Levin, unlike Benjamin, actually became a Protestant. As a newspaper editor in Philadelphia and then as a three-term congressman, Levin had raised hatred of immigrants and especially Catholics to a new level of virulence in American politics. He saw the Irish in particular as exhibiting the same insular clannishness that had turned him away from the Jewish community in which he was raised. Before going mad and dying in an insane asylum, Levin built a brief but impressive career as a barnstorming demagogue warning against a Catholic conspiracy to "overthrow American liberty" and submit the republic to the rule of Rome.

Though he had been born in a British territory, Benjamin, too, had dabbled with that first wave of nativism in the 1840s. He feared that an influx of foreign-born immigrants into Louisiana would undermine the institution of slavery. Newcomers would be less attached to bondage.

Yet whether it was because his own wife and daughter were Catholic or because he himself was foreign-born, Benjamin ultimately rejected the Know-Nothings as a political dead end. He did not trust them to support slavery—indeed, many would later join the antislavery Republican Party—and he ridiculed the idea that "to know if you wanted a man to serve you faithfully in any office of trust or emolument, you must find out first by what priest he was baptized, and what faith he professed!" Any party that would pose such a test was not the party for him. He told the Senate in 1855 that he eagerly awaited the "fast approaching time when not only Louisiana but the entire South, animated by a single spirit, shall struggle for its dearest rights."

Sparring with antislavery spokesmen like Charles Sumner of Massachusetts, Benjamin became more aggressive in his defense of slavery. He saw the violence that accompanied Northern attempts to shield alleged runaway slaves from arrest as proof there could be no peaceful resolution to the conflict. Such obstruction amounted to "a course of direct war upon the South." Compromise was out of the question. With the onset of violence in Kansas, Benjamin began to talk about the Constitution in the past tense. He even hinted of war. He promised to "assist in averting that last, lamentable catastrophe," but became "every day more and more persuaded it is becoming inevitable." Unless something miraculous happened, he would soon have to bid "good bye to this glorious Union of States."

In a different corner of the continent and for very different reasons, Ernestine Rose was coming to the same conclusion. Yet Benjamin was certain that no peaceful dissolution of the Union could be possible. Once the final crisis came, he warned, "dreadful will be the internecine war that must ensue."

In Kansas, August Bondi was doing everything he could to help bring the war on. Everywhere men went armed, most with rifles, some with hand grenades and swords. Secret signs and handshakes revealed carefully concealed allegiances. After the proslavery mob's attack on the free-staters in Lawrence, posses went from house to house in the Osawatomie part of the territory, where August Bondi and the Brown family lived, warning antislavery men and their families to leave or risk lynching. Bondi, regretting having sold a double-barreled shotgun to pay for his journey westward, hastily tried to hide his property and cattle deep in the woods, broke down his store, and, grasping his 1812 musket, prepared himself for war.

Furious at the proslavery assaults, John Brown called for volunteers to exact vengeance. Seven agreed, Theodore Wiener among them. Wiener—"a big, savage, bloodthirsty Austrian," as one of Brown's sons described him, who "could not be kept out of any accessible fight"—had lived in the South for years. Until recently, he had considered himself a proslavery man. In Kansas, some on the proslavery side tried to get him to publicly ally with them, but Wiener said that he had come to Kansas to make money, not to get involved in politics. Meeting John Brown and his sons had changed him, as had a brawl with "Dutch Henry" Sherman's brother, "Dutch Bill," who, angered by Wiener's neutrality, attacked Wiener in Bondi's store. Wiener managed to pin Sherman, then took his gun, emptied its contents, and kept beating him up. He finally threw the gun at Sherman and told him to get lost. "After that," Bondi recalled, "Wiener acknowledged himself Free State." He supplied food for the antislavery forces marching to relieve their besieged comrades in Lawrence. Three days later, Wiener was with Brown and six other men when, an hour before midnight, they grabbed five proslavery settlers from their cabins and hacked at them with broadswords. One had his throat slit for good measure. Others were shot and stabbed. Dutch Bill was one of the victims. The next morning, he was found at the edge of Pottawatomie Creek with a hole in his chest and his skull cracked open, his brains washed away by the burbling brook.

Bondi could never get Wiener to talk about what happened on the prairie that night. The attack was immediately controversial, even among some free-staters who feared, with good reason, that it gave the federal government an excuse to intervene and crush the antislavery militias. As for Bondi, he recalled being "astonished but not at all displeased" on learning of the violence. Responding nearly fifty years later to the charge that the Pottawatomie killings amounted to cold-blooded murder, Bondi held firm: "John Brown and his handful of men only executed upon those scoundrels a just sentence of death for the benefit of many unprotected families." Brown's attack served notice that free-staters would stand up for themselves.

After the Pottawatomie killings, the simmering tensions in Kansas exploded into an all-out civil war. There were raids on outlying farms, ambushes on lonely prairie roads, cold-blooded killings, pitched battles between organized forces lined up across a field, rockets and hand grenades and brass cannons loaded with rusty nails aimed at one another. One free-stater called for the Southern scoundrels to be "shot as mad dogs." A proslavery settler slept with his rifle, revolver, pistol, hatchet, and axe to protect himself from "the midnight attacks of the Abolitionists." Bondi once saw a proslavery militia hauling wagons loaded with dead bodies, arms and legs dangling over the sides. At a well-traveled crossroads, he and his friend Jacob Benjamin came across the body of one of John Brown's sons, murdered by a Southern militia. Bondi's log cabin was burned to the ground and his cattle stolen, all while federal troops, openly allied with the proslavery mob, silently looked on. Theodore Wiener's store was plundered and destroyed. Jacob Benjamin was taken prisoner with two of the Brown brothers, their arms painfully chained to their feet. By the time the fighting died down in the late 1850s, each side had suffered as many as one hundred fatalities.

For the rest of his life, August Bondi was proud to have participated, that summer of 1856, in the first battles between North and South. The free-state cause would have failed if not for the "small and starving and ragged crowd" that "stay[ed] together in the primeval Kansas forest with John Brown." Years later, he still vividly recalled the "torment of hunger," the "sleepless days and nights . . . and continuous mosquito torture." Bondi described the surprisingly rules-based atmosphere of the outlaws' camp: Brown warned his fighters never to target women or children, nor to take anything they could not use, and never to destroy property unnecessarily. Captured horses and cattle were to be the "common property of the Free State army." Enemy prisoners always ate first. Profanity was forbidden. Blessings were said every morning and evening and over every meal. Brown told one visitor he would "rather have the small-pox, yellow fever and cholera all together in my camp, than a man without principles." One night after dinner, Bondi and other members of the company discussed a far-fetched scheme for free Kansas to secede from the slavery-corrupted United States. "We were very enthusiastic," Bondi recalled, "but when John Brown was informed of our project he soon cooled our fervor by his cool, simple words, 'Boys, no nonsense.'"

"He showed at all times the most affectionate care for each of us," Bondi remembered of Brown, and the men, in return, showed strict obedience to the leader who "in the depths of the wilder-ness . . . prepared a handful of young men for the work of laying the foundation of a free commonwealth."

5

"Israelites with Egyptian Principles"

"H. LEHMAN," READ THE SIGN, A SIMPLE, ROUGH-HEWN shingle. The humble store's twenty-three-year-old proprietor had left Bavaria little more than a year earlier, as Hayum. After landing in New York in 1844 and adopting the name Henry, he headed for Alabama, where his agricultural knowledge—he came from a family of cattle dealers and wine merchants—fit him well for Southern life. From Mobile, Henry set off as so many Jewish immigrants did, making his way through the state selling pots and pans from a wagon. Within a year, he found his way to Montgomery, home to six thousand people, one-third of them enslaved. Despite its unpaved streets, its swarms of flies, its deadly outbreaks of yellow fever, the newly designated state capital may have reminded Henry of Rimpar, the inland German river town where he had grown up. He saw the city's potential and hung up his wooden sign.

For the first few years, he led a solitary existence, living in the store's back room, working by the meager light of oil lamps late into the night. Awed by his industry, locals called him "our little monk." "There is money to be made here," Henry wrote home to Germany, "if the Fever does not get me first."

Along with the dozen or so other Jewish men in Montgomery, he helped form a congregation. When a brother, Mendel (Emanuel in America), joined Henry, they replaced the sign with a new one: "H. Lehman & Bro.," and when another, Mayer, came after the 1848 revolution, the sign changed once more, to "Lehman Brothers."

The business grew quickly, and slavery, from the beginning, was central to its success. The South's thriving cotton economy supported a swelling professional class of insurance brokers, speculators, lawyers, merchants, and shippers. The Lehmans leapt at the opportunities.

The firm that began in a dusty shop with goods lined along open shelves soon moved to a huge new building in a more prominent location, just across the street from Montgomery's auction block. By 1850, Henry Lehman owned two people, a fifty-year-old man and a forty-five-year-old woman; a few years later, he added a fourteen-year-old girl. Mayer Lehman is listed in the 1860 census as the owner of seven people, ranging in age from five to fifty.

Before long the brothers began trading in cotton, accepting burlap-wrapped bales as barter for shirts, shoes, sheets, rope, fertilizer, and tools. Often they simply jotted down a customer's promise of future deliveries once the crop came in. Those lines of credit turned the firm into something of an informal bank, one that specialized in finding increasingly creative ways of making money off the cotton market, especially by trading in debts and mortgages backed by human chattel as collateral. The brothers would sometimes take ownership of enslaved people in lieu of payment, then sell them off for cash. Mayer Lehman, the brains of the operation once Henry died, just as he had feared, of yellow fever, proved tenacious in learning the ins and outs of the cotton business, "mastering every intricacy and nuance of the trade," as one historian of the family put it, "with the same patience and persistence his ancestors had applied to the Talmud."

———

Like the Lehmans, many Jews found the antebellum South a comfortable and congenial home. Jews in the region achieved success as mayors, congressmen, state representatives, editors, bank presidents, railroad directors, and prominent businessmen. Christians in the South donated to Jewish community funds for building and maintaining synagogues or assisting persecuted Jews overseas. Southern governors attended fancy balls to benefit Hebrew schools. Southern Jews did not have to hide their Jewishness. But a tacit agreement lay behind their tenuous welcome. As one resident of Richmond, Virginia, observed, the city's Jews had learned they could prosper only by remaining "as quiet and unostentatious as possible." Above all, they had to keep quiet about slavery.

Many of the new immigrants first encountered bondage as traveling peddlers. On the road, they learned everything they needed to know about their new homeland, its language and its people, what to say and what not to say, especially about slavery. Lazarus Straus, patriarch of the family that later owned Macy's, experienced for himself the surprising benefits of arriving on American shores already carrying in his pigmentation all the credentials he needed to succeed. According to his son Oscar, later a member of Theodore Roosevelt's cabinet, Lazarus, though a foreigner, had felt welcomed by the plantation masters: "[T]he existence of slavery drew a distinct line of demarcation between the white and black races. This gave to the white [Jewish] visitor a status of equality that probably otherwise he would not have enjoyed to such a degree."

When they stopped at plantation mansions, after pitching the residents on the goods in their packs—and occasionally having to show whether they in fact, as rumored, had horns—Jewish peddlers were sometimes put up for the night in rooms set aside just for them, accepted as the guests, if not quite the social equals, of native-born whites. "During those nights in the 'big house,' in the parlors and kitchens of the slaveowning classes," the historian Hasia Diner has written, "the peddlers learned firsthand the meaning of whiteness." In this far-famed land of opportunities, perhaps the most significant, for the new arrivals, was the presence of a permanent underclass whose members were, by definition, their inferiors.

Even so, Jewish peddlers were sometimes reviled, even harassed, for violating the Sunday Sabbath or for trading illicitly with the enslaved, particularly for selling alcohol to them or accepting goods stolen from masters in exchange for new wares. In a pair of popular books about his travels through the South in the 1850s, Frederick Law Olmsted, still a few years away from designing New York's Central Park, wrote of a "swarm" of Jewish peddlers, "many of them men of no character," who preyed on enslaved people. Often such claims of illicit dealing were advanced by gentile merchants jealous of their Jewish competitors. Some Southern whites feared that Jewish peddlers were disseminating antislavery literature or encouraging enslaved people to run away. By 1860, Isaac Leeser, the editor of the influential *Occident* newspaper, felt compelled to "warn all our brothers residing in the Southern states against making themselves obnoxious by violating the ordinances against dealing with the bondsman of that part of the republic." Early the following year, amid the upheaval of the secession crisis, ten peddlers were thrown out of Mississippi after raising a panic among the locals that they were in fact "Abolitionists, endeavoring to stir up an insurrection."

Despite such suspicions, a few Southern Jews managed to succeed in the slave economy. In Richmond, the Davis family established what one historian has called "something of a Jewish slave-trading dynasty." Two blocks from the state capitol designed by Thomas Jefferson, brothers Hector, Benjamin, John, Robert, and Solomon owned a two-floor slave auction house as well as what they deemed a "safe and commodious jail," where men, women, and children were held pending sale. In her *Key to Uncle Tom's Cabin*, a nonfiction compendium detailing the sources she drew on in writing the 1852 bestseller, Harriet Beecher Stowe quoted a letter about the Davis firm: "They are Jews, came to that place many years ago as poor peddlers . . . These men are always in the market, giving the highest price for slaves. During the summer and fall they buy them up at low prices, trim, shave, wash them, fatten them so that they may look sleek, and sell them to great profit." In one week in 1859, the Davis brothers of Richmond made the equivalent today of more than four million dollars in profit. They sold anywhere from seventy to one hundred individuals on an average day. Other Davis brothers established slave-trading outlets in Alexandria and Petersburg. In 1854, Ansley Davis of Petersburg signed a bill of sale for "a female slave named Savry about 15 years of age warranted Sound and Healthy." The buyer was also Jewish—Abraham Tobias of Charleston—as was the witness who validated the sale.

Jewish slave ownership in the 1850s went far beyond traders and plantation owners. Jewish butchers owned slaves. Jewish lawyers owned slaves. Bookkeepers and brokers and hoteliers owned slaves. A Jewish dentist in Charleston owned twelve people. Some masters held one or two workers to help out with the business; others invested in the ownership of people to make some extra money by renting them out to others. Both the native-born and new arrivals owned slaves; by one calculation, the former tended to own twice as many as the latter, an average of ten compared to five. In the antebellum South, slave ownership was the ultimate mark of success. A credit report from Georgia in 1860 showed that a German Jewish immigrant named Alexander Baum, a sack-burdened traveling salesman only eight years earlier, was now "going on big scale, buying negroes and land."

Most of the Jewish immigrants who settled in the South would have known of the existence of slavery in the region before their arrival and would likely have moved to the North if they had a problem with it. Arriving in America in 1847, Aaron Hirsch traveled through Mississippi and Alabama as a peddler. Slavery was "not so great a wrong as people believe," Hirsch reflected. "The Negroes were brought here in a savage state; they captured and ate each other in their African home. Here they were instructed to work, were civilized and got religion, and were perfectly happy." Julius Weis, who arrived at the age of nineteen, was startled when he first saw a slave stripped and whipped by an overseer. But before long, Weis bought a slave for himself—a "negro man, a fine looking mulatto." A successful cotton and dry-goods merchant in New Orleans, Weis claimed he "always felt a pity for the poor slaves" and never punished his human property as he had seen done in the street that day. But he never denounced bondage.

In Charleston, South Carolina, one of the richest men in the city, Benjamin Mordecai, kept his own slave pen next to his warehouse and once purchased $12,000 worth of human beings in a single sale; in 1840 he put forty people, including three children, up for sale at one time. A few blocks away, Grace Peixotto, the Caribbean-born daughter of a former cantor at Congregation Beth Elohim, ran Charleston's notorious three-story "Big Brick" brothel, where high-class gentlemen, sailors and laborers, and even free and enslaved Black men mingled and sampled the wares, a rare instance of racial mixing in a city devoted to slavery and segregation. A visiting Englishman, critical of both prostitution and slavery, called Peixotto a "notorious woman who has kept the worst kind of a brothel for years, where harlots of all shades and importations break the quietude of night with their polluted songs." Peixotto herself, objecting to a police description of her bordello as disorderly, boasted of having "the most quiet, respectable, ladylike whores south of the Mason-Dixon Line." By 1860, she personally owned seven women between the ages of six and forty-five.

Religious leaders were supportive of the institution. Maurice Mayer, the rabbi at Charleston's Beth Elohim through most of the 1850s, was a veteran of the 1848 revolution in Germany. Charged with "armed rebellion and high treason," convicted and sentenced to death, he had somehow escaped to America. Though an outspoken adherent of the more radical strain of Reform Judaism and a close ally of the antislavery Baltimore rabbi David Einhorn, Mayer saw no contradiction between his support for liberal revolution in Europe and his embrace of slavery in the United States. He married into a family of Southern Jewish slaveholders and wrote to friends in Germany that living in a slave society did not bother him, for he considered the issue "not relevant to the core of Jewish interest."

Opposing abolitionism, however, *was* relevant to Jewish interests. For Mayer, the Christian-tinged radicalism of the abolitionists boded ill for the safety of American Jews. "It does not take a prophetic clairvoyance to claim that Jews will never be the last chosen as fanaticism's victims once it prevails," the rabbi observed. "This is regardless of the shape it takes, be it political or religious or whatever name it might bear . . . it will always threaten the Jews." Contrary to the "slanderous claims of the northern fanatics," however much the abolitionists attacked the institution on the basis of "a misguided philanthropy," Mayer argued, slavery was in fact "a charity," far more humane than the treatment of white laborers in Europe and the Northern states.

Jacob N. Cardozo, a prominent editor and economist in Charleston (his first cousin's grandson would be the Supreme Court justice Benjamin N. Cardozo), made similar arguments. "The institution of slavery is a harmonizing bond of union and sympathy," he contended, offering a "reciprocity of protection and obedience" that benefited both owners and owned. The chief risk to the system, in Cardozo's view, was the masters' overly indulgent treatment of their bondsmen. He called for "reduc[ing] the standard of comfort of our slaves" in order to ensure slave owners "receive a fair remuneration of living profit on our capital."

Just as Haym Salomon's supposed financing of the American Revolution would be invoked by subsequent generations of American Jews eager to identify with the nation's founding, Uriah P.

Levy's stewardship of Monticello has served a similar function. In 1836, Levy, a career naval officer who faced decades of religious bigotry in the service—he was court-martialed six times and once killed a man in a duel over an insult—plowed his profits from successful investments in New York real estate into the purchase of Thomas Jefferson's beloved mountaintop home in Virginia, which had fallen into disrepair since the master's death a decade earlier. Levy, a native Philadelphian who admired Jefferson's commitment to religious liberty, purchased nineteen slaves to refurbish the property. They cleared leaves and branches, hauled away the garbage and scattered debris, landscaped the grounds, cleaned out the well, fixed the roof and exterior walls, repainted the interior, repaired the clock in the front hall, and refurbished the carriage that Jefferson had taken to Philadelphia in 1776. Levy's role in "saving Monticello" has gone down in American Jewish lore. Fictional portrayals have imagined him harboring private regrets about owning slaves on account of his own people's history of oppression, but there is no evidence for such reluctance. A bachelor until the age of sixty-one, he married Virginia Lopez, the widowed daughter of his own sister. Levy died in New York in 1862, shortly after the Confederacy seized Monticello—and its nineteen slaves—on account of Levy's refusal to renounce his US citizenship. Virginia outlived her uncle and husband by more than sixty years. Shortly before her death, she reminisced about her years at Monticello, where "the darkies were very amusing."

By the end of 1857, proslavery forces in Kansas were outnumbered by free-state settlers. The Border Ruffians could only win control of the territory through yet another election so blatantly fraudulent their opponents would stay home in disgust. That accomplished, they held a convention in the tiny outpost of Lecompton to draw up a proslavery constitution. Then they sent it to Congress, asking for Kansas to be admitted to the Union as a slave state.

The Lecompton Constitution put the president, James Buchanan, in a tough spot. Along with others in the Democratic Party, the proslavery Pennsylvanian had embraced the doctrine of popular sovereignty, which held that the people on the ground should decide whether to allow slavery in a new territory or state. But the open fraud and intimidation in Kansas made a mockery of the idea. Even many of the South's leading Northern sympathizers urged the president to reject the Lecompton document as undemocratic. Buchanan's Southern supporters, in turn, framed the issue as a test of the party's commitment to slave-state interests. If freedom prevailed in Kansas, slavery's political power would decline. From throughout the South came threats to leave the Union if Kansas failed to legalize slavery.

As so often happens in American history, the intimidation worked. Buchanan followed the South-friendly strategy that had earned him the presidency in the first place. A "Northern man with Southern principles," as the expression went—a fierce defender of bondage though he came from a free state—Buchanan endorsed the Lecompton Constitution and recommended that Congress admit Kansas as a slave state.

On March 11, 1858, Judah Benjamin, now more comfortable speaking before the national legislature, rose in the Senate to defend the Lecompton Constitution and the institution of slavery. As the sectional struggle escalated in the 1850s, Benjamin had become even more convinced that emancipation had to be avoided, lest "our property, now kept in proper subjection, peaceful and laborious, would be converted into an idle, reckless, criminal population, led on to their foul purpose by inflamed passions." He feared "the gravest of social perils" if the slaves suddenly went free. Abolition posed a threat not merely to Southern property but to "existence itself, because the history of Hayti is written in characters so black, so dark, so prominent, that we cannot be ignorant of the fate that awaits us if measures similar to those which have produced that result there are also to be inaugurated in our Southern states." References to the specter of the Haitian Revolution were commonplace in Southern rhetoric, but Benjamin had a special connection to it: His in-laws had fled the uprising. Even after his wife's departure for France, her father, Auguste St. Martin, would sometimes stop by social gatherings at Bellechasse to "tell the young folk thrilling tales of the horrors of the great West Indian slave insurrection," as Benjamin's first biographer, Pierce Butler, wrote. Benjamin himself, as a ten-year-old boy, may have seen the alleged conspirators of Denmark Vesey's uprising hanging in the Charleston streets.

In his five years in the Senate, Benjamin had become an ally of hard-core proslavery Southerners like Jefferson Davis of Mississippi. They were an unlikely pairing—Benjamin an urbane sophisticate, an immigrant, and a Jew; Davis a rural planter with Southern roots going back to the American Revolution—and at first they rubbed one another the wrong way. Once, during a heated exchange in the Senate over federal appropriations, Davis dismissed Benjamin's scrupulous inquiries about War Department expenditures as those of a "paid attorney." Benjamin asked if he had heard Davis right. Davis replied that he had. At that, Benjamin invited Davis to a duel. Remarkably, Davis, a decorated hero of the Mexican-American War, declined and, though he did not quite apologize, acknowledged on the Senate floor that the perceived insult had been based on a regrettable misunderstanding. A perpetual outsider, Benjamin constantly felt he had to prove his credentials as a member in good standing of the white Southern aristocracy.

Addressing the Senate on the controversial Lecompton issue, the most accomplished lawyer in the Senate—"the most brilliant perhaps of the whole of the famous Southern orators," one journalist believed—Benjamin defended slavery not only on moral and political grounds but as legally and constitutionally unassailable.

According to American common law, a Black person "was merchandise, was property, was a slave," he said. Even if the Northern states passed legislation banning it, they could not force the Southern states to follow suit. Compelled to choose between slavery and the Union, the South would not hesitate—and neither would he.

Two days later, Benjamin Wade, a radical antislavery senator from Ohio, fired back at Benjamin and took indirect aim at his opponent's Jewish origins. Recalling the time "when old Moses . . . enticed a whole nation of slaves, and ran away, not to Canada, but to old Canaan," Wade mused that the pharaoh and his ministers must have thought the rebel leader "a most furious abolitionist." Even then, Wade went on, there were some among those newly freed Hebrews, wandering in the desert, murmuring against Moses, who glorified the days of bondage and sought to return. "They were not exactly Northern men with Southern principles," Wade snickered, "but they were Israelites with Egyptian principles." And so, too, the elaborately veiled yet unmistakable insult implied, was the gentleman from Louisiana, Judah P. Benjamin. The nation's most famous representative of a people who celebrated their liberation from slavery was also one of its foremost defenders of the enslavement of others.

He was not the only one. There were plenty of Israelites with Egyptian principles in the 1850s. All three Jewish men elected to the House of Representatives that decade were strong supporters of human bondage. Others pushed the proslavery line in the press. After Mordecai Manuel Noah's death in 1851—Morris Jacob Raphall, the Orthodox rabbi who had recently arrived from Birmingham, England, delivered the eulogy at his funeral—Robert Lyon was perhaps the most prominent Jewish journalist in the country. A London-born former umbrella manufacturer, Lyon founded and edited both the

Asmonean, a Jewish weekly that opened its pages to advocates of religious reform (Isaac Mayer Wise helped edit it before starting his own paper), and the *New York Mercantile Journal*, an organ devoted to the interests of the city's commercial elite. Following Noah's model as a self-appointed defender of Jewish interests, Lyon criticized abolitionists and warned of the economic consequences of a rupture over slavery. The *Asmonean* condemned "Frederick Douglass, the nigger"; ridiculed Black suffrage (a "more wild and a more preposterous idea never yet entered the brain of man"); and called on all Americans, including Jews, to "crush out for once and forever the attempt to plunder our Southern citizens of their property."

The newspaper also supported enforcement of the Fugitive Slave Act, which required all citizens to assist in the return of runaways to bondage. In 1851, shortly after the law's passage, a Bavarian-born, Yale-educated physician named Sigismund Waterman explained in the *Asmonean* why it had to be obeyed: the Torah itself endorsed "the principle of reclaiming the absconded slave." Though Jews themselves had experienced slavery and knew well "the sorrow of the man of servitude," slavery existed whether they liked it or not. Jews could purchase a slave in order to grant him his freedom, but they could not jeopardize "national and even international peace by gaining his freedom through violence." American Jews depended on the stability of the Union for their security, Waterman warned. They had a special responsibility to "stand by the constitution, now and forever," and that meant complying with the new law.

––––––––––

Most American Jews tended to follow the dominant opinion of their region. But Northern Jews were far more free to express support for slavery than Southern Jews were to express opposition. Oscar Straus recalled that growing up in the Talbotton, Georgia, home of his father, Lazarus, served by enslaved people his family first rented and then bought, he never questioned the institution. Nobody else did either. To criticize slavery would "subject one to social ostracism."

Many years later, the Cincinnati merchant Louis Stix recalled a conversation he had with a fellow Jew, a Southerner, when they met at a boardinghouse in New York City just before the Civil War. The boardinghouse was about evenly split between Northerners and Southerners. An "outspoken opponent of all involuntary serfdom," as Stix called himself, he had lost Southern customers due to his antislavery position, and he felt unsafe traveling in the slave states. In New York, however, he thought he could express his opinions freely. When the other man told Stix that "Southerners could not live without slavery," Stix replied with a barbed criticism of the hypocrisy of Southern Jews. The man "drew his pistol to compel me to take back my words." Stix refused. A fellow Northerner, siding with Stix, took out his pistol in return, and the Southerner slunk away. A half-century later, Stix wrote that he hoped the Southern man had since revised his opinions or returned to Europe, "where he was almost a slave himself."

Some Southern Jews did bravely criticize the institution, though they knew doing so could bring severe repercussions. In 1856, Henry Harrisse, a French-born Jewish professor at the University of North Carolina, later famous as a biographer of Columbus, was fired by the college for defending a colleague who had expressed support for a ban on slavery in the western territories. "You may eliminate all suspicious men from your institutions of learning," Harrisse warned Southerners after his termination, "but as long as people study, and read, and think among you, the absurdity of your system will be discovered and there will always be found some courageous intelligence to protest against your hateful tyranny."

For Jews as for others in the South, any criticisms they did offer of slavery tended to question its economic merits rather than its moral failings. In 1849, Solomon Heydenfeldt, a Charleston-born lawyer and politician who had moved to Alabama, addressed a pamphlet to the state's governor advocating an immediate end to the importation of additional slaves. Heydenfeldt was no abolitionist. "Born and reared at the South," he assured the governor, he opposed any "sickly sympathy for the condition of the slave." He believed that slave labor depressed wages, starved the economy, and turned off new immigrants, an argument later put forward, to more explosive effect, by the Southern-born Hinton Rowan Helper in his controversial 1857 book *The Impending Crisis*. If the population of slaves in the Lower South continued to grow, Heydenfeldt contended, the region would become "the St. Domingo of the Continent"; it would suffer the fate of Haiti. The South had to free itself from the burden of human bondage, or else the federal government would step in, likely without compensating the slaveholders.

Despite Heydenfeldt's assurances of his loyalty to the South, the pamphlet ended his Alabama career. Limiting the supply of slaves, one critic noted, would increase the cost of purchase. Most whites who aspired to slave ownership would be locked out of the market. Within a year, Heydenfeldt decamped for San Francisco, where he would go on to serve on the state supreme court. (In 1861, Heydenfeldt argued that California should side with the Confederacy. When the state opted to remain in the Union and forced all lawyers to swear a loyalty oath, he retired from the bar.)

An even more idiosyncratic antislavery perspective came from the pen of Marx Lazarus, scion of a prominent Southern Jewish family (his grandfather had been a Virginia plantation owner and the president of Richmond's Beth Shalome congregation). Raised in Wilmington, North Carolina, and educated at the state university (the first Jewish student to enroll there), Lazarus was drawn to social reform movements like vegetarianism, homeopathy, and socialism. He spent time at both the Brook Farm commune outside Boston and the North American Phalanx in New Jersey, radical experiments in group living inspired by the French utopian socialist

Charles Fourier. ("[T]hey have made him a menial and a drudge," one relative wrote scornfully to another, "but . . . he enjoys it, cleans cow stables, waits on the table, takes orders from the cook, ploughs, helps the Ladies iron clothes, etc.") An eccentric even among utopians, a manic mystic with long black hair and jet-black eyes, Lazarus advocated free love, most notably in an 1852 book, *Love vs. Marriage*. Like Ernestine Rose, he saw women's role in conventional marriage as a form of "systematic slavery, an immolation of one's personal predilections and pursuits on the altar of . . . domestic comfort."

Yet even in the book, Lazarus acknowledged that he was writing those words in the Alabama home of his aunt and uncle, the enslavers of numerous people. These slaves, Lazarus claimed, "have never known aught but comfort, security, the mild yoke of well-assorted labors, and that elevating influence which the Caucasian race, superior in intellect and culture, invariably extends over the negro when this superiority is accompanied with the Christian character."

Born Jewish yet committed to his own utopian visions, Lazarus was keen to repeat to his presumably white Christian readers nostrums prevalent in the broader culture about the nation's predominant religion and its privileged race. (His uncle had converted to marry a Christian woman.) But even he must have known it was not true that his family's slaves had only known comfort and security. Twenty years earlier, after the Nat Turner revolt in Virginia, fear of a similar insurrection swept through Marx's native Wilmington. The Lazarus family hid in their home while nine-year-old Marx's father, Aaron, a prominent businessman, patrolled the streets as part of the civic guard. Two slaves who worked in Aaron's warehouse were accused of participating in the plot; Marx's older brother, Washington, recently admitted to the bar (and himself the owner of thirty people), defended two of them in court, unsuccessfully. They were executed and Aaron was compensated for the loss of his property. Marx's mother, Rachel, concluded that the only solution to the problem of slavery was to send all Black people back to Africa. "Till this is resolved on and executed," Rachel wrote her sister, "we can have no security but in a state of unremitted vigilance." Rachel found it impossible to live in a place where "soon or later we or our descendents will become the certain victims of a band of lawless wretches who will deem murder and outrage just retribution" for their years in bondage.

By 1860, then living in Cincinnati, Marx Lazarus was arguing for abolition. He wrote in an essay that Black slavery amounted to the "prolonged crucifixion of a martyr race." It should be ended, but that was not all. Slavery was but one form of unjust economic control—"free" labor was another. Abolishing bondage but maintaining wage labor would change "the form, but not the facts, of slavery and oppression." Emancipation had to mean something "more humane than the liberty of selling oneself by the day, the cut-throat competitions of labor for wages, the outrages sanctioned by prejudice against color, careworn indigence or paralyzed pauperism." A year later, when the Civil War broke out, this utopian Jewish socialist, a sworn opponent of slavery in all its forms, enlisted in the Confederate Army.

After the war, Lazarus lived alone in a hilltop cabin in Alabama, having fallen "victim," as his obituary stated, "to communistic views, which ultimately exiled him from society." Known locally as the Sand Mountain Hermit, he subsisted on goat milk and wild roots and occasionally rode a bull into town for supplies, wearing red flannel pajamas and no shoes. He died sometime around 1895, aged seventy-three or seventy-four years old.

———

African Americans in bondage often saw themselves as spiritual descendants of the ancient Hebrews. As early as 1774, the enslaved poet Phillis Wheatley mocked American slaveholders as "our modern

Egyptians." In a fiery 1843 address calling for a violent revolution against slavery, the militant abolitionist Henry Highland Garnet, himself born into slavery, said it was time for enslaved Black Americans, "like the children of Israel, to make a grand exodus from the land of bondage." For enslaved people who could not read—just as for David Einhorn and other proponents of Reform Judaism—the Bible lived not in the text itself but in the spirit. Jewish scripture became the basis for Black folklore. In the "sorrow songs," as W. E. B. Du Bois called the traditional slave spirituals, often based on biblical stories, "there breathes a hope—a faith in the ultimate justice of things." Harriet Tubman, known to all as "Moses," used the song "Wade in the Water"—with its reference to "the leader of the Israelites" guiding his people across the parted sea—to remind the fugitives in her charge to stick to rivers and swamps so as to throw patrol dogs off their scents. In 1862, at Fortress Monroe, a Union outpost on the Virginia coast, a white missionary recorded some lines he heard sung by the first runaways to seize their freedom amid the chaos of war: "When Israel was in Egypt land / Let my people go."

Through the Civil War and beyond, Black Americans invoked Exodus to denounce American slavery and segregation more often and more consistently than did American Jews. If today we see a contradiction in the fact that Jews once owned slaves, it is partly because Judaism has itself reabsorbed the Black interpretation of Exodus, an appropriation of an appropriation.

Occasionally, Black identification with the Jewish tradition went beyond the metaphorical. Some slaves owned by Jews adopted the faith of their masters, as those owned by Christians adopted that of theirs. In the colonial-era Caribbean, especially before 1800, many African slaves were circumcised, in the case of men, or immersed in the ritual *mikveh* bath, in the case of women, partly to make them able to prepare kosher food. The historian C. L. R. James wrote that Jewish masters in the West Indies "spared no energy in making

Israelites of their slaves," unlike Christians, who generally denied religious instruction to their bondsmen. For those enslaved in Spanish colonies, conversion to Judaism put them, along with their crypto-Jewish masters, at risk of execution by the Inquisition.

By the late eighteenth century, as many as one in ten Jews in the Americas were people of color. In some communities, such as the Dutch colony of Suriname, they may have been up to half of the Jewish population. In time, religious authorities on both sides of the Atlantic, Christian and Jewish, felt compelled to come up with rules dealing with the phenomenon. Catholic authorities tried to block the circumcision and conversion of slaves owned by Jews, while rabbis drew up "responsa," or religious opinions, in reply to requests by Jewish slave owners for clarification of the thorny issues involved.

In some of the larger Jewish communities, slaves who converted to Judaism were initially welcomed as full members of Jewish society. But over time the development of the colonies and the growth of racial slavery seemed to require the imposition of a firmer hierarchy. To ensure they were counted among the whites in societies increasingly defined by racial distinctions, Jewish communities began adopting more rigid restrictions on the status of Jewish-owned slaves. A formerly mixed synagogue in Suriname established a separate, less-than-equal classification for Jews of color, then banned them from sitting in shul, reading from the Torah, or being buried in the Jewish cemetery. Eventually, slave conversions were prohibited entirely.

But those rigid distinctions were not always easy to enforce. Sexual relations between Jews and Black slaves or free people of color—both consensual and, as we have seen, shockingly predatory—were known from the earliest days of the colonial period. Some Jewish masters converted their female slaves to Judaism in order to marry them as Jews. Others lived with non-Jewish women of color in what were effectively common-law marriages, frowned upon by neighbors, perhaps, but tolerated by the law. In 1822, David Isaacs, a

German-born Jewish shopkeeper in Charlottesville, Virginia, and a free woman of color named Nancy West, a successful baker, were indicted by a grand jury for "umbraging the decency of society and violating the laws of the land." Five years later, they were acquitted, as convicting them would only have exposed how common such partnerships were. Indeed, it is possible that Isaacs's Jewishness—he was a founder of Richmond's first synagogue—protected him, since white neighbors may have felt a foreign-born heathen did not need to be held to as high a moral standard as a native Christian.

Despite his flouting of the South's racial mores, Isaacs was fully enmeshed in Charlottesville society. A friend of Thomas Jefferson, Isaacs sold meat, cheese, and butter to the former president and sent him books about Judaism. In 1832, one of the couple's children, Julia Ann Isaacs, married Eston Hemings, a son of Jefferson's slave and mistress Sally Hemings. Eston, likely fathered by Jefferson during his presidency, was freed after the master's death. Julia and Eston later moved to Wisconsin, adopted the last name Jefferson, lived as Christians, and passed as white.

Jews of color in the antebellum period faced difficulties that white Jews did not, especially related to death. When an enslaved Black woman named Lucy Marks died in Philadelphia in 1823, the family that had owned her contended that her faithful devotion to Judaism should entitle her to burial in Congregation Mikveh Israel's Spruce Street Cemetery. Other members of the synagogue objected, but the Marks family won out, citing Lucy's legally acceptable conversion. Lucy was interred in a plot not far from Haym Salomon, Jewish hero of the American Revolution. The controversy was revived a few years later, however, when Mary Gratz, a member of the congregation born to a Jewish father and a Christian mother, lay dying, and her family asked to bury her in the cemetery. The president of the congregation denied the request on the grounds that by the rules of matrilineal descent, Mary was not strictly Jewish. Rebecca Gratz, Mary's well-connected aunt and a founder of numerous Jewish institutions in the city, was horrified. If "a Negro servant in a Jewish family living a religious life was allowed the privilege of burial in our ground," she argued, surely "a pious confirming Jewess" ought to be granted the same privilege. But the president held firm and refused to admit Mary Gratz to the graveyard.

Billy Simons of Charleston was similarly preoccupied with whether he would be buried beside his fellow Jews. In 1820, just before the revolt of the young reformers, Congregation Beth Elohim had adopted a rule stating that "people of color" could not become members. An exception was made, however, for "Uncle Billy." Apparently born in Madagascar around 1780, he was sold into slavery, transported to the United States, and bought by the publisher of the *Charleston Courier*. Billy worked as a paper carrier for nearly two decades and was known around town. Described as "universally respected by his coreligionists," Billy claimed his father had told him they were descended from Rechabites, a biblical clan of nomadic tent dwellers. Maurice Mayer, the proslavery Reform rabbi of Beth Elohim in the 1850s, noted in one of his letters home to Germany that Uncle Billy was "the most observant of those who go to synagogue." He always sat in the front row. "Only one thing worries him, as he has often told me," Mayer wrote, "namely that, when he has passed away, by some oversight, he may not be buried in the Jewish cemetery. If God lets me survive him and if it is only in my power, he shall rest among his co-religionists instead of among the slaves or the free persons of color." As no place of burial is listed for Billy in the city records, it is possible he was indeed quietly entombed in Beth Elohim's cemetery.

Biographers of the Lehman brothers have noted in their defense that it would have been difficult for immigrant Jews to take a different approach to slavery in the antebellum South, especially in Alabama. Yet others in something close to their position did just that. In *The Kidnapped and the Ransomed*, a remarkable 1856 fugitive-slave narrative written in the third person with the aid of a white friend, Peter Still recounted how he and his brother, Levin, as six- and eight-year-old children, had been kidnapped from their New Jersey home along the Delaware River and brought to Kentucky to work on a plantation. Like so many enslaved kinsmen, they were eventually split apart. Levin died in bondage from injuries sustained when his master beat him for marrying without permission. Peter vowed to find his way home. His quest for freedom was guided not by abolitionist pamphlets or busybody sermonizers, he emphasized in the narrative, but by memories of sweeter times in the past and the hope they might return.

When Peter was around eighteen, his owner moved to a vast plantation in northern Alabama, near the small town of Tuscumbia. Peter worked mostly as a field hand. He married, built a cabin, raised chickens, and had children. When the master died and a new one took over, Peter was even allowed to hire out his own labor and keep some of the pay. He spent more time in town, working odd jobs for teachers, shopkeepers, booksellers, even a Presbyterian minister. He gathered information and waited for the chance to reclaim his freedom.

Peter's story might seem indistinguishable from numerous other slave narratives. Indeed, his tale serves as the inspiration for Ta-Nehisi Coates's 2019 novel, *The Water Dancer*. But while in that novel the narrator's deliverance is effected through supernatural means— memory-fueled waterborne travel across impossible distances in the blink of an eye—Peter Still won his freedom by a more prosaic method: a matter-of-fact business agreement with a pair of Jewish brothers, hardworking storekeepers whom Peter had come to trust.

Joseph and Isaac Friedman had moved from Cincinnati to Tuscumbia, where it took the brothers a few years to overcome the initial hostility of locals. They were accepted as part of the community. Yet they mostly kept to themselves. Peter found himself "mysteriously attracted towards these somewhat isolated brothers," he recalled. The Bavarian-born Friedmans were observant Jews, active members, back in Cincinnati, of Congregation B'nai Jeshurun, the synagogue where only a few years later Isaac Mayer Wise would be hired as rabbi. Three other brothers, Levi, Solomon, and Raphael, remained in Cincinnati to run the family business, which largely supplied peddlers with goods. Joseph Friedman, the older brother in Alabama, whom Peter described as "small in stature, with the black hair and keen eyes peculiar to his race," addressed the enslaved man with a degree of respect that other whites rarely showed. For once, Peter felt treated "as *a man*."

Desperate to gain his freedom, terrified of uttering the wrong word to the wrong person, Peter decided that the Jewish brothers offered his best chance. Joseph Friedman never denounced slavery outright, Peter recalled—that would have been far too dangerous—but he did occasionally let slip "some careless sentence, which revealed his sympathy with the suffering, and his hatred of injustice and oppression."

Other whites in town, fond of Peter, tried to warn him not to get too close with the Friedmans. Southern Christians were often suspicious of the foreign-born, and many told the enslaved that Jewish masters were especially cruel. (Inspired by the teachings of white preachers, one Black spiritual included the lines, "Virgin Mary had one son / The cruel Jews had him hung.") Peter watched the brothers closely, however, and concluded that such rumors were baseless. But he had to be absolutely certain. He knew of others who had been promised they could buy their freedom but had been cheated of their money and sold off, their hopes dashed forever. Peter did not think the Friedmans were capable of such treachery. With trembling knees and a throbbing heart, he summoned the courage to broach the subject of their purchasing him in order to free him; Peter would later repay them. To his joy and relief, the brothers agreed.

Such an arrangement was illegal in Alabama; both Peter and the Friedmans were taking an immense risk. Feigning illness, Peter convinced his master to sell him to the Friedmans for $500. He was ostensibly owned by the Jewish brothers—and he did continue to work for them, shining their boots, sweeping the store—but now he was allowed to save all his earnings. Peter managed within the year to raise the money to pay them back. But since buying his own freedom was illegal, he needed to find a safe way to flee the South. In 1850, when Joseph Friedman followed the Gold Rush to California and Isaac Friedman decided to return to Cincinnati, Peter realized his chance had come. He had to leave behind his wife and children, but, traveling as Isaac's enslaved servant, he finally made it to freedom. Once in the North, Peter set off for Philadelphia, where he hoped to get help finding his long-lost birth family. He traveled under a false name: Peter Friedman.

Arriving in Philadelphia that August—amid heightened enforcement of the newly passed Fugitive Slave Law—Peter went to the offices of the local Anti-Slavery Society, headquarters of the network of activists who shepherded runaways to freedom along the Underground Railroad. Convinced he was about to fall into some trap laid by slave catchers, he nervously began telling his tale to the man in charge, whose ears perked up at some of the details. A central organizer of the fugitives network, William Still realized that the desperate runaway standing in front of him was his own long-lost brother. William took him to see their aged mother and siblings at their home in New Jersey. Amid their joyous, tear-filled reunion, Peter was taken aback by the relative comfort of their lives as free people in the North, far different from the nightmarish depictions that Southern whites had circulated to frighten those in bondage. He had not until that moment realized just how thoroughly *"slavery had kept him ignorant and poor."*

Relishing his own freedom, Peter set to work trying to get his wife and children out of slavery. Again, Isaac Friedman proved helpful, giving him a pass to travel back to Alabama. He also offered to forward Peter the money to buy his family and even to negotiate on his behalf. But Peter's new abolitionist friends in Philadelphia convinced him to turn the offer down so as not to contribute another dime to the masters' pockets. Instead, with the help of a white abolitionist "wholly insensible of fear," Peter tried to wrest his family free by force. After a dramatic escape, the group was seized by slave catchers in Indiana. The body of the white accomplice, tied up in heavy chains, was found at the bottom of a river. Peter decided that buying his family was the only viable option. For two years, he traveled around the North telling his story and receiving endorsements from antislavery luminaries like William Lloyd Garrison, Horace Greeley, and Harriet Beecher Stowe, and raising the necessary funds. In 1855, the family was reunited in Philadelphia. The narrative of his enslavement and escape was published the following year.

Not much is known of the Friedman brothers once they left Alabama. After a spell at the gold mines in Northern California, Joseph Friedman opened a cigar and tobacco business in San Francisco, then lost his stock in two devastating fires. He recouped his money through real estate investments in the Bay Area and died a wealthy man. Isaac S. Friedman appears to have joined his brother in California at some point in the 1850s, but died shortly thereafter.

In addition to showing the remarkable resilience of a man who risked everything to escape bondage, the story of Peter Still and the Friedmans proves there was nothing inevitable about the Lehmans'— or anyone else's—unquestioning complicity with bondage. At least one set of Jewish brothers in the South found ways to undermine slavery, or at least to help free one of the enslaved.

6

On Native Grounds

FROM THE EARLIEST DAYS OF THE REPUBLIC, MOST Jews had aligned with the Democratic Party. For the handful qualified at the time to vote, Thomas Jefferson's Democratic-Republicans offered a more congenial partisan home than the Federalists, led by George Washington, John Adams, and Alexander Hamilton. Jefferson, seen as a champion of the common man, had long supported immigration. As early as 1776 he had scrawled "Jews advantageous" on the back of a bill proposed in the Virginia assembly to allow the foreign-born to become citizens. Jefferson went on to support religious freedom in Virginia and the disestablishment of the Anglican Church, while his own idiosyncratic religious views and association with known Jacobins, though held against him by more conservative Americans, counted as a plus in the eyes of those who appreciated the French Revolution's 1791 emancipation of the nation's Jews. Jefferson's Federalist opponents occasionally used anti-Jewish themes in their political campaigns. In 1795, an editor denounced the merchant Solomon Simpson, vice president of the Democratic Society of New York, as "of the tribe of Shylock." Three years later, President Adams signed the Alien and Sedition Acts, which threatened the position of immigrants in American society. Noting that only in a republic could Jews become full citizens, Benjamin Nones, a veteran of the American Revolution, asked, "How then can a Jew but be a Republican?"

Leading Jews of the early nineteenth century helped shape the coalitions that became the backbone of the Democratic Party. In New York, several helped found and lead Tammany Hall, the powerful political machine. When Jefferson's party split, Jews gravitated toward the new party founded to support Andrew Jackson's bids for the presidency. Isaac Harby of Charleston, South Carolina, a prominent journalist and leader of Jewish reformers in the city, heralded the legendary Jackson as having "fought in the same holy cause" as the founders of the republic.

Jackson's opponents, the generally upper-class Whigs, tended to be more hostile to the foreign-born. They were also more likely to support missionary societies seeking to convert Jews and government intervention in matters of religion and morality, such as laws banning commerce on Sundays, an issue of particular concern to Jewish merchants. Democrats, by contrast, were more open to naturalized citizens and mass participation in political life. Nearly every Jewish officeholder before the Civil War was a Democrat.

But in 1854, after the passage of the proslavery Kansas-Nebraska Act drove a wedge between Northern and Southern Democrats and killed off the Whigs, two new political formations began to cohere. The first was the Know-Nothing Party, a powerful vehicle for the previous decade's increasingly fierce strain of nativism. Between 1845 and 1854, nearly three million immigrants had arrived in the United States. Foreign-born residents came to make up one-quarter of the US population. The influx of new arrivals—a torrent of which Jews represented only a trickle—provoked a vicious backlash among the native-born, even those whose ancestors had arrived only a few generations back. Nativists believed that immigrants took low-wage jobs from American citizens, distorted the outcome of elections through nearly uniform support for the Democratic Party, and failed to assimilate into mainstream white Protestant society. Though its bigotry was primarily directed at Irish Catholics—nearly two dozen Catholic churches were burned in this period—the rise of the anti-immigrant Know-Nothing Party suggested it might not be long before Jews, too, came under attack.

Yet at the same time another new party was taking shape, the first mass antislavery coalition in world history: the Republican Party. Though the party included some nativists in its ranks, many immigrants, especially German speakers, decided that stopping the spread of slavery to the western territories was vital for preserving the opportunities that their adopted homeland promised for ordinary white farmers and laborers, and even the rawest of recently arrived immigrants saw themselves, and wished to be seen, as white. Most Jews would remain Democrats through the Civil War and beyond, but many veterans and supporters of the failed revolutions of 1848 opted to join the nascent party, which seemed to offer a second chance to achieve in America what they had failed to accomplish in Europe.

The first chapters of the new party were organized in the Upper Midwest, where thousands of European refugees had only recently settled. In Michigan, three Jewish residents participated in one of the party's first conventions and signed a call for the Northern states to unite against the "aggression of the slave power." One, Michigan pioneer Edward Kanter, was a member of Detroit's Temple Beth El, where the rabbi, another European exile named Liebmann Adler, spoke out against slavery and reportedly encouraged the rescue of runaway slaves. Stories have long circulated in the Detroit Jewish community that other Beth El members—including a city policeman—aided fugitives heading to Canada. Direct participation in such efforts was rare for American Jews, but not unheard-of. In 1853, a Jewish plumber in Chicago named Michael Greenebaum gathered a crowd to help an alleged runaway free himself from custody.

In 1856, foreign-born Republicans stumped the country for the party's first presidential candidate, the charismatic explorer John C. Fremont, and Jews in large cities and small towns joined the campaign. In the proslavery *Asmonean*, whose editor Robert Lyon had endorsed the Democratic presidential candidate, James Buchanan, a letter from one reader, MACCABEE, connected the issues of the campaign to the themes of Jewish history and asked how Lyon or any other Jew could be anything but "inflexibly hostile to the perpetuation of human slavery."

> Have they read the harrowing history of their ancestors' bondage in Egypt, to no purpose? Have the merciless persecutions and unutterable tortures of the dark ages not yet opened their eyes and enlarged their heart for the alleviation of their fellow men's woes?
>
> Will they, on their escape from the oppression of the old land, lend aid and comfort to the tyrant of the new world[?]
>
> No! the Jew cannot support a party, that would condemn our fellow men for the mere accident of color, to a more than Egyptian bondage in the free soil of the West. He must be active, and eager, and zealous on the side of freedom and freedom's candidates—he must enlist with warmth in the ranks of the party, who, religiously observing the constitutional rights of the South, will oppose the extension of chattel slavery over another *inch* of free territory.

The only place for a Jew in the political struggle of 1856, MACCABEE believed, was in the Republican Party.

Another early Jewish convert to the party was Lewis Naphtali Dembitz, who as a fifteen-year-old had left Europe with his family amid the turmoil of 1848. They settled in New Orleans, but he continued on to Louisville, Kentucky. While waiting to pass the bar exam, Dembitz edited a daily newspaper, *Der Beobachter am Ohio*—"The Observer on the Ohio"—in which he serialized his own German translation of *Uncle Tom's Cabin*, the first to be produced in the United States. An accomplished theologian, a talented mathematician, an amateur astronomer, and an avid swimmer, the barely five-foot-tall Dembitz could read in twelve languages, including Sanskrit and Aramaic. A fierce opponent of slavery though he lived in a slave state, he served as a Kentucky delegate to the first national Republican convention, in 1856. In Louisville, Dembitz wrote, "the most intelligent, most honest and most cultivated people are all more or less openly on the side of Fremont," and against the Democrats, those "ballot-box-stuffers, baggage-smashers, shoulder-strikers, pothouse-brawlers."

A week after election day, Dembitz's older sister, Frederika, married to fellow exile Adolph Brandeis, gave birth to a boy, whom they named Louis, in Dembitz's honor. "My uncle, the abolitionist, was a lawyer," Louis Brandeis later recalled, "and to me nothing else seemed worthwhile." As a teenager, the future Supreme Court justice changed his middle name from David to Dembitz to honor the uncle who not only inspired him to pursue a legal career and hold liberal political opinions but who also offered the future Zionist leader, whose parents were unobservant, his only early connection to Judaism. Brandeis vividly remembered the sacred feeling of Friday nights in his uncle's Louisville home. The joys of the "Sabbath peace," Dembitz told his nephew, offered a weekly "foretaste of heaven."

———

In the fall of 1856, at the height of the election season, the American Jewish conscience was pricked by an illustrious visitor: Gabriel

Riesser, the foremost champion of Jewish emancipation in Germany and throughout Europe. In his short-lived periodical *Der Jude* and influential pamphlets, Riesser had advocated equal rights and the end of religious restrictions. In the frustrating decades after Napoleon's armies scattered seeds of emancipation that had yet to bear fruit, Riesser was a dashing, romantic figure, a hero and inspiration for young Jews. During his visit to the United States, Jewish communities across the country held banquets in the great man's honor. In some places, however, Riesser's comparison of European tyranny with American slavery left his audiences uncomfortable. To Riesser, it was a scandal that a republic founded in the name of liberty continued to sanction the practice of slavery. He was appalled to find in Washington, DC, the supposed "capital of freedom," the legal existence of human bondage, "the deepest outrage of man." The *New York Tribune* described the eminent visitor as "horror-stricken at the spectacle of a Slaveholding Democracy."

Though a Riesser admirer from his boyhood, Isaac Mayer Wise found that spectacle somehow easier to stomach. The Reform rabbi resisted the growing antislavery movement and the Republican Party. He responded to the struggle over slavery not only as a Jew and a proud American but as a Cincinattian, poised on the tenuous border between free and slave states, fearful of war and willing to compromise at almost any cost.

Slavery was illegal in Ohio, but reminders of its existence were not far away. Many of Wise's congregants had close business and family ties to the slave states, and roughly half the subscribers to his newspapers lived in the South. Wise himself had firsthand experience with the institution. During his 1850 visit to Charleston, Wise had been happily waited on by enslaved people. Five years later, again seeking to restore his ever-fragile health, Wise boarded a steamship heading up the Ohio River to Wheeling, Virginia, where "the negro servants in the hotel swarmed about us like satellites," he recalled. It seems likely that Wise felt, in such moments, more

American than he ever had before. On the same river trip to Wheeling, he met Henry Wise (no relation), the rabidly proslavery candidate for Virginia governor. The two joked about their shared name and how it meant they were both, as the rabbi put it, "very wise and white (*weiss*); a highly important necessity at that time."

Through his long career, Wise would change his mind on many religious and political questions, yet making sure that American Jews were seen as white would always be a necessity for him. On occasion it could rise to the level of obsession.

Anxious about divisions in the country and among Jews, Wise was dismissive toward abolitionists. Having lived in Europe under a Christian government that watched closely over the religious lives of its subjects, Wise was appalled by the explicitly religious nature of the antislavery campaign. Wise denounced the abolitionists as "demons of hatred and destruction," "red republicans who feed on excitement and delight in civil wars." The movement against slavery was a joint project between "German atheism and American puritanism," sealed by "visionary philanthropists and wicked preachers" who knew "no limits to their fanaticism," almost as if he were taking aim at partnerships such as Ernestine Rose's alliance with William Lloyd Garrison. War and devastation would be the consequence of their agitation, as would growing enmity toward Jews.

Like Maurice Mayer, the 1848 revolutionary and proslavery rabbi of Charleston's Congregation Beth Elohim, Wise's hostility to abolitionism was also based on what he saw as an unholy alliance between nativists and antislavery activists. He noticed how many who opposed slavery because it suppressed the wages of white workers often criticized immigrants for the same reason. In 1859, a popular referendum in the abolitionist stronghold of Massachusetts banned foreign-born citizens from voting or holding public office for two years after they were granted citizenship, which itself required five years of residency. Wise, who had become a citizen in 1851, compared the measure to one of the czar's anti-Jewish decrees. "Where are the abolitionists, freesoilers, republicans, negro worshippers and liberty jobbers of Massachusetts?" he asked. "Is this State in the United States, or in Russia?" He derided antislavery activists for focusing so much on the plight of oppressed Black people while ignoring hostile measures aimed at new immigrants: "Men who embrace the distant negro, cry furiously for bleeding Kansas, are intolerant enough to sully their own Constitution [with] intolerant laws."

In fact, Wise was wrong about the nativist tendencies of the leading abolitionists. Though some, like Wendell Phillips, had dabbled in anti-immigrant invective to score points with their New England audiences, others had no patience for such demagoguery. Garrison's *Liberator* denounced the new law restricting immigrants from suffrage as "an act of political injustice." The *Liberator* did, however, criticize any foreign-born citizen who clamored for the rights of fellow immigrants, yet who "cares nothing that four millions of *native-born Americans* are stripped of every right, ranked with the brutes, bought and sold as property, and subjected to insults, outrages and tortures innumerable. His love of liberty," the editorial concluded of such a person, "is nothing but personal selfishness."

For Wise, the threat that nativists posed to law and order had appeared frighteningly close to home. During municipal elections in April 1855, a year after he arrived in town, Cincinnati's streets devolved into urban warfare as Know-Nothing mobs, angry their candidate appeared to have lost the mayoral election, marched on the immigrant-dominated "Over-the-Rhine" neighborhood, seized control of the polling places, and destroyed ballot boxes. German radicals, many of them 1848 revolutionaries, erected barricades, fortified homes, posted sharpshooters, and even fired a cannon at their native-born assailants. The fighting lasted three days before the nativists withdrew. Twenty-two people were killed.

The riots marked the end of nativism as a viable political force in Cincinnati, but in the rest of the country, the Know-Nothing Party remained strong. Similar clashes broke out that year in Columbus, Ohio, and in Louisville, Kentucky, both cities with many German-speaking immigrants, including Jews.

Wise was out of town and then ill for much of the month and did not comment on the riots in the *Israelite*. Perhaps he did not want to draw the mob's attention to himself. But the episode likely shaped his developing views on American politics. Salmon P. Chase, the governor of Ohio and a founder of the new Republican Party, tried to convince Wise to join, but Wise refused and turned against Chase when the governor published an official Thanksgiving Day message with what Wise considered anti-Jewish undertones. (Chase had stated that observation of the Thanksgiving holiday was a custom "highly becoming a Christian people.") Instead, the rabbi identified more and more openly with the Democrats. Antislavery was merely a cover for the Republicans' quest for power, Wise believed, and he doubted the exercise of that power would be beneficial for American Jews.

"We are not apologists for slavery," Wise explained in 1859. He opposed letting bondage spread to the West. But he also believed the "abolitionist agitation" threatened the Constitution that had given Jews unparalleled liberty. As one biographer summarized Wise's position, "it was the Union, blemished slightly though it might be by negro servitude, which had guaranteed freedoms to whites who had fled the shores of Europe, and that came first."

————

David Einhorn saw things differently. Instead of complacently accepting the country's flaws, Jews fortunate enough to have found refuge in the United States should work to make it better, for everyone.

"Does the Negro have less ability to think, to feel, to will? Does he have less of a desire to happiness?" Einhorn asked. "Does the

Negro have an iron neck that does not feel a burdensome yoke? Does he have a stiffer heart that does not bleed when . . . his beloved child is torn away from him?" Judah Benjamin had asked similar questions back in 1842, but only because it advanced the interests of his legal clients. Ernestine Rose also called for empathy with the enslaved, but she did so from the podium at socialist meetings and atheist conventions. Einhorn said it from the pulpit in shul: "Slavery is immoral and must be abolished."

Unlike Wise, Einhorn saw the fight against nativism as linked to the fight against slavery, and he argued that the rights of Jews in America would be insecure so long as either form of prejudice held sway. His home state of Maryland had become a bastion for the Know-Nothings. In Baltimore, murderous gangs like the Red Necks, the Rip Raps, the Black Snakes, and the Blood Tubs—named for their preferred tactic of dunking the heads of Democrats in vats of animal gore—prowled around the city and its outskirts starting fights and breaking up picnics, shooting and sometimes killing the foreign-born. Know-Nothings and Democrats battled in the streets at nearly every 1850s election, killing dozens. As one Jewish resident of Baltimore later wrote in a memoir, "A foreigner could only cast his vote by running through a gauntlet of pistols, knives, and clubs." In the especially violent canvass of 1858, Thomas Hicks, a Know-Nothing candidate, was elected governor of Maryland. He used his inaugural speech to attack the foreign-born for trying to "change the national character." Einhorn condemned the nativists, for even if Jews were not the target, that could swiftly change. "Once we start to evaluate people by the country of birth, next will come an evaluation by religion," he warned, "and in this case, surely, the Jews, the so-called crucifiers of the crucified, will be in danger." Arguments about the inferiority of one group could easily be applied to another. "The defeat of the Know Nothing," Einhorn pronounced, "will be the victory of the fundamental Mosaic law of equality of the stranger with the native before the law."

Many Baltimore Jews disagreed with the rabbi's political positions or thought it was not a religious leader's role to speak out on secular issues. Einhorn's Har Sinai congregation was itself divided, with some members holding leadership positions in the Democratic Party while others joined the Republicans. Slave ownership among Baltimore Jews, as in Maryland at large, had sharply declined by 1860. It was difficult for new arrivals to gather the capital needed to invest in human property. Between 1840 and 1855, Baltimore's Jewish population had grown sevenfold, to nearly seven thousand people. But even the new immigrants who did not own slaves benefited from being accepted as white. Most spoke German and were part of the city's larger German-speaking community, the leading newspaper of which, *Der Deutsche Correspondent*, reminded its readers "never to forget that the Constitution of the United States in support of which every adopted citizen of the Republic has sworn an oath of loyalty, sanctions and protects the institution of slavery."

To Rabbi Einhorn's nervous congregants, the threat to Jews seemed far from theoretical. Only thirty years had passed since the 1826 passage of Maryland's "Jew Bill," which finally—a half-century after the adoption of the Constitution—granted Jews in the state political and civil rights. It was far from inconceivable that the surge of nativism could bring back such restrictions. In a nation verging on civil war, in a state caught in between, it was no time for an already isolated group of immigrants to draw attention to themselves.

For Einhorn, however, the freedom that Jews had found in America would be worthless unless they used it to denounce inequality and injustice. In 1856, as August Bondi camped out with John Brown in Kansas and Judah Benjamin threatened secession in the Senate, while Ernestine Rose barnstormed against slavery and Isaac Mayer Wise condemned agitators like her as irresponsible firebrands, David Einhorn denounced bondage as "the cancer of the Union." Devoutly religious in his own way, the rabbi arrived at the same position as the avowedly atheist Rose. "[I]f the Union is based on immoral foundations," Einhorn concluded, "it is not fit to survive, nor is it worth surviving."

The same was true of Judaism, whose mission was not merely to survive but to be a light unto the nations. Einhorn was not interested in compromising the radicalism of this vision for the sake of accruing followers for his movement or influence for himself. While Wise told immigrants to learn English as quickly as possible—for only by doing so could a Jew "gain the proud self-consciousness of the free-born man"—Einhorn stubbornly continued to write and speak in German, deeming it the only suitable means for communicating the refined ideas he espoused.

Despite his outspokenness, Einhorn was beloved by his Baltimore congregation. A witty conversationalist, he had bright, beaming eyes that shone, as one former pupil remembered, "with a light not of this earth, tender with sympathy, melting in sorrow, twinkling with wit, burning with indignation, withering in scorn, flashing with anger, radiant in devotion." When he rose to the pulpit to offer his weekly sermon, silence engulfed the synagogue. "The very soul of sincerity breathed in his words," the student recalled, even if many listeners had a hard time following the rabbi's "artistic" language and "flawless, inexorable logic." One could see at a glance he was "a very exceptional man, whose solemn gravity and intense fervor indicated a life steadfastly given to the spreading of his inmost convictions." He lost his temper only once, when he arrived before a class of young Torah scholars and found the synagogue's sexton had allowed the fire to go out, leaving the children to wait for him in the cold.

Others remembered a darker side to Einhorn: "the kind of anger," as one scholar put it, "that went beyond prophetic urgency or . . . righteousness." During his time in Baltimore, Einhorn "seemed to be arguing with everyone, about everything." Esteemed by his followers, Einhorn did little to make himself loved by the wider Jewish community. He had none of Wise's gifts for politicking, for organizing a diverse community around common goals. In 1859, when Benjamin Szold, a young and energetic Hungarian-born rabbi, arrived in Baltimore to take charge of an Orthodox synagogue, Einhorn denounced the upstart in his monthly *Sinai* in the most personal and insulting terms: "Herr Szold is not able to think clearly, to speak in an orderly manner, to write correctly . . . There is only one excuse, Herr Szold does not know what he is talking about . . . A chick barely out of the egg wants to play the role of a roaring lion . . . a man who cannot distinguish his right hand from his left." Szold retorted in an eighteen-page pamphlet titled *Einhorn Unmasked*, in which he condemned his critic as "arrogant, conceited, a man without honor, who insults Judaism as no enemy of the Jews before him had ever done." Szold predicted that Einhorn's name would be "execrated with an eternal curse by the entire world." Einhorn, of course, had to have the last word, denouncing the "incompetent Szold" as an "ignorant youngster."

David Einhorn never swerved from his principles, but the perilous times ahead would reveal the risks of his self-isolation, finally making it impossible for him to ignore the world outside his study and his shul.

———

Starting with the breakaway Reformed Society of Israelites in Charleston in 1824, a cascade of congregational separations occurred throughout the country, as Jews following particular rituals or observing specific requirements of biblical law (while ignoring others) sought to start their own synagogues. A German speaker familiar with Ashkenazi practices deemed it an insult to have to worship according to the strange Sephardic ways of the oldest American synagogues, still dominated by descendants of Spanish and Portuguese exiles. Yiddish speakers from Poland found little in common with either. "Each society," Robert Lyon, editor of the *Asmonean*, complained in 1855, referring to different synagogues, "is an independent organization, irresponsible to all . . . [and] assumes an indifference to outside impressions." Many Jewish immigrants had more in common with Christians from the same European countries than with fellow Jews from other lands.

American Jews feared that forming communal institutions would give the impression of separatism just when they were trying desperately to blend in. It would also limit congregational autonomy. In 1841, when one Orthodox leader circulated a "plan for establishing religious union among the Israelites of America"—a leadership council of three men and an assembly of delegates—Southerners rejected the effort to institute top-down control as distressingly akin to the federal government's threats to state sovereignty. Abraham Moise of Charleston observed that any effort to form a tighter union of Jews in America would "keep away all Jews south of the Potomac," and the city's Congregation Beth Elohim rejected the plan as "wholly inconsistent with the spirit of American liberty." Subsequent efforts by Isaac Mayer Wise, such as the ill-fated Cleveland Conference of 1855, had likewise come to naught. For most American Jews on the eve of the Civil War, unity seemed neither necessary nor desirable.

Yet the limitations of such an approach became clear when controversy erupted over a treaty the US government signed in 1850 with Switzerland. The treaty acknowledged the right of the Swiss Confederation's twenty-two cantons to bar non-Christians from their territories. American diplomats sought assurances that the exclusion would never be enforced against American citizens, but when a Jewish businessman from Boston was deported from one of the cantons, American Jews demanded that the federal government defend the rights of its citizens. "Slaves and cowards only will submit to such an outrage," Isaac Mayer Wise warned. "We are men and must be treated as such."

When he took office in 1857, James Buchanan promised to push the Swiss to overturn their exclusions. But he did not push hard. The president's Southern allies were reluctant to upset Switzerland, a buyer of American cotton and tobacco. Not until 1874 would Switzerland change its constitution to bar such restrictions. Though the campaign against the treaty by American Jews fell short of success, the combination of mass petitions, protest meetings, and delegations to Washington seemed to offer a template for future action.

A fresh opportunity to implement those tools came in the summer of 1858, when police in Bologna, Italy, acting on the orders of papal authorities, broke into the home of Momolo Mortara, a Jewish merchant, seized his small, weeping six-year-old son Edgar, and sent him to Rome. A former nursemaid of the boy claimed she had secretly baptized Edgar, and the Church argued that made the Mortaras unfit to raise him in their home. Medieval-style anti-Jewish persecution, seemingly relegated to the past, had returned.

Jews throughout Europe mobilized to pressure the Catholic Church to free the boy. In the United States, they once again lobbied Buchanan to take action, and not only Jews. The Know-Nothings, already a diminished force by 1858, riven in two over slavery, seized on the scandal in a bid for new relevance. But while Buchanan agreed the abduction was unjust, he refused to pressure the Church. The United States government had "neither the right nor the duty," the president told one Jewish petitioner, "to express a moral censorship over the conduct of other independent nations."

To opponents, the president's reasoning was obvious: Irish Catholics overwhelmingly supported his Democratic Party, especially in the Northern states, and Buchanan and other Democrats refused to challenge their own voters by openly criticizing the Church. As one letter in the *Jewish Messenger* of New York put it, "It is not that they love the Jewish vote less, but because they love the Irish—i.e., the Catholic—vote more, that the administration refuse any manifestation of sympathy for so glaring a wrong."

Even more importantly, Buchanan feared that if he denounced the separation of the Jewish child from his parents as a violation of human rights, the Vatican and other European powers could point out that American slavery regularly separated Black children from their parents. Far from criticizing slavery, one Chicago paper observed, Buchanan's party "glorified it as a moral and religious institution." Had the administration protested to the pope about the Mortara case, another journal noted, France and Britain could make an issue out of the "habitual child stealing, women whipping and baby selling" that went on every day in the Southern states. David Einhorn was furious at Buchanan's inaction, describing the president as "sly as a fox," before reflecting that the president's stance was consistent with his politics. After all, how could someone "who approves of slavery . . . deliver a moral sermon to the pope?"

Among Jews, Einhorn was nearly alone in speaking out against both the abduction of the Jewish boy in Bologna and the abduction of Black children in the United States. When Northern rabbis like Morris Jacob Raphall and Isaac Mayer Wise—opponents in every other respect—organized a mass petition drive to demand that Buchanan press Rome for Mortara's return, the Jewish communities of New Orleans, Mobile, and Charleston abstained. If the federal government could interfere in the local laws of the Papal States—or, for that matter, the Swiss cantons—it could, by the same logic, interfere in the local laws of the Southern states. While sympathetic to the plight of their coreligionists abroad, Southern Jews recognized the domestic implications of the foreign policy debate. In this first real instance of organized Jewish engagement in American politics, complicity with slavery compelled many Jews to keep silent.

———

In his 1858 Senate speech defending the proslavery Lecompton Constitution—the one for which a Northern colleague mocked him as an "Israelite with Egyptian principles"—Judah Benjamin had attacked the antislavery settlers in Kansas as a "miserable rabble of insurgents . . . seeking naught but violence and bloodshed." Among that miserable rabble, unbeknownst to Benjamin, was his coreligionist August Bondi, who for months had camped out with John Brown's free-state militia, fighting pitched battles with proslavery forces and raiding enemy farms. As one American Jew in the United States Senate called for the extirpation of free-state settlers in Kansas, another fought among them.

But by the time Benjamin spoke before the Senate, Bondi had split from Brown. One night around the campfire, as the group hid out from federal soldiers and Border Ruffians, the leader suggested to his exhausted crew that if proslavery militia forced them to leave the territory, maybe they should sneak down to Louisiana and stir up a rebellion among the enslaved.

Bondi was idealistic, but also practical. As a new immigrant in St. Louis, he had adopted antislavery politics not out of "sympathy for the negro slave [but] antipathy against the degradation of labor." He did not go to Kansas seeking to join the front lines of a civil war between freedom and slavery so much as he went looking for adventure. In moving to the frontier, even in fighting the proslavery invasion of Kansas, Bondi may not have been fighting to overthrow white supremacy so much as to secure his own right to benefit from it. He disagreed with Brown's plans for a nationwide slave revolution, and said so.

The last time Bondi set eyes on John Brown, the old man had traveled alone on horseback before dawn to say goodbye. Bondi insisted on repaying Brown a dollar he owed him. When Brown, after leaving Kansas to raise funds and arms in New England, returned two years later, he camped a few yards from Bondi's cabin but did not stop by to say hello, nor did he invite Bondi to rejoin the posse. He was traveling with eleven people he had helped free from bondage in Missouri. He planned to guide them to Canada. Brown knew that his former comrade "did not sanction an increase in the colored population north," as Bondi would remember, "and I suppose he never forgot my opposition to his Negro insurrection plans." Brown even told locals from whom he received provisions to keep his presence in the area secret from Bondi.

A year after leaving Kansas for the last time, the grizzled fighter devised a spectacular attack that he hoped would rouse the South's enslaved people to revolution and shock the country out of its complacency. Just before midnight on October 16, 1859, Brown and twenty-one men crept away from their rented farmhouse in western Maryland and marched five miles south to the well-stocked federal arsenal at Harpers Ferry, Virginia, hoping to make off with weapons and other supplies before heading into the Appalachian Mountains to launch an insurrection among the enslaved. Brown lingered too long in the arsenal and his plan, such as it was, collapsed. The next day, Colonel Robert E. Lee led a company of federal troops to put down the rebellion. It was over in a flash. Seventeen men died in the raid, including ten of Brown's accomplices, two of them his sons. Six weeks later, he was hanged.

If Brown's "insurrection was to be regretted," Ernestine Rose observed, "the cause that produced it was infinitely more so." She expected the nation, unless it acted quickly to abolish slavery, "would have to regret many more unhappy results springing from the same miserable cause."

Even while they quarreled with his chosen methods, many Northerners hailed Brown for his antislavery ideals. Southerners were furious, less at the raid itself than what they took to be the North's approval of his revolutionary agenda and what that implied about the future of slavery in the Union. In a Congress sharply split among Democrats, Know-Nothings, and Republicans, decorum broke down so severely in the winter after Brown's raid that the election of a new Speaker of the House was delayed by eight tense and grueling weeks. After forty-three ballots, the nation's business remained ground to a halt.

Curiously, it was only in that menacing atmosphere of political gridlock, amid the looming clouds of national dissolution and civil war, that a rabbi was invited for the first time to offer the customary prayer before the House of Representatives began its daily work. ("In Washington," Ernestine Rose had scornfully observed a few months earlier, "chaplains pray open Congress, while the members prey upon the people.") In the wake of the Mortara controversy, Congressman Schuyler Colfax, a Republican from Indiana, wanted to show a concerned Jewish constituent that the rights of American Jews "were certainly equal to those of any other denominations." He first invited the rabbi of Washington's newly organized synagogue to deliver the opening prayers, but his English was inadequate. A more palatable choice was Morris Jacob Raphall of New York's B'nai Jeshurun, one of the most prominent and establishment-friendly Jewish religious leaders, America's first "glamor-rabbi," as historian Jonathan Sarna has called him. On February 1, 1860, Raphall appeared in full rabbinic garb, with a velvet skullcap and a white prayer shawl, dazzling the initially skeptical congressmen by intoning a blessing in Hebrew. Then, in the strong, eloquent, English-accented voice for which he had become famous, Raphall thanked the Almighty for "Thy bounties to this highly-favored land," a land that, just over a year later, would be drenched in blood.

Later that day, the gridlock in Congress was broken. For the first time, a Republican was elected Speaker of the House.

Some press accounts of Raphall's appearance jokingly attributed to the rabbi the sudden break in the political impasse. "The Rabbi did it today," a report in the *New York Times* began, "Christianity, so far as the House is concerned, having proved a failure." *Frank Leslie's Illustrated Newspaper* welcomed the occasion as "a striking feature of the times, evincing the triumph of an enlightened religious opinion over the vulgar prejudices of the world." Less charitable critics mocked Raphall's appearance or deplored it as sacrilege. The *New York Herald* wanted to know what the nation's representatives would be treated to next: the ecstatic dance of a quivering Shaker? A sermon from Mormon leader Brigham Young, "surrounded by his harem, threatening to send the administration to hell"? An Episcopalian journal expressed "extreme sorrow, and almost disgust," arguing that Raphall's prayer represented "the official rejection of Christianity by the Legislature of the country." William G. Brownlow of Tennessee, an editor and Methodist preacher, said he was horrified that congressmen would invite a benediction from "one of the *murderers of Christ.*"

Others understood the event in the context of the era's political turbulence. Disunion, once a distant possibility, suddenly seemed imminent. The upheaval opened up opportunities for those who had been excluded. Ben Perley Poore, a distinguished Washington journalist, quipped to a fellow reporter that Raphall's precedent-shattering appearance was "the result of the irrepressible conflict—the crush between the North and the South having at length squeezed out the 'juice.'"

Outrages like the Mortara case helped push even more wavering Jews to abandon what one called "the Catholicized Slaveocratic Party"—the Democrats—and sample the other options on offer. One Know-Nothing leader implored a Jewish New Yorker to join the anti-Catholic movement, noting that "surely there is no sect of the whole human race that has a greater reason to protest against Popery than the Israelites; they have suffered greater persecution, from time immemorial, than any other people." In Albany, some Jews attended Know-Nothing meetings calling on the state legislature to pass resolutions supporting the Mortara family.

Far more American Jews, however, abandoned the Democrats for the Republicans. Days after Raphall offered the prayer before Congress, on a snowy night in late February, as Abraham Lincoln spoke in the cavernous hall of the Cooper Union in New York to effectively kick off his campaign for the Republican Party's presidential nomination, Abram Dittenhoefer, a savvy twenty-four-year-old lawyer and political operative, sat behind him on the stage, applauding as the candidate urged his audience to "have faith that right makes might."

Dittenhoefer had just met Lincoln for the first time that afternoon. He was not exactly awestruck. "His large, gaunt body was like a huge clothed skeleton," Dittenhoefer would later recall. "No artistic skill could soften his features nor render his appearance less ungainly, but after he began to talk he was awkwardness deified."

Born in Charleston, son of a wealthy merchant and staunch Democrat, Dittenhoefer had absorbed what he called "the sentiments and antipathies of my Southern environment." The family soon moved to New York, however, and Dittenhoefer began to question those prejudices. His father tried to convince him to join the Democrats; doing so would advance his career in Tammany-dominated New York politics. A recent graduate of Columbia College, Abram was ready to follow his father's advice until one day he read newspaper reports of Judah Benjamin's proslavery speech on the Lecompton Constitution and Benjamin Wade's description of him as an "Israelite with Egyptian principles." His "convictions . . . irrevocably changed," Abram decided he could not join a party that upheld slavery. "It struck me with great force," he would remember, "that the Israelite Benjamin, whose ancestors were enslaved in Egypt, ought not to uphold slavery in free America, and could not do so without bringing disgrace upon himself."

Despite facing "obloquy from and ostracism by acquaintances, my clients, and even members of my own family," Abram joined the

Republican Party and committed himself to the antislavery cause. In the 1860 election, he marched with fellow Lincoln supporters and delivered campaign speeches to convince New York's German-speaking population to back the Republican. Even his father cast aside old allegiances and voted for Lincoln.

Dittenhoefer was far from alone among Jews in supporting Lincoln. The rail splitter was the friend, colleague, and acquaintance of a remarkable number of Jews, from clothiers in Springfield to clients of his law practice. They and others played important roles in electing him to the presidency. At the 1860 Republican convention in Chicago, Lewis Dembitz of Louisville, Kentucky, the translator of *Uncle Tom's Cabin* and uncle of the future Supreme Court justice Louis Brandeis, formally nominated Lincoln for the presidency. Another delegate at the convention, Moritz Pinner, the Prussian-born son of a poor small-town rabbi, was the editor of a boldly antislavery newspaper in Kansas City. Pinner contended that only with slavery's abolition could "this Confederacy . . . become in fact what it now only is in name, 'the Home of the Brave, and the Land of the Free.'"

One of Lincoln's closest friends, Abraham Jonas, was an English-born Jew who settled in Cincinnati in 1819. He and his brother Joseph founded the city's first synagogue (indeed, the first west of the Appalachian Mountains). After the death of his wife, a daughter of the religious leader Gershom Mendes Seixas, Jonas moved to Kentucky and then to Illinois, where he served in the state legislature. It was likely there, in the capital of Springfield, that he first met Lincoln, a fellow Whig. Both converts to the new Republican Party, Jonas and Lincoln barnstormed Illinois together in 1856 to support John C. Fremont's candidacy. The pair once worked in secret to liberate a member of Springfield's small free Black community from imprisonment in New Orleans after he was arrested for not carrying papers identifying him as a free man.

Born in an Orthodox family, Jonas was not religiously observant.

He ate oysters with Lincoln and fellow Illinois politicos. A canny political operator, Jonas helped organize Lincoln's unsuccessful 1858 Senate campaign and was one of the first to encourage his friend, inclined to retire from politics, to consider a run for the presidency. After helping to orchestrate Lincoln's surprising victory at the Republican convention in Chicago in 1860—"I have got the thing all fixed," Jonas reportedly told an associate about an especially canny maneuver—Jonas stayed in touch with Lincoln into his presidency, even warning the president-elect about a conspiracy to assassinate him before his inauguration. Four of Jonas's sons wound up fighting for the Confederacy, while two fought for the Union. In 1864, Lincoln freed one of the rebel Jonases from a Union prison camp so he could be at the deathbed of his father, "one of my most valued friends," as Lincoln said.

At the 1860 Republican convention in Chicago, Lewis Dembitz and Moritz Pinner were joined by a third Jewish delegate, a hometown Chicagoan named Abraham Kohn. Born in Bavaria, Kohn had arrived in the United States in 1842 at the age of twenty-three and hit the road with a bundle full of goods. The peddler's life was hard, Kohn wrote in a diary. America was an unforgiving country, a "land of hypocrisy, guile, and fraud." He regretted leaving home only to roast in the heat and freeze in the cold. "It is hard, very hard indeed to make a living this way," Kohn wrote. "Sweat runs down my body in great drops and my back seems to be breaking, but I cannot stop; I must go on and on, however far my way lies."

Devoutly religious, Kohn regretted how difficult it was to observe Jewish dietary laws and Sabbath rituals. On Saturday mornings, he had no choice but to hoist his pack and make the open fields his synagogue. Other times, like many peddlers, Kohn bowed to the prodding of his customers and reluctantly attended church.

"O youth of Bavaria," Kohn wrote, "if you long for freedom, if you dream of life here, beware, for you shall rue the hour you embarked for a country and a life far different from what you dream of. This land—and particularly this calling—offers harsh, cold air, great masses of snow and people who are credulous, filled with silly pride, cold toward foreigners and toward all who do not speak the language perfectly."

Despite such complaints, Kohn persevered. He came to harbor a deep love for his new country. Within two years of his arrival, Kohn had cast aside his bundle and opened a shop in the rough frontier town of Chicago. In 1847, he helped found its first synagogue. He organized local opposition to the Swiss Treaty and spoke out against slavery. A Democratic paper in Chicago called Kohn, soon elected city clerk, "one of the blackest Republicans and Abolitionists." Late in 1860, as the storm clouds of the secession crisis gathered, a mutual friend took the new president-elect to meet Kohn at his store. The Abrahams hit it off, chatting about politics, the election, and their shared love for the Hebrew Bible.

In the weeks between his election and his departure by train for Washington, Lincoln received countless letters and gifts from supporters and well-wishers. One he cherished was a satin banner that Abraham Kohn had woven and painted in the colors of the American flag, then carefully scrawled six lines of Hebrew scripture across the white stripes, a pep talk from God to Joshua, as he is about to assume his solemn duties: "As I was with Moses, so I will be with thee; I will not fail thee nor forsake thee . . . Be strong and of a good courage; be not afraid, neither be thou dismayed; for the Lord, thy God, is with thee whithersoever thou goest."

The message must have appealed to the biblically inclined Lincoln. On February 11, 1861, when the president-elect bid farewell to his friends and neighbors at the Springfield train depot, he asked for the assistance of a "Divine Being" with qualities markedly similar to those of the one invoked by Kohn. "Trusting in Him who can go with me, and yet remain with you and be everywhere for good," Lincoln vowed, "let us confidently hope that all will yet be well."

––––––––

In Kansas, August Bondi turned respectable . . . mostly. After breaking with John Brown, he helped lay out the town of Greeley— named for the luminary whose editorial had beckoned him to Kansas in the first place—and built its first commercial building, his new store. He served as town postmaster until he was fired for shooting at a marshal trying to execute warrants issued against free-staters by a proslavery grand jury. When his store failed, Bondi took up farming.

He also gave refuge to runaway slaves. "Our house, or rather cabin, was close to a big body of timber which, in case of necessity, provided a good shelter," he would recall. Two years after rejecting Brown's schemes to free enslaved people, now he, too, was helping fugitives escape to freedom. Bondi never explained what made him change his mind. Perhaps, like other white Kansans, he realized he could not consistently fight for white liberty while neglecting the claims of Black people.

After a new election in early 1858, Kansas voters rejected the proslavery Lecompton Constitution, then ratified one banning slavery. Thanks in part to John Brown, who showed, as Bondi put it, that "the Border Ruffians could be met in the field and defeated with proper energy and pluck," the free-staters had won. Slavery would be illegal in Kansas. Bondi's parents moved to the territory. In 1860, he married a woman whose brother had been introduced to him by a Jewish acquaintance from St. Louis. At the wedding, talk around the dinner table turned to politics. If Lincoln won the election, the groom confidently predicted, the South would secede and there would be a ghastly civil war.

Judah Benjamin was in San Francisco on legal business the day of Lincoln's election. Through the campaign season, he had rejected any suggestion that the South would leave the Union to protest a Republican victory. Benjamin was not among the hard-core "fire-eater" faction of Southerners whose increasingly frantic demands for the protection of slavery—even reopening the long-banned Atlantic slave trade—had finally split the Democratic Party. In May 1860, days after the party convention in Charleston adjourned without nominating a candidate, Benjamin clashed with more radical pro-slavery Southern senators—including Jefferson Davis—when he declared his support for appropriating funds to help enslaved people who had been confiscated from illegal slave-trading ships return to Africa. There were roughly 1,200 such captives in federal confinement in Key West, Florida, and Benjamin believed the federal government's obligations to suppress the slave trade as laid out in a treaty with Britain included the responsibility to provision the victims with the basic necessities of existence, if only for a time. Notably for such a proslavery Southerner, Benjamin invoked "the dictates of humanity" in explaining his support for the bill. "[S]omething else must be done with these slaves," Benjamin insisted, "besides putting them back in the hands of the slave-traders and slave-dealers." Jefferson Davis replied that his constituents would "object to paying taxes to this Government for any other than its legitimate purposes."

Though Benjamin had supported the Southerners' refusal to back Stephen Douglas for president, he later joined other relative moderates in urging a reconciliation with the Northern wing of the party. When that failed, he stayed aloof from the Southern Democrats' campaign to elect Buchanan's vice president, John C. Breckinridge, and focused instead on his law practice. In the fall, he sailed to San Francisco to argue an important case in court. The day after the election, the loquacious senator told an audience in the city that he hoped secession could be avoided, for he could not help but "look with kindling eye and glowing heart and quick-beating pulse upon the majestic march of our Union," which, like the Mississippi River he lived beside, gathered diverse streams into "one common reservoir of wealth and power." Even after Lincoln's election, it was not too late for the sections to find some peaceful path forward. The American people had a responsibility to preserve "the priceless heritage of our liberties and our union," Benjamin said, "as they have acquired both, by the pledge of life, of fortune, and of sacred honor." Those were the last words Benjamin uttered in public before, on November 11, 1861, boarding a ship to take him home.

Even after his return to Washington a few weeks later, Benjamin continued to oppose secession "except in the last resort," as the *New Orleans Picayune*'s correspondent in the capital reported. A rumor that he would soon deliver a major pro-Union address went uncontested during a few crucial days in early December, as Southern senators huddled to figure out what to do. But soon Benjamin realized how swiftly events had overtaken him. The tide of Southern radicalism had turned so sharply and suddenly that he could only swim with the current to avoid being swept out to sea. On December 9, Benjamin wrote to a friend that "the wild torrent of passion which is carrying everything before it . . . is a revolution . . . and it can no more be checked by human effort . . . than a prairie fire by a gardener's watering pot." Five days later, he and thirty other Southern senators signed a letter stating that secession had become the only option. Benjamin, one Washington journalist observed, "evidently feels the ground giving way under him."

And so, on the last day of 1860, Benjamin rose to announce his imminent departure from the Senate in which he had served for eight years and from the country that had raised him from obscurity to the heights of power and fame. He had long predicted the time would come to say "good bye to this glorious Union of States."

Now that fateful day had arrived. With one hand in his pocket while the other toyed with the chain of his pocket watch, Benjamin implored the citizens and politicians of the North to let the South depart in peace. There should be no invasion, no bloodshed. Even if war came, and the rebel states lost, and their cities lay in smoking ruin—even if "furious fanatics" stirred the slaves to rebellion and the institution crumbled—even then, the South would never be subjugated. "You never can convert the free sons of the soil into vassals, paying tribute to your power," Benjamin thundered. "And you never, never can degrade them to the level of an inferior and servile race." The audience was silent. Benjamin turned to take his seat, then pivoted back to face his soon-to-be-former colleagues: "Never! Never!"

Up in the galleries—packed with visitors swarming into Washington to take in the spectacle of a country tearing itself apart—the crowd erupted into shouts and applause so raucous it offended even Benjamin's Southern allies, though they were then in the midst of seceding from the Union. They moved to adjourn for the evening, but only once the galleries had been cleared, in order to ensure, as one honor-bound rebel put it, that "the dignity of the Senate is vindicated."

Benjamin's words would be studied and revered by generations of Southern schoolchildren as the glorious expression of a noble cause. Yet for Benjamin, resisting Northern efforts to "convert" the white South may have had a special, private meaning. Only by joining the slaveholders' rebellion could he prove himself as a free son of the Southern soil, rather than the profoundly conflicted member of an inferior and servile race. He could become fully American only by leaving the United States behind.

PART II

"We Are Still in Bondage"

7

Battle of the Rabbis

IN THOSE STATES STILL IN THE UNION, THEIR RANKS rapidly dwindling, the first Friday of 1861 was an unusual and memorable day. Three weeks earlier, the lame-duck president, James Buchanan, had summoned the American people to "assemble . . . according to their several forms of worship" and observe "a solemn Fast." They were not to work, travel, or eat. They were to pray. "In this the hour of our calamity and peril," Buchanan asked, "to whom shall we resort for relief but to the God of our fathers? His omnipotent arm only can save us from the awful effects of our own crimes and follies."

Coming from an aged statesman whose submissiveness to pro-slavery Southerners had, in the minds of many, done much to bring on the crisis of the Union, Buchanan's call for solemn reflection would be widely ridiculed as far too little and much too late. Southern rebels had used the two months since Lincoln's election to seize federal forts, mints, customs houses, and other property. Surely the president's own follies—even, to some, his crimes—deserved repentance more than those of other Americans. Even Isaac Mayer Wise, despite his staunch hostility to abolitionism, ridiculed Buchanan's invitation to "pray away the sins of James Buchanan."

Still, come January 4, 1861, a huge swath of the Northern public heeded the president's summons. In Boston, Detroit, and Chicago, in Baltimore and Philadelphia, even in Southern towns like Portsmouth, Virginia, and Lexington, Kentucky, crowds filed into churches and synagogues, temples and cathedrals, to ask the creator of all to step in and accomplish what the nation's politicians had failed to do: stitch the country back together and stave off a civil war.

In Manhattan, commerce slowed to a halt. Streets were empty. Days later, a letter in the *Jewish Messenger* asked why observance of the Sabbath could not be so widespread. Jewish businessmen who insisted on keeping their stores open on Saturdays had willingly closed them on the Fast Day. "I cannot understand why these people are so anxious to please an earthly authority," the writer complained, "but disregard so openly the Divine behest."

Perhaps it was because as the government faltered, American Jews realized how much they owed to its earthly authority: to the Constitution, with its guarantees of religious liberty, and to the Union, which had saved them, as well as hundreds of thousands of others, from misery and oppression. They had much to lose, perhaps more than most, if the American experiment came to an early and violent end.

Shortly before eleven o'clock that morning, the well-heeled members of New York's Congregation B'nai Jeshurun, along with curious visitors, filed into the opulent synagogue building on Greene Street in Manhattan. Some of the visitors were residents of Charleston, where South Carolina's secession from the Union had been declared two weeks earlier. The men sat in the nave, the women in the balconies. After the synagogue's cantor finished reciting the morning prayers, the rabbi, Morris Jacob Raphall, rose to the podium and began his address. As the members of a bitterly divided Congress had done less than a year earlier, the audience listened with "the most profound attention," the *New York Herald* reported the next day. In his usual ornate and elevated prose, Raphall echoed Buchanan's appeal for help from a higher power and lamented the failure of the nation in its moment of crisis to produce leaders equal to the task of peaceful reconciliation, "men . . . capable of rising above the narrow horizon of sectional influences and prejudices."

In their absence, Raphall offered himself for the role. The question of whether slavery was "a sin before God" lay at the center of the nation-rending controversy, Raphall observed. It was a question not for lawmakers but for theologians.

Slavery was older than the biblical flood, he said. Indeed, master and slave was the oldest form of human relationship other than husband and wife or parents and children. Given that all the Hebrew patriarchs owned slaves, it was a "pernicious fallacy" to suggest that God had any problem with human beings enslaving one another. To those who said it was a sin, like the famous Brooklyn minister Henry Ward Beecher, who had delivered his own sermon on the subject a few days earlier, Raphall asked, "Does it not strike you that you are guilty of something very little short of blasphemy?"

The rabbi acknowledged that slaves in ancient Israel were treated better than those in the American South, and that the system of slavery practiced in the United States did not meet the biblical standards laid out in the law code of Moses. According to the Torah, Raphall noted, "the slave is a *person* in whom the dignity of human nature is to be respected; *he has rights*." Southern slavery, by contrast, "reduces the slave to a *thing*, and a thing can have no rights."

Though he criticized its brutality in practice, Raphall had no problem with the racial theories that supported American slavery. He corresponded with early proponents of scientific racism like Josiah Nott, the thickly goateed Alabama slave owner who argued for polygenesis, the idea that different races were created for different reasons at different times. Nott quoted Raphall in his influential

1854 book, *Types of Mankind*. Raphall did not embrace polygenesis, but rather endorsed the centuries-old idea of the "Curse of Ham," a reading of the passage in Genesis in which Noah cursed the descendants of his son Ham because Ham had seen his father naked. Raphall, like many proslavery Christian preachers over the years, saw Ham as the ancestor of Black people. One only had to observe the present-day condition of the "fetish-serving, benighted African," the rabbi contended, to prove that their enslavement was favored by God.

———

What was Raphall trying to accomplish in so boldly seizing the secession-winter limelight? He was surprised, or so he claimed, to find himself giving a proslavery address. He had been urged to do so, he explained, by non-Jewish friends. Raphall delivered his sermon in the belief that he was offering a sober, sensible intervention in a debate that had grown far too impassioned. He expected to be congratulated, and at first he was.

In just over a decade of living in America, Raphall had combined his equally impressive Jewish and secular learning, rigid adherence to traditional beliefs and practices, and exceptional oratorical skills to become one of the foremost intermediaries between religious Jews and other Americans, particularly the moneyed and powerful. Raphall often seemed to prefer basking in the applause of gentiles to dealing with his fellow Jews, who he tended to think were either too hidebound and intellectually incurious (as when he had criticized the "mystics of Poland" for blocking access to secular education) or much too willing, like Isaac Mayer Wise, his opponent in the Charleston debate of 1850, to dispense with traditional laws and practices. He could be pompous and argumentative. As an obituary would later put it, Raphall usually seemed "wrapt in his own affairs and in profound meditation to an extent that created a barrier between him and the unlearned." He was a teacher and a preacher, not a leader of men.

To be sure, Raphall's private affairs in the late 1850s would have been preoccupying for anyone. A grown son died in 1857, one of four of their six children he and his wife, Rachel, would bury. They decided to raise their son's children as their own, but Rachel died the following year. Such personal tragedies do not explain Raphall's decision to deliver the proslavery sermon, but they undoubtedly affected him deeply. In depriving him of happiness in his private life, they may have prodded him further to seek approval from the public.

Only two months before his Fast Day sermon, Raphall had been chastised by the board of his synagogue, B'nai Jeshurun—with whom he otherwise enjoyed warm relations—for involving himself in a political controversy. A thoroughgoing conservative, Raphall had publicly endorsed a local Democratic judge for the position of city recorder. While avowing himself "no party-man," Raphall argued that the judge's election would go a long way toward "reducing the mass of crime and criminals, by which this city is disgraced." The synagogue's Board of Trustees admonished Raphall to avoid "the impropriety of any intermeddling with politics, as we firmly believe such a course to be entirely inconsistent with the Jewish clerical character, calculated to be of serious injury to the Jews in general, and to our Congregation in particular." Raphall was not convinced. Openly courting another chastisement, he may have seen his Fast Day sermon, in part, as a counterthrust to the synagogue's board, a challenge to its right to dictate to the rabbi what he could and could not say.

Raphall did not see silence in public as part of the rabbi's role. He yearned for the approval of non-Jewish elites, especially in New York City. By January 1861, those elites were desperate to find a way to avoid a civil war. They knew business with Southern clients would be cut off in the event of war, and so would any chance of the city's businessmen recouping some $200 million in debts owed by Southerners to New York firms. Abram Dittenhoefer, the Jewish Republican who sat on the stage behind Abraham Lincoln at Cooper Union, described New York in 1860 as "virtually an annex of the South," a city whose merchants, Jews and gentiles alike, had put their principles up for sale along with their merchandise. Many of the city's forty thousand Jews had risen from their impoverished immigrant beginnings to achieve some success, particularly in the garment trade, which specialized in making cheap clothing for the enslaved workers on cotton plantations. New York had voted overwhelmingly against Lincoln in the presidential election: by a factor of two to one in the neighborhoods where most Jews lived.

In the weeks after Lincoln's election, the New York economy had plummeted into depression, leaving many firms bankrupt and some ten thousand workers unemployed. *"Alles ist beendet!"* Emanuel Lehman scribbled in his notepad as the South's secession loomed: *All is lost!* He had moved to New York a few years earlier to oversee the Alabama firm's increasingly finance-oriented Northern operations. War would mean disaster for Lehman Brothers. The New York office headed by Emanuel would lose access to Southern cotton, while the Montgomery office would forfeit all business with Northern and British manufacturers. The Lehmans were far from alone in fearing the financial consequences of disunion. A few weeks after Raphall's sermon, a committee of New York merchants—led by Emanuel B. Hart, a Tammany-connected Jewish ex-congressman—took a train to Washington, where they delivered a petition signed by thousands of New York businessmen pleading that the "perpetuity of the Union" was more important than the Republicans' call for banning slavery from the territories. The businessmen shared their Southern customers' views on slavery and states' rights and were willing to strike any compromise to reunite the country.

Some of those businessmen were congregants of Raphall's B'nai Jeshurun, and others, including non-Jews, were his friends. Sharing their aversion to abolition and fear of upheaval, Raphall spoke not merely for "us handful of peaceable Union-loving Hebrews" but for all such Americans everywhere.

Raphall's foray into public controversy was also motivated by his unwavering commitment to Orthodoxy and scorn for his Reform opponents. Throughout his career, Raphall had objected to any efforts to parcel through the Jewish tradition for what could be discarded and what should remain. It was all the direct word of God, and none of it could be stripped away without violating the central commandments of the faith. When he asked, in his Fast Day sermon, at what point slavery had become a sin, he was reiterating his oft-stated objection to the Reformers' loose interpretation of scripture on other matters as well. Raphall distrusted the belief that the mere passage of time lessened the demands of biblical laws and divine commandments. He and his fellow Orthodox rabbis granted no theological importance to the progress of human history. Indeed, for them, there could be no such thing, religiously speaking, as change over time. That which was forbidden in biblical times remained forbidden now, and that which was permitted then remained permitted now. One could not morph one's religious principles to fit preexisting political commitments, arbitrarily changing a millennia-old tradition for the sake of trivial, worldly concerns.

The argument that scripture sanctioned slavery was far from new. Ever since colonial times, the debate over slavery had been in large part a debate about the Bible. Every Sunday in the antebellum South, preachers of various Christian denominations invoked the holy text, both the Old and New Testaments, to prove that the enslavement of Black people was ordained by God.

But endowing that argument with the prestige of Orthodox Judaism was new. Jews in America had often been asked to answer their neighbors' questions about the Hebrew Bible. Oscar Straus recalled in his memoir that his father was called on even by Christian clergy to translate passages from the ancient text and weigh in on biblical debates. The endorsement of the proslavery reading of the Bible by such a prominent Jewish leader, one already well-known as a scholar, thrilled Southern propagandists. In the self-proclaimed independent republic of South Carolina, the pro-secession *Charleston Mercury* called Raphall's speech "one of the most powerful arguments put forth north or south." A Protestant minister in Westchester County, New York, complained that Raphall's sermon left "the impression on the minds of some . . . that he must know the Hebrew of the Bible so profoundly that it is absolutely impossible for him to be mistaken on the subject of slavery; and that what he affirms respecting it is as true almost as the word of God itself." The rabbi's seal of approval lent greater credence to the claim.

"It is a singular fact," one North Carolina paper commented, "that the most masterly expositions which have lately been made of the constitutional and the religious arguments for slavery are from gentlemen of the Hebrew faith," citing not only Raphall's sermon but Judah Benjamin's farewell speech to the Senate a few days earlier.

Above all, Raphall seems to have intended his sermon as a last-minute peace proposal, an audacious effort to patch up the differences between North and South, and to use Judaism as the glue. Raphall offered a bargain: the North would refrain from condemning slaveholding as a sin, while the South would adopt the more humane form of bondage practiced, he believed, in ancient Israel. Though Raphall could not have seriously thought his sermon, with its acerbic, occasionally insulting tone, would be enough to draw the parties to the negotiating table, he may have wished to be seen as doing his part to forge some sort of compromise. Careful to take a position between the extremists of both sides, he reproached Southerners who defended their institutions to the point of tarring and feathering suspected opponents, as well as Northern abolitionists—those "impulsive declaimers, gifted with zeal but little knowledge"—willing to push the nation over the brink on the basis of bad theology and self-interested politics.

As soon as he finished speaking, the Southerners in the audience leapt from their seats to offer the rabbi their warm congratulations. Two weeks later, a group of prominent pro-South citizens, organized as the American Society for Promotion of National Unity, invited Raphall to repeat his sermon at the New-York Historical Society. Samuel F. B. Morse, the artist and telegraph inventor, chaired the proceedings, which concluded with the collection of funds to publish Raphall's sermon as a pamphlet. The board of Raphall's congregation chastised him for once again entering the political sphere but did not take issue with the substance of his remarks.

———

The sermon horrified abolitionists. They felt the descendants of slaves should know better than to endorse slavery. A Black-owned newspaper, the *Weekly Anglo-African*, observed that Raphall's sermon was intended to make Jews "forget that they themselves have been in the house of bondage, and that they have had to beg for their emancipation at the hands of almost every nation in Europe." A poem in the New York–based *Independent* offered up a tidy couplet: "He that unto thy fathers freedom gave / Hath he not taught thee pity for the slave?"

Antislavery Jews were especially angered by Raphall's speech and furious that many Americans seemed to assume he spoke for all Jews. The rabbi had brought disgrace not only on his congregation, argued Michael Heilprin, a Polish-born exile from the 1848 revolutions, but on the whole American Jewish community and on Judaism itself. An encyclopedia editor in New York, Heilprin penned a rapid-fire rebuttal of Raphall's arguments and published it in the *New York Tribune*. Denouncing "the sacrilegious words of the Rabbi," Heilprin said he was astonished to find Raphall being celebrated for his defense of slavery. "Day after day brings hosannahs to the Hebrew defamer of the law of his nation," he lamented. Heilprin did not fear that Raphall's sermon would convince anybody of the righteousness of human bondage, but it might confuse some into thinking that "the God of the Jews" was "a God of Slavery." Alluding to Benjamin Wade's insult of Judah Benjamin, Heilprin asked, "Must the stigma of Egyptian principles be fastened on the people of Israel by Israelitish lips themselves?"

Rabbi David Einhorn of Baltimore had already courted controversy by denouncing both nativism and slavery from his pulpit and in the pages of his monthly German-language magazine, the *Sinai*. To Einhorn, even if the letter of the law countenanced slavery, the spirit of the Torah and of Judaism—particularly the idea, expressed in the first chapter of Genesis, that all human beings were created in the image of God—clearly opposed human bondage.

Einhorn lived an isolated existence. He was well aware, as he acknowledged in his response to Raphall, that he resided in "the chief city of a slave state." Many prominent citizens in Maryland were intent on joining the other slaveholding states in a new Southern Confederacy. A year earlier, in the wake of John Brown's raid on Harpers Ferry, the state legislature had resolved that if the Union broke up, Maryland would "cast her lot with her sister states of the South and abide their fortune to the fullest extent." Only the mildly pro-Union governor, Thomas Hicks, a staunch Know-Nothing, stood in the way of secession.

Few Baltimore Jews supported Einhorn's antislavery stance. Most had voted for John C. Breckinridge, the Southern Democratic presidential candidate, in the 1860 election, both because they agreed with his states' rights views and because a coalition led by Democrats had recently ousted the anti-immigrant Know-

Nothings from positions of prominence in the city. The Jews, like other new arrivals, were grateful. Einhorn's rival rabbis in Baltimore either embraced slavery or did not want to get involved. In his own sermon on the day that President Buchanan had asked Americans to set aside for fasting and prayer, the leading Orthodox rabbi in the city, Bernard Illowy, had asked, "who can blame our brethren of the South" for seceding from a union "kept together . . . by an ill-regulated balance of power and heavy iron ties of violence and arbitrary force?" So long as the federal government "can not, or will not, protect the property rights and privileges of a great portion of the Union"—the slaveholders' property in their fellow men—it made sense for Southerners to want to form their own nation.

Other Baltimore rabbis were less avowedly pro-secession yet far from antislavery. Benjamin Szold, whom Einhorn had tangled with a few years earlier, expressed hope that the states would eventually be "reconciled and reunited in love and good faith." Abraham Rice, the first ordained rabbi to move to the United States twenty years earlier, wrote in a private letter that he could only ask God to "guard us in these times from all troubles and misfortunes." As Rice's wife clarified in a handwritten note appended to the letter, the elderly rabbi simply wished that "the whole thing should pass peacefully for the Jews."

Amid such equivocations and outright embraces of slavery, Einhorn's response to Raphall stood out sharply. The radical rabbi framed his response to Raphall's sermon not only to discredit the Orthodox leader but to challenge the more general political complacency of American Jews. Einhorn saw a community looking after its own immediate interests, willing to be silent about the oppression of others, frightened into complicity and acquiescence. Rising to his Baltimore pulpit a few weeks after Raphall's New York appearance, Einhorn acknowledged that many of his congregants did not want him to speak out. He understood their position. "The Jew has special cause to be conservative," Einhorn acknowledged, "and he is doubly and triply so in a country which grants him all the spiritual and material privileges he can wish for." It made sense for Jews to cherish peace and pray for the Union, "like a true son for the life of a dangerously sick mother."

Yet while sharing his congregation's "patriotic sentiments," Einhorn could not allow Judaism to be "disgraced . . . and in the holy place!" To enlist the Torah on behalf of slavery, as Raphall had, betrayed the core ethical principles on which the religion had persisted for thousands of years. "This pride and renown, the only one which we possess, we will not and dare not allow ourselves to be robbed," Einhorn said. If a Christian minister in Europe had said what Raphall had, they would be criticized as bigots and enemies of the Jewish people. "And are we in America to ignore this mischief done by a *Jewish* preacher?" Einhorn asked. Raphall's speech had been motivated by a love of money and fame, he said: "Only such Jews, who prize the dollar more highly than their God and their religion, can demand or even approve of this!"

The "learned Rabbi," as Einhorn contemptuously called Raphall, had completely missed the point. The Torah was a product of its time. Because ancient slavery could not be abolished immediately, the Mosaic law had introduced rules to make it more humane and to limit suffering. Its antislavery bent was unmistakable. Einhorn could not understand how someone who "praises the Lord daily for the deliverance out of [the] Egyptian yoke of slavery, undertook to defend slavery." The first line of the Ten Commandments identifies God as the being "who brought thee out of the land of Egypt— out of the house of bondage." To Einhorn, Raphall's remarks were nothing less than "a profanation of God's name."

The point of finding a refuge in America could not be to give up the ethical principles Jews had developed through centuries of subjugation, disempowerment, and exile, to slough them off like a burden and eagerly take part in the oppression of others. If Raphall's sermon were accepted as the official Jewish position on slavery, Einhorn warned, it would allow the enemies of the Jewish people to declare, "Such are the Jews! Where they are oppressed, they boast of the humanity of their religion; but where they are free, their Rabbis declare slavery to have been sanctioned by God."

To Isaac Mayer Wise, the point of Jews finding a refuge in America was to enjoy and preserve it, even if that meant keeping quiet about the oppression of others. Whereas Einhorn felt that Jews would never find security so long as slavery and racism continued to exist, Wise seems to have seen the subjugation of Black people as a kind of substitute for the oppression of Jews. The two groups were locked in permanent competition over which would be ranked lower in the American social hierarchy. The welcome the Jews had received in America was predicated on their embrace of the Constitution and acceptance of the "peculiar institution" it protected. To denounce slavery not only violated that implicit contract, but it endangered the refuge the Jews had found.

Wise considered Lincoln's victory in the 1860 election "one of the greatest blunders a nation can commit." But he expected that the crisis would die down once Northerners and Southerners alike realized the consequences of a national rupture. "People care very little for abstract ideas, extreme views or false conceptions of honor when their material interests are neglected or even ruined," Wise mused in the weeks after the election. Because his own principles were so adaptable to circumstances, Wise imagined that others valued their own no less highly. Like many, he assumed the Southerners were bluffing, holding out for a new bargain: "Politics in this country means money, material interests, and no more . . . Philosophize over it as you please . . . it remains a vulgar business." The supposed ethical principles of Northern abolitionists were merely a pretext. What they really cared about was power.

In valuing the Union above all else, Wise drew on his experiences back in Europe, where the fragmentation of Italy and Germany into competing fiefdoms had contributed to a general atmosphere of political backwardness and to the oppression of the Jews. He imagined a disunited America falling prey to standing armies and soaring taxes, economically devastated, turned into a vast ruin. European aristocrats would rejoice that America's republican experiment had reached the end they had always predicted for it.

Yet the secession of the Southern states caught Wise in a dilemma: Judaism could only thrive in a united America, but he could not bring himself to support the means required to keep America united. Like Buchanan and other Northern Democrats, Wise opposed both Southern secession and the use of force to keep the South in the Union. He understood the slaveholders' position and sympathized with it, asking whether the Southern states owed loyalty to a government whose leading officers they could no longer hope to have any role in selecting. Wise deplored South Carolina's secession but argued that the state had the right to leave the Union. "Force will not hold together this Union," Wise said. "It was cemented by liberty and can stand only by the affections of the people." He could only hope that some statesman in the mold of those great men he had seen in Washington a decade earlier, hammering out the Compromise of 1850, would miraculously appear with a plan to hold the country together.

When none did, Wise blamed "the fanatics in both sections of the country" for "destroying the most admirable fabric of government." He thought Buchanan's embrace of the extreme proslavery position on the Kansas turmoil had divided both the Democratic Party and the country at large. Yet Wise held Lincoln and the Republicans primarily responsible for the crisis at hand. When Buchanan called for the day of prayer, Wise scorned the invitation from a man he considered "one of the principal agents in this calamity."

But then he echoed the rebels' own ultimatum: "Pray, Sir? No, it is too late. Either the Republican Party must be killed off forever . . . or the Union be dissolved."

Addressing the uproar over Raphall's proslavery sermon, Wise explained in a brief note in his weekly, the *Israelite*, that he disagreed with Raphall's position. He described the rabbi's "curse of Ham" theory as perhaps the "greatest . . . among all nonsense imposed on the Bible," "blasphem[y]" against "the all-just Deity." But Wise refused to criticize Southern slavery itself, and he did believe, along with Raphall, that whites were inherently superior to Blacks; he just disagreed that it had anything to do with Noah. If making slavery permanent was necessary to keep the Union together, that was fine with him.

In February 1861, Wise watched as enthusiastic crowds descended on Cincinnati's train station to welcome the president-elect as he stopped on his way to Washington. The rabbi was appalled, comparing the mass to a horde of "Philistines" worshipping their pagan god. He could not comprehend the excitement. Wise described Lincoln as looking "like a country squire for the first time in the city," an ironic comment coming from someone who not fifteen years earlier, when he landed in New York, had found himself in a similar position. Now Wise fancied himself more worldly and sophisticated than the gangly rail splitter from the sticks. "We have no doubt he is an honest man and, as much as we can learn, also quite an intelligent man," Wise told his readers, "but he will look queer in the White House, with his primitive manner."

It had become clear by then that no miracle would be forthcoming. Lincoln would be inaugurated, and a civil war would likely commence. When it began, with the Confederates firing on Fort Sumter in April, Wise published his brief editorial titled "Silence, Our Policy." He pledged to remain impartial as the nation devolved into armed conflict. Calling himself "the servant of peace, not war,"

Wise explained to his more than five thousand *Israelite* subscribers, roughly half of whom lived in the South, that no option remained but a vow of silence on political matters:

> What can we say now? Shall we lament and weep like Jeremiah over a state of things too sad and too threatening to be looked upon with indifference? . . . Or should we choose sides with one of the parties? We can not, not only because we abhor the idea of war, but also we have dear friends and near relations, beloved brethren and kinsmen in either section of the country, that our heart bleeds on thinking of their distress, of the misery that might befall them.
>
> Therefore silence must henceforth be our policy, silence on all the questions of the day, until a spirit of conciliation shall move the hearts of millions to a better understanding of the blessings of peace, freedom and union.

Wise's stance may have reflected an age-old strategy, adopted by generations of European Jews: stay quiet on secular issues in exchange for toleration. Unlike his longtime antagonist, David Einhorn, who thought Jews should enter the public square as Jews and on behalf of explicitly Jewish principles, such as supporting equality and aiding the oppressed, Wise thought Jews should be Jews in the home and synagogue but indistinguishable from other Americans outside it. Through four years of war, Wise would largely keep his vow of silence on political matters. A reader of the *Israelite* between 1861 and 1865 would not learn much about the Civil War from Wise's pages, and even then, only that which directly concerned Jews.

Ernestine Rose must have heard about Raphall's sermon and the uproar that ensued. She lived at the time on Grand Street in

Manhattan, mere steps from B'nai Jeshurun's building on Greene Street, in the heart of the city's lively Jewish neighborhood. As an engaged activist, she could not have missed coverage of the episode in the city's leading newspapers. Her public speeches in the ensuing weeks and months suggest the outspoken atheist and abolitionist took a more than passing interest in the debate raging among her former coreligionists. Her activities and writings during the Civil War itself would display a greater degree of familiarity with—and sympathy for—the Jewish experience in America than she had ever before revealed. While undoubtedly sincere in rejecting any affinity for the religion of her upbringing in Poland, she likely continued to see herself, in some sense, as Jewish, and her radical vision for America as bound up with the still-uncertain status of her fellow American Jews.

As war loomed, Rose turned fifty years old. Her trademark black curls, uncovered as always, were beginning to gray. A brief trip to Europe in 1858, intended to help her recuperate from exhaustion and other physical ailments, had offered only a temporary reprieve from her grueling schedule of lectures, conventions, reformist meetings, and picnics. The next year she took a nasty fall down the stairs, spraining her wrist and bruising her head. When the war broke out, the women's movement took a yearslong hiatus. While she never would have said so, Rose must have been grateful for the respite.

She had never seriously believed the Southerners would follow through on their long-standing threats to secede from a Union that had always served them well. It was all bluster, she thought, "a sheer political trick," meant to intimidate the North into caving to the slaveholders' demands. While some, like Isaac Mayer Wise, hoped a new bargain could be struck in order to bring the Southern states back into the fold, Rose thought such a deal would ruin the best chance to strike a fatal blow against the South's immoral institution. So long as human slavery remained legal in America, no progress could be made on the other causes so dear to her heart. At the annual dinner in honor of Thomas Paine's birthday, in late January 1861, Rose likened the union between free and slave states to "that of husband and wife; with all the rights on one side and all penalties on the other." The South had gotten far more out of the marriage than the North. The central issue now was "whether a vile mob, headed by corrupted and treacherous politicians . . . shall be allowed to trample the dignity, the manhood and the liberties of the North in the dust—whether we shall barter away the rights, the progress and the civilization of the free States for the inestimable blessing to belong to South Carolina."

Like Wise, Raphall, and Judah Benjamin, though for very different reasons, Rose thought the South should be allowed to secede in peace: "[L]et the watchword be, 'No more compromise!'" Without the North's constitutional obligations to return fugitive slaves and help put down insurrections, slavery would die out on its own. "The danger . . . is not the secession of the South from the North," Rose said, "but of the North from herself, from the self-evident truth of man's right to life, liberty and the pursuit of happiness."

Speaking a few weeks after Raphall's proslavery sermon, Rose ridiculed how President Buchanan, faced with the gravest crisis in the history of the Union, "being too cowardly and inefficient to weather the storm he helped to raise, took refuge in fasting and prayer." Nothing could be more embarrassing and inadequate, to Rose's mind, than for the elected leader of a free government to implore a fictional deity to save humanity from a crisis of humanity's own making. Anticipating Lincoln's Second Inaugural Address, Rose observed that each side was asking God for assistance against the other: "One party for secession, the other for non-secession . . . One side claims the Bible for and the other claims it against slavery, and they are both right. That book is so accommodating that it proves and disproves anything you choose."

Condemning both sides for appealing to an antiquated, contradictory, and ultimately irrelevant authority, Rose nonetheless believed that Raphall had the better case. The Bible did, on its face, countenance slavery, as well as incest, polygamy, and mass murder. If those positions conflicted with modern morality, the appropriate thing to do was to dismiss the Bible entirely as the product of a primitive period in the development of civilization, and come up with new guidance for the present age. Rose had long felt that religion was "a hindrance to the elevation and progress of the race." Never had that been more true than in the winter of 1861, as dogmatic adherence to a millennia-old book compelled otherwise thoughtful people to endorse human slavery and had driven the country to the brink of civil war.

On April 10, 1861, two days before the firing on Fort Sumter, Rose delivered a speech in Boston titled "A Defense of Atheism." Later published in book form, the speech drew on biblical texts, recent scientific discoveries, and examples from daily life to argue, as the young girl in the Polish shtetl had contended in debates with her rabbi father, that there was no God, and that religion, far from a guarantee of good morals, encouraged the worst, most violent forms of human behavior. "Look at the present crisis at the South, with 4,000,000 beings in slavery, bought and sold like brute chattels under the sanction of religion and of God," Rose observed. There had to be another way: "Teach man to do right, to love justice, to revere truth, to be virtuous, not because a God would reward or punish him hereafter, but because it is right . . . Let him feel the great truth that our highest happiness consists in making all around us happy; and it would be an infinitely truer and safer guide for man to a life of usefulness, virtue, and morality, than all the beliefs in all the Gods ever imagined."

Rose had little hope that her words would alter the nation's trajectory, but it seemed important that somebody stand unequivocally, even if alone, for reason, equality, liberty, and humanity. Maybe she would have some barely detectable influence. Maybe not. But at least she would not feel that she had kept silent at a moment when her principles compelled her to speak up. In that way, she was not much different from David Einhorn, her religious opposite, who also spoke from a position of resolute commitment and profound isolation and who was about to encounter something Rose had many times before: the rampaging violence of an American mob.

Six years after his arrival in the United States, Einhorn was finally making a name for himself outside Jewish circles. The Baltimore rabbi's response to Raphall's sermon was picked up and translated by the *New York Evening Post*, then published as a pamphlet by Jewish booksellers. He found little support among Jewish leaders, who, like Isaac Mayer Wise, entirely avoided the issue or sided with the proslavery position. The Orthodox *Jewish Messenger*, refusing to publish readers' letters on the debate Raphall had started, flatly stated that its editors had "no desire to take part in a controversy of this nature." Isaac Leeser, the Philadelphia editor of the influential *Occident*, who had spent formative years in his youth living in Richmond, Virginia, agreed with "nearly all" that Raphall had said on the subject of slavery, yet he urged his fellow Jews not to encourage "the destruction of the temple in which human freedom had dreamed to have found a refuge." Leeser vowed not to raise "any political theme" in his newspaper, "but simply matters belonging to us as a religious community." Yet he published several proslavery articles during the secession winter, while refusing to print Einhorn's antislavery sermon.

Einhorn faced even greater hostility closer to home. After years of fighting off vicious attacks by nativist gangs, the Jews of Baltimore were not eager to give the unruly mobs new reasons to target them. After the publication of his response to Raphall, Einhorn's critics in the city called a protest meeting to denounce his irresponsible behavior. Some in his congregation even told Einhorn that his antislavery views demonstrated, as the rabbi put it, "unheard of daring, bordering on madness." Einhorn explained that he was aware that anything blamed on one Jew was usually—and unfairly—attributed to all of them, yet it was precisely his desire to save the community from prejudice that led him to speak out when he saw it directed at others.

By April 1861, civic order in Baltimore had deteriorated to the breaking point. The convergence of multiple railroads in the city, without direct connections between them, meant that anyone traveling from the North had to cross through downtown, close to the city's rowdy, bustling wharves, to get to the vulnerable capital at Washington and points farther south. One by one, each train car had to be dragged by horses from one depot to another through the clogged city streets. That February, the month Einhorn published his critique of Raphall, the Washington-bound president-elect had been forced to sneak through the city in the middle of the night to evade a rumored assassination attempt.

On April 19, 1861, eighty-six years to the day after the British marched on Lexington and Concord, another revolution broke out, this time in the streets of Baltimore. A week earlier, Fort Sumter had surrendered to the seven-state Confederacy. When Lincoln asked for seventy-five thousand troops to put down the rebellion, four more states, including Virginia, seceded in protest. Maryland seemed likely to be next. Northern troops made their way south to protect the federal capital from invasion, but that meant passing through Baltimore, where support for secession was growing by the day. When a regiment of Massachusetts troops attempted the perilous cross-town journey, hundreds of proslavery residents, cheering for Jefferson Davis and the Confederacy, set up a barricade of ship anchors hauled from the nearby docks and attacked the troops, hurling cobblestones and firing pistols. The soldiers fired back. When the smoke cleared, four soldiers and twelve civilians lay dead on the pavement, the first combat victims of the Civil War. Six people were arrested, including Joseph Friedenwald, son of a prominent member of the Baltimore Hebrew Congregation, where Rabbi Illowy, a few months earlier, had defended slavery and secession.

The federal troops continued on their way to Washington, leaving drunken mobs to tear through Baltimore, burning and pillaging homes and businesses associated with Lincoln supporters and critics of slavery. David Einhorn hunkered down at his home with a clutch of armed volunteers standing guard. His name, he was told, appeared prominently on a list of targets. The printing press that published his *Sinai*, just around the corner from Pratt Street, where the Union soldiers had been attacked, had already been demolished. Now the mob was coming for the rabbi himself. Friends, family, congregants, even federal soldiers begged him to flee. Einhorn resisted, not wanting to abandon his congregation. Finally he gave in. Two supporters, a pair of brothers, took the rabbi and his family, including his pregnant wife, sixty miles by carriage to the safety of York, Pennsylvania, then to Philadelphia.

A decade earlier, in Europe, Einhorn had lost his job as rabbi in Pest, forced out by the strong arm of autocratic power. Now he was once again run out of town, only this time it was by a democratic mob.

A few weeks later, with Baltimore restored to an uneasy calm under federal occupation, Einhorn prepared to go home. He wanted to be back in time for Shavuot, the feast commemorating the day God gave the Torah to the ancient Israelites. But just as he was about to set off, a letter arrived from the president of his congregation, a tobacco dealer, reporting the outcome of a recent meeting of the members. The letter asked Einhorn, when he returned, to refrain from public comment on the "explosive questions of the day." For the sake of his safety and their own, Einhorn's congregants wanted him to keep silent about slavery. The rabbi refused and resigned his position. To a supporter, Einhorn bitterly denounced his opponents, who seemed more interested in loosening dietary laws than adhering to moral ones: "There is nothing so loathsome, indeed, than this riffraff of bacon reformers. The light of the Rabbis becomes a destroying torch in the hands of such people."

Einhorn never returned to Baltimore. Instead, he accepted leadership of what he called "a braver congregation" in Philadelphia, which imposed no restrictions on his speech. Though he had lost his job and his home, Einhorn had no regrets. As he wrote in the first issue of the *Sinai* he published in Philadelphia, "I could not and would not keep silent in the face of such a defamation of Judaism, no matter what might follow."

Later that summer, the first of the war, Einhorn's wife gave birth to a son. "The boy started out by being anxious to take a look at the world of America at the very moment they fought at Bull Run," the rabbi explained to a friend weeks later, as Rosh Hashanah and Yom Kippur approached. "Now comes the Holy Season and I hope that the Southern rebels will be sent to perdition. Amen!"

8

"No More Pharaohs . . ."

AUGUST BONDI HAD GROWN USED TO FRONTIER LIFE. Years had passed since he battled with proslavery posses on the western plains. His side, at last, had won. In January 1861, as Judah Benjamin and his fellow Southerners took their leave from the Union, putting Northerners firmly in control of Congress, Kansas entered the Union as a free state. Bondi spent his days hauling butter and eggs to market, tending to his cattle and his corn.

His sense of peace and contentment would prove short-lived. Domestic duties kept Bondi from enlisting when the war broke out, as he badly wanted to do. His first child, a girl, was born two weeks after the firing on Fort Sumter. But come fall, as soon as the harvest had been reaped and he had readied the homestead for his absence—wood chopped, hay stored, "my hogs killed and pickled"—Bondi got ready to join the fight. His father encouraged him to go; his mother offered to help care for the newborn. She told him that "as a Jehudi" he was obligated "to defend the institutions which gave equal rights to all beliefs." In November 1861, Bondi left his family with enough oxen, cows, horses, and pigs to see them through the winter. Along with two neighbors, he set off for the nearest federal fort.

The Civil War proved a pivotal moment not only for the United States but for the small but growing Jewish community. The country's 150,000 Jews participated in the culminating struggle between slavery and freedom in both blue and gray uniforms, filling the ranks from lowliest cannon fodder to cigar-chomping, campaign-plotting generals—in all, some six thousand Jewish men would serve in the Union forces, about half that number in the Confederate ranks—but also as blood-spattered medics and army-chasing sutlers, illicit cotton traders and ocean-crossing financiers, seagoing blockade runners and shape-shifting spies. On both home fronts, Jews contributed to relief organizations and gathered donations of tobacco and tea, flour and grits and biscuits, pens and paper, socks and shirts and soap. Women knitted clothes and bandages, nursed the wounded, filled sandbags for fortifications, rolled and filled cartridges for rifles. Rabbis exhorted their congregants to join the fight and said Kaddish over the slain.

Jews from far-flung communities holding widely diverse ideas about religion and politics responded differently to the long-dreaded outbreak of war, and especially to what Lincoln called its most "fundamental and astounding" consequence, the abolition of slavery. But they also had much in common. The Civil War has been described as an Americanizing experience for Jews. Those who served in the armies lived for the first time in close quarters with other Americans, and by fighting for their chosen country or even dying for it, demonstrated that it was their country, too. The war offered Jews a chance to show their patriotism to one side or the other, to demonstrate to their fellow citizens their willingness to sacrifice themselves for a larger cause. Seeing Jews march off to battle in the same Union blue or Confederate gray as their own fathers and sons may have convinced otherwise skeptical gentiles that the differences between

Jews and Christians were of little importance. In 1863, Myer S. Isaacs, the son of a New York rabbi, delivered a Thanksgiving sermon in his father's synagogue on Wooster Street in Manhattan. The war had brought Jews closer to the mainstream of American life, Isaacs observed. Jews and gentiles were now "working together, fighting together the battles of the Union, pouring their blood on the battlefield." Whether they sought in those battles to destroy the Union or preserve it, they hoped that blood might serve as a down payment on belonging.

Several decades after the Civil War, Jewish historians keen to counter depictions of Jews as fundamentally disloyal compiled vast (and in some cases inaccurate) lists of Jewish soldiers who fought for the Union and the Confederacy. Oft-repeated claims about Jewish Medal of Honor recipients, all-Jewish army units, Passover seders held in the wilderness, and home-front contributions shaped a story of Jewish participation in the conflict as a triumphant moment of sacrifice and accomplishment, acceptance and assimilation.

In fact, while some of these stories are true, many were exaggerated or misrepresented. Charitable fundraising was inconsistent, while supposedly all-Jewish units only had a small fraction of Jews in their ranks. It may be that the Civil War did as much to differentiate Jews from their fellow Americans as it did to integrate them into the larger population. The historian Adam Mendelsohn, whose work has begun to chip away at such pieties, diagnoses a "tendency to trumpery" in early accounts of American Jewry and the Civil War. Dwelling on precisely how many Jews fought in the armies or how Jews fought back against efforts to exclude them tends to obscure more difficult topics like how Jews thought about slavery and abolition and how wartime outbursts of antisemitism continued to affect American Jews after the conflict ended. To a large extent, the Civil War was a devastating experience for American Jews, one that shaped the community in profound and not altogether positive ways for many years to come.

Despite their hesitation during the secession crisis, their fears for a country teetering on the brink of violence, many Jewish leaders in the North were eager to be seen demonstrating their patriotism once the war began. Even those who had deplored the prospect of war now embraced loudly and publicly the need to fight it, as if they feared the consequences should they remain silent. Only a few months after his proslavery sermon, Morris J. Raphall presided over an elaborate ceremony that culminated with the Stars and Stripes being raised over his Manhattan synagogue. American Jews knew the "difference between *elsewhere* and *here*," Raphall insisted. While he did not retract his earlier comments in defense of the biblical legitimacy of slavery, he now affirmed that the Bible also offered "abundant warrant for denouncing rebellion as a sin before God."

Blaming secession on "foul stimulants of selfish, ambitious leaders" who had led Southerners astray, the rabbi urged his congregants to defend their Union "at the peril of life and limb." Little did he know how close to home that peril would strike. Weeks later, Raphall's thirty-one-year-old son, Alfred, enlisted in the 40th New York Infantry. One day in the summer of 1863, as the rabbi was about to lead his congregation in services, Raphall was shocked into an "attack of apoplexy," the *New York Times* reported, by the sight of Alfred, newly returned from the Battle of Gettysburg, missing his right arm.

In so loudly declaring his loyalties, Raphall was part of a larger trend. After arriving in New York and addressing a massive crowd in Union Square, Robert Anderson, the army major who had bravely held out at Fort Sumter before surrendering it to the Confederacy, agreed to pay a visit to Temple Emanu-El, a Reform congregation. The organist usually charged with rapping out German hymns on the second-largest set of pipes in the country played "The Star-Spangled

Banner" as Emanu-El's members crowded around the first Northern hero of the war.

Months earlier, Samuel Isaacs, a traditionalist rabbi and the editor of the *Jewish Messenger*, had refused to discuss the controversy over Raphall's sermon. Now Isaacs urged his readers, whatever their feelings about slavery, to support the Union and embrace the flag: "Whether native or foreign born, Christian or Israelite, stand by it, and you are doing your duty, and acting well your part on the side of liberty and justice." Like many Northerners, Jews and gentiles, Isaacs supported going to war for the sake of restoring the Union, but not for abolishing slavery. A week later, noting David Einhorn's flight from Baltimore, the *Messenger* ridiculed the antislavery rabbi for "mistaking his vocation, and making the pulpit the vehicle for political invective." Trumpeting one's support for the Union was not politics, but denouncing slavery was.

Despite his criticism of Einhorn, Isaacs's milder salvo against secession still went too far for his subscribers. So many canceled their subscriptions that the weekly *Messenger* had to cut its frequency in half. A group of secession-supporting Jews in Shreveport, Louisiana, sent a petition condemning the *Messenger* as a "black republican paper" and rebuked Isaacs for asking them to "act as traitors and renegades to our adopted country." They, too, would stand by the flag, their new flag, that of "the Union and Constitution of the Southern Confederacy."

Still, Isaacs was unmoved. He contrasted his firm stance with that of Isaac Mayer Wise, who, even after Fort Sumter, remained suspicious of Lincoln and stubbornly neutral in the pages of his *Israelite*. "We conceive, there is no neutral ground, just now," Isaacs said, "and the loss of a portion of our subscribers shall not induce us to passively sympathize with those who would overthrow the UNION, which we love." Those who disagreed were welcome to end their subscriptions, so long as they "spare us their 'protests'" and paid up what they owed on their bill, "with as few words as possible."

───────────

The secession crisis called forth displays of patriotism not only from rabbis and editors but public figures well positioned to make a difference. In Missouri, a crucial border state, a businessman named Isidor Bush, a native of Prague, helped keep the state in the Union. After the 1848 uprisings, Bush's family, like August Bondi's, had made their way to America. Bush opened a bookstore in New York and published a short-lived weekly, *Israel's Herold*, the first Jewish newspaper published in German in the United States. Bush then moved west to St. Louis and opened a store in the same immigrant-heavy neighborhood where the Bondis lived. But while they struggled to find a footing, Bush prospered, investing in real estate and wine making, then banking and railroads. An outspoken abolitionist, he served as a delegate at the state convention called in 1861 to consider whether Missouri should secede from the Union. Bush argued not only for staying in the Union but for emancipating all slaves in the state right away, and for doing so without any compensation to the masters:

> They tell us that the Negroes would be but one great band of idlers and vagabonds, robbers, murderers, and thieves . . . I have no such words for such slanders against poor human beings, so much sinned against. It is not enough that you hold them in bondage, toys of your whim and your lust, but you must charge them with crimes they never committed and never dreamt of. I pray you have pity for yourselves, *not* for the Negro.

Bush's influence at the convention was pivotal; he helped design the program of uncompensated emancipation that Missouri ultimately enacted, an astonishing turn of events in the state whose proslavery citizens had invaded neighboring Kansas a decade earlier, igniting the sectional dispute into armed conflict. Early in the war, Bush served as an aide to John C. Fremont, the presidential candidate–turned–Union general whose 1861 proclamation freeing the slaves in his Missouri district put Lincoln, desperate to keep the border states in the Union, in a difficult position. Bush implored the president to support Fremont: "Act Sir, act freely—according to the dictates of your honest heart." During the darkest days of the war, Bush gave antislavery speeches at Congregation B'nai El, the synagogue that August Bondi's parents had joined, and later advocated for Black suffrage and fought racial segregation in the state.

Rising Jewish stars of the financial world likewise stepped in to aid the Union cause. August Belmont, the American agent of the Rothschild banking family and the powerful chairman of the now-fractured Democratic Party, had opposed Lincoln's election and long argued for respecting the rights and interests of the slave South. But he was horrified by the Confederate attack on Fort Sumter and, like Morris Jacob Raphall, loudly proclaimed his loyalty to the Union. Married to the Christian daughter of the famed seaman Commodore Matthew Perry, Belmont had little to do with the Jewish community. Still he was widely recognized—and often disparaged—as a Jew. Pledging himself chiefly interested "not as the Banker & Correspondent of foreign Banking firms but as an American citizen, anxious to do his share in the crisis which has overcome our dear Country," Belmont offered Lincoln advice on how to fund the war and lobbied the British government not to recognize the Confederacy. He even opened his ample private art collection to the public and donated the proceeds from admission fees to the Sanitary Commission, a forerunner of the Red Cross.

Yet Belmont's closeness with the Lincoln administration cooled as the Rothschilds, like many in Europe, began to doubt the Union's ability to win the war, and they curtailed their financial support. "The sooner the great European powers recognize the Confederacy," Salomon de Rothschild wrote home from America during a prolonged visit, "the sooner they will have fulfilled a mission of peace and humanity." Belmont himself began calling for "an earnest effort towards reconciliation and peace." In the 1864 election, he campaigned as vigorously to eject Lincoln from the White House as he had to prevent him from entering it in the first place.

Into the vacuum left by Belmont's disaffection rushed the Bavarian immigrant Joseph Seligman and his seven brothers, partners in a wide variety of continent-spanning businesses from dry-goods importing and merchandising to banking based on reserves of California gold. Consciously modeling himself after Belmont and his easy access to the highest rungs of the New York social ladder, Joseph, the eldest brother, saw the war as his family's chance to rise into that refined echelon. After withdrawals by Southern banks depleted the coffers of the federal treasury, the Seligmans offered sizable donations to stabilize the government, a goodwill gesture that helped the firm secure contracts to supply the Union Army. Ironically, the outbreak of war brought a windfall to the same garment manufacturers in New York who had feared calamity in the event of disunion. Instead of making clothes for slaves, they now made uniforms for Union soldiers.

Paid in federal bonds, Joseph Seligman traveled to Europe to sell them off for as much as he could, more of a self-interested endeavor than the purely patriotic mission often depicted (Seligman's efforts were "scarcely less important than the Battle of Gettysburg," according to one breathless chronicler). In London, Seligman crossed paths with Emanuel Lehman, who was also in England attempting to sell American bonds, but on behalf of the Confederacy. Joseph despaired of success, his own and the Union's. At a low point, he wrote home that he was inclined to sell off his own personal stake in the bonds, remain in Europe, and thereby "keep my hands clear of the present degenerated American race." He resisted the temptation, and before the war ended had gathered enough capital to realize a long-standing dream: the founding of an international banking firm bearing his family's increasingly well-regarded name. As was true of countless other merchants and manufacturers lower on the economic ladder, the war contributed more to the success of the Seligmans than they did to the success of the war.

The most convincing way to show one's patriotism was to enlist in the army, and in those early days of the war, Jews did so in droves. Nearly as many Jewish men signed up to serve on April 19, 1861—the day pro-secession rioters forced David Einhorn to flee Baltimore—as in all of 1863, a mostly dismal year of the conflict for the North. The roughly six thousand Jews who fought for the Union did so for many reasons. Some, like August Bondi, believed wholeheartedly not only in preserving the Union but in fighting against slavery. Leopold Blumenberg, a veteran of the Prussian army who quickly rose to the rank of major in the 5th Maryland Infantry, was a long-standing supporter of David Einhorn at Har Sinai Congregation in Baltimore, an active Republican who agreed with the rabbi's antislavery views and, on the day of the riots, likewise hid out from the rampaging mob, which he believed was intent on hanging him. Shot in the thigh at Antietam, Blumenberg suffered from his wounds for fourteen years until he finally succumbed. Edward Salomon, who had arrived in Chicago at the age of nineteen and risen within five years from working as a clerk in a hat store to being elected the city's first Jewish alderman, served as a lieutenant in the 82nd Illinois Infantry, led by Friedrich Hecker, a veteran of the 1848 revolutions in Germany. While back home in Chicago on leave from the army in the summer of 1862, Salomon helped rescue a free Black man from being beaten to death after he refused an omnibus driver's order to disembark.

Other Jews fought not because they hoped the war would lead to the abolition of slavery but despite the fact that they feared it would. And some who enlisted for one reason stayed in the army for another. The son and grandson of rabbis, Marcus Spiegel had been born in a small town on the Rhine. After joining the uprising against the Prussian monarchy, he sailed for America in 1849 at the age of nineteen. Like so many Jews of his generation, he hoisted a pack and sold goods in the Ohio countryside. At one farmhouse he met a pretty sixteen-year-old named Caroline, daughter of a Quaker family, and after repeated visits asked her to marry him. At first Spiegel's family was resistant to the marriage, but Caroline won them over by converting to Judaism and studying up on the German language and Jewish cuisine.

By 1860, the Spiegels were living in Millersville, Ohio, a thriving village at the end of a branch-line railroad thirty miles outside Toledo. Marcus invested in warehouses for storing wheat, oats, and corn, but he overextended himself and was on the brink of bankruptcy when the outbreak of war offered a near-miraculous path out of trouble. Ohio law dictated that those who enlisted were not liable for their debts for the duration of their service. Enlistment offered Spiegel immediate relief from his financial embarrassments. He hoped to find a "bombproof" job in the army, so he could make enough money to settle his debts without putting his life at risk for a cause that he, an outspoken Democrat, only half-heartedly believed in. As he wrote Caroline in March 1862, "for the Constitution, the Union and the Flag of my country I will fight to the last . . . but it is not necessary to fight for the darkies, nor are they worth fighting for." In another letter, Spiegel promised to bring home "a nice a litte He nigger [*sic*]" as a gift for his son.

In the course of his two and a half years in the army, however, Marcus Spiegel changed. Along with vivid descriptions of long marches, moonlit camps, and tight rations (often several different kinds of pork, which Spiegel, like most Jews in the field, even traditionally observant ones, had little choice but to consume), Spiegel's letters to Caroline, impatient for her husband's return, show how the experience of war made him a different person. He turned out to be a capable officer, was quickly promoted to colonel of the 120th Ohio Volunteer Infantry, and was beloved by his men and fearless in battle. Wounded at Vicksburg and sent home in a freight car, Spiegel made his way back to the front as soon as he could, though able to walk only with the use of a cane.

The war also transformed his political views. As the war ground on, Spiegel's letters show his prewar prejudices on an ever shakier foundation. Firsthand glimpses of the realities of bondage, and encounters with newly liberated former slaves (including Black soldiers of the United States Colored Troops), changed his beliefs about the issue that had caused the conflict. South of Memphis, Spiegel and his men were "hailed by darkies in the most cheering spirit and great manifestation of joy." Spiegel was sympathetic, even if he still believed the proslavery propaganda that depicted slaves as only discontented due to abolitionist meddling:

> The poor devils frequently by signs, gestures and so forth imploringly ask to be taken out of bondage. That seems hard to see and not to comply; yet if all the agitation had never been and those poor and unfortunate men been left in their once happy state of carelessness, there is no question but they would have been more benefit to humanity in a social, philanthropic and humane Auspice but as it is, it seems hard to deny a privilege to be free. Yet when on the other hand you see thousands of the Contrabands pulled away in the same manner from their masters, in a miserable and starving and filthy condition, then in a spirit of philanthropy you will say, better be in slavery than such freedom as I can give you.

Days later, the Emancipation Proclamation made the freeing and arming of the enslaved both an objective of the war and an essential means for winning it. Despite his growing doubts about slavery, Spiegel reacted like many of his fellow Democrats: with disdain. The "whole Army is discouraged and very much dissatisfied," he wrote in January 1863. The Proclamation "fell like a thunderbolt among the troops." He was not sure many of them would pick up a weapon if asked, he told Caroline, and he would try to find an honorable way to leave the army as soon as he could: "I do not . . . want to fight for Lincoln's Negro proclamation one day longer than I can help."

Further brushes with formerly enslaved people in the Deep South, especially in Louisiana, where his regiment was sent as part of Grant's Vicksburg campaign, made him less indifferent to their fate and more willing to fight for slavery's abolition. As friends and neighbors in Ohio offered violent resistance to the military draft and angrily denounced the Emancipation Proclamation, Spiegel recoiled. He began to resent the home-front politicians decrying the war though far from the field of battle, and disavowed an attempt by Ohio Democrats to nominate him for office. In a letter to his brother-in-law, Michael Greenebaum, the Jewish plumber in Chicago who had helped rescue a fugitive slave back in 1853, Spiegel denounced the Democrats for seeking to end the war short of a Confederate surrender. Much as he wished the war to end, Spiegel wrote, "I do not want to see it close until the enemies of my beloved country are conquered and brought to terms." The Confederates had to be shown that the United States, "although a noble country to live in peaceably, yet it is a powerful government to rebel against." While he believed that the Emancipation Proclamation had "strengthened the enemy," Spiegel knew it was vitally important to stamp out the rebellion once and for all. Let the demand for peace first be heard from Richmond, Charleston, and Vicksburg, along with a surrender of arms and acknowledgment of the national government: "Then and not until then, will I say peace."

He had grown in the war as a man, as a soldier, even as a Jew. Spiegel rejoiced in encountering Southern Jews and took every opportunity he could to enjoy Sabbath and festive meals. He could usually tell who was Jewish, "by the name as well as *ponim* [face]." He would greet them in Hebrew, then "see them jump and ask 'Yehudah?'" Once, while stationed in northern Kentucky, he crossed the Ohio River to attend services at Isaac Mayer Wise's Cincinnati synagogue. Reminded by a fellow Jewish soldier he bumped into that Rosh Hashanah and Yom Kippur were approaching, he implored the converted Caroline to make sure that she and the children observed the holidays "for my sake, and let us pray to the Lord God of Israel for the deliverance of this once happy Country and the Peaceful enjoyment of our family Circle at the End of this unhappy war."

By early 1864, Spiegel, seemingly on the verge of being promoted to brigadier general, told Caroline he now considered himself "a strong abolitionist." This conversion, he assured her, was "no hasty conclusion but a deep conviction" informed by all he had witnessed while at war: "Since I am here I have learned and seen more of what the horrors of Slavery was than I ever knew before and I am glad indeed that the signs of the times show towards closing out the accursed institution." He did still favor somehow "making the negro work at all events, inasmuch as he is naturally lazy and indolent, but never hereafter will I either speak or vote in favor of Slavery." Abolition, he now saw, was "for the best interest of the white man in the south and the black man anywheres."

On May 3, 1864, a boat that Spiegel's regiment was taking up the Red River in Louisiana to relieve an isolated Union outpost was ambushed by Confederate cannons hidden behind the levee. As one survivor recalled, "such a torrent of shot and shell as was poured into the boat I never saw before and never want to witness again." As he made his way to the deck to wave a white flag of surrender, Spiegel took a bullet to the stomach. He suffered in agony for twenty-four hours, then died. His men buried him in a riverbank, but the shifting course of the stream soon washed away the grave.

Like August Bondi, Marcus Spiegel felt he had a special obligation to fight for the land that had taken him in. "[I]f anything does happen to me," he once told his wife, "I am only offering a small sacrifice for my beloved country, which always so generous and kind, has opened her arms to receive the down-trodden of other nations."

By the time something did happen to him, Spiegel had come to feel obligated to fight for the downtrodden of his adopted nation as well.

———

"No more pharaohs and no more slaves." This one line from August Bondi's posthumously published memoir of nearly two hundred pages, much of it drawn from a diary he kept through his three years of service in the Union Army, has been quoted in online articles about "the Jewish conductor on the Underground Railroad"—his participation, in fact, lasted at most a few months—and even in historian Simon Schama's celebrated two-volume, millennia-spanning survey, *The Story of the Jews* (2017). Bondi allegedly wrote the line in celebration of the Emancipation Proclamation while camped out with his men in eastern Arkansas. The only problem is that he never did. What Bondi actually put down in his notebook on January 1, 1863, was far more prosaic: "No more slaves returned to their masters."

The misquotation has proven popular because it offers an appealingly concise statement of the Jewish-tinted antislavery politics shared by August Bondi, David Einhorn, and others. Having engaged in some of the first active fights against the forces of slavery, Bondi rejoiced in the abolition of Southern bondage. Yet the diary he kept of his Civil War experiences does not explore his emotional

or intellectual reactions to what he was seeing, nor does it emphasize the death and terror he must have seen all around him. None
of that was new for Bondi, who as a fourteen-year-old had seen
friends fall dead in front of him on Vienna's blood-soaked streets.
Rather than linger on the gore, Bondi's diary is filled with matter-
of-fact descriptions of battles, pickets, scouting expeditions, impass-
able roads, frostbitten feet, and unfathomable hunger. A talented
forager, Bondi bragged about occasionally adding raccoon to his
company's rations.

The action Bondi saw in Arkansas and Missouri, two states split
between Unionist and secessionist populations, resembled the small-
scale Bleeding Kansas fighting he was familiar with from a decade
before more than it did the massed engagements of brigades and
divisions at Shiloh, Chickamauga, or Gettysburg. Guerrilla bands,
roadside executions, rampant pillaging and cattle stealing, combat-
ants disguised as civilians: Bondi had seen it all before. He was more
interested in writing about the moments when the fighting ceased,
such as the time his regiment and the rebels called a brief truce
so they could gather the juicy harvest of a watermelon patch. For
one blessedly peaceful afternoon, enemies mingled together in the
fields, and even sat down for a "social game," likely poker.

One source of consternation for Bondi was the refusal of two
other Jewish soldiers in his company to acknowledge that they were
Jews. In the Union Army, such denials were a common tactic to
avoid unwanted scrutiny. As the *Jewish Messenger* observed, many
Jewish soldiers feared that if their religious identity was known, "it
would expose them to the taunts and sneers of those among their
comrades who have been in the habit of associating with the name
of Jew, everything that is mean and contemptible." Bondi only confirmed his suspicions about one of his fellow soldiers after the man
died of illness and Bondi was handed a letter the dead man's parents
had written him in Hebrew informing him of the upcoming dates
of the High Holidays. Bondi regretted that if the man had only

acknowledged his Jewishness, he might have helped save his life. He had made a habit of going out of his way to help his coreligionists, once returning horses some of his men had stolen from Arkansas Jews, a mitzvah that landed Bondi an invitation to Rosh Hashanah dinner, where he happened to run into an old acquaintance from his St. Louis days.

During his time in the army, Bondi rose to first sergeant and found, like Marcus Spiegel, that he had an aptitude for leadership. On Christmas Day in 1862, Bondi comforted his men, who wondered if they would ever see home again. "I encourage all hands to keep up good spirits," Bondi wrote in his diary. "Sooner or later the war will end and the United States be an united free people, the strongest nation on earth."

Bondi's war ended one morning in September 1864, outside Pine Bluff, Arkansas, at a crossroads where his troops came across a large detachment of Confederates. Bravely halting a retreat in order to secure the federal guns, Bondi took a bullet to his left thigh, then another in the scrotum, before a third ricocheted off the metal plate of his belt and knocked him off his horse. Two fellow soldiers carried him until the pain became too great and he asked to be dropped beside a log. He gave them his weapons. He would not need them anymore. Speaking became difficult, then impossible. Some Confederate soldiers came by and promised to see he was well-treated. One tried to take his money, another his boots, but Bondi resisted and they moved on. Through a long, late-summer day, he roasted in the sun. Darkness fell, and feral hogs began prowling around the battlefield, rooting among the bodies. Bondi knew that if he passed out they would eat him. He tried to yell but could not. He tried to slither a few yards but could not do that either. He was about to give up when he saw a light approaching him in the dark. An elderly Freemason with sons in the rebel army and a young soldier home on sick leave helped Bondi onto a horse and led him to the older man's home. They cleaned and fed him until a federal detachment looking for bodies to bury came to retrieve him and carried him along bumpy roads to an army hospital, where, defying a nurse who told him he would not survive, he recovered. Helped by Ed, "a colored boy" he had "picked up" during the war, Bondi finally made his way home by ambulance, steamship, railroad, and buggy. When he appeared outside the humble Kansas farmhouse he had left three years earlier, his daughter, whom he had last seen as a six-month-old, vaulted into his arms.

9

"A Storm, Vast and Terrible"

IN JUNE 1862, AS THE UNION ARMY CREPT UP THE VIR-
ginia Peninsula toward Richmond, a rabbi in Chicago mulled a
difficult question. A few years earlier, Bernhard Felsenthal had gotten in trouble with the board of his synagogue in southern Indiana for endorsing John C. Fremont's antislavery campaign for the
presidency. He then declined to apply for a rabbinical post in Mobile
because accepting it would have required staying silent about human
bondage. Now at the helm of a Reform congregation in Chicago,
Felsenthal felt free to speak his mind on the issue tearing the country apart, and the American Jewish community along with it.

Felsenthal's article, "Die Juden und die Sclaverei"—*The Jews and
Slavery*—ran in the *Illinois Staatszeitung*, a popular journal among
German-speaking Republicans, both Jews and gentiles, who, still
fired up with the fervor of revolutionary ideals from 1848, tended
to be pro-Union and antislavery. Yet, as Felsenthal observed with
chagrin and bafflement, Southern Jews were overwhelmingly supportive of both slavery and the Confederacy. "How is it possible,"
the rabbi mused, "that members of a tribe, which for millennia
has been oppressed, persecuted, and enslaved . . . are defenders of

the most shameful institution on earth, slavery, and enemies of the struggle for freedom?"

Felsenthal was mystified, as generations of American Jews have been ever since, that a community haunted by its own history and still oppressed in Europe would support the perpetuation and extension of bondage in a land supposedly devoted to liberty and equality. It was astonishing, he wrote, that "people, who, each morning and each night thank God for freeing their fathers from Egypt's enslavement; whose brothers and relatives . . . in the Old World, today still have to petition and agitate for their own emancipation, here reveal themselves as fanatic apologists for Negro slavery!"

It still surprises many to learn that Jews living in the Confederacy embraced breaking up the Union at least as fervently as their brethren in the North supported its preservation. By 1861, Jews could be found in every prominent Southern city and most of the larger towns, even in remote backwoods outposts. Many were shiftless salesmen wandering from farm to farm, town to town, peddling their wares. Others had graduated to shopkeeping. A rare few were teachers, lawyers, and doctors; some were planters. Native-born Jews and new arrivals alike felt grateful to the states and the section that had accepted them, even more than in the North, as fully credentialed members of society; that is, as white.

Southern Jews did not support the Confederacy or join its armies solely because they wished to curry favor with their neighbors. They were part of the South. They shared the principles, practices, and prejudices of other whites. Right up to 1865, Southern Jews used their claimed property as cooks and maids, as assistants in their businesses, and as fieldhands. Some even hauled their slaves with them to the front lines.

The rate of slave ownership among Jews in the South had dropped by more than half between 1850 and 1860, from 38 percent of Jewish adults owning slaves to 17 percent, partly because less wealthy immigrants who had a harder time raising the capital to purchase human beings came to make up a larger percentage of the region's Jewish population. But whether they owned slaves or not, most Southern Jews, like other whites, felt invested in the slave system and terrified of the consequences of abolition. The vast majority of Jews in the South supported the Confederacy, sincerely and wholeheartedly. There is little evidence to suggest they were engaged in an elaborate performance intended to convince others of a commitment to slavery they did not in fact possess. There is instead plenty of evidence showing Jews, even in private, embracing the Confederate cause—both the perpetuation of slavery and the secession seen as necessary to secure it—with as much passion and pride as other Southerners. Some even felt that as historically marginalized immigrants in the Old World they had more at stake than most in ensuring that another class of people filled that role, instead of them, in the New. In a letter to his family, one Jewish soldier from Mississippi said he sympathized not with the enslaved but with "the poor victims of abolition despotism."

While some Jews in the North saw the struggle against slavery as an outgrowth of their attempts to overthrow European absolutism in the 1848 revolutions, immigrants who had settled in the South compared the Lincoln administration to the tyrannical regimes they had escaped. What was Lincoln's attempt to beat the slave states into submission but an American version of Emperor Franz Josef's vicious suppression of the campaign for Hungarian independence? In Savannah, Jewish immigrants joined with other German speakers at a meeting in May 1861 to proclaim their allegiance to the Confederacy. Just as Jews and Christians together had manned the barricades in Europe to beat back the hired soldiers of despotic governments, the immigrants vowed they were again "ready with heart and hand to defend the home of their choice": the Confederacy.

If some Southern Jews may have had qualms about the peculiar institution or doubted the prudence of secession, most saw their aspirations as linked with the war for Southern independence and the establishment of a new nation dedicated to preserving the rights and privileges of whites, a favored class among which they were pleased to find themselves, for once, included. Jacob Weil, a cotton merchant in Montgomery, Alabama, had bought slaves to help establish his cotton-dealing business in his new hometown, then freed them as soon as he could, believing, as he wrote his brother in Germany, that "one man never has the right to own another man." But he also did not think the North had the right to take away property that had been legally purchased. Writing in the war-mad weeks after Fort Sumter, Weil rejected both extremes, the fire-eating Southern secessionists and the antislavery Yankee meddlers. "In this dispute for a man of reason is no place left," Weil sighed. "Of two evils, I choose the one more familiar."

Victory for the South might augur good things for the Jews, perhaps even a new golden age. Defeat promised only more of what a long-suffering people needed least: immiseration and subjugation. Like many Jews in the slave states, Jacob Weil felt grateful to the South and figured he owed something to it in return, maybe even his life. That was why he enlisted in the Confederate Army, he told his brother: "This land has been good to all of us."

Southern Jews could be found everywhere in the Confederacy, from the moment of its birth. Institute Hall in Charleston, where South Carolina's secession from the Union was declared in December 1860, had been built by a Jewish contractor, David Lopez, the owner of some fourteen slaves who helped with his construction work. A long-standing member of Congregation Beth Elohim, Lopez had also built its neoclassical sanctuary, in 1840, complete with the controversial organ. Great-nephew of the eighteenth-century Newport slave trader Aaron Lopez, David Lopez would go on to

August Bondi photographed in his hometown of Salina, Kansas, between 1884 and 1889, shortly after he began writing his memoirs. (Kansas Historical Society)

An engraving of Ernestine Rose from a daguerreotype by William Wellstood. (Massachusetts Historical Society)

Judah P. Benjamin, photographed by Mathew Brady in Washington, DC. (Library of Congress)

The ruins of Judah Benjamin's Bellechasse plantation house, beside the Mississippi River near New Orleans, photographed in 1926 by Robert Tebbs. (Louisiana State Museum)

The younger Isaac Mayer Wise. (Jacob Rader Marcus Center of the American Jewish Archives)

A lithograph of Morris Jacob Raphall as he appeared in 1850, the year of his move from England to America. (Library of Congress)

A black-and-white print of a drawing of Rabbi David Einhorn (artist and date unknown).
(Jewish Museum of Maryland)

The original interior of Charleston's Congregation Beth Elohim, constructed in 1793–94 and destroyed by fire in 1838. Lithograph by Solomon Carvalho.
(College of Charleston)

Mayer Lehman, the brains of the early Lehman Brothers operation. (Columbia University Rare Book & Manuscript Library)

The Peddler's Wagon, by C. G. Bush, appeared in *Harper's Weekly* in 1868. (Library of Congress)

Marx Lazarus, the antislavery anarchist and free-love advocate who fought for the Confederacy, lived out his final days as a mountaintop hermit in Alabama. (Labadie Collection, University of Michigan)

This first picture of Abraham Lincoln with his newly grown beard was taken by Samuel G. Altschuler, a Jewish photographer in Chicago, just after the 1860 election. (Library of Congress)

This depiction of the silk flag given by Abraham Kohn to Lincoln in 1861, inscribed with passages from the Book of Joshua, appeared in *History of the Jews of Chicago* (1924), edited by Hyman L. Meites. (Chicago History Museum)

RIGHT: The sermon by Rabbi Morris Jacob Raphall that ignited the debate over slavery and Judaism in early 1861. (Library of Congress)

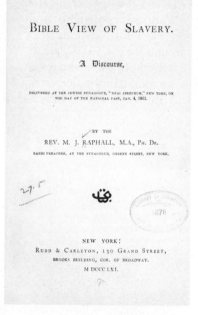

BIBLE VIEW OF SLAVERY.

A Discourse,

DELIVERED AT THE JEWISH SYNAGOGUE, "BNAI JESHURUN," NEW YORK, ON
THE DAY OF THE NATIONAL FAST, JAN. 4, 1861.

BY THE

REV. M. J. RAPHALL, M.A., PH. DR.

RABBI PREACHER, AT THE SYNAGOGUE, GREENE STREET, NEW YORK.

NEW YORK:
RUDD & CARLETON, 130 GRAND STREET,
BROOKS BUILDING, COR. OF BROADWAY.
M DCCC LXI.

The building of Congregation Har Sinai in Baltimore, where David Einhorn served as rabbi from 1855 to 1861. (Jewish Museum of Maryland)

The Soldier's Dream of Home, a lithograph by Louis N. and Max Rosenthal, two Jewish brothers from Poland who moved to America in 1850. (Harry T. Peters "America on Stone" Lithography Collection, National Museum of American History)

The only piece of American currency that has ever featured the image of a Jewish person: Judah Benjamin, a member of the Confederate cabinet. (National Numismatic Collection, National Museum of American History)

LEFT: The Moorish-style Plum Street Temple of Rabbi Isaac Mayer Wise's Congregation Beth Elohim in Cincinnati. Built in 1866, it still operates as a house of worship. (College of Charleston)

RIGHT: The elder Isaac Mayer Wise, painted by Morris Goldstein. (National Portrait Gallery, Smithsonian Institution)

BELOW: A cartoon in *Puck* magazine ridiculing the anti-semitic policies of the Saratoga Springs hotelier who excluded the Jewish financier Joseph Seligman. (Library of Congress)

build fortifications and large-gun carriages for the Confederate Army. As South Carolina's superintendent of state works, he oversaw the construction of a vast armory churning out carbine rifles, bayonets, cannon parts, and bullets by the thousands.

Within days of South Carolina's secession, Benjamin Mordecai, a prominent Charleston merchant and slave trader, donated $10,000 to the newly independent Palmetto Republic, and offered the labor of his enslaved servants for whatever purpose the government saw fit. The secession convention thanked him for his "liberality and patriotism." Mordecai later organized a "Free Market" that helped support six hundred families in Charleston. He invested his life savings in Confederate bonds, and lost everything.

Jews served as delegates at the state conventions that declared independence from the United States and as traveling commissioners sent by slave states that had already seceded to convince those that had not to take the fateful leap. When the fighting began at Fort Sumter, a Jewish lieutenant manned the batteries that fired at the island garrison. The Jewish chief of the Charleston fire department helped douse the smoldering fort, and a steamship owned by Benjamin Mordecai transported the defeated Union troops to the federal fleet floating offshore. Later that year, a Jewish Charlestonian named Charles Moise convinced the designer of the Confederate battle flag to replace the original's top-down St. George's Cross with a diagonal St. Andrew's Cross, a less obviously sectarian symbol. (The scholar Anton Hieke notes the irony that the Confederate battle flag is thus "a symbol of both racism and tolerance.") When the Union and Confederate armies met in battle for the first time in July 1861, the routed federals, adopting the water-based naming practice they would prefer throughout the war, called the action "Bull Run," after the languid muddy stream that initially separated the two sides. The Confederates, by contrast, used the names of nearby towns or settlements, in this case one that originated with an eighteenth-century Jewish innkeeper whose tavern was a favored resting place for travelers venturing through a pass in the Appalachian foothills, Manasseh's Gap: *Manassas.*

Some two to three thousand Jews served in the Confederate forces, as privates and officers, cooks and foragers, sharpshooters and scouts, prison guards and sentinels. As in the North, Jewish soldiers in the Confederacy found themselves scattered across units dominated by gentiles. A few companies boasted unusual clusters of Jews; in the Richmond Grays, a light infantry unit, they represented fifteen of the ninety-nine members, while disproportionately Jewish units were raised by communities in Macon and West Point, Georgia. Whether grouped with fellow Jews or all on their own, Southern Jewish soldiers fought in every major engagement. They were wounded, they deserted, they were captured, and they died. The thick accent so noticeable when a new immigrant spoke would have been imperceptible when they screeched, along with thousands of fellow soldiers, their piercing rebel yells.

Some who were religiously observant tried their best to adhere to the traditional rituals and restrictions. An Arkansas private who fought under Nathan Bedford Forrest (later first Grand Wizard of the Ku Klux Klan) carried with him two separate mess kits, one for meat and the other for dairy. Most gave up any pretense of piety for the duration of their service.

While August Bondi, like many Northern Jewish soldiers, believed he had an obligation to fight for the Union because he was a Jew, others joined the Confederate forces for the same reason. Philip Whitlock, a member of the Richmond Grays, reflected after the war that if he had neglected to serve "it would unfavorably reflect on the whole Jewish race and religion." Isaac Hermann, a French-born Jewish immigrant in Georgia, enlisted along with a number of his friends. He had arrived only a few years earlier, but Hermann was convinced by Southern arguments for independence. "I found in this country an ideal and harmonious people," he would write in a memoir; "they treated me as one of their own." Hermann's country, as for Whitlock, was not the United States but the South as he saw it, "the land of Canaan where milk and honey flowed."

Like their compatriots, Jewish Confederates set off for the war full of high hopes. Isaac Hermann recalled how his neighbors gathered to bid the men "Godspeed and a safe return." Hermann would always relish the memory: "It was a lovely day and patriotism ran high."

Fighting was not the only way Jews could serve the Confederacy. David Camden De Leon served as Confederate surgeon general, while his brother Edwin was sent to Europe to seek recognition of Southern independence. Those with commercial experience made ideal commissaries and quartermasters, positions responsible for gathering up necessary supplies and ensuring they made it where they were most needed. Given the South's weak economic base and the ever-tightening Northern blockade, these jobs proved difficult. The officers in charge of handling and transporting provisions often took the brunt of criticism when soldiers had to go without shoes, blankets, food, or horses. Southern troops eventually resorted to stripping garments and boots from the bodies of dead Union men.

When Louisiana seceded in January 1861, Col. Abraham Charles Myers, a West Point graduate and descendant of the first president of Charleston's Beth Elohim, handed control of the federal arsenal in New Orleans to Confederate authorities and resigned his hard-earned US Army commission. But he would be amply rewarded: Myers became quartermaster-general of the entire Confederacy. He eventually won control of all the Confederacy's railroads, until Jefferson Davis fired him in 1864 after Myers reportedly referred to Davis' dark-complexioned wife, Varina, as a "squaw."

Another prominent supply officer, Raphael J. Moses, was the

owner of a vast hilltop plantation in Columbus, Georgia, and forty-seven enslaved workers to reap the bounty of the land. Born and raised in Charleston, Moses had grown up with slavery; his mother once sent him to collect $500 from the sale of a young girl. After starting out as a peddler, Moses worked his way up from railroad clerk and small-time merchant to become a top commercial lawyer in the South and a successful planter as well. Known fondly as the "peach man," Moses was the first farmer in Georgia to success-fully market the fruit out-of-state (a feat made possible by packing them in baskets originally intended for champagne, which left the fruit in better shape than the crushed charcoal that others had used before him). An outspoken secessionist long before most Southern-ers embraced independence—John C. Calhoun once congratulated him in a letter for his fierce defense of Southern rights—Moses had immediately volunteered to help the Confederate forces however he could. He served as chief commissary on the staff of Gen. James Longstreet, tasked with securing supplies for one of the Confed-eracy's most important divisions. As the troops marched through Tennessee, Virginia, and Georgia, Moses embarked on wide-ranging foraging expeditions, buying up (or just taking) whatever quantities he could find of cattle, bacon, and flour. All three of Moses's sons also served in the armies. One was shot in the head at Seven Pines, outside Richmond, in the spring of 1862, the first Southern Jew to lose his life in battle. Yet Moses never doubted the righteousness of the cause. Even in 1893, when he died at the age of eighty-one, the grizzled old rebel was still handing out calling cards identifying himself as "Major Raphael J. Moses, C.S.A."

On the home front, Southern Jewish women did what they could to show support for the war effort. In New Orleans, sixteen-year-old Clara Solomon, whose father was away supplying the Southern armies, lamented every Confederate setback and mourned every Union advance. One day her sister brought home a tiny Con-federate flag. The girls cherished it and displayed it prominently in their home. "It is but a *very* miniature one, and yet I love it," Clara wrote. "I placed it there with my own hands, and in the invasion of the city, dare any Federalist lay his polluted hand upon it . . . Yes, with my own hands, will I slay him. There it floats, yielding gracefully to every breath of air. 'Forever may it wave over the land of the free and the home of the brave.'"

Jews as well as non-Jews often had close family ties across enemy lines, and many faced wrenching choices about which side, if either, they should support. When the secession crisis broke out, Alfred Mordecai, a North Carolina native and an accomplished weapons engineer who held the rank of major, was in charge of the federal arsenal at Watervliet, New York, just north of Albany. Thousands of Southern-born soldiers and officers resigned from the army to fight for the South, but Mordecai had married a Philadelphia woman and raised his children in the North. He could not imagine helping one side or the other make the bullets that might kill his kin. Mordecai's son and namesake—like him, a West Point graduate—ended up in the Union Army, while four of his nephews would fight for the South.

With forty years of army service behind him, Mordecai agonized over his decision through the winter and spring of 1861. Family members from the South begged him to aid the rebellion, while Confederate officials offered him plum jobs in the army. "All eyes of the South are turned towards you," Alfred's sister Ellen wrote from Richmond. His older brother George, the owner of one hundred human beings, argued that every Southerner had an obligation "to take a firm decided stand" against Lincoln's "absurd and violent measures."

Alfred spurned every admonishment and declined every offer. He tried to explain himself to his family, noting that even as a boy he had considered slavery "the greatest misfortune and curse that could have befallen us." He had once purchased a woman— Eugenia Hemings, Sally Hemings's niece, once owned by Thomas Jefferson—only to set her free a few years later.

He was sure the South would be better off without the institution. But he also believed that Southern masters had to give up their property willingly. They could not be forced. Mordecai opposed disunion, he wrote, for a nation split "into incoherent fragments [would] become the inveterate foes of each other, and the scorn and contempt of the rest of the world." But if the Southern states wanted to leave the Union, they should be allowed to go in peace. He would not fight to stop them.

Even after the firing on Fort Sumter, Mordecai held on at the New York arsenal as long as he could, though under suspicion of his loyalties. When he could postpone his decision no longer, he resigned his post, but refused to join the Confederacy. He moved his family to Philadelphia and sat out the war. To his Southern relatives, Alfred was a traitor. In an anguished letter, Mordecai's eighty-five-year-old mother told him that he had never before disappointed her, "until now."

Other Jewish parents guilted their sons for betraying them not by avoiding service but by enlisting. Philip Kohn of South Carolina, an immigrant from Bavaria, begged his twenty-year-old Theodore not to enlist, blaming "eager demagogues, parsons, hussies and wenches" for misleading the impressionable boy. "I got him away from the old world, from the old 'rust' fatherland," Philip wrote, "so that he has not to serve as a soldier-slave for an unjust cause. For what?" Theodore signed up anyway. He had already become a Southerner.

The Friedenwalds of Baltimore were similarly split. One brother, Joseph, was among those in the city arrested for attacking Union soldiers at the outbreak of the war. Another brother, Aaron, though critical of "debauched, black Republicanism," considered the Union "a holy institution . . . against which no hand can be directed but in sacrilege." When a third brother, Isaac, joined the Confederate Army, Aaron wished him "nothing else but a small shot in . . . you know where."

Septima Levy Collis of Charleston, a Jewish woman who had married an Irish-born Philadelphian just before the war and accompanied him into the field, later wrote, "I never fully realized the fratricidal character of the conflict until I lost my idolized brother Dave of the Southern army one day, and was nursing my Northern husband back to life the next." Asked near the close of the war by a one-legged Confederate general why she supported the Union, Collis replied that she had "only followed the example of many other Southerners—I had gone with my state, mine being the state of matrimony."

Julius and Bertha Ochs, both German immigrants, had met in Natchez, Mississippi, lived for a few years in Tennessee, then settled in Cincinnati. Julius sided with the Union. He abhorred slavery, having once seen "a poor wretch so horribly beaten that tears of pity gushed from my eyes." His wife, Bertha, who as a young student at the University of Heidelberg had supported the 1848 uprisings, opted for the Confederacy and reportedly smuggled quinine, used to treat malaria, across the Ohio River to help Southern troops. When a warrant went out for her arrest, Julius used his political connections to have it quashed. Years later, when Bertha died, the Confederate flag was draped over her casket, while her husband, for his own burial, arranged to have the Stars and Stripes prominently displayed. (In 1896, their son, Adolph Ochs, purchased the *New York Times*.)

Perhaps the most explosively divided Jewish household was that of former Alabama congressman Philip Phillips and his wife, Eugenia. Natives of Charleston, the pair had moved shortly after their marriage to Alabama, where Philip became a congressman. He helped write the Kansas-Nebraska Act but fell out of step with the increasing radicalism of his fellow Southerners and soon left poli-tics to practice law in Washington. He opposed Alabama's secession from the Union, warning it would lead to war.

Eugenia, a child of well-heeled Southern Jewish aristocrats, felt differently. A strong supporter of secession, she helped funnel aid to Southern prisoners and provided information to rebel authori-ties. Worse, even while living in Washington, she expressed her pro-Southern opinions, as her husband later wrote, "openly . . . and, considering the times, indiscreetly." One quiet morning in August 1861, as Eugenia hosted a friend, federal agents raided the Phillips house on I Street. Eugenia managed to have her maid smuggle out under her dress a clutch of incriminating letters. She and her daugh-ters were placed under house arrest in the home of an acquaintance also accused of espionage; "thrust into two dirty, small, attic rooms, evidently where negroes had lived, with no comforts of any kind." They lived closed off from the rest of the world. "Again I ask myself what is my crime?" Eugenia wrote in a diary. "If an ardent attach-ment to the land of my birth and expression of deepest sympathy with my relatives and friends in the South constitute treason—then I am indeed a traitor! If hostility towards Black Republicanism, its sentiments and policy—is a crime—I am self-condemned!"

After three weeks of confinement, Philip managed to secure Eu-genia's release, so long as the couple exiled themselves to the Con-federacy. Eugenia was eager to return to "a land where our hearts will beat with sympathy to all around us." As a summer storm raged on the Chesapeake, the family leapt, "yelling and screaming with de-light," from a Union boat to a small Confederate vessel that had come to meet them. They stopped in Richmond to share with the Confed-erate government everything they knew about Union strategy—and some papers Eugenia had "enveloped" around her body—then made their way to New Orleans, where they assumed, as Philip put it, they would "be freed from the complications of the war."

No such luck. Six months after their arrival, a fleet of Union war-ships steamed up the Mississippi. Chaos engulfed the city as people raced screaming out of their homes, desperate to escape. Bales of cotton, barrels of molasses and sugar, whole wharves and even ships were torched to keep them from falling into federal hands. Union troops threatened to burn the city unless the Stars and Stripes went up over city hall. The people wanted to fight but bowed to the mayor's pleas and surrendered. Yet the conquest was not entirely peaceful. A man who cried "Hurra for Lincoln" was torn to shreds on the street, while a boy who raised a Confederate flag on the levee was shot from a Union boat. "[A] gloom has settled o'er my spirit," the teenager Clara Solomon wrote in her diary, "a gloom envelopes our dearly-beloved city."

Infuriated by insults hurled at his soldiers, the presiding fed-eral officer, Gen. Benjamin Butler, ordered that any woman in New Orleans who disrespected Union troops should be treated as a prostitute. Eugenia ignored the order and was seen laughing at a funeral procession for a Union soldier. Butler condemned her as "a uncommon, bad and dangerous woman, stirring up strife and incit-ing to riot" and ordered her imprisoned on an island in the Gulf of Mexico, where she would be fed only thin rations of "beans and spoiled meat." Eugenia's imprisonment was not, as she wrote in a memoir, "the greatest outrage of the War," but neither was it easy. Though he blamed his wife's troubles on her own "imprudence," Philip went to the Lake Pontchartrain docks every night to look for ships steaming into the harbor, desperate for news from the island. Released three months later, Eugenia walked into her New Orleans home, shocking her family, who had not been informed of her re-lease. After embracing her children, she collapsed on the floor.

Undaunted by her stints in captivity, Eugenia supported the Southern cause to the bitter end, lamenting only that "Providence in his wisdom decided against us." Her husband disagreed. The end of slavery would bring new and better things for the South, Philip believed: "I regard it as the greatest blessing."

———————

Jews largely felt at home in the Confederate Army and faced little discrimination in its ranks. In 1864, Robert E. Lee promised to do everything he could to "facilitate the observance of the duties of their religion by the Israelites in the army." He even let Jewish soldiers leave the front to observe Jewish holidays. Unlike in the Union, Jews were allowed to serve as Confederate Army chaplains from the beginning of the war. None actually did, but not because, as initially in the North, it was against the law.

Southern rabbis supported the cause from the presumed safety of their synagogues. Responding to Buchanan's call for fasting and prayer in January 1861, George Jacobs, the Jamaican-born leader of Richmond's Ashkenazi congregation, Beth Ahabah, asked God to remind all Americans "how good and how beautiful it is for us to dwell together in unity." But if disunion came to pass it should be without "the horrors of civil warfare." Instead, "an equitable and peaceful separation" should be negotiated.

Across town, Rabbi Max Michelbacher, the long-serving leader of Richmond's Sephardic synagogue, Beth Shalome, compared Southerners to the Israelites who crossed the Red Sea in their flight from Egypt. If "union and peace may not be preserved, because of perpetual and opposing interests," Michelbacher prayed, "grant, Father of all, that a way may be opened whereby we, the people of the South, may pass with dry feet safely to the position of peace and plenty, attended with the protection which Thou gavest to thy chosen people of old."

A year later, Michelbacher published a special prayer for Jewish soldiers serving in the Confederate Army. The blessing asked God to frustrate the North's "wicked" attempts to "beguile . . . the man servants and maid servants Thou has given unto us" into running away or even killing their masters, and to ensure that Northern soldiers "fall into the pit of destruction." "Here I stand now," the rabbi urged Jewish Confederates to pray, "with many thousands of the sons of the sunny South, to face the foe, to drive him back, and to defend our natural rights. O Lord, God of Israel, be with me in the hot season of the contending strife; protect and bless me with health and courage to bear cheerfully the hardships of war."

As the war expanded and the Union armies marched through the South, even synagogues did not remain safe havens for long. Rabbi James K. Gutheim was the leader of a New Orleans synagogue when federal troops occupied the city in 1862. Born in Germany, Gutheim had arrived in America in the early 1840s and first served in Cincinnati before moving to New Orleans and adopting the local view of the coming struggle. "A storm, vast and terrible, is impending," Gutheim warned his congregation after Lincoln's election. Jews had a special interest in the triumph of the Southern cause, for after enduring centuries of "tribulation and misery," they had finally found a home where God's blessings "have been showered upon us."

Those blessings turned into a curse, however, when the Union Army arrived in New Orleans. Pressured, like all residents, to swear allegiance to the United States if they wanted to remain in the city, many Jews chose to flee. Rabbi Gutheim was among them, refusing to pay fealty to "the Dictator in Washington." After one final Sabbath sermon to a nervous and fearful congregation, the rabbi found his way to Montgomery, where he pledged undying loyalty to "our beloved country, the Confederate States of America." Gutheim denounced the Union's "lust for gain and dominion," and called on all Southerners to see that the "unrighteous invaders be repulsed on every side." Liking what they heard, the Montgomery congregation hired Gutheim full-time.

In Charleston, the old Jewish neighborhood long clustered near the tip of the peninsula, easily within range of federal batteries, suffered near daily bombardment and all but emptied out for the duration of the conflict. Beth Elohim, the beachhead of Reform Judaism in America, sent its Torah scrolls, chandelier, and organ to the state capital at Columbia for safekeeping. All were destroyed in the inferno that engulfed that city in early 1865. Shearith Israel, the Orthodox synagogue that had broken from Beth Elohim to protest the organ, had also sent what it could to Columbia. Its rabbi, Henry S. Jacobs, bemoaned the loss of nearly all his belongings, "clothing, furniture, books, manuscripts, provisions, even my canonicals and prayer shawls—everything except hope and confidence in our Heavenly Father." Jacobs picked through the burning rubble and found only one partly burnt Torah and a single bell that had graced the ornate finials atop the scroll. He brought them back to Charleston "as Sacred Relics." The two long-feuding congregations lost so much property and so many members in the war they had no choice but to merge back together after it was over. When Isaac Leeser visited Charleston in 1866, he found the Beth Elohim structure so severely damaged "as almost to render it useless as a place of worship." The ceiling had been punctured by bombshells and broken glass littered the floor.

———

Had Judah Benjamin's counsel been heeded from the beginning, the Confederacy may well have won the war. LeRoy Walker, Jefferson Davis's first secretary of war, later remembered that at the first meeting of the rebel cabinet, only the new attorney general came with any kind of practical plan for defending the slave states' independence against the coming federal onslaught. Benjamin proposed buying up as much Southern cotton as possible and shipping it to England before the North was able to impose a naval blockade. Some of the stockpile could be sold for guns and bullets while the rest would serve as security for loans. Others in the meeting thought it would be better to hold the cotton as a form of blackmail: European dependence on the crop would ensure recognition of their breakaway nation. They deemed Benjamin's proposal too hasty. There probably would not even be a war, and if there was it would be over quickly. Benjamin alone predicted that the rebels faced a long and protracted struggle. "All the rest of us fairly ridiculed the idea of a serious war," LeRoy Walker told a friend years later. "Well, you know what happened."

Benjamin has been called "the brains of the Confederacy," and with justice. At key moments, especially at the beginning and end of the conflict, he resisted being swept away by the strains of romantic slaveholding nationalism that warped the thinking and strategic capacities of others. He was too canny and too worldly—far better traveled than most of the South's provincial leaders—to fully buy into their wishful thinking. He had been warning for more than fifteen years that the struggle over the future of slavery in America would end up dividing the country in two. He had come to embrace secession as the only solution.

But Benjamin had never imagined the rupture could be accomplished peacefully. When he bid his final farewell to the Senate in early February 1861—five weeks after the dazzling New Year's Eve speech in which he refused, as a "free son of the soil," to be "converted" into a "vassal"—the decidedly unmartial Benjamin spoke with a pistol holstered at his side.

From Washington, Benjamin sailed home to New Orleans to spend time with his sisters, settle his business affairs, and plot his next moves. He did not have to wait long. He was soon summoned to Montgomery, the capital of the newly birthed Confederacy. One newspaper even mentioned him as a potential vice president of the new nation.

On George Washington's birthday, February 22, Benjamin spoke to some twenty thousand fellow New Orleanians gathered at the city's racetrack to honor a local artillery company. While other Southern politicians were reassuring the people that secession would be accomplished without conflict, Benjamin pointedly told the crowd that Southern independence could not be achieved "without the shedding of blood." Perhaps, unable to silence his own lingering doubts, he was subtly trying to sow some in the minds of others. Days later, Benjamin left for Montgomery. He would never see New Orleans or his sisters again.

Benjamin had not been close with the brooding Mississippi planter chosen as the Confederacy's first president. They had sometimes clashed and once nearly fought a duel. But Benjamin's hard-earned self-assurance and sense of gentlemanly propriety on that and other occasions had impressed Jefferson Davis. Keen to have in his cabinet one man from each of the rebel states, Benjamin seemed a natural choice to represent Louisiana. As he was known as an accomplished lawyer, Davis appointed him attorney-general. But it quickly became clear that his talents were being wasted. Diligent as ever, Benjamin set to work churning out legal opinions for the new government. His first concern was whether lemons, oranges, and walnuts would be subject to import duties. Lemons and oranges should be exempt, he decided, but walnuts would be taxed.

Within months, Davis recognized his mistake. When LeRoy Walker resigned, Davis appointed Benjamin to be secretary of war. This was, in effect, a promotion—and was warmly greeted in the Southern press—but somehow an even worse fit. Other than during his toddler years in the Caribbean during the Napoleonic Wars, the pudgy, effete Benjamin had never found himself within a few hundred miles of a battlefield. He knew nothing of tactics, strategy, armaments, and supplies. He had always been a quick study, but in taking such a crucial job in the months after Manassas—a chaotic but encouraging victory followed by a boneheaded failure to chase the enemy back to Washington—while the South readied itself for a stronger Union advance, Benjamin could hardly master all the intricacies of Confederate operations from New Mexico to Virginia, Kentucky to the Florida Keys.

His sole qualification, other than a famously tireless work ethic, was that his inexperience meant he would never challenge Davis's own authority on military affairs. A decorated hero of the Mexican War and secretary of war under Franklin Pierce, Davis needed an underling who could be trusted to enact his will. The ever-obsequious Benjamin, always struggling to fit in among the Southern squires, seemed to fit the bill. Davis could use his aide to issue orders that the prickly generals found distasteful, and let Benjamin take the blame.

Sure enough, Benjamin soon clashed with already legendary Confederates like Stonewall Jackson and P. G. T. Beauregard, conqueror of Fort Sumter, who complained to Davis about Benjamin's "unusual and offensive style" in his official correspondence, derided "that functionary at his desk," and asked the president to "shield me from these ill-timed, unaccountable annoyances." It had perhaps been a mistake for Benjamin, in congratulating Beauregard on his victory at Fort Sumter earlier that year, to self-deprecatingly admit he knew "nothing of war." The generals never respected their refined civilian overseer. Clueless in his management of military men, Benjamin alternated between his usual ingratiating tone and an overcompensating standoffishness. He seemed unaware of the real-world limitations of what he had gleaned solely from reading books.

Yet whenever the generals appealed to the president to intervene, Davis always backed Benjamin. He came to trust his judgment implicitly. According to Varina Davis, one of Benjamin's closest friends through the war, he and her husband spent ten to twelve hours each day together. In Richmond, where the Confederate capital was moved in May 1861 (another unwise decision Benjamin had opposed), their offices were just down the hall from one another on the second floor of the former US Customs House. Benjamin would work in his own quarters until about three o'clock in the afternoon—maps and battle plans tacked to the walls, the department's hired staff slave keeping up the fire—then go help Davis with whatever he needed. The pair worked "like galley slaves early and late," Varina recalled. The president was tense, high-strung, often ill; his neuralgia had grown so bad he lost vision in one eye. Benjamin, ever attentive, worked daily to ease the president's troubles. Benjamin possessed a "kind of electric sympathy with every mind with which he came into contact," Varina wrote. He recognized Davis's constant need for approbation and reassurance. He worked hard, and his efforts were recognized. "Mr. Benjamin is one of the most extraordinary men in America, and is almost indispensable to the Confederacy," the *Richmond Courier* observed. "No public man has a larger share of the confidence of the President." Throughout the war, Benjamin's bearded countenance stared out from the increasingly worthless Confederate $2 bill, the only time the face of a Jewish person has ever appeared on American currency.

He won that confidence, in part, by running interference for Davis, serving as scapegoat for nearly every Confederate setback: food shortages, losses on the battlefield, the imposition of martial law in blockade-starved Richmond. In early 1862, when the Union threatened Roanoke Island in North Carolina and the general in command asked repeatedly for reinforcements, Benjamin refused to send any, saying they were needed elsewhere. He withheld the real reason because it might have reached the enemy: he did not have any to send. When the invasion came, Southern troops were badly outnumbered, with some 2,500 taken prisoner and a hundred more killed or wounded. Many of those stationed at Roanoke were from Richmond, and the popular outcry against Benjamin, stoked by increasingly tense relations with the generals, became unignorable. Opponents of the Davis administration seized on the opportunity to bring the rebel chieftain down a peg. Henry S. Foote, a short, bald, zealous Confederate senator from Mississippi, denounced "Judas Iscariot Benjamin" as the "Jewish puppeteer" pulling the strings of the "Davis tyranny." Seeking to undermine the president's faith in his war minister, critics derided Benjamin as the "fat Jew sitting at his desk," in the words of a descendant of a popular young Richmonder killed at Roanoke Island, and they questioned his allegiance to the cause.

Benjamin took full responsibility for the Roanoke episode, but it was not enough. Davis decided to replace him as secretary of war. He would not get rid of Benjamin, however; Davis felt he could not afford to. Sensitive to what Varina called the "injustice" of the criticism Benjamin faced, Davis promoted him further, to secretary of state, a position for which, at last, the impeccably mannered, multilingual Benjamin, well-known in European financial and intellectual circles, was supremely well-qualified. As secretary of state, Benjamin became the most powerful figure in the Confederate cabinet, chief administrator of the government, even effectively serving as acting president when Davis was ill or out of town. Benjamin wrote most of Davis's speeches and consulted with him on every important decision.

His main objective in the new role was to win recognition of the Confederacy from France and Great Britain. That proved far more difficult than he or anyone else in the Confederate government had expected. They had believed Southern cotton would determine the outcome of the war. But keeping the ships running across the Atlantic would have required Britain and France to sever ties—and possibly start a war—with the United States. New sources of the valuable crop in European colonies such as India and Egypt offered a ready substitute for the diminished American supply. The best Benjamin could hope for was to keep Europe neutral and to secure essential loans for continuing the fight.

On that score Benjamin's European connections came in handy. He appealed to a Parisian banker, Emile Erlanger, who had risen from a clerk in the Rothschild firm to running his own bank. Like Benjamin, Erlanger was a disaffected Jew married to a Catholic (the daughter of Benjamin's former mentor in Louisiana politics, John Slidell, now Confederate envoy to France). Negotiated in French, Benjamin's agreement with Erlanger gave the Confederates access to much-needed funds, some three million francs, albeit at interest rates widely denounced in the South as usurious. But Benjamin hoped that the deal might lead to further European involvement in the war.

Through numerous personal difficulties—the expulsion from Yale, the casual insults he faced as a Jew in the antebellum South, the estrangement from his wife—Benjamin had learned to hide behind what the poet Stephen Vincent Benét would later call the "Perpetual smile he held before himself / Continually like a silk-ribbed fan." Now he managed to do so even on the darkest days of the war. Benjamin always seemed "fresh and buoyant," Varina Davis noted, while her husband was "a mere mass of throbbing nerves, and perfectly exhausted."

That endlessly renewable vigor seems all the more impressive given that Benjamin's personal life had once again been plunged into turmoil just before the war. In 1859, he convinced his long-estranged wife, Natalie, to return from her nearly fifteen years of living in Paris to join him in Washington. With his two terms in the Senate and his successful career as a Supreme Court lawyer, he had finally achieved the wealth and success he had sought. To make the marriage work—if only for the sake of appearances—he rented one of the most fabulous homes in Washington, just across Lafayette Square from the White House, and filled it with expensive paintings, sculptures, sofas, and chandeliers. Natalie shipped items she purchased from the estate of King Louis Philippe, the French monarch deposed in the revolution of 1848.

The experiment ended disastrously. Natalie barely spoke English. She knew nothing of the capital's byzantine code of rituals and mo-res. When the leading ladies of the city, after debating among them-selves whether it would be proper to call upon a woman so tarnished by rumors of infidelity and ill-behavior, condescended to stop by and leave their cards, Natalie never bothered to return the favor. She may have resented being seen as just another of Benjamin's expensive adornments. Her return to America lasted only two months before she took off, allegedly following an affair with a German officer. Benjamin, once again, was humiliated. He gave up the house and put everything up for auction; "everyone in Washington . . . thronged to see the beautiful things," as one senator's wife put it. The wife of Benjamin's friend David Yulee of Florida, the only other Jewish-born senator, bought up the bulk of the collection. Benjamin left town to avoid the indignity. A rare misstep, the fiasco may have been motivated by Benjamin's desperation to quash rumors unbecoming a gentleman, and, on account of his Jewishness, an already suspect one at that.

If so, his lifestyle in Confederate Richmond did the opposite. Benjamin's ebullience, his sophistication, his mellifluous voice, his unflickering bullishness about the cause (at least in public) made him an instant hit on the besieged capital's surprisingly lively social circuit. A famously witty and well-mannered conversationalist, he stood ever ready with long and vivid recitations of historical anecdotes or ancient and modern verse. A canny observer of people and events, he was a prized ornament at what, amid the deprivations of war, passed for Confederate soirees and salons. In a tense city short on basic foodstuffs, swarming with sick and wounded soldiers, Benjamin insisted on finding ways to enjoy himself. The *Richmond Examiner*, reporting a crackdown on a gambling den in the capital, noted that "a cabinet minister, who was in one of the inner chambers reserved for distinguished guests, effected his escape by jumping from a window," a likely reference to Benjamin.

There were other rumors as well. There always had been. During the war, Benjamin would sometimes beg forgiveness for having to leave one gathering or another on account of the "dear little fellow, who will be lonesome if I do not go home." Varina Davis remembered her shock on learning that the "dear little fellow" was not, as she had imagined, "a very charming boy of twelve or fifteen years old," but a full-grown thirty-year-old man. For years, Benjamin had had an unusually close relationship with Jules St. Martin, his wife's younger brother, born after her marriage to Judah and raised for a time almost as if he were their own. In Richmond, Jules and Judah lived in a rented house, where the two hosted friends in what Varina called "as elegant a manner as blockaded *bon vivants* could do." Benjamin even managed to land a job for Jules as clerk in the War Department so he would not have to go off to war. Once, during a dinner at the Davises', Benjamin stopped himself in the middle of a disquisition on the recently published *Les Miserables* to explain that he was not enjoying his dinner, "for Jules would like these dishes so much." He stood up, wrapped some choice items in a napkin, and slipped out the door, as Varina recalled, "beaming with the hope of conferring pleasure upon his beloved Jules."

Such rumors had swirled around Benjamin for years, but now he had more enemies than ever. In a letter to his wife, Howell Cobb, a prominent Georgia politician and a rival to Jefferson Davis, derided Benjamin as "an eunuch," then added: "The poor fool to try and hide it, married . . . This is the 'on-dit' [gossip] of the city." The diarist Mary Chesnut, an admirer of Benjamin's and the wife of a Davis-aligned Confederate politician, wrote that a visiting colonel once referred to Jules St. Martin as a "sinner." Chesnut asked, "Why 'sinner'?" The colonel insinuatingly replied, "Ain't he Benjamin's brother-in-law? &c&c&c."

Yet Benjamin's critics more often took aim at the other trait that set him apart from his fellow Southerners. Benjamin had struggled his whole adult life against any association with Jews and Judaism. He wanted to be seen as a lawyer, a planter, a senator, and finally as a founder of the new Confederate nation, the genius of the operation if not its titular leader. Now at the peak of his accomplishments, Benjamin's all-but-forsworn Jewishness came back to haunt and define him. Thomas Cobb, a leading Georgia politician (Howell Cobb's cousin), commented in a letter in early 1862, "A grander rascal than this Jew Benjamin does not exist in the Confederacy." What one thought of Jefferson Davis tended to dictate what one thought of Benjamin. Those who opposed the president saw his chief adviser as a malevolent traitor. "The mob calls him 'Mr. Davis's pet Jew,'" Mary Chesnut wrote in her diary, "cheap, very cheap, &c&c." A letter in the *Richmond Enquirer* called it "blasphemous" for a Jew to hold such a high position in the Confederacy and suggested Benjamin was personally responsible for God's refusal to answer the prayers of the beleaguered nation.

At some point, Benjamin began concocting a plan, if and when the rebellion failed, to separate his own fate from that of the others.

10

"You Are Jews"

EDWARD ROSEWATER FASTED TWICE IN 1861, FIRST IN January, on the day President Buchanan set aside for reflection and prayer, and again, as was the Bavarian immigrant's custom, on Yom Kippur, as the armies dug in for what all Americans by then realized might not be such a short war after all. The day the war began, Rosewater had mused in his diary about the uncertainties of the coming months: "oh what may this Book of my fate be destined to contain!" He had reason to worry: Rosewater was an antislavery Jew caught behind enemy lines.

When the South broke away, the twenty-year-old had been working as a telegraph operator in Alabama. He was soon transferred to Nashville. When federal troops occupied the city in early 1862, Rosewater pledged his loyalty to the Union and volunteered for difficult and dangerous work, stretching telegraph wires across rugged mountains and untamed rivers, sometimes in enemy territory. By that fall, Rosewater was in Washington, working in the War Department's telegraph office, next door to the White House. In boastful letters home to the Cleveland girl he was courting, Rosewater reported that "Old Abe," keen for war news, would drop by at eight o'clock nearly every morning, wearing white satin slippers, concealing grave concern with his usual irrepressible humor. Rosewater wrote that Lincoln, with whom he once shared a lunch of beer and crackers, howled so loudly at his own frontier-flavored yarns that his cackles could be heard a half-mile away.

A story has been told—including in a 1957 television special produced by the American Jewish Committee and aired on CBS before Passover—that on the first day of January 1863, Edward Rosewater was sitting at his desk in the telegraph office when the president walked over and handed him a paper requiring immediate transmission over the wires. It was the Emancipation Proclamation. With Lincoln looking over his shoulder, Rosewater, a Jewish immigrant from Bavaria, tapped out the dots and dashes that officially informed the world that all slaves belonging to Southern rebels would be "thenceforward, and forever free."

Alas, that did not happen. As with August Bondi responding to that same Proclamation with the line "No more pharaohs and no more slaves," the story turns out to be a wholesale invention. Rosewater did see Lincoln that New Year's Day, not at the war office but at the White House, when hordes of civilians were allowed in to pay their respects. "The crowd was large," Rosewater wrote in his diary, in the terse style of a telegraph operator, "& Old Ladies young ladies babies children Soldiers & Civillans were all mixed & jammed kept off by squad of Soldiers with Bayonets . . . The Pres[iden]t looked rather cheerfull . . . [he] remarked to me. How do you do sir."

Only later that night did Rosewater venture over to the office to see what was doing. The Proclamation had already been published; he read it in a Washington newspaper. "Certainly a new era for liberty," Rosewater reflected, "but what will be changed?"

More useful than these facts, however, has been the legend, which perfectly encapsulates how American Jews would prefer to remember their role in the nation's history. The story of Lincoln handing the world-changing document to Rosewater served as another illustration, along with the old yarn about Haym Solomon "financing" the American Revolution and George Washington's letter to the Newport Jews, of a historically outcast people not only finding a home in the United States but participating in its march of continual progress, the fulfillment, in due time, of the great promises of its founding.

In reality, the Emancipation Proclamation could not have come at a more uncomfortable moment for American Jews, just as their claim to equal rights as United States citizens had come under threat as never before.

———

The Civil War brought an unprecedented explosion of antisemitism on both sides of the conflict. As many had feared, the hostility long targeted against the Irish was now turned, amid the carnage and uncertainties of war, against the Jews. Northerners and Southerners alike blamed Jews for their respective woes. Newspapers published cartoons depicting villainous Hebrews trading with the enemy and undermining the war effort. The "pork-hating descendants of Abraham" refused to fight, the *New York Times* said, and instead focused on profiteering off those who did.

In the North, much of the wartime bigotry was directed at prominent Jewish bankers and businessmen. After Fort Sumter, the *New York World* speculated that an "unrevealed southern Rothschild" might be behind the mischief, while a Republican speaker at a rally in Philadelphia denounced August Belmont, the Democratic Party chairman, as "the Jew banker of New York." As the 1864 elections drew near and George B. McClellan, the general twice fired by Lincoln, stood a decent chance of winning the presidency, the *Chicago Tribune* asked, "Will we have a dishonorable peace in order to enrich Belmont, the Rothschilds, and the whole tribe of Jews?" During the New York City draft riots of July 1863, a horrific three-day rampage mostly directed at Black people, a few Jewish businesses and homes were also targeted. Abram Dittenhoefer, the antislavery lawyer who had sat on the stage behind Lincoln at Cooper Union in 1860, watched as a crowd gathered in front of his Thirty-Fourth Street townhouse chanting, "Down with the abolitionists! Death to Dittenhoefer!" The police arrived just as the mob was about to break down his front door.

On the Senate floor, Henry Wilson of Massachusetts, a leading antislavery Republican, took aim at "curbstone Jew brokers . . . who fatten upon public calamity." A columnist in *Harper's* condemned Jews as having "no native, no political, no religious sympathy with this country. You are here solely to make money . . . [Yo]u are inevitably a Secessionist, a Copperhead, and a Rebel." A Detroit newspaper observed that "the tribe of gold speculators" was composed "exclusively of the people who look up to Abraham as their father." Such "hooked-nose wretches speculate on disasters and a battle lost to our army is chuckled over by them, as it puts money in their purse." One Jewish soldier was bullied so relentlessly by his fellow soldiers that he deserted and reenlisted in a different company.

Amid soaring inflation and corruption scandals, Jewish merchants and chance-seeking speculators offered ideal scapegoats for widespread suffering and deprivation. Soldiers shivering through winter in ragged clothing and ramshackle tents blamed Jewish contractors for outfitting them with unusable weapons, moldy biscuits, rancid beef, and "shoddy" coats and blankets. A term for scraps of wool swept off the factory floor, "shoddy" became a new slur against Jews. A prominent New York humor magazine ran a serialized mock-epic poem centered on the character of "Mr. Shoddy," a treasonous, money-grubbing tailor. The poem accused Jews of "bleeding the country, but not bleeding for it!" Reporting on the capture of three Jews suspected of smuggling letters and medicine across Confederate lines, an Associated Press reporter in New Orleans called for all Jews in the South to be "exterminated."

For some ardent Christians, the war offered an opportunity to correct a glaring error dating back to the founding of the republic: the separation of church and state. A growing Protestant movement, organized as the National Reform Association, sought to amend the Constitution to acknowledge "the Lord Jesus Christ as the Ruler among the nations." Observing that a "Christian nation with an atheistical Constitution is an anomaly," the group argued that "*now* is the time to make this correction of fundamental error when God is baptizing the nation in blood, in order, as we trust, to purify it from destructive evils, so as to preserve our nationality and give us in the end peace and prosperity." Senators, governors, college presidents, judges, and other prominent citizens signed on to support the movement. American Jews had long feared a drive to formally make America a Christian nation, and they now saw the movement's rise as an ominous sign. The initiative could not be dismissed as isolated or fringe, Isaac Leeser warned in his monthly *Occident*. It was "indicative of a coming storm."

By the summer and fall of 1862, the Union's early victories in parts of the South along the Atlantic coast and in the Mississippi Valley raised a slew of thorny questions: Should slaves who fled to federal lines be returned to their masters? How should the conquered regions be governed? Would trade be permitted between the North and the newly reoccupied areas?

Lincoln's blockade of the Confederacy banned all commerce with the enemy, but administration policy held that once the Union Army took over an area, the blockade no longer applied. Trade should follow the flag. Southerners could freely sell their cotton. The president hoped that letting at least some cotton through the lines would help win allegiance from planters and keep cotton-hungry Europe from siding with the Confederacy. Ulysses S. Grant, whose vast military district encompassed northern Mississippi and western Kentucky and Tennessee, deplored the trade in cotton, which, by funneling gold to the South, helped the Confederates fund the cannonballs and bullets that were slaughtering his men by the thousands. The federal campaign was being undermined, he complained to his sister, by "speculators whose patriotism is measured by dollars & cents."

The general could not help but notice that many of these border-crossing traders were Jewish, and he was not alone. Marcus Spiegel, the Ohio officer who as the war progressed grew more sympathetic to the enslaved and supportive of abolition, noted in a letter to his wife while passing through Union-occupied Memphis that it was "a beautiful City, full at the present of trading Yehudim . . . the Cotton buying attracts many men here and often large fortunes are made in a short time." "The Israelites have come down upon the city like locusts," reported a *Chicago Times* journalist. Another scribe, writing after the war, recalled that "the long dining-hall of the principal hotel at Memphis, looked at meal-times like a Feast of the Passover." That was surely an exaggeration. Yet even the pro-Confederate Reform rabbi of Memphis, Simon Tuska, a scholarly Hungarian steeped in Greek and Latin literature, compared Jewish speculators in his city to "greedy birds of prey." He advised them to leave, lest "the Gentiles . . . become infuriated against thee."

To be sure, plenty of the cotton traders were not Jewish. Some who had themselves profited from corruption-fueled speculation saw it as useful to blame their Jewish competitors. Even Union Army officers were not immune to the cotton fever. "Every colonel, captain, or quartermaster is in secret partnership with some operator in cotton," wrote Charles Dana, Lincoln's assistant secretary of war, who had himself planned to ship cotton north before deciding not to partake in the frenzy. "Every soldier dreams of adding a bale of cotton to his monthly pay." Benjamin Butler, the Union general in command of New Orleans, asked the secretary of war to keep "the Jews from gathering up all the gold in the country to exchange it with the Confederates for cotton"; never mind that Butler had helped his own brother get rich off the trade.

Fed up with the speculators in his district, Grant told his officers to stop anyone from coming South with gold in their belongings. Jews "should receive special attention," Grant added. He soon banned Jews from traveling south by railroad: "They may go north and be encouraged in it; but they are such an intolerable nuisance that the department must be purged of them." Yet when a colonel in his department moved to do just that, ordering "All Cotton-Speculators, Jews and other Vagrants" to leave the vicinity of the Union supply depot at Holly Springs, Mississippi, or be "sent to duty in the trenches," Grant overturned the fiat as "manifestly unjust."

Nine days later, Grant changed his mind, provoked apparently by the arrival of his shiftless father, Jesse, along with Henry Mack, a Bavarian-born Jewish clothing manufacturer from Cincinnati, a congregant of Isaac Mayer Wise, who in the 1850s had recruited the Reform rabbi to move to the Midwestern city. In less than twenty years, Mack had risen from peddling knickknacks to supplying tens of thousands of uniforms for Ohio troops. But now he was running out of cotton. Mack and the elder Grant had struck an agreement to buy cotton from Southern plantations under Union control. Letters and passes from Jesse's son would smooth the operation. Jesse Grant would receive 25 percent of the profits.

But the son refused to go along. Grant put Mack on a train back to Ohio, then, on December 17, 1862, ordered all Jews, traders and residents alike, in his district to be deported immediately and arrested if they tried to return or appeal to him for exemption: "The Jews, as a class, violating every regulation of trade established by the Treasury Department, and also Department orders, are hereby expelled from the Department." So read Grant's General Order No. 11, which applied to a large swath of Mississippi as well as parts of Kentucky and Tennessee.

Grant's underlings got to work, clearing Jewish merchants and even regular inhabitants from northern Mississippi. Some, banned from using the railroads, had to walk the forty miles to Memphis. One man was arrested merely for trying to telegraph Grant. Thirty long-residing Jewish families in the Ohio River port town of Paducah, Kentucky, none of them speculators in cotton and with two Union Army veterans among them, were given twenty-four hours to leave their homes, then sent on a steamship to Cincinnati. Only a pair of sick women were allowed to stay. "You are Jews," a brigadier general explained to one couple, "and . . . neither a benefit to the Union or the Confederacy."

In all, around one hundred people were displaced by Grant's decree, a fraction of the district's Jewish population. It could have been worse; the order's execution was delayed by strained lines of communication as Confederate forces went on the attack. At least one of Grant's subordinates refused to implement what he believed to be an unjust and unconstitutional edict. Others may have intentionally slow-walked enforcement. A Jewish officer in the Union Army resigned his position in protest, explaining that he could "no longer bear the taunts and malice of those to whom my religious opinions are known, brought on by the effect that that order has instilled into their minds."

Wasting no time, Cesar Kaskel, a Jewish merchant in Paducah forcibly exiled by Grant's troops, traveled to Washington to lobby Lincoln to rescind the order. "So the children of Israel were driven from the happy land of Canaan?" Lincoln reportedly asked Kaskel. Just two weeks after Grant issued his order, Lincoln rescinded it. "I do not like to hear a class or nationality condemned on account of a few sinners," he explained to Jewish community leaders, including Isaac Mayer Wise, during a White House meeting.

Seldom mentioned in accounts of Lincoln's intervention, however, is that he knew of Grant's earlier order banning Jews from the railroads and did nothing to stop it.

The nation's representatives in Congress heard testimony from Paducah's Jewish refugees and considered censuring Grant over the episode, but ultimately they voted against it along party lines. Republicans sought to drop the issue as embarrassing to one of the most promising Union generals. A congressional ally of Grant—an Illinois representative who had himself likely benefited from a friend's participation in the cotton trade—considered the edict "the wisest order yet made by a military command, and . . . necessary."

For Jews, both those born in America and more recent arrivals who had embraced their new home, Grant's order and Congress's refusal to censure the general raised unpleasant questions. How far had they progressed from centuries of exclusion and banishment? To the well-connected Washington lawyer Simon Wolf—himself briefly arrested on suspicion of Confederate sympathies—the wartime outburst brought to mind the "darkest days of superstition and the Spanish Inquisition." The *Jewish Messenger*, which had nearly put itself out of business by adopting a staunchly pro-Union position, lamented that Grant's order had been overturned without "the slightest apology . . . the slightest reparation."

The paper was careful to warn Northern Jews not to let their anger be co-opted by Democratic opponents of the Lincoln administration and sympathizers with the Confederacy. "[S]hall we, the loyal Israelites of the United States, permit ourselves to be made tools of . . . by men who have no love for us, no love for the Union, no respect for constitutional government? . . . We *must* love the Union—we cannot avoid it."

Whichever side won, there was no guarantee that the new hostility toward Jews would end anytime soon. After decades of growing optimism, Isaac Leeser observed, the once-promising position of Jews in American life seemed only to be getting worse: "We are still in bondage."

It took several days for news of Grant's decree to filter out from war-wracked Mississippi. In much of the country, reports of both Order No. 11 and the Emancipation Proclamation, issued two weeks apart, were published nearly simultaneously. One Memphis paper printed the two texts on the same page. It was impossible, for some American Jews, not to notice the implicit contrast of Black Americans liberated from bondage at just the moment Jews felt targeted, thrown back into a history of oppression they thought they had escaped. Community leaders feared that the timing of Grant's order and Lincoln's proclamation was no coincidence, but signaled the arrival of a future long feared: the downgrading of American Jews as foreign and unwelcome, the replacement of racial slavery with religious persecution. Might the country only have room for one historically oppressed group, such that progress for one could only come at the expense of the other? Would Jews replace newly emancipated Black people as the lowliest class in a newly reunited nation?

If the struggle against Grant's expulsion order marked the birth of American Jewish politics, as has been claimed, it was a politics defined from the beginning by a sense of zero-sum competition between Black and Jewish Americans. "Are Israelites slaves?" one letter to Isaac Leeser's *Occident* asked. The writer had received news of the decree just before being asked to attend the funeral for a fallen Union soldier who had died alone in a Philadelphia hospital. As he helped carry the coffin, the writer could not help but wonder: Were Jewish soldiers dying "in a contest designed by those in authority to give freedom to the negro, only to bring expulsion from the Union territory to the descendants of the Hebrews? . . . Why are tears shed for the sufferings of the African in his bondage, by which his moral condition has been immensely improved . . . whereas for the Hebrews every one has words of contempt or acts of violence?"

"We know not how to speak in the same breath of the negro and the Israelite," the New York–based *Jewish Record* commented in a January 1863 editorial:

> There is no parallel between such races. Humanity from pole to pole would scour such a comparison. The Hebrew was *originally* free; and the charter of his liberty was inspired by his Creator. The Negro was never free; and his bondage in Africa was simply duplicated in a milder form when he was imported here . . . Alas, that the holy name and fame of the Prophet Moses should be desecrated by a comparison with the quixotic achievements of President Lincoln!

To compare the suffering of Black slaves to millennia of oppression and exclusion endured by the Jews would be to "insult the choice of God himself."

On learning of Grant's decree, Isaac Mayer Wise called on all American Jews to protest an "outrage, without a precedent in American history." This was no time for a policy of silence. He traveled to Washington to personally lobby the president to overturn it. Long skeptical of Lincoln's antislavery convictions and his fitness for office, Wise was impressed by his swift action to overturn the unjust edict. The president "knows of no distinction between Jew and Gentile," Wise told his readers, and "feels no prejudice against any nationality."

From his initial misgivings in 1861 about whether Lincoln, "with his primitive manner," was fit to serve as president, Wise's attitude toward Lincoln would continue to evolve to near-deification after the president's death. But even after the repeal of Grant's discriminatory order, Wise remained skeptical of the Union war effort, and especially suspicious of the Emancipation Proclamation. "If so many Negroes had been injured as were Hebrews by the order of General Grant," Wise told Northern abolitionists, "you would have cried as loudly as the people of Sodom and Gomorrah; but for the white Hebrew who gave you a God and a religion, you had not a word to say." More than a decade after joking with Virginia politician Henry Wise about their shared surname and how being white (*weiss*) was a "highly important necessity," Wise continued to insist that Jews were as white as their Christian neighbors and therefore deserved equal protection of the laws.

In 1863, antiwar Ohio Democrats fired up by opposition to the Emancipation Proclamation nominated Wise to run for state senate on the same ballot as Clement Vallandigham, an ex-congressman arrested the previous year for treason and exiled to the Confederacy, now orchestrating his campaign for governor from across the Canadian border. But Wise's congregation, already frustrated with their leader's intransigent opposition to the war, stepped in to block the rabbi's bid for public office. Wise had fallen out of step with the Cincinnati Jewish community. The bonanza of supply contracts that benefited Jewish merchants in Cincinnati—like Jesse Grant's business partner Henry Mack—had, as in New York, led to a swift turn toward supporting the Union. The synagogue's trustees, most of them Republicans, "politely, but most emphatically" instructed Wise to decline the nomination or resign from the position of rabbi.

Reluctantly, Wise bowed to the pressure and withdrew his name, lamenting, with typical immodesty, a lost opportunity to "render some services to my country, not altogether unessential." Throughout the war, Wise continued to describe Southerners as friends, denounce abolitionists, and plead for a "soft," forgiving peace. He sought without success to win the release of Jewish Confederate

soldiers confined in Northern prisons and as late as 1864 insisted
there was no ethical question at stake in the struggle over slavery,
nothing "absolutely unjust" in buying "savages" from Africa in order to "place them under the protection of law, and secure them the
benefit of civilized society." Echoing Morris J. Raphall's distinction
between slavery as practiced in ancient Israel and in the South, Wise
argued that if American slavery had respected the laws of Moses, it
would have "tended to the blessing of the Negro race." He chafed
against the polarized politics of the moment, which forced everyone
to choose between extremes: "Either one must believe the Negro
was created to be a beast of burden to others, or you must say he is
just as good as you are."

Wise would not say that. He lived another thirty-six years. He
never would.

———

For Wise's frequent antagonist David Einhorn, the rabbi who had
been run out of Baltimore in April 1861, equality between the races,
and indeed all people, was not a radical position to be rejected out
of hand. It was a fundamental principle of Judaism.

Exiled to Philadelphia, Einhorn remained unchastened by his
near-lynching and appalled by his former congregation's request
that he stay silent on the "excitable" issues of the day. In the first
issue of his monthly *Sinai* published after his flight, Einhorn wrote
that he had no patience for "these pious gentlemen," rabbis like
Wise and Leeser, "men of the pseudopeace," who argued for keeping politics out of the pulpit. Invoking the biblical prophets, who
recognized no artificial distinctions between politics and faith, Einhorn warned that Jews must never adopt "an attitude of indifference" on a question so relevant to their core tenets. "Can a religion
which contains regulations with regard to one's treatment of an
overloaded animal pass by, cold-bloodedly and unfeelingly, a human

being who has been mercilessly enslaved?" Anyone who thought, like Isaac Mayer Wise ("that swindler in Cincinnati"), that they could simply wait the war out merely demonstrated the "mendacity which has, unfortunately, seized upon the whole religious life." They were living proof of why Judaism had to be radically overhauled and renewed.

For Einhorn, the Civil War represented the signal moment proving the providential assignment to both Judaism and the United States. Just as the Jewish people had a divinely appointed mission, the Union likewise bore the God-given burden of spreading liberty and equality to every land on earth. The founding of the country represented "the most sublime moment in the evolution of recent world history," Einhorn said, promising "an international salvation." America would in time become "the most powerful lever" for bringing on "the kingdom of the Messiah." It only had to be permitted to continue, not merely for the Jews, who, after millennia of wandering the globe, had finally found a secure refuge, but for all mankind. "It would be petty selfishness to think only of the innumerable blessings which the Stars and Stripes have brought to our coreligionists," Einhorn said, "while it has become the shining banner of redemption for the enslaved of all nations."

The only blemish on that banner had been slavery itself, a "black spot" that had turned into a "threatening, storm-laded cloud." In fighting to preserve slavery, the rebels sought to replace "the principle of the innate equality of all beings created in the image of God" with a principle of "innate servitude," the idea that might makes right. "If this diabolical undertaking should succeed," Einhorn asked, "who would have more to fear than Israel, the very ancient slave of slaves? And should the religion of Israel . . . not have a word of indignation to say against such an outrage? Should it have no encouragement to utter on behalf of the highest possessions of mankind, and to struggle against the kingdom of lies and of malice?" Like the prophets of old, Einhorn at once trumpeted a

vision of national greatness and purpose and castigated his listeners
for failing to live up to their holy assignment. "Any Jew who lifts
his hand against the Union," Einhorn warned, "is as a Jew to be
considered equal to a parricide."

Einhorn spent the war years as rabbi at Philadelphia's Kenes-
eth Israel congregation, delivering sermons in his usual soaring and
scholarly German, especially on presidentially designated fast days
and national holidays like July Fourth and Thanksgiving. He continued to publish the *Sinai* until he could no longer afford to do so.
It ceased publication in 1863, seven years after he had started it. The
paper "dies in the battle against slavery," Einhorn wrote. Non-Jews
recognized the rabbi's brave advocacy of the antislavery cause and
the suffering he had endured in consequence. Philadelphia's Union
League Club elected him an honorary member and published one of
his sermons, from Thanksgiving 1863, as a fundraiser for the Sanitary Commission. A week after Lincoln delivered the Gettysburg
Address, Einhorn had closed with a prayer. "Bless Israel," Einhorn
implored, "imbue it with a spirit of devotion and thankfulness towards this land, the first that broke the chains its children wore for
centuries."

Four decades had passed since Ernestine Rose had left Poland to
avoid an arranged marriage set up by her father. She had since become an internationally known advocate for an uncompromising
brand of atheism, a self-proclaimed "Infidel" who rejected any form
of supernatural belief. Though she lived in a neighborhood swelling
with Jewish immigrants, Rose had never associated herself with the
Jewish community in New York. She showed little attachment to
the religion of her birth and never used her powerful, widely praised
oratory to defend the people who still adhered to it. Yet as the Civil

War raged, amid rising animosity toward Jews, Rose finally spoke up on their behalf, and, implicitly, her own.

Rose had felt isolated as the only reformer to denounce not only slavery and women's oppression but the systematic mental enslavement she deemed organized religion. During the war, that sense of loneliness was exacerbated. The conflict subsumed much of the energy and zeal that had formerly gone into the social reform movements in which she had long been a respected leader. While her fellow activists cheered that the North was finally taking a stand for human rights, Rose refused to relent.

When the war broke out, women's rights activists suspended their conventions and organizing activities for the sake of building support behind the Union. Many were still basking in the glow of the movement's greatest accomplishment yet: the passage in 1860 of a New York state law granting women the right to retain property accumulated during marriage (such as wages), not merely, as the 1848 law that Rose pushed had provided for, property held before marriage. Rose saw a lesson in the victory. "How has all this been achieved?" she asked one audience. "The answer is, by agitation . . . Agitate! agitate! ought to be the motto of every reformer." While her fellow activists were willing to let the issues raised by the war take precedence, Rose would not relax her labors even for a moment. "Agitation is the opposite of stagnation," she insisted, "the one is life, the other death."

Rose even fell out of step with the antislavery movement, the cause to which she had devoted most of her attention in recent years. With the goal he had long dreamt of in sight, the abolitionist leader William Lloyd Garrison grew less eager to attack the Lincoln administration, which, though it was not doing everything it could to end slavery, had done more than anyone in power ever had. The logic of civil war, Garrison believed, would make abolition necessary, if not as an act of justice then simply to bludgeon the rebels into submission.

Garrison changed the banner atop his *Liberator* newspaper from his longtime rallying cry, "No Union with Slaveholders," to a verse from the Book of Isaiah, "Let the Oppressed Go Free."

After the Emancipation Proclamation, Rose criticized Lincoln for only banning slavery in areas "in rebellion against the United States," and not the slave states that had remained loyal to the Union (Delaware, Maryland, Kentucky, and Missouri). The Proclamation was a "mockery," Rose contended, since it only freed "slaves we cannot reach." She rejected Lincoln's reasoning that freeing slaves under Union control was both unconstitutional and ill-advised, since it might lose the border states to the Confederacy. "If the President cannot move without pushing, push him on," Rose told one antislavery audience. "I stand here to push you on." But when she went on to question Lincoln's honesty, the typically friendly audience hissed and booed at Rose, who replied that being so treated was always how she could tell she was right.

To Rose, all the expense of the war, measured in dollars and lives, had to buy more than a reunited nation. Was the point of the bloodshed simply to patch up the nation as soon as possible, or to end slavery everywhere, once and for all? Long after Garrison had given up his call for breaking up the country to cleanse the North of complicity with slavery, Rose continued to espouse her prewar doctrine of disunion if the alternative meant binding the country back together with the peculiar institution, at least in some places, still intact. The point was the abolition of human bondage, not the maintenance of specific constitutional arrangements. "Why this hue-and-cry for Union, *Union*, UNION, which is like a bait held out to the mass of people to lure them on," Rose asked. "I would rather have a small republic without the taint and without the stain of slavery in it, than to have the South brought back by compromise."

In public, Rose seemed to embrace her own isolation. In private, it saddened her. Lucretia Mott told a relative in 1863 that Rose had

"suffered from the bigotry of very fr[ien]ds." They were mostly bigoted against her atheism, but some had taken aim over the years
at her Jewishness and foreign birth. Now Rose's stubborn radicalism put her at odds with even the most committed of reformers.
When women's rights organizers formed a Loyal League to demonstrate their support for the Union, Rose told the group she was "not
unconditionally loyal to the Administration." No woman should
be, since "the law has never yet recognized us." The chair of the
convention, Lucy Stone, Rose's longtime nemesis in the movement,
criticized Rose's comments, declaring that "all the loyal women"
owed Lincoln "words of cheer and encouragement." Then she hastily adjourned the meeting for the night.

Rose's most dramatic confrontation during the war was with
her community of freethinkers. The atheist movement had declined
as the brewing sectional conflict provoked a religious resurgence.
By 1860, attendance at the annual Thomas Paine birthday celebrations that Ernestine and William Rose helped organize had fallen
by three-fourths from the glory days twenty years earlier. During
the war itself, what remained of organized atheism underwent a
further split. Rose continued to demand the immediate abolition of
slavery while many of her former allies questioned the connections
she made between religious dogmatism and racial oppression. At
an Infidel Convention in 1862, Rose introduced a resolution stating that as "Religion is the primary cause of all slavery . . . it is the
bounden duty of every lover of freedom and justice . . . to aid in
emancipating the slave wherever found, and of whatever color." The
proposal ignited a raucous debate. One attendee said that slavery
was "irrelevant" to the question of religion, while another objected
to "running the country into a prolonged civil war" only to free
Black people, "foreigners by nature, and . . . undoubtedly of an inferior quality." A letter in the *Boston Investigator*, a freethought paper
that Rose had long supported (it once published a poem about her
praising "the sight of thy soul-lit 'Jewish' face!"), complained that

"E. L. Rose" and other rabble-rousers, committing "the Christian error of attributing the war to slavery," were trying to get the atheists "to do service for abolitionism."

The split over slavery and the war widened into a more personal confrontation with the *Investigator*'s editor, Horace Seaver, a longtime ally of Rose who in 1859 had called her "a lady of fine abilities." Five years later, Rose trained those abilities against Seaver himself. Reflecting the spirit of the times, and eager perhaps to rescue the freethought movement from its wartime doldrums, Seaver lamented the conversion of a former Universalist church in Boston into a synagogue, then took the opportunity to denounce the ancient Israelites for their "ridiculous customs, murderous propensities, disgusting ceremonies, and determined scoundrelism." He went on to attack Judaism itself as "bigoted, narrow, exclusive, and totally unfit for a progressive people like the Americans."

Weeks later, Rose, surprised and disappointed that nobody else had spoken up before her, wrote a letter defending both the religion and the people from which she had always tried to keep her distance. Seaver published her letter along with a testy reply, and the two went back and forth for months. Drawing on her personal knowledge of Jews and Judaism—"they act just about the same as other people . . . they progress just as fast as the world will permit them"—to refute Seaver's attacks, Rose demonstrated a surprising familiarity with the tenets of Reform Judaism, noting that many Jews had grown less dogmatic in their adherence to traditional beliefs and rituals. Some did not even observe the Sabbath and enjoyed organs and singers in their synagogues. "As a people, they are sober, industrious, good citizens," Rose explained. "They interfere with no one, hunt after no proselytes, follow the even tenor of their ways, glad to be left alone." Closing one letter, Rose implored her fellow "Infidels" to be careful and "not add to the prejudice already existing towards the Jews, or any other sect."

Rose likely would have sprung to the defense of any group

she felt was being unfairly maligned, yet she did so in the debate with Seaver with added passion and a claim to personal authority. "[W]hatever you may know of the ancient, you evidently know nothing of the modern Jews," she wrote the editor. Rose initially engaged in the debate with her usual jovial tone, bantering with a fellow freethinker that Judaism had one advantage over Christianity from the atheist perspective: "if the belief in one [god] is bad, the belief in three is three times as bad." But Seaver touched a nerve when he alluded to the possibility of his critic "turning Jew," reverting to the faith in which she had been reared. With that, the exchange turned tense. "Is it not mean and cowardly to insinuate where there is not even a shadow of a shade to base the insinuation upon?" Rose asked. Seaver, undaunted, continued to taunt "our too sensitive sister," dubbing her "the Jewish champion."

But was there, perhaps, a shadow of a shade? Though she vehemently denied Seaver's insinuations, perhaps her decision to speak out had something to do with what she was seeing around her at the time, the liberation of another oppressed people from their centuries-long bondage. Now that the immediate goal of emancipation for Black Americans was on the way to being achieved, Rose may have felt she could turn some attention to another long-suffering group facing renewed persecution in a land supposedly devoted to liberty and equality, a group that happened to be her own. Following Rose's bitter exchange with Seaver, the *Jewish Record* observed that even if Rose had long ago disavowed any connection to the Jewish religion, she still possessed "some of the leaven of the Jewish spirit." That had always been true, but it had taken the upheaval of the Civil War to draw from her even the most indirect acknowledgment.

During his presidency, as in his younger days, Lincoln frequently came into contact with American Jews: visiting delegations who sought to protest exclusionary acts like Grant's Order No. 11 as well as individual supplicants seeking jobs, promotions, passes, or pardons. Some of his closest friends were Jewish, as were photographers who took his picture, clothiers who made his suits, and opticians who made his eyeglasses.

And so was the podiatrist who did wonders for his feet. In the fall of 1862, Lincoln met Issachar Zacharie, an English-born Jew raised in Philadelphia and Charleston who had recently made a name for himself in Washington by curing the corns and bunions of several prominent citizens, including the secretary of war. Without any training, armed only with a fake degree from a Cuban medical school, made-up letters of recommendation, and someone else's book he reprinted under his own name, the mysterious Zacharie had a knack for earning the trust and confidence of the powerful. He knew how lonely and isolated Lincoln felt and offered himself as a friend and informal adviser. They were an odd pairing, the lanky, disheveled president and the stout, stylishly dressed podiatrist, a diamond brooch pinned to his shirt, his hair smoothed back with oil. Zacharie smelled "sweeter than the winds that blow from Araby," according to one acquaintance.

Yet their relationship soon shifted toward matters beyond Lincoln's foot pain. The *New York World* reported that "the President has often left his business-apartment to spend an evening in the parlor with this favored bunionist." Just four months after first meeting Zacharie, the president sent his foot doctor on a top-secret spying mission to occupied New Orleans, where he was to serve as intermediary between the army commanders and the city's Jewish population, alienated from the Union due to Eugenia Levy Phillips's imprisonment and other perceived insults and abuses. In doing so, Zacharie would work toward Lincoln's ultimate goal of easing Louisiana's return to the Union.

To get Zacharie to New Orleans, Lincoln sent an order to Gen. Nathaniel Banks on November 25, 1862, "excepting his case from a general prohibition which I understand to exist," likely referring to Grant's ban on Jews traveling south by railroad. Once in New Orleans, between dabbling in various speculative ventures and reportedly taking bribes from all comers, Zacharie hired a few loyal Jews and disguised them as peddlers before sending them into the countryside to gather sensitive information about the enemy.

At some point Zacharie became convinced that he could heal the breach not only between New Orleans Jews and the occupying federal troops but between the warring nations themselves, a goal of personal importance for Zacharie, whose family lived in the South. He persuaded Lincoln to send him on another secret mission, this time to Richmond, to explore the possibilities of a negotiated settlement to end the war. Again, Zacharie's religion made him a valuable messenger for the president. In Richmond, the doctor met twice with Judah P. Benjamin, first with other cabinet members present, then, later that night, alone. It is not known what the two discussed, likely some version of a much-rumored, widely ridiculed scheme for the South to rejoin the Union and for Jefferson Davis to be installed as president of a newly reconquered Mexico. The next day, Zacharie sent Benjamin a note marked "confidential," sharing his hope that Benjamin would "never regret the interview we had last night."

Following Union victories on the battlefield, Lincoln's cabinet opposed the negotiations, the president stalled for time, and the foot doctor's peace plan went nowhere.

Zacharie next turned to organizing American Jews behind Lincoln's reelection in 1864. He met with Republican figures and traveled widely in the Northeast to line up votes. "As regards the *Isrelites*," the doctor wrote Lincoln a few days before the November 8 election, "with but few exceptions, they will vote for you . . . My men had been all the week seeing that their masses are properly Registered so that all will go right on the 8." When newspapers began reporting that Jewish emissaries had traveled to Washington to pledge the Jewish vote to Lincoln—a rumor denied by the White House—the *Jewish Messenger*, fearful of a popular backlash, insisted there was no such thing as a Jewish vote, and that "the Jews, as a body, have no politics." Each would vote his conscience.

And so they did: Thanks to Grant's expulsion decree and past comments by Lincoln's new running mate, Andrew Johnson of Tennessee, who had once accused Judah Benjamin of belonging to "that tribe that parted the garments of our savior," many American Jews saw the Republicans as hostile. Like other immigrants in Northern cities, they worried that newly freed Black people would take their jobs. Zacharie's final mission for Lincoln, like his effort to heal the breach with the South, was a failure. In the Jewish neighborhoods of Manhattan, Lincoln's opponent won more than two-thirds of the vote.

Though Jews in the North began the war with a surge of patriotism—or at least conspicuous displays thereof—many soured on the conflict, especially after the near-simultaneous promulgation of Grant's Order No. 11 and Lincoln's Emancipation Proclamation. Enlistment plummeted as Jews balked at sacrificing themselves for a country unwilling to treat them as equal citizens. Throughout the war, Jews served at much lower rates than both native-born citizens and other immigrants. (According to Adam Mendelsohn, nearly 15 percent of all German immigrants in New York signed up to serve, compared to just 1.7 percent of Jews.) Though some, like Marcus Spiegel, saw joining up as an opportunity to attain badly needed financial security, others thought staying out of the fight offered the better deal. Newly arrived immigrants trying to find a sure footing were not eager to risk all in a conflict they barely understood. Merchants and clothiers who had only recently left the hard life of peddling stood to benefit from wartime supply contracts. Why don a uniform when you could make them? The gusher of federal spending opened by the war offered a stimulus for ambitious businessmen to scale up their efforts. If some, like August Bondi, cited their Jewishness as a spur to fight, others saw the peculiar burdens of their marginalized identity and their struggles as new immigrants as ample reason to look out for themselves.

The uncomfortable fact is that many American Jews did sit out the war. Religious and community leaders all but encouraged them to do so. The conflict was largely absent from the most widely read Jewish newspapers of the time—Isaac Mayer Wise's *Israelite* and Isaac Leeser's *Occident*—except when an issue related directly to Jews. Leeser, who had opposed the war from the beginning, observed when it ended that while slavery's abolition had "conferr[ed] benefits on millions," it had also "deprived millions of others of their vested rights."

Morris Raphall, the Orthodox rabbi who had supplemented his secession-winter defense of slavery with a nervous post-Sumter call to defend the Union "at the peril of life and limb," soon returned to his more conservative prewar position. He had grown dejected even before his son Alfred lost his arm at Gettysburg. In May 1863, five months after the Emancipation Proclamation, Raphall blamed "demagogues, fanatics and a party press" of both sections for plunging the country into "a destructive but needless sectional war." He found "consolation" in the reflection that the cause of keeping the Union together was "the worthiest in the field," but he did not see the end of slavery as a necessary part of that endeavor.

Jews in the Northern states had no way of knowing whether the staggering hostility they suddenly faced would continue after the fighting ended. Isaac Mayer Wise warned his followers after Grant's expulsion order that the next time the Jews' constitutional liberties were threatened, "we could have here another Spain." The movement to make the United States an officially Christian nation showed no signs of slowing down.

They also had no way of knowing how the war would end. If the Union lost, as at moments seemed likelier than not, the prejudice against the Jews in the North might have exploded into actual violence, mob-driven terror like that of the Draft Riots of 1863, but directed at Jews instead of (or in addition to) Black Americans. It might have become unsafe for Jews to live in a defeated and demoralized Union tearing itself apart over who to blame, while their cousins in the South, counted among the privileged class of whites, could well have enjoyed a more comfortable and prosperous existence as citizens of the Confederate States of America than any other Jews in the world.

11

"This Otherwise Blessed Land"

THOMAS WENTWORTH HIGGINSON, A WHITE ABOLI-
tionist from Boston who led the first Black soldiers into battle
against their former masters, recalled in his 1867 memoir that many
of his men, fresh from slavery and largely illiterate, possessed little
knowledge of the wider world apart from "a vast bewildered chaos
of Jewish history": the characters and tales of the Old Testament,
especially the Book of Exodus.

Higginson was crudely simplifying the understanding of his
men. Yet it was true that many of the newly freed slaves saw themselves in the story of the ancient Jews' flight from Egypt after four
hundred of years of oppression. Delivered from the house of bondage, desperately hoping the much-vaunted promised land of America
would finally be opened to them, Black Americans sensed a biblical
current coursing through their times. "The magnificent trumpet
tones of the Hebrew Scripture, transmuted and oddly changed, became a strange new gospel," W. E. B. Du Bois would write. Emancipation was a world-historical event in which the long-ago stories of
the Bible were suddenly, in their own time, becoming real.

Even if August Bondi did not respond to the Emancipation Proclamation by writing "no more pharaohs and no more slaves" in his
diary, many Black Americans cheered it in similar terms. When the
news reached Boston, one preacher led his worshippers in a hymn:

Sound the loud timbrel o'er Egypt's dark sea,
Jehovah hath triumphed, his people are free.

"No wonder God sent war on this nation!" a former slave remarked
after the end of the war. "It was the old story of the captivity in
Egypt repeated. The slaveholders were warned time and again to let
the black man go, but they hardened their hearts and would not,
until finally the wrath of God was poured out upon them and the
sword of the great North fell upon the first-born."

Black Americans were not the only ones who understood the
Civil War as somehow an essentially Jewish experience. The themes
and images of Exodus had long shaped American political thought,
from the New England Puritans, who saw themselves as modern-
day Hebrews fleeing oppression to form a new, more righteous
nation, to American revolutionaries like Benjamin Franklin, who
proposed as the official seal of the United States the figure of Moses
lifting his rod as the Egyptian army drowns in the sea. (Thomas Jefferson suggested instead the band of wandering Israelites following
the pillar of fire through the desert.) Ezra Stiles, the president of
Yale College (and a friend of slave trader Aaron Lopez), called the
new republic "God's American Israel." Early settlers named their
towns Canaan, Goshen, Bethel, and Salem. Invocations of ancient
Israel were standard in American rhetoric after the Revolution. The
lore and literature of the once-mighty Hebrew nation, eventually
split in two and conquered by invaders, offered both a model for the
early republic and a warning of how disunity could lead to disaster.

Yet more than any other event in American history, the Civil
War called to mind Old Testament echoes, not least because it

brought ruin and devastation of biblical proportions. Americans of all kinds felt they were living, as the Hebrews had, through an era of divine intervention, judgment, abandonment, or salvation. The divided America of the Civil War period was "a culture with Jews on the mind," Adam Mendelsohn observes. Northerners and Southerners alike used Jewish language and symbolism to explain to themselves and others what the fight was all about. That was part of what made the presence of actual Jews in their midst both a source of curiosity and, for some, an unwelcome inconvenience.

Interestingly, given the identification of their Black bondsmen with the ancient Israelites, white Southerners also imagined themselves as latter-day Hebrews fleeing the Pharaoh named Lincoln. Others preferred to think of the Confederate armies as legions of zealous conquerors, and the God-fearing Stonewall Jackson as the Joshua of the Old Dominion. Robert E. Lee's wool-and-cotton headquarters flag, signaling his location in the field, featured thirteen stars—the eleven states of the Confederacy, plus Missouri and Kentucky—arranged in the shape of the Ark of the Covenant. Lee's "fighting parson," Confederate Army chaplain J. William Jones, often began his prayers by invoking the "God of Abraham, Isaac and Jacob, God of Israel, God of the centuries, God of our fathers, God of Jefferson Davis, Robert Edward Lee, and Stonewall Jackson, Lord of Hosts and King of Kings."

Jews in the Confederacy embraced the comparison with a special enthusiasm. In his "Prayer for Peace," written four months after Gettysburg, Samuel Yates Levy, a Jewish lawyer and playwright from Savannah serving as an officer in the Confederate Army, implored the "King of Kings" to "smite the Armies of the Cruel North," just "as thou led'st thy chosen people forth / From Egypt's sullen wrath." After the Southern armies instead were smited, Southern Jews compared the Northern occupation of the rebel states to the destruction of the first Jerusalem Temple and the expulsion of the Jews to Babylonia. "As Israelites," Henry Hyams, the former lieutenant governor of Louisiana, wrote soon after the war, "we are passing through another captivity which relives and reenacts all the troubles so pathetically poured forth by the inspired Jeremiah. Let us hope with him that the days of Bondage will have a permanent end and that freedom will again reign in our unhappy land."

New Englanders, meanwhile, retained their Puritan ancestors' conception of themselves as, in the prewar words of Herman Melville, "the peculiar, chosen people—the Israel of our time." In 1862, Oliver Wendell Holmes Jr. wrote a poem after dropping out of Harvard to join the Union Army: "To Canaan, to Canaan / The Lord has led us forth, / To blow before the heathen walls / The trumpets of the North!"

Abraham Lincoln, the Union's theologian-in-chief, regularly invoked biblical language and casually cited the stories of the Hebrew patriarchs and the words of the prophets. In his presidential communications, he seemed to go out of his way to use non-Christian terms for the divine, such as "He, from Whom all blessings flow," possibly to avoid giving offense to Jews. By the final weeks of the war, Lincoln had found his way to something like an Old Testament take on the conflict: stark, severe, punitive. In his Bible-suffused second inaugural address—a "sacred effort," Frederick Douglass observed, more a sermon than a political oration—Lincoln suggested that the astounding bloodshed was divine retribution for the national crime of slavery. Quoting Psalms, he vowed that even if the war continued indefinitely, "as was said three thousand years ago, so still it must be said, 'the judgments of the Lord are true and righteous altogether.'" On the day of his assassination, Lincoln told his wife that he wished to see Jerusalem before he died.

———

The South had never been an especially hostile place for Jews. Because they were generally seen as white and had not made themselves odious by criticizing slavery, Jews had been accepted, more or less, as equals. Outnumbered, in many areas, by the Black people they enslaved, white Southern Christians needed all the allies they could get. Even if they held to inherited notions of far-off Jews as perfidious, Satan-serving Christ killers, they tended to be respectful toward those who lived in their midst. They differentiated, as Jonathan Sarna has written, between "the mythical Jew" and the "Jew next door." The former deserved only scorn and damnation, the latter a hearty welcome, or at least the benefit of the doubt.

In the early days of the war, the South did not see the explosive rise of bigotry that Jews faced in the North. No Southern general even entertained the idea of expelling unoffending Jewish civilians from their homes. Indeed, Southern papers disparaged Grant's 1862 edict as one more example of Yankee perfidy. "It is worthy of the dark ages," the *Richmond Dispatch* commented, "and of the darkest and most hypocritical despotism now in existence in the civilized globe."

Yet despite the surface-level friendliness, hostility to Jews had long lingered just below the surface of Southern life. In the tense atmosphere of the sectional crisis, it burst to the surface. On the same day in December 1860 that South Carolina seceded, a rabble of young men in Greenville, in the far western part of the state, decided to force their Jewish neighbors to leave town. One merchant even had his beard shaved. An observer in Greenville told a relative that the attack was "much to the satisfaction of the majority of our citizens."

As the Union naval blockade, combined with the dedication of what little industrial capacity the South had to military production, led to severe shortages of goods and astonishing levels of inflation, Southerners looked around for a scapegoat. Counterfeit currency circulated widely. Speculators hoarded stocks of necessary items, then sold them off at outrageous prices. Anyone who managed to smuggle goods across enemy lines—running cotton to the North and anything at all to the South—stood to make a fortune.

Heyman Herzberg of Atlanta found he could not resist. As in any war, the reality—long stretches of pure drudgery punctuated by sheer terror—often disappointed the initial optimism. After serving in the Confederate Army for six months, Herzberg hired a sixty-year-old to serve in his place, then bribed his senior officer with a gold watch to let him leave. Dodging the bullets of Confederate recruiters, he traveled by foot, buggy, and train to New York and Philadelphia to pick up a stock of goods before returning south to sell them at "fabulous prices." Arrested by both armies, Herzberg always managed to get off, once by bonding with his captors over their shared affection for Freemasonry, another time by offering a taste of his loot.

As with Northern cotton traders in Grant's western district, not all the Southern smugglers were Jewish, but many were. That certain merchants had the craftiness and the connections to sneak badly needed goods through the lines proved useful both to desperate Southern citizens and Confederate officials facing rising unrest. But performing that service, in a time of deprivation, also made Jews vulnerable to charges of price gouging and treachery. Confederate papers depicted Jewish merchants as "un-Southern," as "scavengers" preying on the vulnerable. In Savannah, one citizen noted that "some of the best property in this City . . . has been purchased by German jews who were lately the poorest of the city." A letter in the *Richmond Examiner* denounced those "specimens" of the "accursed race" who "fatten upon the calamities of the very people who are giving them a home."

John Beauchamp Jones, a Southern novelist working as a War Department clerk (he loathed his boss, Judah Benjamin), wrote in his diary that if the Confederates somehow managed to win, "instead of being vassals of the Yankees, we shall find all our wealth in the hands of the Jews." Noting the robbery of a Jewish-owned store in Richmond, Jones wrote, not without excitement, "The prejudice is very strong against the extortionists, and . . . may contribute to produce a new Reign of Terror."

As the possibility of a quick victory receded, hatred of Jews became an outlet for Confederate anger, bitterness, and fear. A former peddler turned successful merchant and slave owner, Lazarus Straus thought he had been accepted as a member of the community of Talbotton, Georgia. His son, Oscar, would write in his memoir about the warm welcome his father had received, for "the existence of slavery drew a distinct line of demarcation between the white and black races." But now that the existence of slavery was in question, the line of racial demarcation no longer seemed quite so distinct. In 1862, a Talbotton grand jury denounced the "evil and unpatriotic conduct" of Jewish businessmen and called for a boycott. The elder Straus was shocked by the grand jury's statement—he was only one of a handful of Jews living in the town—and made it known he planned to leave. That, in turn, surprised the townspeople, who had thought they were blaming those hypothetical "mythical Jews" for their suffering, not the kindly businessman who had helped their town grow. They begged Straus to stay, but he decided to move to nearby Columbus, a thriving commercial town with a larger Jewish population, including Raphael J. Moses, the peach man of Georgia. At least there he would not feel so dangerously alone.

Two hundred miles south of Talbotton, in Thomasville, Georgia, citizens at a public meeting voted to ban Jewish peddlers from entering the town and ordered the three Jewish families who lived there to leave within ten days or be expelled by force. A Confederate colonel and former congressman, J. L. Seward, accused the Jews of circulating fake money, hoarding goods, and "demanding exorbitant and ruinous prices." The offending families left for Savannah, where they asked their fellow Jews to help them fight the ouster. Savannah's Jews called a meeting to protest the "wholesale slander, persecution and denunciation of a people," while Jewish soldiers in Georgia's

32nd Regiment met at a battery south of town to condemn the Thomasville expulsion as an insult to those Jewish Confederates who, "armor buckled, enduring all toils and hardships of camp life, [are] ready to shed our blood for the defence of our country."

The South's wave of wartime hostility was mostly an expression of popular frustration rather than an organized campaign against Jews. Still, it was concerning. A letter to the *Richmond Sentinel* noted with "sorrow and dismay" how a once-welcoming Southern society had joined in an "unholy and unjust denunciation" of the Jews. Gratz Cohen, the son of a prominent Savannah businessman and slave owner, lamented to his father how "intolerance & prejudice cast their baneful seed throughout the land."

Still, that did not stop Cohen from giving his life to the cause. The first Jewish student at the University of Virginia, Cohen brought his enslaved servant Louis to the front. This "faithful servant," as Cohen described him, soon ran away, leaving his master bereft. In a poem he mailed a relative during the war, Cohen invoked a "God alike of White & Black" and imagined a world in which "the oppressor and / Oppressed shall cease & all be equal and men . . . drawn together, race with race / Commingled." Gratz Cohen died in battle in March 1865, two weeks before the end of the war, in an apparent case of friendly fire.

At first, the prominence of Jews among Confederate leaders stirred more bigotry in the North than in the South. After South Carolina's secession, an upper-class Boston newspaper blamed the crisis on Southern Jews like Judah Benjamin, noting that "this peculiar race . . . having no country of their own," hoped to see "that other nations shall be in the same unhappy condition." Following Benjamin's thunderous farewell to the Senate, Henry Wilson of Massachusetts had called the Louisianan part of a "foul and wicked plot . . . to overthrow the government of his adopted country which gives equality of rights even to that race that stoned prophets and crucified the Redeemer of the world." When Benjamin, as Confederate secretary of war, ordered William Brownlow, the avowedly pro-Union "fighting parson" of eastern Tennessee, deported across enemy lines, Brownlow barnstormed the North denouncing the "little Jew of the bogus Confederacy."

In the North, however, the wartime surge in antisemitism began to ebb as soon as the tides of war turned against the Confederacy in late 1864, as Sherman marched to the sea and Lincoln to a re-election that had seemed unlikely only months earlier. Treacherous Jewish traders could no longer be blamed for thwarting a campaign now poised on the cusp of victory.

In the collapsing Confederacy, prejudice against Jews took longer to recede. Benjamin offered too appealing a bogeyman for distraught Southern patriots. Henry S. Foote, sworn opponent of the Davis administration and a leading critic of Benjamin, suggested in the Confederate Congress that Benjamin had personally given permission for fellow Jews to engage in illicit trade. Immediately after the South's victory, Foote confidently suggested, he would move to ban Jews from coming within twelve miles of the Confederate capital. The proposal was met with cheers.

An acclaimed orator of the antebellum period, Benjamin remained unusually quiet during the war. He gave not a single public speech through nearly four years of fighting. He stayed behind the scenes, allowing Jefferson Davis's opponents to depict him as the true power behind the rebel throne. Benjamin's position required him to take no notice of the prejudice he faced. He had to act as if he did not feel like an outsider, even if he was constantly being reminded that was just what he was.

As secretary of state, Benjamin's primary objective had been to win diplomatic recognition, maybe even military aid, from the European powers. That was how the Americans had won their independence from Britain in the Revolution and it was the only way the Southerners could win theirs. But though the governments and upper classes of Britain and France tended to sympathize with the South, the people deplored slavery. As Union victories mounted, foreign intervention only grew more unlikely.

Stymied in his diplomacy, Benjamin turned his attention to another job Davis had tasked him with: overseeing the Confederate secret service. Benjamin organized a ring of spies, smugglers, and secret agents to burn bridges, buildings, and ships and encourage "fierce and passionate dissensions . . . among the Northern people." From their perch just across the border in ostensibly neutral Canada, Benjamin's emissaries reached out to antiwar politicians in the Midwest and made connections with secret organizations like the Knights of the Golden Circle, rumored to boast a membership hundreds of thousands strong across the North. These peace groups organized resistance to the draft, protected deserters from arrest, and even contemplated more radical measures to stop the war, including revolution.

Yet those "fierce and passionate dissensions" were never as widespread in the Northern states as Benjamin wanted to believe. His agents' schemes to break Southern captives out of Union prisons, launch insurrections in the Midwest, and burn down Northern cities never amounted to much, mostly due to haphazard conception, slipshod execution, and a lack of support among locals who, tired of war, were not eager for it to be brought to their doorsteps. In October 1864, Confederate agents invaded St. Albans, a quiet village in northern Vermont. They robbed a few banks and roamed aimlessly up and down the elm-lined Main Street, firing pistols in the air.

Early in his efforts to stir up trouble in the North, Benjamin had warned an underling that all covert actions should be "strictly legitimate, honorable and proper." An aide later recalled that Benjamin's agents were told to adhere to "the accepted methods of civilized warfare." But such commitments waned as the Confederates grew more desperate and as reports of Sherman's march across Georgia filtered out and riled up the forlorn rebels. Top government officials regretted not having been more ruthless and ingenious in their stratagems. One Confederate sympathizer, a handsome and celebrated actor who had been spending time with Benjamin's associates in Washington, Baltimore, Boston, and Montreal, began devising a plan to go beyond such strictures. What Benjamin might have known of his plan has been a matter of conjecture ever since.

————

The Confederacy was running out of time. If the rebellion was going to have any chance of success, desperate measures, once unthinkable, would be required. Neither France nor England would acknowledge the South's independence so long as the Confederacy remained devoted to slavery. Absent some move toward emancipation, the cause would surely be lost.

It was a long shot, but Benjamin began to see that long shot as the South's only hope. An old friend from New Orleans had written to him in the summer of 1863, a month after the devastating losses at Gettysburg and Vicksburg, proposing the arming of slaves and, ultimately, their emancipation. Benjamin replied that the cost of compensating the owners would be too high, and the South could not afford to lose the agricultural output of slave labor. Food was scarce enough already. But he was far from horrified by the proposal, as other Southern leaders would have been. He told the writer he offered his objections merely as "food for thought." He welcomed the suggestion as "an evidence of patriotism."

A year later, Benjamin began to reconsider his objections. After starting the year of 1864 with the "sincere conviction" that its end would not come without the slaveholders' republic being "welcome[d] into the family of nations," by late autumn he saw that the rebellion was in serious jeopardy. He sent a few hundred bales of cotton to England as an insurance policy, something to start a new life with, as he had already had to do several times before.

With Confederate prospects looking gloomy, Benjamin began arguing behind the scenes for the radical measures that only a few months earlier he had rejected. If the Union Army could offer freedom to slaves in exchange for military service, the Confederates should do the same. Alone among top Confederates, Benjamin understood that the rebels faced a stark choice: emancipation or surrender. He pushed for the former as much as he could without risking his position in the cabinet. An administration-backed Richmond paper, which often published editorials likely ghostwritten by Benjamin, commented in October 1864 that the South "would sooner sacrifice slavery a thousand times than to be conquered by the Yankees and have it sacrificed by them." The issue, ultimately, was a simple one, Benjamin told a friend: "Is it better for the Negro to fight for us or against us?"

In private, Benjamin convinced Davis that it was worth losing their slaves if that meant escaping Northern domination. But Davis knew the Southern public was not ready for a step that threatened the very premises of the Confederate nation. Eugene Henry Levy, a Jewish private from New Orleans, rejected the rumored emancipation plan, noting that the idea "that slaves are in their proper sphere as they are at present situated . . . is one of the grand incentives to the waging of war against the United States." David Yulee, Benjamin's friend and former Senate colleague, who spent most of the war at his Gulf Coast plantation, objected that arming slaves would entitle them to "the prerogatives of the citizen," an outrage under what was supposed to have been "a white man's Government." "If slaves will make good soldiers," one of Benjamin's critics ventured, "our whole theory of slavery is wrong."

Benjamin may have suspected for a long time that the theory was wrong. He had said as much in his arguments before the Louisiana Supreme Court in the *Creole* cases back in 1842. "What is a slave?" he had asked. "He is a human being . . . His heart, like the heart of the white man . . . ever cherishes the desire for liberty." Of course, the gifted attorney had only presented that argument because it served the interests of his clients. Benjamin surely believed in slavery, in white domination, in the Southern "way of life," and he had personally benefited from the institution since he was a boy. But as a worldly traveler well-connected in antislavery European intellectual circles, life without slavery was likely not inconceivable to him. It would be too much to say that Benjamin's Jewishness lay behind his emancipation proposal. But that Jewishness *had* rendered him an outsider among Confederate leaders, and only an outsider would have been willing to introduce such a subversive idea and risk the kind of public opprobrium to which Benjamin had long grown accustomed. Slavery, for Benjamin, had always served as a means to his own chosen ends, rising as an unprivileged immigrant to the commanding heights of the Southern aristocracy. In 1852, the year he won appointment to the United States Senate, he had sold his plantation once it had served his purposes. Now he suggested the South, too, get rid of slavery in order to have a chance of ensuring what had come to matter, at least to him, far more: freedom from Yankee rule.

By the end of 1864, Savannah had fallen, and Sherman was getting ready to march north toward Richmond. Jefferson Davis remained unwilling to put the emancipation plan forward himself, so in February 1865, Benjamin broke his four-year public silence with a speech to some ten thousand people crowded inside and outside the capital's cavernous African Church, the largest assembly hall in Richmond, often borrowed from its Black members for public meetings. He did not hide that the situation facing the South was grim: "We now know, in the core of our hearts, that this people must conquer its freedom or die."

All the South needed was sufficient resources to keep up the fight. "Are they in this country?" Benjamin asked. "If so, they belong to the country, and not to the man who chances to hold them now." He needed their cotton. Would they give it? He also needed their tobacco. He needed their bacon. "I want one other thing," Benjamin prodded the audience, as he would a jury, to follow his line of thought. He needed men, whoever and wherever they could be found. The South had suffered staggering losses. Thanks to the concentration of immigrants in Northern cities, the Union had far more bodies to throw into battle. "Our resources of white population have greatly diminished," Benjamin coldly informed a crowd that had felt that diminishment in the loss of their own sons and fathers and limbs. "But you have 680,000 black men of the same ages." A murmur rose as the audience began to understand where he was going. Benjamin made his meaning clear: "Let us say to every negro who wishes to go into the ranks on condition of being made free, 'Go and fight—you are free.'" Anticipating the objection that the North had enlisted Black men and been damned by the South as barbaric scoundrels for it, Benjamin replied, "Let us imitate them in this. I would imitate them in nothing else."

Someone in the crowd shouted, "No! Never!" while another countered, "Send in the slaves!" Benjamin knew the proposal would be controversial, and in the speech anticipated a moment in the future when Southerners would regret not having adopted his proposal: "I feel that the time is rapidly coming on when the people will wonder that they ever doubted."

Two months earlier, Benjamin and Davis had sent an emissary to Europe with a new offer: emancipation in exchange for diplomatic recognition. For the Europeans, however, the offer came too late. The Union was almost certain to win. For white Southerners, meanwhile, emancipation was too much to swallow. Already under suspicion on account of his Jewish background, Benjamin's speech brought the wrath of the exhausted and terrified would-be nation down on his own head. The Confederate Congress debated a resolution stating that "Judah P. Benjamin is not a wise and prudent

Secretary of State and lacks the confidence of the country." Benjamin offered his resignation to Davis, who refused it.

Had the rebel cabinet acted on his plan, four bloody years earlier, to ship cotton to England, the war might have taken a very different course. Now the Confederacy as a whole failed to seize on Benjamin's bold proposal to save their nation from impending doom by sacrificing the very institution it had been founded to secure.

On the morning of Sunday, April 2, 1865, Robert E. Lee sent a telegram to the Confederate War Department, with a message for Jefferson Davis. The president received the news while sitting in his pew in church: Union forces had broken through the rebel lines. Richmond had to be evacuated by nightfall. Federal soldiers would be in the capital by the following day.

Though not averse to attending Christian services from time to time, Judah Benjamin was not in church that morning. He learned of the capital's imminent capture while at home, then rushed to the office. He had work to do. In the preceding weeks, once the need for an evacuation had grown likely, Benjamin had boxed up many of his personal belongings and official documents and shipped them south for safekeeping. But now he had more sensitive papers that needed to be disposed of: those related to his management of Confederate spies and agents, including strictly secret schemes cooked up only in the last few months. With Grant's forces about to seize the Confederate capital, that work had to be put on hold. The ring of conspirators, if they chose to go ahead, would have to proceed without further guidance from Richmond.

That morning, Benjamin summoned the French consul in Richmond, a man named Alfred Paul, to his office. The two had become friends during the war. Paul offered Benjamin a connection to his wife and daughter, whom he had not seen in years, in faraway Paris. As Benjamin packed up boxes and tossed papers into the fireplace, he told the French diplomat that the Confederate government's departure from Richmond was "simply a measure of prudence." They would likely return in a few weeks.

Paul knew that was not true, and he marveled that someone of Benjamin's intellectual caliber could say something so patently implausible. He was only unsure, the consul wrote in a letter shortly after the conversation, whether Benjamin's baseless optimism was motivated by "persisting illusion or by a lack of sincerity, two things which characterize this statesman."

It remains a tantalizing question: Was Benjamin a true believer to the end, deluded but loyal, or was he a skilled dissembler? Was he putting on a show of bravado for the European's benefit and perhaps, as he knew his words would be recorded, for history's? The question, ultimately, is unanswerable, thanks to Benjamin's penchant for consigning his papers to the flames. What we do know is that by that evening, when he along with Davis and the rest of the cabinet boarded the Danville train out of an increasingly chaotic Richmond, Benjamin had already devised an elaborate getaway plan. With a fake Confederate passport, the former master of Belle-chasse had invented a new persona for himself: Monsieur Bonfals, from the Louisiana Creole for "good disguise." He would not be taken alive.

Southern Jews felt the sting of the Confederacy's fall just as painfully as did their Christian neighbors, and women on the home front as much as men on the front lines. In the final months of the war, whole communities of Jews fled or were forced out of Atlanta, Savannah, and Charleston, as each fell under bombardment and occupation by Sherman's troops. "In one night," Eleanor Cohen, a dentist's daughter in Columbia, South Carolina, wrote, "we were brought from comparative wealth and luxury to abject poverty." The family watched from the top floor of their house as fires rose over the city. Then a change in wind sent the inferno barreling toward them. For days, the Cohens wandered the streets without food, clothing, or shelter. Twenty-four-year-old Eleanor was supposed to be married later that month; the festivities would have to be postponed. But that was less of a tragedy than seeing her hometown under hostile occupation. "Yes, we are again in the hated Union," Cohen wrote in her diary, "and over us again floats the banner that is now a sign of tyranny and oppression."

Phoebe Pember, the widowed daughter of one of the most prominent Southern Jewish families (her sister was Eugenia Levy Phillips, twice imprisoned for siding with the South), ran the Chimborazo military hospital outside Richmond. She nursed thousands of wounded Confederate soldiers, dressed wounds, read the Bible to bedridden men, killed chickens to make soup, and presided over disbursements of whiskey. As the government fled and the capital fell, Pember stayed at her post. She considered herself blessed for "being born of a nation and religion that did not enjoin forgiveness on its enemies," she wrote. Her Jewishness left her free, unlike her Christian friends, to pray "an eye for an eye, and a life for a life."

Emma Mordecai lived for most of the war on a small family farm five miles north of the Confederate capital, along with her sister-in-law (whose three sons had donned the rebel gray) and several enslaved servants. Unlike her brother Alfred, who at the war's outset had quit his job in the United States Army yet refused to fight for the South, Emma believed in the righteousness of both slavery and the Confederate cause. "We are fighting and suffering for independence," she wrote in her wartime diary. "I shall stand by the Flag of *Home*, & will die by the graves of my ancestors."

Emma continued to attend synagogue in Richmond all through the four years of fighting. Even as it became clear things were going badly, the unmarried fifty-three-year-old had come to rely more than ever on her faith in "the great Disposer of events."

That faith did not keep Emma from being stunned by certain of His dispositions, especially the fall of Richmond. She had just spent a week in town with friends. None had any hint of the calamity about to befall them. Early on the morning after the evacuation, as Judah Benjamin and the rest of the fleeing government rumbled south along rickety, torn-up tracks, Emma was jolted out of bed when the house shook from a gigantic explosion in the city, the vast reserves of gunpowder at the Richmond arsenal going up in a massive fireball. As Union troops overran the surrounding countryside, Emma and her sister-in-law hid out on their farm. One by one, their enslaved servants began to slink off. A man named Cyrus told her "there was to be no more master and mistress now." Emma was astonished, for she had thought the servants shared her view of bondage as beneficial to slaves and masters alike. Some left without even saying goodbye to "one of the kindest of mistresses," as Emma considered herself. A man who had fled late one night returned a short time later, but only to take with him a cart, a mule, and all the corn in the barn. "Nothing to be done but to submit," sighed Emma, soon reduced to "doing drudgery" herself.

But Emma prided herself on her pluck and would not submit to certain slights. When a Black soldier—"an insolent-looking negro, dirty and ragged"—seized her family's horse, Emma ventured into the burned-up city to try to retrieve it. Richmond was hardly recognizable from just a week earlier. The town was full of rubble. Cannons and shells burst all around her. Union officers cheered their hard-won victory, the formerly enslaved their newfound freedom. The white residents "all looked disconsolate, desolate, and defiled." Emma was appalled. "Everything looks unnatural and desecrated," she wrote in her diary.

As she picked her way through the smoldering, glass-strewn

streets, a huge eruption of celebratory gunfire signaled the arrival of Abraham Lincoln on his triumphant tour of the former den of treason. Disgusted, Emma turned for home. On the road out of town, she was stopped by another soldier with the United States Colored Troops, "the blackest man I ever saw." When Emma brazenly ignored his orders to halt, then cursed under her breath, the soldier pointed his rifle at her and cocked the hammer. "You haven't got things here no longer as you *have* had them," he told her. "Don't you know that? Don't you know *that?*"

Mortified, Emma scurried back to the farm, where she faced the unpleasant task of preparing for Passover, for the first time in her life, without the help of her slaves.

———

The festival commemorating the ancient Hebrews' escape from bondage began the day after Lee's surrender to Grant at Appomattox, just as news flashed through telegraph wires across the land that the long bloody strife had at last reached its end. Jews and gentiles alike were moved by the coincidence. "As the forefathers of the Jews passed over the Red Sea," the *New York Herald* observed, "so also the American people . . . have passed over and beyond the red sea of blood which has been spilt so freely during the last four years."

In Chicago, Liebmann Adler, a Reform rabbi who years earlier, while serving a congregation in Detroit, had allegedly helped fugitive slaves escape to Canada, reflected on the war's outcome. "Slavery was a disaster in this otherwise blessed land," Adler told his congregants on the first day of Passover. "It was a bad spirit from the first of this republic until now." But it was time to move on, and to welcome the rebels back in the Union: "At the return of this holiday"—by the following year's Passover—"may all hate and misgivings disappear between citizen and citizen, house and house, state and state," Adler prayed. "May the wound be healed and the tears be dried. May peace reign for all the victims of the war and may men be free in all this land!"

Come Shabbat morning, however, it was all too clear that healing the wounds of the war would not be so easy. Just as many Jews headed to synagogue, news of Lincoln's assassination raced across the country. Some heard about it as they entered the sanctuary, others as they took their seats. A rabbi in San Francisco, handed the report as he ascended to his pulpit, burst out crying, rendered "senseless" by the news. He composed himself enough to inform his congregation that "the twice anointed high priest in the sanctuary of our Republic . . . is no more." Samuel Adler of New York's Temple Emanu-El attempted a few words of consolation, but was so overcome with grief he could not go on. At the end of the services, the congregation spontaneously rose to recite the Mourner's Kaddish for the slain president—an honor never previously extended in American synagogues to non-Jews.

A week later, Jews were prominent participants in the official memorial ceremonies. At the massive citywide gathering in New York's Union Square, five Jewish leaders sat on the platform—the outspoken Lincoln critic Morris J. Raphall among them—and some seven thousand Jews from at least twenty congregations and other Jewish organizations participated in the somber procession up Broadway. The arks in the city's synagogues were decked in black banners. In their eulogies, rabbis compared the president to biblical figures like Moses, David, and, of course, his patriarchal namesake. From his Philadelphia pulpit, David Einhorn described Lincoln as "the Messiah of his people," though he did fault him for "excessive leniency towards the rebels."

The outpouring of grief by American rabbis and other Jews was all the more remarkable given that so many had opposed Lincoln during his presidency and likely voted against his reelection only six months earlier. Leading Jews who had mocked and scorned Lincoln in life now embraced him in death, and even tried to claim him as one of their own. Benjamin Szold, the Baltimore rabbi who had argued during the secession crisis for letting the South go, praised Lincoln as "so loyally devoted to [freedom]," he should be considered "a son of Israel." Isaac Mayer Wise's personal encounters with the president, including when Lincoln rescinded Grant's discriminatory order, had only slightly moderated his opinion that the former rail splitter was unfit for high office. Now he implausibly claimed that Lincoln—"the greatest man that ever sprung from mortal loins"—had once claimed in conversation that he himself had Hebrew ancestry.

In his own understated tribute, Morris Raphall praised Lincoln's final public statements for offering mercy to the defeated rebels, but criticized him for having "lock[ed] up many a courageous American" who had opposed the war. He also blamed Lincoln for having unwisely exposed himself to danger by appearing unguarded in public. After "stumbl[ing]" through most of his term, the president had "perished for the sake of America, and perished with all his sins upon his head."

Lincoln's death may have so profoundly distressed the American Jewish community because he had been such a constant friend, ever responsive to complaint or petition, remarkably free of the bigotry so prevalent at the time. But the outpouring of grief may also have been an expression of guilt for not having sufficiently supported him while he lived. The cult of Lincoln that developed with particular zeal among Jews in the United States in the years after his assassination may have been a way of atoning for the realization that the Great Emancipator had in a sense been more Jewish—more faithful to the lessons of Exodus and the spirit of the Hebrew Bible—than they had been themselves. On the morning of April 14, the day of Lincoln's assassination, Rabbi Max Lilienthal, a German-born rabbi and friend of Isaac Mayer Wise, acknowledged to his congregation that he and other Jews had been wrong not to denounce slavery more forthrightly before the war, as the abolitionists had done, only to be met with scorn. "Right must be right," Lilienthal concluded, "whatever may be the consequences."

In his own eulogy for Lincoln, a week after the assassination, Wise seemed to similarly acknowledge that he had gotten the major questions of the war wrong, and that Lincoln, whom he had opposed nearly every step of the way, had gotten them right:

> Let us carry into effect and perpetuate the great desires which heaved the breast of Abraham Lincoln; let us be one people, one, free, just and enlightened; let us be the chosen people to perpetuate and promulgate liberty and righteousness, the union and freedom of the human family; let us break asunder, wherever we can, the chains of the bondsman, the fetters of the slave, the iron rod of despotism, the oppressive yoke of tyranny; let us banish strife, discord, hatred, injustice, oppression from the domain of man, as far as our hands do reach, and we secure to Abraham Lincoln a perpetual reign and dominion everlasting; we set him the most durable monument in the hearts of the human family; then he is not dead, not removed even, from our midst, and will live forever.

When news of Lincoln's assassination caught up with the fleeing Confederate government, Judah Benjamin knew he had to evade capture. Northerners were convinced the leading rebels had a hand in the conspiracy and that Benjamin, especially, bore the blame for the president's demise. The *New York Times* argued that in retribution for their suspected role in the assassination plot, Davis and Benjamin "should die the most disgraceful death known to our civilization—death on the gallows." Secretary of State William Seward, severely wounded by one of Booth's accomplices, believed that Benjamin alone in the Confederate cabinet had communicated

with and encouraged the conspirators. Given both the seething anger over Lincoln's killing—martyred on Good Friday, no less—
and the anti-Jewish sentiments of the war years, Benjamin's escape
plans may have been influenced by his assumption that he would
not receive a fair trial were he captured. Powerless to resist the mob,
Northern leaders might use the occasion to rally the reunited country around the hanging of the Jewish traitor.

Yet if Benjamin feared for his own life, he refused to show it.
As the Confederate leaders crept down the muddy backroads of the
inland South, a curtain of doom seemed to descend over the traveling party, except for the lone member who somehow maintained
"his pleasant smile," according to a fellow cabinet secretary, while
smoking Cuban cigars and swirling his gold-tipped cane, always
exuding an air of "careless confidence." Benjamin passed the time
by ticking off a list of nations in the past that had faced starker odds
and yet prevailed. One night, when his carriage got stuck in a rut—
everybody else rode a horse; he refused—Benjamin was overheard
reciting from memory some lines of Tennyson's elegy for the Duke
of Wellington:

> *Let us bury the Great Duke*
> *To the noise of the mourning of a mighty nation;*
> *Mourning when their leaders fall,*
> *Warriors carry the warrior's pall,*
> *And sorrow darkens hamlet and hall.*

Asked once by Varina Davis how he kept calm whatever storms and
sufferings came his way, Benjamin cited his belief in a "fate in the
destiny of nations." That faith convinced him it was "wrong and
useless to distress one's self and thus weaken one's energy to bear
what was foreordained to happen."

At the last Confederate cabinet meeting, at Abbeville, South
Carolina, on May 2, 1865, while every other secretary counseled

surrender, Benjamin alone supported Davis's delusional idea of regrouping somewhere to the south and west, perhaps in the vast expanses of Texas, to fight another day. In the coming days, he stayed with Davis even as other cabinet members slipped away. When he finally decided it was time to go, he told Davis it was only to help arrange Confederate affairs in Cuba and the Bahamas, and that they would meet up again in Texas. In private, however, Benjamin had already confided to one cabinet member that he planned to travel to "the farthest place from the United States . . . if it takes me to the middle of China."

For all his stoicism in the face of misfortune, Benjamin did not passively suffer the fate of his fallen nation, nor that of its other leading figures, nearly all of whom were eventually captured. Bidding farewell to his chieftain, Benjamin put into effect the plan he had hatched over the previous months. As Monsieur Bonfals, a roving Frenchman journeying through the South, he made for Florida, where he hoped to find a ship to take him to the Caribbean and then to Europe. He traveled with Henry J. Leovy, ostensibly his translator but actually a Jewish lawyer and newspaperman who had supported Benjamin's early political career in New Orleans. Together they made their way along ruin-lined roads crowded with fellow refugees: Confederate deserters, wounded soldiers, displaced families, and former slaves. The pair traveled at night and hid out, as best they could, during the day. Leovy, like Benjamin's earlier companions, was struck by his friend's uncomplaining endurance of the hardships of the fugitive's life: "With all his plans shattered and without definite hope for the future, his superb confidence and courage raised him above all."

Once in Florida, Benjamin dropped the Bonfals disguise and turned himself into a South Carolina planter looking for land to settle. He donned a denim-blue suit made for him by a friendly farmer's wife and hid in the woods to wait out federal search parties. When he reached the Gulf Coast, Benjamin arranged with a sympathetic

Confederate veteran to take him six hundred miles around the Keys to the island of Bimini, halfway between Miami and the Bahamas. He subsisted on fish, turtle eggs, and milk from coconuts. Once, when their boat was stopped by Union sailors who hopped on board to inspect it, Benjamin slathered himself in kitchen grease and pretended to be a cook. One of the Union officers was overheard commenting as he left that he had never before seen a Jew doing manual labor.

Benjamin finally seemed to be on his way to safety, but it was hurricane season and the boat got caught in a storm. Waterspouts churned on all sides of the vessel and threatened to throw him and the small crew overboard. When the boat filled with water, Benjamin helped bail it out with his hat. "This is not like being secretary of state," he joked.

The boat finally made it to Bimini, but then Benjamin's ship to the Bahamas split at the seams after some sponges in its hold filled with water. The vessel went down without warning. Benjamin barely had time to grab a newly cooked pot of rice and a small keg of water before jumping into a one-oared skiff the ship had been towing. "I found myself at eight o'clock in the morning," he wrote to his sister, "with three negroes for my companions in disaster, only five inches of the boat out of water, on the broad ocean, with the certainty that we could not survive five minutes if the sea became the least rough."

Did the hated and hunted Jewish fugitive see some spur to reflection in finding himself, in the wake of the nation-rending catastrophe, in the same leaky boat with three Black people as his "companions in disaster"? Not quite. Later that morning, the survivors were picked up by a passing schooner. After enduring, incredibly, one more shipwreck, Benjamin made it at last to England. As Jefferson Davis wallowed in a dank Union prison, the near-penniless Benjamin set about once more making a new life for himself, in exile. He was fifty-four years old. The cause was lost. He would never set

foot in America again. Yet his narrow escape had left Benjamin fortified, more sure of himself than ever. Despite having spent several
weeks "exposed to the tropical sun . . . utterly without a shelter or
a change of clothes," he had suffered not "one minute's indispo-
sition nor despondency," Benjamin assured his sister. Instead, he
was "rather pleased by the feeling of triumph in disappointing the
malice of my enemies."

12

"Into the Light"

FAR FROM CONVINCING AMERICAN JEWS THEY HAD found a secure and stable home, the Civil War disrupted what had to that point seemed a general shrugging acceptance of them as equal members of American society. It would have been hard for communal leaders and laymen alike to ignore that public expressions of bigotry against Jews had risen to a pitch unprecedented in American history. Grant's Order No. 11 expelling Jews from his military department was particularly unsettling. Though the general labored with some success to woo Jewish voters in the 1868 presidential election, then appointed several to top positions, many Jews found it difficult to shake the sense of vulnerability the decree had evoked. America had seemed a more promising haven than Europe, but what if that was wrong? The horror of seeing their claims to full equality called into question—and at just the moment when the abolition of slavery promised equality to Black Americans—helped fuel a lingering sense of insecurity that rippled out far from American shores. In 1912, Max Nordau, the Hungarian-born cofounder with Theodor Herzl of the World Zionist Congress, cited Grant's half-century-old expulsion order in arguing for the necessity of a separate Jewish homeland. The decree was evidence, Nordau said, of "how thin the floor between Jews and Hell was (and most probably still is) even in enlightened free America . . . What an object lesson to Jewish optimists."

Most American Jews in the postwar period simply wanted to move on. They tried to forget a conflict most had opposed in the first place partly out of a suspicion that the upheaval would not serve them well, a suspicion events seemed to confirm. In 1869, the *Jewish Messenger* complained that the observation of Decoration Day (forerunner of Memorial Day) "keeps up the feelings of war time—and cannot in this serve a good purpose—all recollections of hostilities during a civil war should, if possible, be obliterated."

Early histories of Jews and the Civil War largely ignored the darker aspects of the conflict, emphasizing, for example, the overturning of Grant's order as a moment of Jewish accomplishment rather than the order itself as a source of lingering pain, even trauma. Such starry-eyed interpretations seemed all the more necessary when it became clear that the explosion of wartime antisemitism would not go away with the return of peace. The themes of 1860s propaganda—that Jews were disloyal scavengers, only interested in devising new ways of plundering and profiteering off the sacrifices of hardworking native-born Americans—reappeared and made life increasingly unpleasant for those Jews who had lived through the war and for the many more who would arrive in America in the decades to come.

In 1859, a year before his appearance in a bitterly divided Congress, Morris Jacob Raphall published a short book, *The Path to Immortality*, about the Jewish conception of the afterlife. For all his scholarly accomplishments and robust defense of Orthodox Judaism, Raphall himself would be remembered by posterity for a single sermon, his "Bible View of Slavery," delivered in January 1861. The sermon had not staved off war. Nor had it halted the rise of Reform Judaism, which many flocked to in the coming years precisely because it did not ask them to espouse such outdated ideas as that there was nothing wrong with one man holding another as property. Instead of offering a vision of enlightened tradition guiding Jews through the wrenching social issues of the time, Raphall's sermon served as a warning of the perils of hewing too closely to inherited dogmas and millennia-old texts as a guide to the politics of the present. Raphall's health, already faltering during the Civil War, gave out soon after it ended. He retired in late 1865 and died three years later. Memories of his infamous sermon likely muted the commemorations. Even Isaac Mayer Wise, who had refused to denounce slavery during the war, observed that Raphall's defense of "an inhuman institution" had been "a great blunder."

Five years after fleeing the proslavery mob in Baltimore for refuge in Philadelphia, David Einhorn, the fiercest critic of Raphall's sermon, moved to New York and became rabbi of a Reform temple. Einhorn rejoiced that Jews could finally live freely in a land that no longer forced them to be complicit in the enslavement of others. The newly reunited republic stood on the brink of an unprecedented era of progress, he thought. Yet even with the blemish of slavery removed from the Union's "shining banner of redemption," the nation still fell short of its world-redeeming potential. After the Civil War, Einhorn pivoted from criticizing slavery to denouncing Gilded Age materialism and inequality. Observing that the architecture of synagogues had grown increasingly ornate—as in the over-the-top, Moorish-style temple dedicated by his rival Wise's Cincinnati congregation in 1866—Einhorn warned that as the buildings grew more elaborate, the worship inside seemed more hollow. American Jews "not only worship the golden calf," Einhorn scoffed, "but pick up the pieces of the broken tablets and try to sell them." As they grew more prosperous and comfortable, they risked losing their souls.

The final years of Einhorn's life were some of the calmest he had known. In 1869, a conference of Reform rabbis in Philadelphia adopted Einhorn's statement of the movement's principles, as well as his proposal to abolish all rules excluding women from rituals and full rights in marriage and divorce. Einhorn's ideas formed the basis of the enormously influential Pittsburgh Platform of 1885, in which Reform leaders agreed it was the responsibility of all Jews to "participate in the great task of modern times, to solve, on the basis of justice and righteousness, the problems presented by the contrasts and evils of the present organization of society." Einhorn's commitment to social justice became a central pillar of American Reform Judaism and laid the basis for later generations to see a commitment to social justice as an essential part of what it means to be a Jew.

Yet the irascible rabbi had never fully felt at home in America, a land he found culturally and intellectually shallow. Einhorn did not enjoy traveling the country, as Wise did, and had always remained an outsider. He had none of Wise's flair for showmanship—Einhorn dismissed his rival as the "Barnum of the Jewish pulpit"—a vital ingredient for success in late nineteenth-century America. He longed for Germany and still believed it might have a crucial role to play in the future of the Jewish people and religion. "As proud as I am of my adopted citizenship," Einhorn said in his last sermon in 1879, "I will never forget that the old home is the land of thinkers, presently the foremost land of culture, and above all the land of Mendelssohn, the birthplace of Reform Judaism . . . If you sever from Reform the German spirit or—what amounts to the same thing—the German language, you will have torn it from its native soil and the lovely flower must wilt." As it turned out, Einhorn's stubborn allegiance to his native land would prove to have been misplaced.

Though he personally felt ill at ease in America, Einhorn recognized that the country offered the most congenial home the Jews had yet found. Yet he had always held that Judaism could not survive in America—and would not deserve to—unless it remained committed to the ideals of justice and equality that he believed lay at the heart of the ancient tradition. Stripping everything else away made it easier to appreciate what really mattered: loving one's neighbor, whatever their race or religion, as oneself. In a sermon delivered a year before he died, Einhorn surveyed all that his fellow Jews had achieved in the United States and all they had left to do:

> Here in America, the sons of Judah are no longer pushed around like strangers. Full of strength, they step forth out of darkness into the light, out of slavery into freedom. Half a century ago, they were treated like slaves . . . Now they sit and consult with the highest officials of the land and fully participate in its culture. Here in our great republic, they raise their heads, freely and proudly. So many of us suffered under Pharaoh-like laws in our old homeland. We had to crawl before the police . . . and here we live in proud palaces. And we will be even greater here, if we bring about an aristocracy of the spirit, rather than an aristocracy of gold.

After the carnage, Southern Jews were as resentful over the end of slavery as their neighbors, perhaps, for their own particular reasons, even more worried about what it might mean for the future. The mere existence of Black bondage, whether they had directly profited from it or not, had eased Southern Jews' acceptance into antebellum society. They feared its abolition would upset the status quo and make their lives in the South more insecure.

Those who had directly profited by owning slaves gave them

up altogether unwillingly. "I, who believe in the institution of slavery, regret deeply its being abolished," wrote Eleanor Cohen, the daughter of a South Carolina dentist, forced to postpone her marriage when Columbia burned. "I am accustomed to have them wait on me, and I dislike white servants very much." Solomon Cohen of Savannah, whose son Gratz died in battle just before Appomattox, wrote a letter a few weeks later, addressed to his sister-in-law, Emma Mordecai—recently stopped by the "blackest man" she ever saw on the road outside Richmond—noting that slavery had benefited the white master and the Black slave alike: by lending the former "an elevation of sentiment and ease and dignity of manners" and raising the latter "from barbarism," helping him "develop the small amounts of intellect with which he is endowed." Jacob Cardozo, the Southern Jewish journalist and economist who had argued before the war that an excess of kindness shown by masters toward their slaves was the primary threat to the slave system, lamented that abolition had brought a total reversal in social relations: "The owner of two hundred to five hundred slaves, with a princely income, has not only to submit to the most degraded employments, but he frequently cannot obtain them. In some instances, he has to drive a cart, or attend a retail grocery, while he may have to obey the orders of an ignorant and coarse menial. There is something unnatural in this reverse of position—something revolting to my sense of propriety in this social degradation."

For the next century and more, memoirs, family histories, and other nostalgia-tinted chronicles of Southern Jewish history would emphasize stories of the loyalty allegedly shown to former Jewish masters by the people they had claimed as property. Biographers of the Lehman brothers would relate that a woman once enslaved by Mayer Lehman followed him to New York after the war as evidence of his kindly treatment. Raphael J. Moses, the Georgia "peach man" who gathered supplies for Longstreet's army, saw forty-six of his forty-seven slaves steal away during the war and in the days that followed. The only one who remained is the one Moses ensured posterity would know about: "Old London," an elderly man who, informed by Moses that Lincoln had set him free, supposedly replied that he had seen Moses buy him at auction and would not abandon him until Lincoln personally repaid the cost of his purchase.

Like other white Americans, Southern Jews enjoyed hearing and repeating these flattering tales of servants refusing to budge from their owners' sides. Within families, however, stories circulated privately that hinted at the not-so-subtle forms of coercion behind such relationships, even into the era of emancipation. While I was working on this book, a friend shared with me an oral history interview conducted in the 1970s with her great-great-grandmother, a New Yorker born in Louisville, Kentucky, in 1881. At the interviewer's prompting, the ninety-six-year-old reads aloud from a letter her cousin sent her concerning a woman once owned by their mutual grandfather, a Jewish immigrant from Hesse and coproprietor with his brothers of one of the largest men's clothing stores in Louisville:

> Our grandfather bought a little seven year old slave girl and she was raised with his eleven children. When she was a young woman—this was right after the war—Grandma taught her housework and cooking (or the other house-servants did). Then one day Grandpa heard that some of her relatives were nearby, across the [Ohio] river, so he asked her if she wouldn't like to go visit them. Of course, she said yes. So he had her driven to where they were. They immediately had her marry one of them, and she gave birth to a boy, Sam.
>
> When she was gone a year, all the children wanted her back— they all loved her. So one day, your mother took a horse and rode across the river to where she was, told Mammy Julie, "I've come for you," took the baby, and rode off with him, knowing that his mother would follow as he had to be fed. Which of course she did.

"She was quite a gal, my mother," the woman being interviewed laughs. Julie and Sam remained in the family's service and followed the next generation to New York.

———

Stories about doggedly loyal servants and the supposed harmony of antebellum Southern life formed part of a package of useful myths and half-truths, a shared civil religion for the war-torn South: the Lost Cause. Southern Jews did not have a difficult time accepting the idea of a nation subjugated by the strong arm of a tyrant and exiled, at least for the moment, from its rightful destiny, yet fated someday to seize it once again. Some named their children after Jefferson Davis and Robert E. Lee. Moses Ezekiel—son of a slave-owning Richmond family and the first Jewish graduate of the Virginia Military Institute—crafted many of the most prominent Confederate monuments put up in the decades after the war, including the towering memorial in Arlington National Cemetery, which after a prolonged legal battle was finally removed in 2024. The base the statue rested on was left intact so as to avoid disturbing nearby graves, including that of its Jewish sculptor, whose descendants had called for the statue's removal.

Embracing the Lost Cause was, in part, a strategic maneuver to head off attempts to blame Jews for the South's defeat. In 1866, the Hebrew Ladies' Memorial Association of Richmond sought funds to build a monument to those Jews whose blood had been spilled "in defense of this glorious cause." The ladies were keen to counter allegations, common during the war, that Jews had stayed out of the fight. "When the malicious tongue of slander, ever so ready to assail Israel, shall be raised against us," the group's fundraising letter stated, "then, with a feeling of mournful pride, will we point to this monument and say, '*There* is our reply.'" The funds went toward surrounding thirty graves of Confederate Jewish soldiers with a wrought-iron fence featuring interlocking swords and laurel wreaths between posts of stacked rifles and the furled Stars and Bars, topped by rebel soldiers' caps. It remains there today, one of the only Jewish military graveyards outside Israel.

At least for the moment, the malicious tongues of slander remained mostly quiet. The Hebrew Ladies' fears were not immediately realized. Religious differences seemed to have melted in the crucible of shared suffering and sacrifice. The enfranchisement of Black men, backed by the presence of federal troops, made Southern Jews important allies for resentful whites. A New Orleans–based correspondent for a Jewish paper in Germany blamed a handful of "nasty voices" for having taken advantage of the "passionate turmoil" of wartime. Now that it was over, he wrote, "public opinion is doing justice to the citizens of the Israelitish faith again." In the decade after Appomattox, Christians contributed to Jewish causes like the construction of synagogues and hailed "our Jewish friends" for sponsoring new churches in turn. Zebulon Vance, a former Confederate governor of North Carolina, delivered a speech hundreds of times across the country praising the Jews—that "scattered nation," as the speech's title had it—as "our spiritual fathers, the authors of our morals, the founders of our civilization." A new constitution adopted by the Reconstruction government of North Carolina in 1868 finally removed one of the nation's last remaining restrictions on Jews holding public office. (New Hampshire would finally do so a decade later.)

Grateful for being included among the South's privileged class of whites, some Jews even embraced the Lost Cause mythology so fully that they served in the white militias that used brute force to reclaim political power in the former Confederate states: beating, kidnapping, or murdering insufficiently deferential Black people along with their white allies. Benjamin Franklin Jonas, a son of Abraham Lincoln's old Illinois friend Abraham Jonas, became a leading anti-Reconstruction politician in Louisiana and likely helped organize a crowd of armed citizens that in 1879 violently took over the state supreme court. In South Carolina's bitter and violent 1876 gubernatorial campaign, Confederate veteran Edwin Moise commanded the paramilitary Red Shirts, which used armed intimidation to wrest the state back from the Republicans. There were even Jewish members of the first Ku Klux Klan. Bernard Baruch, a close adviser to President Franklin Roosevelt and the son of a Confederate veteran, recalled in his memoir that as a child he once came across a Klan robe and hood among his father's clothes. To Bernard and his brother, realizing their father belonged to that "heroic band fighting to free the South from the debaucheries of carpetbag rule . . . exalted him in our youthful eyes."

Just as joining the ranks of the rebellion had been both an expression of earnestly held political views and a reflection of the allegiance Southern Jews felt to the section that had welcomed them in, night riding with the early Klan and other "vigilance" organizations in the postwar period offered a way for Jews in the defeated South to declare that they truly belonged. It was a white man's country, and they were white men. They would fight to keep things that way.

While many Southern Jews who were either born in the region or settled there before the war saw the topsy-turvy social and political world of Reconstruction as a threat to their position, newer arrivals from Europe and the North often considered the chaos an opportunity. Those who had avoided the South because they opposed slavery now had less reason to stay away, and the region sorely needed the commercial expertise and connections that Jews could provide.

The extent of the ruination in the South remains hard to imagine. Whole towns and cities had been burnt to ashes, rail lines ripped up, a generation of potential business and civic leaders cut down in their prime. Farmers needed capital for seeds, fertilizer, equipment, and—after emancipation—labor, but the region was starved for cash. Markets were nonexistent. Shopkeepers had empty shelves and no way to replenish them. In the North, meanwhile, warehouses were stuffed with goods produced to feed the wartime boom. The decimated Southern economy needed new systems of credit for getting crops to market and goods to people's farms and homes, and to get money circulating through the region. Small-town Jewish merchandisers, many of whom had only recently set down their peddlers' packs, saw they had a vital role to play. They helped develop a system in which storekeepers purchased the rights to crops that had not yet been planted in the ground. That gave the farmer capital with which to buy goods, pay his newly freed labor-ers, and invest in planting. The guarantee of future crop deliveries gave the rural storekeeper collateral with which to seek credit from New York financial circles; in the case of a Jewish storekeeper, those circles often involved fellow Jews or even family members. By acting as well-placed middlemen between Northern capitalists and South-ern farmers, many Jewish merchants—both new arrivals and long-standing residents who had been running their crossroads stores for years without much to show for it—found immense success in the postwar Southern economy. While other whites continued to lament the end of slavery and the downfall of the Confederacy, Jews were planning for the future. By 1880, Jewish merchants owned between half and three-quarters of all general stores in the Deep South.

But that very success was what turned some whites against the Jews as the embodiment of all their woes. When the harvest came in under expectations—as it often did in the South after the war—farmers who had put their land up as collateral had to surrender their deeds to the shopkeepers, some of whom built up extensive holdings of farms seized from debtors. Once-humble Jewish mer-chants often did better in the postwar Southern economy than either white planters or non-Jewish Northerners who lacked their extensive networks to draw upon for credit. Jews had been welcome in the South so long as they did not compete economically with other whites. Now they represented a specter even scarier than competition: domination.

Jewish merchants also began to draw the ire of Christian neighbors because many traded openly with the formerly enslaved. Accustomed, back in Europe, to doing business with people from diverse backgrounds, Jews had less of a problem than other whites in moving to largely Black neighborhoods and opening stores. They did so, both near rural plantations and in urban Black neighborhoods in Atlanta and Savannah, Richmond and Norfolk. In 1901, W. E. B. Du Bois noted that Jewish merchants "do a great many things that the white men of the South would not do. They have no objection at all to calling the negro 'mister,' and they are pleasant to him . . . They keep the things he wants in the store." They also often extended credit to Black customers, which most white merchants refused to do.

A few Jews made further trouble for themselves by openly speaking out on behalf of Black equality. Franklin Moses Jr., the son of a prominent Jewish lawyer in Charleston, served in the Confederate Army but underwent a dramatic change of heart after the war. Elected as Republican governor of Reconstruction-era South Carolina, Moses sought to build what his biographer calls "America's first black-Jewish alliance." To counter the murderous Klan, Moses formed a fourteen-thousand-man militia composed largely of former slaves. Moses was not only in favor of political and civil rights for Blacks, but social equality. He forced the integration of the state university, and he gambled, smoked cigars, and drank champagne with Black friends, editors, ministers, and politicians. Though Moses had been raised an Episcopalian, contemporaries associated him with the faith of his father and derided him both as an "Israelite," with a typical "thrifty eye to the main chance," and as a scalawag, a Southerner who supported Reconstruction. Moses's Jewish relatives in the South changed their last name to avoid association with a leader considered by many whites a traitor to his race.

Fueled by economic grievances and persistent doubts about Southern Jews' commitment to white supremacy, the ever-present antisemitism lingering just below the surface of Southern life exploded once again into more explicit displays of bigotry. The relative harmony of the immediate postwar years proved illusory. After all, expressions of affection by Southern Christians for their Jewish "friends" were only necessary because, as even Zebulon Vance had acknowledged in his "Scattered Nation" speech, an "unreasonable prejudice" against Jews remained all too common in the region. As racial tensions mounted, the "nasty voices" of the war years returned. Yet if the outburst of antisemitism during the war had been largely rhetorical, the new wave of persecution could be downright deadly.

By the end of the century, Southern Jews were less often members of night-riding posses than they were their victims. So long as Southern Jews respected the white population's rigid racial hierarchy, they would be left alone. But those who stepped out of line were duly punished.

Samuel Fleishman, a native of Bavaria who had lived in the Florida Panhandle for more than twenty years, ran a small general store in his hometown of Marianna. He was known for hiring and trading with Black people and in 1869 was overheard expressing support for federal efforts to protect Blacks from white supremacist terror. Warned to leave town, Fleishman obeyed. But after aimlessly wandering the countryside for a week, he decided to return to his family. Fleishman's bullet-riddled body was found by the roadside. A local paper argued that he had it coming, for the Jewish merchant had "identified himself with the Radical party [the Republicans] for the purpose of getting the trade of the colored people."

Fleishman's killing was not a one-off incident. A year earlier, Klansmen had murdered S. A. Bierfield, a Russian Jewish immigrant in Franklin, Tennessee, along with the Black clerk he had hired to help out in his dry-goods store. Bierfield had made his liberal racial views and Republican sympathies known, and he paid the price. Even a record of service in the Confederate Army was not enough to protect isolated Jews from meeting a violent end. In 1870, the badly decomposed corpse of Samuel Friedman was discovered under a tree trunk beside a river in Tennessee. He had been shot in the back of the head and his throat had been cut.

In the late 1880s and early 1890s, a severe agricultural depression swelled support across the South and the Midwest for an agrarian protest movement backed by indebted farmers who suspected their dire economic circumstances were the fault of hidden and powerful forces manipulating events to their disadvantage. Unsurprisingly, the Populist movement was accompanied by anti-Jewish invective and in some places violence. In 1892, self-styled Whitecappers—possibly named after the hoods worn by the then defunct Klan—terrorized Jewish merchants in Mississippi and Louisiana, especially those who rented out to Black sharecroppers tracts of land received in foreclosures against white farmers. The members of one club complained that they had been "brought to the verge of ruin by European and Wall Street gold-bugs, backed by a corrupt class who dominate the ballot box, the legislature, and congress." They were joining together to seize "control of the negro labor, which is by right ours," as well as to take revenge on the "accursed Jews." Gangs of impoverished debtors riddled Jewish-owned stores with bullets and posted notices ordering the proprietors to leave the area "under penalty of death." Several complied, including one wealthy Jewish merchant in rural Mississippi, the owner of some four hundred farms, most acquired through foreclosures, who sold his land and fled to New Orleans.

To be sure, most Southern whites opposed violence against Jews. Upper-class business and civic leaders found the presence of Jews in the South advantageous and feared that lawlessness would deter new immigrants from settling in the region. Governors, mayors, sheriffs, and town councils condemned violence against Jews as an illegitimate and irresponsible form of the vigilantism that, when directed at Blacks, they otherwise condoned. In many cases, though not all, the perpetrators were identified, arrested, charged, and convicted.

Yet even if outright violence against Jews enjoyed little support among gentiles, Jewish life in the South was growing less comfortable. Disparaging remarks about Jews became more common in the press, as well as reports of incidents like the 1893 eviction of a Richmond woman solely because she was Jewish. To Southern whites, the Jews in their midst—both isolated peddlers and successful urban merchants—represented everything that was insidious and threatening about the modern age. Jewish merchants and creditors embodied an emerging form of capitalism that had ensnared millions in cycles of debt and robbed them of not only their livelihoods but their sense of ownership over their own lives. Such economic grievances activated older forms of hatred and resentment that helped white Southerners make sense of their changed world. Racially suspect and religiously nonconforming, the Jews' unique position in Southern society challenged the binary premises of Jim Crow–style segregation. No matter how much Southern Jews tried to adapt to local customs—and in the wake of mob violence, they tried even harder—it was never enough to silence suspicion about which side of the color line they belonged on.

Within the first few decades after the Civil War, the South went from being the part of the country most friendly to Jews to the least, a place where Jews, as many had long feared, took their place alongside semifree Black people as hated outsiders in the white Southerners' midst, an enemy within. For some, they were even worse. "The lowest, cheapest thing on this earth aint a nigger: it's a jew," a politician says in William Faulkner's 1931 novel *Sanctuary*. "We need laws against them. Drastic laws."

In the absence of such laws, white Southerners took matters into their own hands. The wave of violence against Southern Jews culminated in the lynching of Leo Frank in 1915. After a jury, on little evidence, convicted the twenty-nine-year-old in the strangulation of Mary Phagan, a young Christian girl who worked in the Atlanta pencil factory he managed, the governor of Georgia commuted Frank's death sentence to life imprisonment. A few weeks later, a mob calling itself the Knights of Mary Phagan—including a former governor of the state—broke into Frank's prison, drove him down some back roads, and hanged him from an oak tree. Three months later, the Knights gathered at Stone Mountain in Georgia and declared themselves the second coming of the Ku Klux Klan. The new formation would prove far more hostile to Jews than its post–Civil War predecessor. The Frank case was not, as one scholar has claimed, "the aberration that proves the rule" of a general acceptance of Jews in the South. It confirmed that a half-century after slavery's abolition, something fundamental had changed.

———

For all their political differences, Ernestine Rose and Judah Benjamin had much in common. They both avoided identifying with Jews or Judaism, yet found they could never fully escape the faith and people they had renounced. Partly because of their Jewishness, both felt isolated within their respective movements. After the Civil War, both felt compelled to leave their adopted homeland, evidently seeing no future for themselves in what it had become. And both lived out their final years in London.

Rose's health declined through the latter years of the war. She was tired from decades on the road, and her acrimonious exchange about Judaism with the editor of the *Boston Investigator* may have deepened her exhaustion. After the war, the women's movement split over whether it was a higher priority to enfranchise Black men or white women. Rose was caught in the middle between longtime friends and allies. Reformers like Wendell Phillips, Frederick Douglass, and Abby Foster advocated for universal male suffrage as the only way to begin to make right the suffering of the newly freed slaves. Elizabeth Cady Stanton and Susan B. Anthony led the women's splinter group. Occasionally, the women's side made blatantly racist appeals, attacking not only Black men but the foreign-born for cutting the citizenship line. In Stanton and Anthony's newspaper, *The Revolution*, one article demanded that "the Jews and Chinese" be prohibited from entering the United States, because "great harm accrues to us from the vast accession of voracious, knavish, cunning traders, especially Jews . . . a race of mere blood-suckers." The other side was hardly better. At a meeting shortly after the end of the war, Rose listened from the stage as Wendell Phillips called on the audience to "trample mistaken Judaism under one foot." When it came to be Rose's turn to speak, she was nowhere to be found. She had "left the platform," an organizer explained, "because she said the subject was exhausted." Rose did not appear in public for more than a year, an unprecedented gap in her career.

Rose wanted suffrage extended to all, white and Black women as well as Black men. She opposed the Fourteenth and Fifteenth Amendments ensuring Black men's access to the ballot for falling short of that goal. That aligned her with Stanton and Anthony, who argued that women had been told to wait long enough. Rose never invoked the racist rhetoric her allies did, but for one exception. On that occasion, an 1869 speech, she complained about those being given the rights of citizenship before women: "We might commence by calling the Chinaman a man and a brother, or the Hottentot, or the Calmuck, or the Indian, the idiot or the criminal, but where shall we stop? They will bring all these in before us, and then they will bring in the babies—the male babies." The sole example of Rose ever using such language, the comment likely reflected the depths of her fatigue.

A few weeks later, Rose and her husband, William, decided to return to England, where they had met more than three decades earlier. The split within the women's movement and the failure of her fellow atheists to denounce the antisemitism of the *Investigator*'s editor apparently disaffected Rose from American reform circles. She may have doubted, even in the wake of slavery's abolition, that the nation she had fought to improve since her 1836 arrival would ever truly embrace the ideals that had motivated her activism. For some reason, Rose chose to accept full American citizenship mere days before her departure. The step was unnecessary, as she had technically gained the status through William's 1845 naturalization, but apparently Rose wanted to do so on her own terms before leaving the country. She also, before embarking, sat for an interview with the *Hebrew Leader*, which described Rose as "an ardent adherent of moral Judaism," despite her atheist beliefs, and deeply interested in the fate of her fellow coreligionists, a daughter of Israel who still spoke fondly of her father, the rabbi.

The Roses set sail on a spring day in 1869, with Ernestine clutching flowers that friends and well-wishers had given her. The couple traveled to various spa towns in Europe, where Rose was pleased to find both her "name and heretical proclivities" known. Taking the waters did wonders for her health, and within a few years Rose was able to engage in public affairs, writing letters and attending reform conventions in London, where she and William settled. The freethought *National Reformer* praised her return to the stump: "The good old lady, with her white curls, her erect, healthy looking body, her clear, distinct voice, her occasional quaint phrases, her stern denomination, and her real genius as a speaker, won from those present a far more hearty and lengthy tribute of applause than was accorded to any one else."

The Roses briefly returned to the United States in 1873, before Ernestine's health again deteriorated, leaving her stricken in bed for weeks. They decided to go back to England. Ernestine followed from afar as Americans commemorated the centennial of the Revolution, writing to Susan B. Anthony that "we must reassert in 1876 what 1776 so gloriously proclaimed and call upon the lawmakers and the law-breakers to carry that declaration to its logical consistency by giving woman the right of representation in the government."

In 1882, William Rose took a fall in the street and died on his way to the hospital. Ernestine was devastated, yet denied herself the usual consolations. "As her long avowed unbelief in a future state forbids her the prospect of meeting him in the future," one acquaintance wrote another, "they say she is very wretched." When Anthony visited Rose the following year, she was stunned by her friend's condition: "It is very sad to see so great and grand an intellect . . . so incapable of making the *best* of the *inevitable*—accepting it cheerfully." Anthony begged Rose to return to America, but Rose did not think she was strong enough to endure a long sea journey. She wanted to be buried alongside William in Highgate Cemetery, indeed, in the same grave.

Rose outlived her husband by a decade, spending much of her time in Brighton, with a sweeping view of the sea. She liked to sit in a chair by the window and feed sparrows or hand out coins to beggars and buskers. She read the newspapers and kept up with public issues. One visitor reported that Rose "still retains her keen interest in all Liberal movements, and her fine face is lighted up when she speaks of America, of which she is proud to own herself a citizen, and recalls the memories of the days when her voice was a trumpet-call to the soldiers of freedom." She told friends she worried that Christian missionaries would try to take advantage of her helplessness and claim her as a last-minute convert. When the end neared, she asked a friend to stay with her to ensure that did not happen. "A woman who ventured to speak against slavery in the slave States," the *London Freethinker* commented, "is little likely to quail on her death-bed before the bogey pictures of a Christian god or a Christian devil."

Ernestine Rose died on August 4, 1892, at eighty-two years old. She was buried, as she requested, in William's grave. One historian has observed that throughout her long and unconventional life Rose sought "a series of alternative communities"—socialism, freethought, abolitionism, women's rights—as a replacement for the ancestral one she had sloughed off at such a young age. Yet in her will Rose left nearly all her property to her Jewish relatives, suggesting she had not only been in communication with them but perhaps achieved some kind of final reconciliation with her own Jewish past.

Rose's influence on American reform movements was forgotten nearly as soon as she died, in fact, even before. She was sidelined in early accounts of the women's rights struggle, including those written by her close friends, Stanton and Anthony. If Rose "had been less honest and conscientious" about her atheism, the journalist Sara Underwood wrote in 1876, "she would today occupy a far higher position in public favor than she does." The *Boston Investigator*, with whose editor Rose had eventually reconciled, observed that Rose was neglected by the movement she helped start because she "is not a Christian, and for this reason is not appreciated by her sex as her merits deserved." Her insistent criticisms of organized religion, meanwhile, proved embarrassing for early American Jewish historians, who mostly left Rose out of their celebratory accounts. "I doubt whether one American Jew in ten thousand has ever heard of her," one journalist commented in the *Forward* in 1927. Only with the reconsideration of abolitionists during the civil rights movement did Rose begin to get the recognition she deserved.

"To enlighten and free all the slaves," Underwood had written in 1876, "that has been the object of Mrs. Rose's life and labors. Slaves of race, slaves of faith, slaves of sex—it mattered not—to each she preached from the same text, 'Knowledge—Liberty.'"

———

Nearing the end of his life, Judah Benjamin told an English journalist who wanted to pen his biography that he would "much prefer that no 'Life,' not even a Magazine article, should ever be written about me." Though he must have known that wish would go unfulfilled, he did everything he could to thwart any attempt. Just as Benjamin burned what he could before fleeing Richmond in 1865, he did so again shortly before his 1884 death.

He had arrived in London in the summer of 1865, fresh from surviving a string of calamities and shipwrecks, with barely a penny to his name. Even the $20,000 he made from the sale of cotton bales he had sent ahead to Liverpool was soon lost in the collapse of the firm with which he had deposited the much-needed funds. But this was hardly his first time starting over. Three decades earlier he had set foot in New Orleans in a similarly deprived state, and before long had climbed to the highest ranks of Southern society. Benjamin was at his best when he had something to strive for. And he did have one advantage: he was already a Crown subject on account of his birth in a British colony in the Caribbean.

He stayed in London for a week, then took a ship to France and saw his family in Paris for the first time since before the war. John Slidell, his old New Orleans friend and political mentor, who had served as Confederate minister to France, offered to connect Benjamin with banking interests in the city, but Benjamin decided instead to return to London and take up his old profession as a lawyer. Remaining in Paris may only have reminded him of the pain and embarrassment his marriage had brought him.

Going back to school, starting out at the bottom, hustling for clients—all to don the English barrister's horsehair wig—was hardly an obvious or easy choice for Benjamin. The imperial capital's legal establishment was even more elite and insular than the Southern planter class. Few advocates in the capital were, like him, the Caribbean-born sons of small-time shopkeepers, and few were Jews. The barriers to success were higher for an outsider in Victorian London than they had been in antebellum New Orleans. Yet sympathy for Benjamin's Confederate past may have smoothed his path. He mingled in aristocratic circles, sought advice from Benjamin Disraeli, and dined with William Gladstone. Describing himself as "a Political Exile, proscribed for my loyalty to my own State," Benjamin skipped quickly through the customary training for a barrister. He was admitted to practice law after only six months of study, rather than the usual three years. As he had once done with his compendium of Louisiana civil court cases, Benjamin labored overtime to produce an impressive thousand-page tome on English commercial law, widely celebrated at the time and still studied today.

The hours were long and the work grueling. Benjamin saved money by subsisting on bread and cheese and dining in cheap restaurants. "I am as much interested in my profession as when I first commenced it as a boy," he wrote to a friend. It was a welcome and pleasing sensation, he reassured his sister, "to have no harassing anxieties to disturb my labors."

Whatever obstacles he faced in his new life, Benjamin knew things could have turned out very differently. As he mingled with "a crowd of titled and fashionable guests" at the opulent country home of a landed baron, his former boss, Jefferson Davis, languished in federal prison. Two days after arriving in London, Benjamin wrote a long, emotional letter to Varina Davis, justifying his not turning back when he heard of the first family's arrest by Union forces. He assured her that he was already working to raise money to help her get by. He was eager to show that his desperate, peril-filled escape to England was neither dishonorable nor proof of insufficient loyalty to the Davises and to the cause. "During this whole time," Benjamin vowed, "I have been incessantly harassed by the most poignant anxiety both on your account and his."

Despite his efforts, those Southerners who had criticized Benjamin during the war hated him even more afterward. His escape and subsequent success seemed to confirm their long-standing suspicions. Louis Wigfall, a Texan who fled to London to raise funds to renew the rebellion, scoffed to a friend that Benjamin "has turned out to be an Englishman." He had never really been a Southerner.

Though he refused to disavow either slavery or secession, the self-exiled Benjamin tried to talk about the Confederacy and the Civil War as little as possible. He gave no public speeches explaining his view of the rebellion and the causes of its defeat, and offered only a few stray comments on postwar politics in the United States. In November 1865, he wrote to an American friend that if the Southern states were left to figure out the problems of Reconstruction on their own, the future of the restored Union could be bright. But "if external influences are brought to bear on the negro and influence his ignorant fancy with wild dreams of social and political equality, I shudder for the bitter future which is in store for my unhappy country."

Benjamin undoubtedly meant every word. Two years later, when a visitor told him about the efforts of the Ku Klux Klan to restore white supremacy in the South, Benjamin reportedly borrowed money to give the visitor so the white-cloaked vigilantes could purchase horses and guns. Yet even though he may have been eager to convince old acquaintances that he was still devoted to the cause, by then his attention was already focused on a new life and career. When Varina Davis replied to Benjamin's offer to help her and her husband "in any way, by any sacrifice," by asking him to publicly refute various lies and slanders that had appeared in the press, Benjamin demurred, offering his opinion that it "would do more harm than good."

Benjamin's lifelong insistence on not dwelling on the past had never proven more useful. In 1868, when the newly freed Jefferson Davis, along with Varina, traveled to London seeking business opportunities, Benjamin hosted the former president at his club. Varina found her old friend "happier than I had ever seen him." Benjamin indulged Davis in one long conversation about the war—Davis may have resented his former aide's flight—but then made it clear he preferred not to talk about it. "In speaking of his grief over our defeat," Varina recalled, "he said that the power of dismissing any painful memory had served him well after the fall of the Confederacy."

As so often before, Benjamin's labors eventually paid off. He again rose to the top of his profession, admitted in 1872 as Queen's Counsel, an honor rarely conferred on outsiders to the legal establishment, or so quickly on anyone. He appeared frequently before the Privy Council, where his command of various systems of foreign law made him especially effective on cases involving the colonies. By the end of the decade, Benjamin was raking in the equivalent today of more than $4 million per year. But that required him to work late into the night, "a necessity against which his whole soul revolted," as one friend later explained. He was still supporting his family in Paris and his sisters in New Orleans.

Approaching seventy years old, Benjamin finally slowed down. He allowed himself to enjoy the pleasures of London society and even vacationed in the Pyrenees with his family. In 1880, Benjamin decided to retire and spend his remaining days with the wife with whom he had not lived for more than a brief stretch in nearly forty years. As he had once renovated both the Bellechasse plantation and the finest home in Washington to try to appeal to Natalie's taste for the finer things, now he built a lavish mansion on one of the great boulevards of Georges-Eugène Haussmann's newly modernized Paris.

That May, however, Benjamin suffered grievous injuries to his head, shoulder, and arm when he fell while jumping from a moving tram. He never fully recovered, and he died on May 6, 1884. Natalie invited a Catholic priest to administer last rites to her husband, even though he had always refused to be converted, and had him buried at Père Lachaise, in the plot belonging to their daughter's French husband's family, listed under the name Philippe Benjamin, which only she had ever called him. Benjamin's unsettled relationship with his own Jewishness followed him into the grave.

***

As in the South, Northern Jews became victims of their own success, or rather of others' resentment of it. Some German-speaking Jews who a quarter-century earlier had arrived penniless and desperate now controlled vast industrial and financial empires. They built mansions in the fanciest neighborhoods of American cities and sought admission to the highest ranks of Gilded Age society. In an age of fierce class conflict, punctuated by two devastating economic depressions (starting in 1873 and 1893), western farmers and urban workers increasingly saw Jewish businessmen as symbols of the capitalism that had made a few rich at the expense of everyone else. Patricians in the East, meanwhile, resented upwardly mobile Jewish parvenus for presumptuously claiming a place at the top of the social heap they plainly did not deserve. Americans claimed to value the traits that made Jewish success possible—ambition, thrift, diligence, a talent for business—but they also distrusted them. Growing rancor toward Jews offered a way for Americans of all classes to process their conflicted feelings about the radical changes afoot in the land, especially industrialization, urbanization, and mass immigration.

The last third of the nineteenth century saw the fairly welcoming atmosphere that Jews had found in America for more than two hundred years turn into something darker and more foreboding. In 1867, a consortium of fire insurance companies in New York

announced they would no longer sell policies to Jews, a population of "swindlers" who, they claimed, habitually committed fraud
by burning down their own buildings. Following the model for
group action first devised a decade earlier during the uproar over
the abduction of Edgar Mortara, Jews across the country organized
meetings and lodged protests with the companies and with elected
officials. The display of such bigotry so soon after the war was a
warning, the *Hebrew Leader* commented: "Let us not indulge in
too secure tranquility—the days of religious proscription and persecution may be brought back for us, even in this country."

The fervor died down only when the insurance companies made
clear that the ban did not affect "respectable Jews," such as Benjamin
Nathan, the former vice president of the New York Stock Exchange,
who led the protest movement, only lower-class "dawdlers, hagglers,
adventurers, war-Jews or any other vagabonds."

The reference to "war-Jews" was telling. The new wave of
persecution was a direct outgrowth of the late conflict, with its
inflamed religious sentiments, economic devastation, and unsettling of the racial status quo. The wartime resentment of so-called
shoddy contractors who lined their own pockets by selling poor-
quality blankets and clothing to the troops laid the foundation for
the particular type of antisemitism that became alarmingly prevalent in the Gilded Age. In 1877, Joseph Seligman, the ambitious,
Bavarian-born merchant who along with his brothers had made a
fortune supplying uniforms to the Union Army and selling federal
war bonds in Europe, became the most famous victim of new exclusionary measures when the proprietor of one of the finest hotels
in Saratoga Springs refused him entry. A national uproar ensued,
but only because Seligman, a personal friend of President Grant (he
had once offered Seligman the post of treasury secretary), was such
a prominent and wealthy citizen. Less privileged Jews also faced
widespread discrimination. They had trouble finding jobs in certain
industries, applying for loans, and renting or buying homes in select

neighborhoods ("Jews need not apply," read ads for boarders). They were turned away from social clubs, private schools, and professional associations, even ones where they had previously been welcome. Two years after the Seligman incident, "Jews as a class"—the same words used in Grant's expulsion decree—were barred from New York banker Austin Corbin's new resort on Coney Island. "If this is a free country," Corbin asked, "why can't we be free of the Jews?"

Even after emancipation, many Black Americans continued to be subjected to working conditions little different from bondage, excluded from politics, banned from public accommodations, and murdered at will. Jews, by contrast, were never systematically barred from the polling booth, the jury box, or public office. But in a nation increasingly obsessed by racial divisions and carefully policed hierarchies—as evidenced not only by Jim Crow segregation but the Chinese Exclusion Act of 1882—Jewish leaders feared seeing their people end up on the wrong side of the racial divide, cast out from the self-sorted ranks of legitimate Americans.

The influx of more than two million Eastern European Jews from 1880 to 1924 further called into question the status of Jews as white people only slightly different from others. Fleeing pogroms rather than the failure of liberal revolutions, the new arrivals were poorer, more religious, and less educated than the German Jews who had preceded them in the 1840s and 1850s, more intent on clustering themselves in Jewish-dominated neighborhoods in the largest American cities. Jews of longer standing in the United States feared the security they had attained—already jeopardized by postwar economic resentments—was being further compromised by this torrent of seemingly unassimilable Yiddish-speaking Jews. While they had once been welcomed as part of the "Great Caucasian Family"—one Christian doctor in the South even went so far as to call Jews "the purest, finest, and most perfect type of the Caucasian race"—they now seemed to be at risk of losing that privileged status. In 1894, when Booker T. Washington mildly suggested that "the black man, like the Jew or white man," should carefully select what sort of business he entered, Isaac Mayer Wise, as pugilistic as ever well into his eighth decade and still haunted by the possibility that American Jews would replace Black people on the lowest step of the nation's social and economic ladder, rebuked Washington for his "scientific blunder"—implying that Jews were not white—and suggested he needed a "lesson in primary ethnology." "All Jewish Americans are Caucasians," Wise insisted. In suggesting otherwise, Washington revealed his essentially "servile nature."

Wise was far from alone in defending the Jews' hard-earned racial status. In 1896, the Atlanta-based *Jewish Sentiment* congratulated the white people of Columbus, Georgia, for ridding the state of "two such scoundrels as those negroes who were hung." When a Jewish paper in Philadelphia likened the Wilmington massacre of 1898—in which scores of Black people were killed by whites trying to overthrow a mixed-race government—to a pogrom, the Richmond-based *Jewish South* retorted that no comparison could be made between Jews and Blacks, who were "intellectually, morally and physically an inferior race—a fact that none can deny." A Jewish paper in Atlanta openly praised the Wilmington coup: "The white man will rule by fair means or by foul."

Twenty years earlier, amid the debate over the ban on Jews from Coney Island, a Black newspaper in Louisiana had commented that African Americans could not get too worked up over the matter, given that so many Jews in the United States supported laws against Black people:

> It seems strange that a people whose history for centuries have been written in tears and blood should here, in this land of liberty, this refuge for the oppressed of all nations, be found

among the foremost in heaping obloquy and opprobrium upon another race whose misfortunes are in some sort similar to their own. It is a melancholy fact that the Jews in this country, in order to curry favor with the ruling classes, are, except in a few sections, classed with the negro haters. It is on this account that we, while battling against class prejudice everywhere, and under all circumstances, are inclined to shed few tears over the discomfiture and humiliations which the Jews are now receiving.

In 1905, when the Senate passed a resolution condemning recent pogroms in Russia, a Black newspaper, the *Voice of the Negro*, bitterly attacked what it saw as naked hypocrisy. "What right has the United States to be horrified? . . . We are having here in America Kishinevs and Bialystoks every day."

American Jews embarked on a frenzy of institution building in the years after the Civil War, much of it led by Isaac Mayer Wise, who had been trying to unite American Jewry under one organizational umbrella ever since his arrival in the United States in 1846. The trials of the Civil War finally made it clear that Jews needed to join together and pool their resources if they were to have any chance of countering efforts like the campaign to add a "Christian amendment" to the Constitution. Newly aware of how susceptible they were, Northern and Southern Jews worked to heal wartime rifts. In the spring of 1865, Southerners picking through the rubble of their homes and synagogues asked their Northern brethren for material assistance, and they received it in the form of thousands of pounds of Passover matzah. "This is no time to look back upon petty differences that may have arisen between communities," the *Jewish Record* commented. The *Jewish Messenger*, which had urged its readers after Fort Sumter to stand by the Union flag, lamented "the ruin

and misery that have become the lot of hundreds of formerly affluent Hebrew families" in the South.

The postwar spirit of bonhomie soon spread from political affairs to religious ones. In 1873, Wise helped to organize the Union
of American Hebrew Congregations, which, though limited to
Reform synagogues, was named ambitiously to reflect his wish for
a fully united American Judaism, without denominational separations. Two years later he founded the Hebrew Union College, based
in his hometown of Cincinnati, the first Jewish seminary in the
United States.

Yet while these institutions are often celebrated as demonstrating the growing strength of the American Jewish community, they
also signaled an increasing sense of difference and detachment from
the mainstream. Unnerved by the antisemitism the war had revealed, Jews became more conscious of themselves as a people apart.
No longer sure they would ever be accepted as equals, they turned
to creating strong, separate institutions as the next best thing, the
legacy not of strength and confidence but of fear and vulnerability.

Wise never apologized for his stance on slavery, nor for his near-
embrace of the Confederacy. He never conceded that the abolitionists had been anything other than irresponsible agitators, and he
opposed federal efforts to safeguard the rights of Black people after
the war. Recounting a journey to Charleston in 1870—twenty years
after he had first visited the city, hosted and feted by slave owners—
Wise condemned what he called "reconstruction with a vengeance."
"As long as the South is interfered with in any way, molested, or
denied any rights or principles which others enjoy anywhere," Wise
wrote in the *Israelite* three years later, "we will be found to stand
with the South." He thought "the negro" should stick to farming
and avoid politics, which would only make him "a demoralized,
lazy and forlorn voting machine, and good for nothing else either
to himself or others."

Though he had succeeded in founding national institutions

and helping to shape the development of Reform Judaism, Wise's final decades were hardly years of triumph. Soon after he and his wife moved to a farm outside Cincinnati overlooking what he called "the grandest scenery imagination can depict," Theresa Wise fell ill, spent nearly two years in bed—"no more herself than the ruin is the castle," Wise grieved—before she died in 1874. Four years later, his daughter Helen eloped with a Presbyterian attorney, a scandal, given Wise's outspoken opposition to intermarriage, that brought international headlines and criticism from traditionalists that such defections were the inevitable fruit of religious modernization. After 1880, the influx of Orthodox immigrants from Eastern Europe imperiled the efforts of Wise and his generation to fit in by discarding from Judaism, as he put it, "whatever makes us ridiculous before the world." Wise was contemptuous of the "half-civilized" new arrivals who "gnaw the dead bones of past centuries" and "read nothing besides their jargon literature." Even in his own Reform circles, the more radical ideas of his archnemesis, David Einhorn, held greater sway over the next generation of leaders than his own.

With pogroms in Russia, the Dreyfus Affair in France, rising antisemitism in Germany, and exclusivist restrictions in America, conditions for Jews in the United States and around the world were getting worse rather than better by the early spring afternoon in 1900 when Wise collapsed after teaching his usual Shabbat class at Hebrew Union College. He died a few days later, just shy of eighty-one years old. "This country," Wise had recently written, "approaches nearest the Mosaic state among all countries known in history." Yet even he would have been forced to admit that the messianic state remained a long way off.

———

For more than half a century after he was saved from being feasted on by wild hogs as he lay wounded on the Pine Ridge battlefield,

August Bondi lived with two ounces of lead in his body. The war changed his life, and not only because the injury later caused him to fall ill from blood poisoning and suffer "for most 15 years . . . more or less invalidated." The war also seems to have sent Bondi back to the religion whose principles he had first imbibed as a boy from his liberal-minded tutor in Vienna. In the fall of 1865, when the high holidays came around, the wounded veteran traveled seventy-five miles, to Leavenworth, Kansas, to attend synagogue services for the first time in years.

Bondi struggled to make ends meet after the war. His travails can sound downright Job-like. He lost one year's corn crop to a hailstorm, another's to grasshoppers. A tornado threw him off his wagon, sending him to bed for six weeks. Once he was attacked by a neighbor's cow, another time by dogs, requiring an even longer recuperation. His second child, another girl, died at nine months old. In 1868, he filed for bankruptcy.

As when he had first settled with his family in St. Louis, Bondi lurched from job to job, working stints as a clerk in the federal land office, then as an insurance salesman. At nearly sixty-three years old, he studied law and was admitted to the bar. He was elected or appointed postmaster, probate judge, and trustee of the Kansas Historical Society, where his papers now reside, along with the lock mechanism of the War of 1812 musket he had been given by John Brown.

As he aged, Bondi worried that the true story of the fighting in Kansas would be left out of the history books. The glory of those few men who had stuck with Brown in the spring of 1856, and who were hunted across the prairie by proslavery Border Ruffians and federal troops, was being overshadowed by the exaggerated claims of "professional abolitionists" who "came to Kansas for a political nest-egg" and mostly stayed out of harm's way, "pure fictions" advanced by men with "political or financial axes to grind." He scrawled letter after letter to the Kansas Historical Society offering details about his time with Brown and his handful of hardy fighters. "Envy and jealousy have . . . tried to detract from their merit," Bondi wrote, but without them the whole course of the national struggle to end slavery would have been different.

Bondi's resentment of those valor-stealing "professional abolitionists," some of whom led the Republican Party in Kansas once it became a state, helps explain the political transformation he underwent in the decades after the Civil War. The former Viennese revolutionary had started out in American politics in the 1850s as an antislavery Democrat, one of the thousands of new immigrants who opposed the expansion of slavery in the West partly because it undermined the economic prospects of white laborers like themselves. Later, Bondi rejected John Brown's schemes to trigger a nationwide antislavery revolution. Swept up in the frenzy of the 1860 election, Bondi briefly sheltered runaways in his Kansas farmhouse, then joined the Union Army because he felt obligated as a Jew to "defend the institutions which gave equal rights to all beliefs." Within a few years, however, Bondi turned against "the reign of Republican boodlers" and returned to the Democrats, the party, after the war as before, more popular among whites in the South. Such defections helped undo Reconstruction. Bondi's recollections, in letters, articles, and in the memoir he began writing in 1884 then expanded in 1903, may have been colored by the more jaded political outlook of his later years. The struggle had always been about white liberty, Bondi insisted. He had only sought "to assist an outraged community of american squatters against nigger-extension efforts, abetted by the national government."

In 1898, Bondi returned to Vienna to attend a fifty-year reunion of veterans of the thwarted revolution that had changed the course of his life. He visited old schoolmates, paid his respects at the graves of his ancestors, toured synagogues, and struggled to understand the antisemitism that had become so rampant in Europe as the century of emancipation ended and a new one dawned.

In his autobiography, the former pig farmer noted that he was "never orthodox but a consistent Jew nonetheless." He had observed "all holy days as symbolic manifestations of the Creator and the creation." Though settled far out on the frontier, "cut off from intercourse with Jews for years," he boasted of having "raised a large family"—nine children grown to adulthood—"*as Jews.*" Salina, Kansas, where Bondi lived out his final decades, did not have a synagogue, but he made sure his daughters were married by the rabbi in Leavenworth. He wanted his account of the Kansas fighting, in particular, to be preserved in order to show "that Jehudim were active at the very commencement of the 'late unpleasantness' between the States."

On September 30, 1907, while on a visit to St. Louis, the city he had first made his way in as a teenaged exile, Bondi had a heart attack and fell dead in the street. He was seventy-four years old. At the end of his memoir, which his family published privately after he died, Bondi asked that at his burial service, which was to mix elements of Jewish and Masonic rituals, "mention be made of my being in the front March 13th, 1848; likewise in Kansas in 1856 . . . and did my full duty in military service of the U.S. for over three years." For Bondi, the revolutions in Europe, the fight against slavery in Kansas, and the American Civil War were but different battles in the same general, unceasing war. "I do not regret a single step or instance in my long life," he wrote, "to further and to assist the realization of my devout wishes that tyranny and despotism may perish, and bigotry and fanaticism may be wiped from the face of the earth."

Conclusion

STRICTLY SPEAKING, THE BOOK OF EXODUS TELLS THE
story of *national* liberation. Seen in that light, the Hebrews' escape
from slavery gave them the freedom to enslave and conquer others,
which, in the text, they promptly began to do. It was this narrow
reading of the tale that allowed some American Jews to sit down to
Passover seders cooked and served by their very own slaves, without
the slightest sense of contradiction or unpleasant pang of guilt.

Yet the story's radical emphasis on lowly origins and the brutalities of despotism has always invited a broader interpretation, even
the adoption of its language and liberatory message by other maligned and oppressed groups. As the philosopher Michael Walzer
has written, "Many men and women, believing in God's mighty
hand, have nevertheless girded their loins, challenged the pharaohs
of their own time, marched into the wilderness—and understood
what they were doing by reading Exodus." In this view, it is an
uplifting tale of *human* liberation and the obligations it entails. Remembering that we were slaves in Egypt, Rabbi David Einhorn said
nearly two centuries ago, should be a spur to fight not only for
ourselves, but "for the whole world."

I have been thinking about American Jews, slavery, and the Civil War ever since I was an undergraduate at McGill University in Montreal. It struck me then that what in part made Jews distinctive as a people—our origins in slavery—was also what helped make the United States distinctive as a country. People who celebrated their deliverance "out of the house of bondage" had found refuge in another, only this time they were not the ones who were enslaved. I wrote a paper on the handful of Jewish abolitionists who, drawing on their own people's history of enslavement and oppression, felt they could not keep silent while others suffered the same.

But the topic continued to gnaw at me, not least because I was surprised to find how rarely it came up at Passover seders I attended. Given that the point of the holiday is to commemorate the Jews' liberation several thousand years ago, did it not make sense to consider how slavery also shaped the country in which we lived? Should we not grapple with the fact that Jews in early America benefited from slavery in direct and indirect ways, and that only a few unsung and forgotten men, and at least one woman, had felt compelled to fight for its abolition?

Nudnik that I am, I would pester my fellow seder guests, between reciting the Four Questions and joyfully incanting *Chad Gadya,* to reflect further on the themes of Exodus and their relevance in the American past and present. One year I passed around copies of a letter from a Confederate soldier detailing his preparations for observing Passover while at war. The next year I read from a moth-eaten volume of local history I found at a thrift store, which showed that the very land on which we sat, in the verdant foothills of the Catskills, pouring each other wine and munching on matzah, imagining ourselves as having been personally delivered from Egypt, had once been worked by people who did not need to use their imaginations to know the terrors of bondage.

I also began seeing signs that a fresh examination might prove useful. The rise of the Black Lives Matter movement seemed to make the task of confronting America's history of racial injustice all the more pressing and ignoring the Jewish angle to the story all the more inexcusable. The subject of Jews and race kept cropping up in the news and in the culture, often in bizarre viral moments and occasionally in gruesome outbursts of violence. In 2018, a racist shooter massacred eleven Jews in a Pittsburgh synagogue because he opposed the work of groups like HIAS, formerly the Hebrew Immigrant Aid Society. Originally founded to help late nineteenth-century immigrants find their footing, the group now works with refugees of all kinds, "not because they are Jewish, but because we are." On that occasion, Jews were killed because they were not white enough. The following year, the problem was that they were not Jewish enough. A radicalized devotee of the Black Hebrew Israelites, a century-old religious group that claims Black people are the true descendants of the biblical Jews and that those who call themselves Jews today are impostors, killed three people at a kosher supermarket in Jersey City. In 2022, the rapper Ye, formerly Kanye West, endorsed that claim and told his more than thirty million Twitter followers that he was going "death con 3 On JEWISH PEOPLE." In the romantic comedy *You People* (2023), an excruciating dinner-table argument between a Black Muslim couple and a white Jewish couple whose children are dating culminates with David Duchovny's character calling Jews "the original slaves—OG slaves," while Nia Long's counters that American Jews' success was based on their profits from the slave trade. "No mainstream voice asks anymore, 'Is the Jew white?'" the scholar Leonard Rogoff observed in 1997. Now that question is once again hotly debated. Some Jews of color, meanwhile, have demanded long-overdue recognition from the larger Jewish community, while others reject the term itself as marginalizing. Hamas's attack on Israel in October 2023 and the subsequent bombardment of Gaza raised a new round of discourse—often simplistic and unenlightening—about whether Jews ought to be classed primarily as victims or as oppressors.

These events encouraged me to return to the topic of my paper, to dig deeper and ask more difficult questions. As I did so, I was surprised to find that the book I wanted to read, tracking the Jewish encounter with Black slavery and the debate over its future from the colonial period through the Civil War and beyond, did not yet exist. Bertram W. Korn, a rabbi and historian (and, as a rear admiral in the Naval Reserve, the first Jewish chaplain to attain flag rank in the US military), came the closest with his landmark 1951 work *American Jewry and the Civil War.* Yet Korn mostly focused on the war itself, especially the home front, and kept to a narrow definition of who counted as a Jew; Ernestine Rose goes unmentioned, August Bondi only in passing. Decades of subsequent research and argumentation, moreover, have complicated some of his findings. While the publication of the Nation of Islam's pseudo-scholarly *Secret Relationship Between Blacks and Jews* in the early 1990s spurred impressive refutations, that work tended to focus on the slave trade itself, not the fight over slavery and the Civil War. Incredibly, some books about Jews in the period have even managed to avoid including an entry for slavery in the index—they talk about the war but not what the war was about—while Robert N. Rosen's *The Jewish Confederates* (2001), otherwise an invaluable resource, is marred by its unapologetically pro-Southern bent. Books about the formation and subsequent fraying of the "Black-Jewish alliance" skip quickly over everything before the twentieth century. Surveys of American Jewish history often mention the dispute over Morris J. Raphall's sermon defending slavery but tend to obscure the context and leave out important details. Perhaps the most insightful recent exploration of the theme appeared in a work of fiction, Dara Horn's *All Other Nights* (2009), which begins with a Confederate seder attended, quite improbably, by Judah Benjamin.

In 2017, on the celebrity genealogy program *Finding Your Roots,* the comedian Larry David learned that his great-grandfather, a German-Jewish immigrant in Mobile, Alabama, owned slaves and fought for the Confederacy. Stunned, playing for laughs, David awkwardly blurted to the show's host, Henry Louis Gates Jr., "I'm so sorry," while Gates gave voice to his guest's embarrassment and confusion: "What part of the Jewish experience is this?!"

As it turns out, a rather important one. Even for the huddled masses who arrived decades after the Civil War, even for those of us who are their descendants, the experience of living as Jews in America has been shaped by the legacy of slavery and by the ideas and laws devised to defend and then replace it. They protect and threaten us still, in this otherwise blessed land.

American Jews at the turn of the twentieth century, their ranks swelling with two million refugees from the latest outbreak of European terror, sought to hold on to the material benefits of whiteness without giving up their cherished self-image as irreducibly different, fundamentally other. Earlier generations of immigrants had come to learn through bracing experience how racial privilege protected them, but for rare exceptions, from bigotry and violence. Newer arrivals often felt less pressure to conform to mainstream expectations. Some brought with them a commitment to political radicalism that the more established crowd feared would draw unwanted attention or even lead to another nation-rending conflict, one even worse for the Jews than the last.

Just as some antislavery Jews had seen an imperative in their own history and religion to fight against bondage, many twentieth-century Jews joined struggles for political reform, economic justice, and equal rights for all Americans. Jewish immigrants filled and often led the ranks of the American socialist and communist movements, advocating for safer working conditions, a social safety net, and nationalized ownership of the means of production, if not outright revolution. Other Jews continued the abolitionists' fight for racial equality, finally helping to seal, partly and fitfully, the alliance proposed by the imprisoned rebel in Jamaica back in 1760. ("You differ from the rest of the Whites, and they hate you. Surely then it is best for us to join in one common interest.") In 1909, the activist Henry Moskowitz, born in Romania, and Rabbi Stephen Wise (no relation to Isaac Mayer Wise), worked with W. E. B. Du Bois and others to found the National Association for the Advancement of Colored People, the NAACP. Two Jewish brothers, Joel and Arthur Spingarn, later served as presidents of the organization. Julius Rosenwald, a part owner of Sears, Roebuck, financed the construction of Black schools throughout the segregated South. In the 1930s, Romanian-born lawyer Samuel Leibowitz defended the Scottsboro Boys, nine Black teenagers falsely accused of rape and convicted by all-white juries. Funded by the Communist Party, Leibowitz faced death threats for upsetting the Southern racial order. A prosecutor screamed at the jurors that "Alabama justice cannot be bought and sold with Jew money from New York."

American Jews continue to pride themselves—and rightly so—on having participated in the civil rights movement of the 1950s and 1960s at rates far out of proportion to their presence in the population. By some estimates (likely high but not far off), two-thirds of the Freedom Riders who ventured south in 1961 to challenge segregation were Jewish. Three years later, Andrew Goodman and Michael Schwerner, two student activists from New York City, were murdered by Klan-affiliated police officers in Mississippi, along with their Black comrade, James Chaney. "Seen in the light of our religious tradition," the rabbi and theologian Abraham Joshua Heschel said, "the Negro problem is God's gift to America, the test of our integrity, a magnificent spiritual opportunity." The image of Heschel marching with Martin Luther King Jr. in Selma, Alabama, in 1965, has become familiar, but Heschel was far from alone among Jewish leaders involved in the movement. Joachim Prinz, a rabbi in Newark, New Jersey, and president of the American Jewish

Congress, who had lived in Berlin until the Nazis expelled him, spoke just before King at the March on Washington in 1963. He had learned as a rabbi in Hitler's Germany, Prinz told the crowd, that "the most urgent, the most disgraceful, the most shameful and the most tragic problem is silence."

Yet not all American Jews supported the civil rights movement, not nearly. The oft-invoked image of Heschel marching with King obscures an unpleasant reality: many Jews embraced a strategy of silence, just as earlier generations had during the struggle over slavery. This was especially, though not exclusively, true in the South. As Jews' sense of belonging in the region came under threat in the decades after slavery's abolition, some feared that freedom for Black Americans would mean its dilution for themselves. "[I]n most Southern towns," the North Carolina journalist Jonathan Daniels observed in 1938, "the direction of racial prejudice at the Negro frees the Jews from prejudice altogether—or nearly altogether."

To protect their privileged position, some Southern Jews joined the White Citizens' Councils that pushed back against desegregation. A Jewish pawnshop owner in downtown Atlanta passed messages between the city's Jewish community and the Ku Klux Klan, to whom he sold pistols and white sheets for their robes. While many Jewish storekeepers continued to cater to a Black clientele, others banned Black customers from their shops and restaurants. Many of the lunch-counter sit-ins that galvanized the civil rights movement in the early 1960s took place at department stores founded as much as a century earlier by former Jewish peddlers; their descendants still owned the businesses and resisted demands for integration. By maintaining racial segregation, Southern Jews could prove they belonged firmly on the right side of the color line. Charles Bloch, the son of an Alsatian immigrant and a legal architect of Georgia's resistance to school desegregation, supported Strom Thurmond's 1948 presidential candidacy, defended literacy tests in court, and published a book titled *States' Rights: The Law of the Land* (1958).

Bloch based his advocacy firmly on his religious faith, arguing that fighting integration was the only way he could "walk humbly before God." When Schwerner and Goodman were killed in Mississippi, a Jewish businessman with roots in the state going back to the Civil War explained that they had it coming. "Sure, I felt sorry for those boys," he said. "But nobody asked them to come down here and meddle with our way of life."

If some Southern Jews stayed quiet because they shared the prejudices of their white neighbors, others did so because they feared violence if they spoke out. The civil rights struggle unleashed a more extreme form of antisemitism than Jews in the South, or anywhere else in the United States, had ever experienced. "There would be no Negro problem without the Jew problem," a prominent segregationist told a Klan rally in 1956. Synagogues in Miami, Charlotte, Nashville, Jacksonville, Atlanta, and Birmingham were bombed—some of the fuses malfunctioned; incredibly, nobody was killed—and death threats were sent to those who dared to speak out. The ghost of Leo Frank haunted Southern Jews with the possible repercussions of inviting white Christian wrath. Many Jews who joined the White Citizens' Councils did so only because, as the historian Clive Webb has written, they "found the $3 or $5 membership fee a small price to pay for safety from reprisal." They could not afford not to join. Likewise, some of the Jewish department store owners targeted by sit-ins wanted to integrate their lunch counters, but felt doing so would invite white boycotts and ruin their businesses, or worse.

Caught between the demands of the protesters and threats from white supremacists, rabbis and other community leaders urged their Northern coreligionists in the movement to stay out of the South. In 1963, nineteen rabbis traveled to Birmingham to join the protests against segregation. A new verse of the protest anthem "We Shall Overcome" included the line, "The rabbis are with us," and one of the clergymen later claimed that yarmulkes became "prized trophies of young Negroes." Unhappy with the intrusion of outsiders, a group of local Jews met with the rabbis and begged them to leave town, lest the gentiles, already suspicious of the civil rights movement as what one called a "Jewish-Communist conspiracy to control the world," took revenge.

As a century earlier, Southern Jews understood that their own security and the still-tenuous welcome they enjoyed required conforming to white society's expectations. "We have to play ball," a Jewish man in Mississippi explained in 1964. "If we said out loud in Temple what most of us really think and believe, there just wouldn't be a Temple here anymore." When a Jewish grocer in Savannah, Georgia, signed a petition supporting school integration, white parents picketed his market and threatened to harm his children.

For some Jews in the South, however, as for David Einhorn in the 1850s, even the instinct for self-preservation was not enough to intimidate them into silence. History seemed to repeat itself in 1967 when Burton Padoll, the Ohio-born rabbi of Charleston's Congregation Beth Elohim, whose landmark building was constructed by slaves, lost his position after congregants complained about his outspoken support for the civil rights movement. In one Passover sermon, Padoll wondered how "Jews, of all people, descendants of slaves, could deny freedom to others." On Yom Kippur, he called on his congregants to atone for their "silence in the face of moral responsibility." "[R]eligion isn't simply Bible tales and explanations of historical practices," Padoll said. "Religion encompasses injustice, immorality, and sin." The Beth Elohim members asked Padoll to keep silent on the controversies of the day, as Einhorn's congregants in Baltimore had asked him a century earlier. Like Einhorn, Padoll refused, arguing that because of their history Jews had a special obligation to defend the rights of everyone.

In 1958, Rabbi Jacob Rothschild of Atlanta, an outspoken supporter of racial equality, was urged by a fellow Southern rabbi to disavow the civil rights struggle. Rothschild was horrified. The strategy of silence had not worked to protect the Jews, as became all too clear only a few months later when Rothschild's synagogue was bombed. The rabbi was moved when the Black inmates of a nearby prison pooled funds to help the congregation rebuild. What might have been yet another traumatic moment in a long history of Jewish suffering turned into one of moral and political clarity. The attack on his synagogue inspired Rothschild—and other Atlanta Jews—to take an even firmer stance on behalf of freedom and equality for all. "How can we condemn the millions who stood by under Hitler or honor those few who chose to live by their ideals," Rothschild replied to the other rabbi, "when we refuse to make a similar choice now that the dilemma is our own?"

Perhaps the legacy of American slavery has not often come up at seders I have attended because the parents of our usual host were themselves once slaves in Nazi Germany who met in a displaced-persons camp after the Second World War. They also did not have to use their imaginations to know the terrors of bondage. Maybe universalizing the Passover story, applying its themes to the experiences of another group, is too much to ask of those for whom the memory of the Holocaust remains so near and so raw.

But for me, coming from a family that has been in this country a few decades longer, I feel called by the words of the Haggadah to turn inward and backward, to reckon with the more discomfiting aspects of the American Jewish story. My great-great-grandfather, along with his wife and five children, fled the early twentieth-century pogroms in Bialystok that the *Voice of the Negro* compared to the daily violence against Black people in America. They settled on the Lower East Side, then graduated to the far reaches of Brooklyn. There my grandmother was born and raised, the daughter of the owner of a Brownsville luncheonette. As more

African Americans filtered into the neighborhood—though not, I am assured, for that reason—my grandparents moved to the sunny, spacious suburbs of Long Island and bought a home, something federal policies and prejudicial lending practices made all but impossible for Black people. Just as assimilating into the antebellum South meant assimilating into a slave society, "making it" in the twentieth-century United States involved benefiting from the country's discriminatory laws and social practices, receiving government assistance at a time, as Ira Katznelson has put it, "when affirmative action was white." That advantaged racial status—conferred not after the Second World War but in one of the first laws passed under the Constitution, the Naturalization Act of 1790—is a crucial part of what has made the United States such a congenial home for Jews.

By the late 1960s, the ever-tenuous Black-Jewish alliance, never as stable or secure as often imagined, was beginning to crumble. For some African Americans, Jewish involvement in the civil rights movement was starting to seem less helpful than inhibitory, limiting the radicalism of groups like the Student Non-Violent Coordinating Committee (SNCC), which banished its Jewish members, along with other whites, in 1966. Two years later, in the Brownsville neighborhood of Brooklyn—a decade after my grandparents left—an intense, monthlong teachers' strike followed the firing of nineteen Jewish teachers and administrators by a Black-dominated local school board seeking "community control." The dispute drove a rift between the communities that never fully healed.

Some tried. In 1969, the civil rights activist Arthur Waskow organized a Freedom Seder, where some eight hundred people gathered around candlelit tables in Washington, DC, and, using an updated Haggadah, reinterpreted the millennia-old Passover tradition with references to the Vietnam War and police brutality, as well as rousing renditions of "Go Down, Moses," one of many Black spirituals inspired by the story of Exodus. Waskow partly succeeded in bringing Black and Jewish communities together by emphasizing what they had in common—a long history of oppression and a shared language for their abiding faith in eventual liberation—but the era's deepening sense of mutual suspicion would not easily be overcome.

In a 1967 essay for the *New York Times Magazine*, James Baldwin reflected on the increasingly tense relations between Blacks and Jews. He argued that Black people resented how Jews had so easily assimilated into American whiteness and reaped the advantages it entailed. "The Jew profits from his status in America, and he must expect Negroes to distrust him for it," Baldwin wrote. "The Jew does not realize that the credential he offers, the fact that he has been despised and slaughtered, does not increase the Negro's understanding. It increases the Negro's rage."

A year after the Brownsville strike, James Forman, a former SNCC leader, published a manifesto demanding $500 million from white churches and synagogues as reparations for slavery. Forman interrupted services at Manhattan's Riverside Church and planned to do the same at Temple Emanu-El, whose leaders invited him to speak in order to head off the confrontation. But Forman backed down when members of the Jewish Defense League, recently founded by Rabbi Meir Kahane and modeled after the Black Panthers, arrived with bats, pipes, and chains, threatening to break Forman's legs if he showed up. "Blacks deserve nothing from us and that is what they will get," Kahane insisted.

In a 1970 essay celebrating Temple Emanu-El's 125th anniversary, Bayard Rustin, the civil rights leader who organized the March on Washington, scorned Forman's bombastic hijinks. A stalwart supporter of Israel and a passionate advocate for Soviet Jewry— "almost all of his best friends were [Jewish]," one biographer has written—Rustin cherished the alliance between Blacks and Jews and honored the influence of the Hebrew Bible on Black culture. "The Jew, from my reading of Jewish history and culture, is truly unique and chosen," Rustin wrote in his essay, "for he has been chosen by God to be His suffering servant and by that experience to obtain the insight and the knowledge to help lift the suffering of others."

Rustin was saddened by the withering of the alliance. Would American Jews really allow "a small minority in the black community, who are reacting to four hundred years of mistreatment, to drive them out of this coalition with anti-Semitic foolishness and confrontationism?" Rustin rejected Forman's approach to the reparations question, but he did not dismiss the idea that American Jews had some special obligation to work for repentance and repair. "I don't want your love, I don't want your affection, I don't want your money even if you offer it," he wrote. "What I want more than anything else is *zadukkah*. Only the Jews have a single word for both charity and justice. The only way that people in this society can have *zadukkah* is by the redistribution of the wealth. They will not have it if charity is given them by an individual, but only if the situation is created whereby they can themselves grow because the society provides the social and economic means for justice."

"That is your heritage," Rustin urged his Jewish readers. "Live up to it! Let nothing tear you away from it. Let nothing or nobody compromise your belief in social righteousness as taught by Isaiah and Jeremiah. And let that belief manifest itself in action. Let us together build a just society."

Notes

Introduction

4   *"Thou shalt not deliver"*: According to Isaac Mendelsohn, the obligation to protect runaways was "most probably drawn up in favor of Hebrew slaves who had fled from foreign countries," and not applied to fugitives from Hebrew bondage. Still, the provision was relatively progressive. In Hammurabi's Babylonia, the penalty for aiding a runaway was death; the fugitive could be put in chains and have the words "A runaway, seize!" inscribed on his face. Mendelsohn, "Slavery in the Ancient Near East," *Biblical Archaeologist* 9, no. 4 (December 1946): 74, 82.

8   *"one of the most secretive"*: Robert D. Meade, *Judah P. Benjamin: Confederate Statesman* (New York: Oxford University Press, 1943), xv.

1. "Emancipation of All Kinds"

15   *August Bondi*: In accordance with a government decree, an ancestor around the turn of the eighteenth century had translated his name, Jomtov, Hebrew for "good day," into the less Jewish-sounding Bondi, which means the same in Italian. *Autobiography of August Bondi, 1833–1907, Published by His Sons and Daughters for Its Preservation* (Galesburg, IL: Wagoner Printing Company, 1910), 3.

16   *"enthusiastic Jew"*: *Autobiography of August Bondi.*

18   *unparalleled promise*: Naomi W. Cohen, *Encounter with Emancipation: The German Jews in the United States, 1830–1914* (Philadelphia: Jewish Publication Society of America, 1984), 9; Bertram W. Korn, "Jewish 48'ers in America," *American Jewish Archives* 2, no. 1 (June 1949): 3–20.

19   *vast sugar plantation*: Bondi relates that he and his family began their journey upriver "on the evening of [November] 8th. On the 9th the tug stopped at a plantation for wood . . . We arrived in New Orleans November 10th."

Judah Benjamin's plantation was located approximately seventy-five river miles above La Balize and fifteen river miles below New Orleans. See *Autobiography of August Bondi*, 24.

20 *Caribbean-born, Charleston-raised*: Biographical interest in Benjamin shifted over the years from studies that focused on his overlooked service to the South to ones more interested in his ambiguous status as an American Jew. See Pierce Butler, *Judah P. Benjamin* (New York: Chelsea House, 1980); Robert D. Meade, *Judah P. Benjamin: Confederate Statesman* (New York: Oxford University Press, 1943); Eli N. Evans, *Judah P. Benjamin: The Jewish Confederate* (New York: The Free Press, 1988); James Traub, *Judah Benjamin: Counselor to the Confederacy* (New Haven, CT: Yale University Press, 2021). See also Richard Kreitner, "Biographical Fallacy," *Jewish Currents* (February 3, 2022), https://jewishcurrents.org/biographical-fallacy.

22 *rumors of insurrection*: Evans, *Judah P. Benjamin*, 9; Meade, *Judah P. Benjamin*, 12–14.

23 *Moving to New Orleans*: Bertram W. Korn, *The Early Jews of New Orleans* (Waltham, MA: American Jewish Historical Society, 1969), 10, 61–62, 88–89, 163; Bertram W. Korn, "Jews and Negro Slavery in the Old South, 1789–1865," *Publications of the American Jewish Historical Society* 50, no. 3 (March 1961): 156–57; S. Frederick Starr, *Bamboula! The Life and Times of Louis Moreau Gottschalk* (Urbana: University of Illinois Press, 1995), 23–24; Saul S. Friedman, *Jews and the American Slave Trade* (New Brunswick, NJ: Transaction Publishers, 1998), 182–83.

24 *Marrying a gentile*: Korn, *Early Jews of New Orleans*, 226; Stephen J. Whitfield, "The Braided Identity of Southern Jewry," *American Jewish History* 77, no. 3 (March 1988): 367; Evans, *Judah P. Benjamin*, 92.

25 *"You might well have written"*: Evans, *Judah P. Benjamin*, 29.

25 *"remarkable for the vivacity"*: Butler, *Judah P. Benjamin*, 44.

25 *"low, full and soft"*: Traub, *Judah Benjamin*, 33.

25 *Joining agriculture with industrial*: Richard Follett, *The Sugar Masters: Planters and Slaves in Louisiana's Cane World, 1820–1860* (Baton Rouge: Louisiana State University Press, 2006), 77–79.

26 *"none but kindly memories"*: Butler, *Judah P. Benjamin*, 62; Evans, *Judah P. Benjamin*, 33; Maury Wiseman, "Judah P. Benjamin and Slavery," *American Jewish Archives Journal* 59 (2010): 109.

26 *Though he bought the property*: Traub, *Judah Benjamin*, 95, 97.

27 *"That man must be indeed blind"*: Traub, *Judah Benjamin*, 45.

28 *By the age of forty*: Meade, *Judah P. Benjamin*, 79.

29 *"The objects of so much"*: Max Kohler surmised that the source of the AFAS report's information about American Jews and slavery may have been "a Mr. Lazar, a German, presumably a Jew," who attended the group's May 11, 1853, meeting in New York. See Kohler, "The Jews and the American Anti-Slavery Movement," *Publications of the American Jewish Historical Society*, no. 5 (1897): 143.

29 *"Frequently a preacher"*: See Maxwell Whiteman, "Introduction," in *The Kidnapped and the Ransomed: The Narrative of Peter & Vina Still After Forty Years of Slavery*, ed. Kate E. R. Pickard (Lincoln: University of Nebraska Press, 1995), 62. In a 1952 paper, Louis Ruchames set out to refute the argument that the abolitionists were anti-Jewish. A quarter-century later, Ruchames

returned to the topic and revised his opinion. See Louis Ruchames, "The Abolitionists and the Jews," *Publications of the American Jewish Historical Society* 42, no. 2 (December 1952): 131–55, and "The Abolitionists and the Jews: Some Further Thoughts," in *Jews and the Civil War: A Reader*, ed. Jonathan D. Sarna and Adam Mendelsohn (New York: New York University Press, 2010), 145–56.

30   *A bombastic journalist and playwright*: Jonathan D. Sarna, *Jacksonian Jew: The Two Worlds of Mordecai Noah* (New York: Holmes & Meier Publishers, 1981), 61–75.

30   *a critic of slavery*: *The Selected Writings of Mordecai Noah*, ed. Michael Schuldiner and Daniel J. Kleinfeld (Westport, CT: Greenwood Press, 1999), 104.

31   *"there is liberty under the name of slavery"*: See Sarna, *Jacksonian Jew*, 108–14.

31   *a "Jewish unbeliever"*: Ruchames, "The Abolitionists and the Jews: Some Further Thoughts," 149; Robert N. Rosen, *The Jewish Confederates* (Columbia: University of South Carolina Press, 2000), 38. Not all the Garrisonian abolitionists were as hostile to Jews as Garrison himself. Lydia Maria Child once visited a synagogue and later excoriated Christians for their treatment of Jews. "As a general thing, Christians have manifested very little kindness, or candour, in their estimate of other religions," she wrote, "but the darkest blot on their history is their treatment of the Jews."

32   *"due partly to her sex"*: Bonnie S. Anderson, *The Rabbi's Atheist Daughter: Ernestine Rose, International Feminist Pioneer* (New York: Oxford University Press, 2017), 63. Paula Doress-Worters and Ellen Carol DuBois contend that Rose may have traveled to Charleston in 1847 to visit Beth Elohim, the first Reform synagogue in the country, and that she did so "to find a community of Jews who embraced a progressive social agenda similar to her own and with whom she would have felt a bond of community and commitment." There is no evidence for this. Reform Jews in South Carolina did not embrace "a progressive social agenda." Indeed, had she bothered to stop by Beth Elohim, Rose would have found that many of its members were slaveholders themselves.

33   *What Ernestine said*: Paula Doress-Worters, "Getting to the Source: Madame Rose: A Life of Ernestine L. Rose as Told to Jenny P. d'Hericourt," *Journal of Women's History* 15, no. 1 (Spring 2003): 192.

33   *"I have not abandoned the trunk"*: Anderson, *The Rabbi's Atheist Daughter*, 20–22.

34   *Contrary to the story Rose liked*: Susan Higginbotham, "The Early Life and Family of Feminist Ernestine Rose: New Findings and an Old Secret," *Journal of Genealogy and Family History* 7, no. 1 (2023): 1–15. Higginbotham subsequently published a historical novel based on her findings, *The Queen of the Platform: A Novel of Women's Rights Activist Ernestine Rose* (2024).

35   *"my poor unhappy country"*: Anderson, *The Rabbi's Atheist Daughter*, 25.

35   *"to infuse the benign spirit"*: Anderson, *The Rabbi's Atheist Daughter*, 33–36.

36   *"a good deal of trouble"*: Anderson, *The Rabbi's Atheist Daughter*, 48.

36   *"whole question of woman's proper"*: Dorothy Wickenden, *The Agitators: Three Friends Who Fought for Abolition and Women's Rights* (New York: Scribner, 2021), 18.

36   *The law finally passed*: Ellen Carol DuBois, "Ernestine Rose's Jewish Origins and the Varieties of Euro-American Emancipation in 1848," in *Women's*

Rights and Transatlantic Antislavery in the Era of Emancipation, ed. Kathryn Kish Sklar and James Stewart (New Haven, CT: Yale University Press, 2007), 284.

37 *"We need no such authority"*: See "Introduction" and "Speech at the Hartford Bible Convention" in *Mistress of Herself: Speeches and Letters of Ernestine L. Rose, Early Women's Rights Leader*, ed. Paula Doress-Worters (New York: Feminist Press at the City University of New York, 2008), 17, 138–39.

38 *"that great incomprehensible inconsistency"*: "Introduction," in *Mistress of Herself*, 23; "New England Anti-Slavery Convention," *The Liberator*, June 8, 1855.

38 *"I would that, instead of speaking"*: "Speech at the Anniversary of West Indian Emancipation," in Doress-Worters, *Mistress of Herself*, 149.

38 *"met me as a brother"*: Anderson, *The Rabbi's Atheist Daughter*, 67.

38 *"Woman is a slave"*: Jacob Rader Marcus, *The American Jewish Woman: A Documentary History* (New York: Ktav, 1981), 165.

39 *"He may compel her return"*: Anderson, *The Rabbi's Atheist Daughter*, 74.

39 *"a Polish lady of the Jewish faith"*: "Speech at the Third National Woman's Rights Convention," in Doress-Worters, *Mistress of Herself*, 121.

39 *"I go for emancipation of all kinds"*: "Speech at the Anniversary of West Indian Emancipation," in Doress-Worters, *Mistress of Herself*, 150.

39 *"a year full of the most interesting"*: "Speech at the Thomas Paine Celebration, 1849," in Doress-Worters, *Mistress of Herself*, 72, 77.

41 *In 1852, angry mobs attacked*: Luke Ritter, *Inventing America's First Immigration Crisis: Political Nativism in the Antebellum West* (New York: Fordham University Press, 2021); Mark Alan Neels, We Shall Be Literally 'Sold to the Dutch': Nativist Suppression of German Radicals in Antebellum St. Louis, 1852–1861," *The Confluence* 1, no. 1 (Fall 2009): 22–29.

42 *Looking for work, Bondi ventured*: Autobiography of August Bondi, 25–33. A year after Bondi left, Galveston elected a Jewish mayor, Michael Seeligson, a Dutch-born shopkeeper who had lived in Texas since 1828, when it was still part of Mexico.

2. Of Hebrew Bondage

44 *an essay in a neo-Nazi magazine*: Richard Bevan, "Early American Jews and the Slave Trade," *New Patriot* (March 1966): 3–12.

45 *The text has been thoroughly discredited*: Seymour Drescher wrote, "At no point along the continuum of the slave trade were Jews numerous enough, rich enough, and powerful enough to affect significantly the structure and flow of the slave trade or to diminish the suffering of its African victims." Seymour Drescher, "Jews and New Christians in the Atlantic Slave Trade," in *The Jews and the Expansion of Europe to the West, 1450 to 1800*, ed. Paolo Bernardini and Norman Fiering (New York: Berghahn Books, 2001), 455; Rosen, *The Jewish Confederates*, 282 note 23; Winthrop Jordan, "Slavery and the Jews," *Atlantic Monthly*, September 1995; David Brion Davis, "The Slave Trade and the Jews," *New York Review of Books*, December 22, 1994; Friedman, *Jews and the American Slave Trade*; Eli Faber, *Jews, Slaves, and the Slave Trade* (New York: New York University Press, 1998).

45 *tens of thousands of individuals*: Drescher, "Jews and New Christians in the Atlantic Slave Trade," 67. As the historian Jonathan Schorsch has written,

"Rebuttal of the anti-Jewish views of extremist black nationalist demagogues does not erase the need to critique problematic biases 'at home.'"
See Schorsch, "American Jewish Historians, Colonial Jews and Blacks, and
the Limits of *Wissenschaft*: A Critical Review," *Jewish Social Studies* 6, no. 2
(Winter 2000): 102–32.

46 *The earliest Jews who settled*: David Brion Davis showed how five world-
shifting developments in fifteenth-century Europe—the fall of Con-
stantinople to the Ottomans, the Catholic reconquest of Spain, the
beginning of oceanic exploration, the rise of the Atlantic slave trade, and
the Inquisition—were all intertwined and were closely related to the Jews.
The Ottoman seizure of the Byzantine capital in 1453 closed off trade between the Black Sea and the Mediterranean, shuttering the slave markets
on which Western European suppliers had depended. At the same time that
a new source of captives was needed, Portuguese explorers began making
contact with tribes on the west coast of Africa, and they slowly succeeded in
diverting the supply of slaves away from the traditional Arab monopoly in
the east. The African slave trade became an overseas instead of an overland
commerce. Demand for slaves in Portugal was also on the rise, because the
wars between Catholics and Muslims had decimated the laboring population. Davis suggests that as Christians, fired up with Crusader fervor,
pushed Jews out of the medieval slave trade, they may have resorted to
mass murder and expulsion as a means to "disguise" the hostile commercial
takeover. There were perhaps "psychological links between the emergence
of a new slave trade in fifteenth-century Spain and Portugal and the culminating expulsion of the Jews." Davis further suggests that those Portuguese explorers who helped open new slave markets and trading routes in
the Atlantic basin were working off Jewish-made maps and nautical instruments that "focused attention on Africa," a continent that Jewish traders
from the Mediterranean had developed special connections to during the
Middle Ages. Over the years, some have even contended that late-medieval
Jews directed European attention to Africa in hopes they would thereby
discover the lost tribes of Israel and bring on the messianic age. See Davis,
The Problem of Slavery in Western Culture (Ithaca, NY: Cornell University
Press, 1966), 43–44, and *Slavery and Human Progress* (New York: Oxford
University Press, 1985), 93–97.

46 *"visited the remnant of his people"*: Stanley F. Chyet, *Lopez of Newport: Colonial American Merchant Prince* (Detroit: Wayne State University Press,
1970), 13–16.

47 *complex financial instruments*: Jerry Z. Muller, *Capitalism and the Jews*
(Princeton, NJ: Princeton University Press, 2010), 20.

47 *Nearly all the Jews*: Faber, *Jews, Slaves, and the Slave Trade*, 3; Friedman, *Jews
and the American Slave Trade*.

47 *In some Jamaican towns*: Faber, *Jews, Slaves, and the Slave Trade*, 65, 117–18.

47 *Access to extensive kinship ties*: Drescher, "Jews and New Christians in the
Atlantic Slave Trade," 56–58.

48 *"You Jews . . . and our nation"*: Edward Long, *The History of Jamaica or, General Survey of the Antient and Modern State of that Island: with Reflections on
its Situation, Settlements, Inhabitants, Climate, Products, Commerce, Laws,*

and Government, vol. II (London: T. Lowndes, 1774), 459–60, quoted in Faber, *Jews, Slaves, and the Slave Trade*, 62.

49   *an escape hatch*: Drescher, "Jews and New Christians in the Atlantic Slave Trade," 70.

49   *Born to a* converso *family*: Chyet, *Lopez of Newport*; Friedman, *Jews and the American Slave Trade*, 120–27; Faber, *Jews, Slaves, and the Slave Trade*, 135–38; Jonathan D. Sarna, *American Judaism: A History* (New Haven, CT: Yale University Press, 2004), 23; Virginia Bever Platt, "'And Don't Forget the Guinea Voyage': The Slave Trade of Aaron Lopez of Newport," *William and Mary Quarterly* 32, no. 4 (October 1975): 601–18; Bruce M. Bigelow, "Aaron Lopez: Colonial Merchant of Newport," *New England Quarterly* 4, no. 4 (October 1931): 757–76; Michael Hoberman, *New Israel/New England: Jews and Puritans in Early America* (Amherst: University of Massachusetts Press, 2011), 121–60.

50   *"eminent Jew merchant"*: Chyet, *Lopez of Newport*, 174.

50   *"very gainful and advantageous"*: Chyet, *Lopez of Newport*, 73.

50   *outbreak of the American Revolution*: Amid the brewing colonial war, Ezra Stiles ridiculed his friend for staying aloof from the protest movement. The war severed Lopez's trading connections and uprooted his family from Newport. His ships were confiscated by both sides, each suspicious of his loyalties. Regretting the "melancholy situation" of his "once happy country," Lopez reflected in 1777 that "there is no real happiness to be expected in this frail world whose vicissitudes . . . must be encountered with a becoming resignation." See Chyet, *Lopez of Newport*, 155–60.

51   *construction of a synagogue*: For the role of slaves in constructing the Newport synagogue, see Max J. Kohler, "The Jews in Newport," *American Hebrew and Jewish Messenger* 61, no. 3 (May 21, 1897): 101. Thanks to Keith Stokes of the Rhode Island Black Heritage Society for bringing this reference to my attention. See also Michael Hoberman, "Hey, I'm Your Cousin," *Tablet*, June 15, 2023, https://www.tabletmag.com/sections/history/articles/im-your-cousin-american-jewish-genealogy.

51   *"gives to bigotry no sanction"*: George Washington, "To the Hebrew Congregation in Newport, Rhode Island [18 August 1790]," *The Papers of George Washington*, Presidential Series, vol. 6, *1 July 1790–30 November 1790*, ed. Mark A. Mastromarino (Charlottesville: University Press of Virginia, 1996), 284–86.

52   *On any given Saturday morning*: Five slaves owned by Jewish families in New York, including the Gomezes, were implicated in the 1740 slave uprising that led to the hanging of eighteen Black people and the burning at the stake of thirteen others. Mordecai Gomez served as Spanish interpreter for the accused. See Howard B. Rock, *Haven of Liberty: New York Jews in the New World, 1654–1865* (New York: New York University Press, 2012), 38–40; "Unwritten History: Reminiscences of N. Taylor Phillips," *American Jewish Archives Journal* 6, no. 2 (1954): 83; Bertram W. Korn, "Black-Jewish Relations in Early American History, 1654–1865," American Jewish Archives, Rabbi Marc H. Tanenbaum Collection, Series E, box 79, folder 6; Friedman, *Jews and the American Slave Trade*, 109; Jill Lepore, *New York Burning*:

Liberty, Slavery, and Conspiracy in Eighteenth-Century Manhattan (New York: Knopf, 2005), 166.

52 *The first Jews in the remote Dutch outpost*: In 1683, "Abraham Franckfoort, a Jew residing in N. Yorck," as the bill of sale describes him, sold a slave to a Dutch settler in the village of Midwout (Midwood) in present-day Brooklyn. See Abraham G. Dunker, "The Sale of a Negro Slave in Brooklyn in 1683," in *Essays in American Jewish History* (Cincinnati: American Jewish Archives, 1958), 63–68; Morris U. Schappes, "The Jews and American Slavery," *Jewish Currents*, May 1954, 17.

52 *"financier of the Revolution"*: In addition to Haym Salomon, other leading Jewish participants in the American Revolution also held slaves. Francis Salvador, who served as an elected delegate to South Carolina's revolutionary provincial congress, owned thousands of acres in the Carolina piedmont and some thirty people to cultivate his indigo crops. Salvador was ambushed by loyalists and their Indian allies in August 1776, making him the first Jewish casualty of the Revolution. See Morris U. Schappes, "Jews in the American Revolution," *Jewish Life*, March 1954, 24. For Haym Salomon, see Nathan M. Kaganoff, "The Business Career of Haym Salomon as Reflected in His Newspaper Advertisements," *American Jewish Historical Quarterly* 66, no. 1 (September 1976): 35–49; Beth S. Wenger, *History Lessons: The Creation of American Jewish Heritage* (Princeton, NJ: Princeton University Press, 2010), 179–209; Morris U. Schappes, ed., *A Documentary History of the Jews in the United States, 1654–1875* (New York: Schocken Books, 1971), 52–53, 578–80.

52 *keeping his kitchen kosher*: Whiteman, "Introduction," 4.

52 *One of Michael's sons, Hyman*: Josh Nathan-Kazis, "Which Side Were We On? Kentucky Slavery, Mine Wars, and Segregation," *The Forward*, June 28, 2015, https://forward.com/culture/310910/which-side-were-we-on-kentucky -slavery-mine-wars-and-segregation/; Krista Smith, "Slaveholders vs. Slaveholders: Divided Kentuckians in the Secession Crisis," *Register of the Kentucky Historical Society* 97, no. 4 (Autumn 1999): 383; Jeremy D. Popkin, email message to author, May 1, 2023.

52 *Even the respected religious leader*: Laura Arnold Leibman, *Once We Were Slaves: The Extraordinary Journey of a Multiracial Jewish Family* (New York: Oxford University Press, 2021), 118.

53 *Roughly one-fourth of Southern Jews*: Korn, "Jews and Negro Slavery," 157.

53 *"engaging in business transactions"*: Korn, "Jews and Negro Slavery," 170.

53 *Abraham Mendes Seixas*: See Theodore Rosengarten and Dale Rosengarten, eds., *A Portion of the People: Three Hundred Years of Southern Jewish Life* (Columbia: University of South Carolina Press, 2002), 80.

54 *Prussian-born Benjamin Sheftall*: Kyle L. McCormick, "Father and Servant, Son and Slave: Judaism and Labor in Georgia, 1732–1809" (MA thesis, University of Nebraska, 2016), 53.

54 *held on a prison ship*: Scraps of a journal kept by Sheftall's friend and fellow captive Reverend Moses Allen reveal Sheftall's effort to keep kosher while imprisoned. "Pork for dinner," Allen recorded. "The Jews Mr. Sheftall & son refused to eat their pieces, & their knives & forks were ordered to be greased

with it . . . It is a happiness that Mr. Sheftall is a fellow sufferer. He bears it with such fortitude as is an example to me." "The Highest Ranking Jewish Officer of the American Revolution, Colonel Mordecai Sheftall, Struggles to Practice Judaism as a Prisoner of War, in Spite of Persecution by the British," Raab Collection, https://www.raabcollection.com/american-history -autographs/shaftell.

55 *In a 1792 letter to his son*: Michael Hoberman, "'The Confidence Placed in You Is of the Greatest Magnitude': Representations of Paternal Authority in Early Jewish American Letters," *Studies in American Jewish Literature* 33, no. 1 (2014): 79.

55 *"due the 1st day of Roshashona"*: McCormick, "Father and Servant, Son and Slave," 49, 60–61, 69.

55 *"kind, indulgent & benevolent"*: McCormick, "Father and Servant, Son and Slave," 74, 76. Abigail Minis of Georgia was one of the few Jewish women to own a slave-worked plantation. She inherited property when her husband Abraham died in 1757, and within a few years had added more land, opened a tavern (where she and her five daughters entertained the elite of Georgia's society), and increased her holdings of slaves from one to nineteen. She supplied Continental troops during the American Revolution, and remained active in her businesses until her death in 1794 at the age of ninety-three. See McCormick, "Father and Servant, Son and Slave," 52; B. H. Levy, "The Early History of Georgia's Jews," in *Forty Years of Diversity: Essays on Colonial Georgia* (Athens: University of Georgia Press, 2011), 172.

55 *Mordecai Cohen was a Polish-born*: Rosengarten and Rosengarten, *A Portion of the People*, 81; Seth R. Clare, "Marx Cohen and Clear Springs Plantation," *Southern Jewish History* 17 (2014): 26.

56 *"keep her at as hard labor"*: See Emily West, *Chains of Love: Slave Couples in Antebellum South Carolina* (Champaign: University of Illinois Press, 2004), 29.

56 *"a great deal said about hell"*: "Recollections of Slavery by a Runaway Slave," serialized in *The Emancipator* (August 23, September 13, September 20, October 11, October 18, 1838). Susanna Ashton has identified the author of the "Recollections" as James Matthews, who eventually settled in Maine, where, seemingly tormented by what he had endured in bondage, he cycled in and out of the insane asylum before ending his life in poverty. See Ashton, "Recollecting Jim," *Common-Place: The Journal of Early American Life* 15, no. 1 (Fall 2014), https://commonplace.online/article/re-collecting-jim/; and Ashton, "Slaves of Charleston," *The Forward*, September 15, 2014, https:// forward.com/culture/205455/slaves-of-charleston/.

57 *Hart had become one of the wealthiest*: Joshua Trachtenberg, *Consider the Years: The Story of the Jewish Community of Easton, 1752–1942* (Easton, PA: Centennial Committee of Temple Brith Shiloh, 1944), 69.

57 *Legend has it that George Washington*: See J. L. Bell, "The Legend of Hanukkah at Easton," *Boston 1775*, February 6, 2007, https://boston1775 .blogspot.com/2007/02/legend-of-hanukkah-at-easton.html.

57 *"[H]e, the said Michael Hart"*: Northampton County Papers, Misc. Mss. 1778–1797, Historical Society of Pennsylvania. See also Francis S. Fox, *Sweet Land of Liberty: The Ordeal of the American Revolution in Northampton County, Pennsylvania* (University Park: Pennsylvania State University Press,

2000), 127–29; Liam Riordan, *Many Identities, One Nation: The Revolution and Its Legacy in the Mid-Atlantic* (Philadelphia: University of Pennsylvania Press, 2010), 102; Cory James Young, "For Life or Otherwise: Abolition and Slavery in South Central Pennsylvania, 1780–1847" (PhD diss., Georgetown University, 2021), 175.

59 *"carried with it social and business"*: Kohler, "The Jews and the American Anti-Slavery Movement," 147.

60 *To take the Bible's legal stipulations*: Davis, *Slavery and Human Progress*, 85. See also E. E. Urbach, "The Laws Regarding Slavery as a Source for Social History of the Period of the Second Temple, the Mishnah and Talmud," *Papers of the Institute of Jewish Studies* 1 (Jerusalem: Magnes Press, Hebrew University, 1964), 1–94.

61 *"Not a single slave"*: Philo likely had no firsthand knowledge of the Essene community and may have concocted a romanticized view of the group in order to make Jews seem more admirable to his Greek readership. Yet other sources validate aspects of Philo's portrait. Pliny the Elder, in his *Natural History*, describes the Essenes as "a people unique of its kind . . . without women and renouncing love entirely, without money, and having for company only the palm trees." The Roman-Jewish historian Josephus, writing thirty years after Philo, claimed to have lived among the Essenes and explained that the sect avoided slavery because it "tempts men to be unjust." Many centuries later, Voltaire, otherwise critical of Jews, wrote admiringly of the Essenes. "If one is prepared to examine Judaism closely," he acknowledged, "one will be surprised to find, in the midst of barbaric horrors, the most extraordinary spirit of tolerance." Voltaire, *On Tolerance* (Cambridge: Cambridge University Press, 2000), 63; Philo, *Every Good Man Is Free*, in *Jewish Life and Thought Among Greeks and Romans: Primary Readings*, ed. Louis H. Feldman and Meyer Reinhold (Edinburgh: T&T Clark, 1996), 246, 254; John J. Collins, *The Dead Sea Scrolls: A Biography* (Princeton, NJ: Princeton University Press, 2012), 33–66.

62 *Solomon Bush, a prominent Mason*: Henry Samuel Morais, *The Jews of Philadelphia: Their History from the Earliest Settlements to the Present Time* (Philadelphia: Levytype, 1894), 155–57; William Pencak, "Jews and Anti-Semitism in Early Pennsylvania," *Pennsylvania Magazine of History and Biography* 126, no. 3 (July 2002): 391.

63 *"I am a Jew"*: Having already fathered a David, a Solomon, an Esther, an Abraham, a Joseph, and an Aaron, Nones named his next son Jefferson. See Bennett Muraskin, "Benjamin Nones: Profile of a Jewish Jeffersonian," *American Jewish History* 83, no. 3 (September 1995): 381–85; Schappes, "Jews in the American Revolution," 24; Edwin Wolf and Maxwell Whiteman, *The History of the Jews of Philadelphia: From Colonial Times to the Age of Jackson* (Philadelphia: Jewish Publication Society of America, 1957), 190–92, 436–37.

63 *Mordecai Myers, a veteran*: As a boy in Boston, Lowell used to see a painting of Myers hanging in the house of a cousin, and commemorated him in the memoir section of his book *Life Studies*: "The artist painted Major Myers in his sanguine War of 1812 uniform with epaulets, white breeches, and a scarlet frogged waistcoat. His right hand played with the sword 'now to be seen

in the Smithsonian cabinet of heirlooms.' The pose was routine and gallant. The full-lipped smile was good-humoredly pompous and embarrassed . . . Undoubtedly Major Mordecai had lived in a more ritualistic, gaudy, and animal world than twentieth-century Boston. There was something unde-cided, Mediterranean, versatile, almost double-faced about his bearing which suggested that, even to his contemporaries, he must have seemed gratuitously both *ci-devant* and *parvenu*. He was a dark man, a German Jew . . . Our Major's suffering almond eye rested on his luxurious dawn-colored fingers ruffling an off-white glove." Robert Lowell, *Life Studies and For the Union Dead* (New York: Farrar, Straus and Giroux, 1999), 15–16.

63 *Judah provided legal assistance*: Schappes, *A Documentary History of the Jews of the United States*, 118–21.

63 *petition from twenty-four Philadelphia Jews*: *The National Gazette and Liter-ary Register* (Phil.), January 30, 1838, 2; Whiteman, "Introduction," 25, 79. The otherwise South-friendly Buchanan defended the right to submit antislavery petitions, and the obligation of Congress to receive them, though he warned that doing so would "light up a flame over the whole country." See *Congressional Globe, Twenty-Fifth Congress* (1838), 2nd sess., vol. VI, 39.

63 *In the 1840s, Rebecca Hart*: The Female Anti-Slavery Society's founding constitution, from 1833, declares that its members "deem it our duty, *as professing Christians*, to manifest our abhorrence of the flagrant injustice and deep sin of slavery." The Christian language was removed by 1845, and it is only after that date that Hart appears in the minutes of the Society. See Philadelphia Female Anti-Slavery Society papers, Historical Society of Pennsylvania.

64 *Hart worked with William Still*: Hart may have had concerns about Garrett's methods. Garrett wrote Still in a letter dated November 14, 1857: "Please say to my friend, Rebecca Hart, that I have heretofore kept clear of persuad-ing, or even advising slaves to leave their masters till they had fully made up their minds to leave, knowing as I do there is great risk in so doing, and if betrayed once would be a serious injury to the cause hereafter." Even so, Hart took an active hand directing Garrett's attention toward bondsmen she believed ready to be assisted to freedom. "If Rebecca Hart will write to me, and give me the name of the boy, and the name of his mother, I will make another effort," Garrett writes in the same letter. See *William Still's Underground Rail Road Records, Revised Edition* (Philadelphia: William Still, 1886), 640.

64 *eccentric merchant and philanthropist*: See C. S. Monaco, *Moses Levy of Florida: Jewish Utopian and Antebellum Reformer* (Baton Rouge: Louisiana State University Press, 2005).

64 *"which by ignorance and superstition"*: Monaco, *Moses Levy of Florida*, 56.

65 *"indolent, deceitful, and vicious"*: Monaco, *Moses Levy of Florida*, 110–11.

65 *"a unique blend of Utopianism"*: Monaco, *Moses Levy of Florida*, 133–35.

66 *"It is not easy"*: Monaco, *Moses Levy of Florida*, 105, 150, 162.

66 *Levy was devastated when his son*: Maurice I. Wiseman, "Railroad Baron, Fire-Eater, and the "Alien Jew": The Life and Memory of David Levy Yulee" (PhD diss., University of Florida, 2011).

3. "First Truth and Then Peace"

69 *Born in a small Bohemian village*: Wise's often unreliable memoir, which only covered the years before 1857, was published in his German-language newspaper *Die Deborah* in 1874 and 1875. David Phillipsson, a fellow Reform rabbi and one of Wise's mentees, translated and published the text as *Reminiscences* (Cincinnati: Leo Wise and Company, 1901). The standard biography remains Sefton D. Temkin, *Isaac Mayer Wise: Shaping American Judaism* (Oxford: Oxford University Press, 1992). See also James G. Heller, *Isaac M. Wise: His Life, Work and Thought* (New York: Union of American Hebrew Congregations, 1965); Aryeh Rubinstein, "Isaac Mayer Wise: A New Appraisal," *Jewish Social Studies* 39, no. 1/2 (Winter–Spring 1977): 53–74; Jacob Rader Marcus, *The Americanization of Isaac Mayer Wise* (Cincinnati, 1931); Ryan Fox, "Isaac Wise and the Path to American Jewish Unity Through American Nationalism" (BA thesis, University of Albany, 2018).

69 *"small, insignificant-looking people"*: Wise, *Reminiscences*, 17–18.

70 *first day's steam up the Hudson*: Wise, *Reminiscences*, 29–30.

70 *"develops far more swiftly"*: Peter Adams, *Politics, Faith, and the Making of American Judaism* (Ann Arbor: University of Michigan Press, 2014), 1.

71 *The idea of reforming Judaism*: Michael A. Meyer, *Response to Modernity: A History of the Reform Movement in Judaism* (New York: Oxford University Press, 1988).

73 *"Wherever you are treated humanely"*: Meyer, *Response to Modernity*, 30. Even before the wave of civic emancipations, European governments had begun to seize more control over internal Jewish affairs. That cut into Jewish communal autonomy and prevented the once-powerful rabbinic authorities from cracking down on signs of dissension from within.

73 *society of religious dissenters*: See Steven R. Weisman, *The Chosen Wars: How Judaism Became an American Religion* (New York: Simon and Schuster, 2018). For the Reformed Society of Israelites, see Meyer, *Response to Modernity*, 228–29; Sarna, *American Judaism*, 57–59. Philip Benjamin's participation is discussed in Evans, *Judah P. Benjamin*, 9–10.

74 *"the abolitionist society and its secret"*: *A Selection from the Miscellaneous Writings of the Late Isaac Harby, Esq*, ed. Abraham Moise (Charleston, SC: James S. Burges, 1829), 94–95. For more on Harby's proslavery politics, including his editorial commentary on both the Missouri Crisis and the Denmark Vesey conspiracy, see Gary P. Zola, *Isaac Harby of Charleston, 1788–1828* (Tuscaloosa: University of Alabama Press, 1994), 94–98; Daniel N. Gullotta, "Jews for Jackson: Isaac Harby, Southern Politics During the Election of 1824, and the Rise of Jacksonian Democracy," *Early American Studies* 21, no. 2 (Spring 2023): 307.

75 *The building was constructed*: Barry Stiefel, "David Lopez Jr.: Builder, Industrialist, and Defender of the Confederacy," *American Jewish Archives Journal* 64, no. 1/2 (2012): 59.

75 *organ became a dramatic symbol*: Sarna, *American Judaism*, 84–85; Weisman, *The Chosen Wars*, 38–61.

76 *"anyone can do what he wants"*: Sarna, *American Judaism*, 45.

76   *"I dwell in complete darkness"*: Isaac M. Fein, *The Making of an American Jewish Community: The History of Baltimore Jewry from 1773 to 1920* (Philadelphia: Jewish Publication Society of America, 1971), 56–57.

76   *Orthodoxy, formerly an uncommon*: Sarna, *American Judaism*, 87.

76   *Wise did not want to err*: Wise, *Reminiscences*, 54.

77   *"Each congregation pursues its own way"*: Weisman, *The Chosen Wars*, 100.

77   *"Some are reformed"*: Sarna, *American Judaism*, 88; Bertram W. Korn, "Factors Bearing upon the Survival of Judaism in the Ante-Bellum Period," *American Jewish Historical Quarterly* 53, no. 4 (June 1964): 341–51.

77   *"a new peculiar destiny"*: Meyer, *Response to Modernity*, 227.

78   *"reformed and reconstructed"*: Weisman, *The Chosen Wars*, 131.

78   *Born in Stockholm in 1798*: The best account of Raphall's career in England is Israel Finestein, *Anglo-Jewry in Changing Times: Studies in Diversity, 1840–1914* (London: Vallentine Mitchell, 1999). For the later years, see Israel Goldstein, *A Century of Judaism in New York: B'nai Jeshurun, 1825–1925* (New York: Congregation B'nai Jeshurun, 1931); Moshe Davis, *The Emergence of Conservative Judaism: The Historical School in 19th Century America* (Philadelphia: Jewish Publication Society of America, 1963), 356–68.

79   *"most eloquent preacher"*: Finestein, *Anglo-Jewry in Changing Times*, 176–77.

79   *"one of the finest minds"*: Finestein, *Anglo-Jewry in Changing Times*, 184.

79   *"the land we live in"*: Finestein, *Anglo-Jewry in Changing Times*, 176.

80   *"a leading rank among the nations"*: Rock, *Haven of Liberty*, 163.

80   *"Jew and gentile, clergy and laity"*: *Charleston Courier*, February 25, 1850, 2.

80   *"Where there are no men"*: Wise, *Reminiscences*, 128–29.

81   *Tired of the constant strife*: Naphtali J. Rubinger, "Dismissal in Albany," *American Jewish Archives Journal* 24, no. 2 (1972): 160–83.

81   *"I was domiciled in splendid rooms"*: Wise, *Reminiscences*, 143.

81   *"grew excited, and declaimed violently"*: Wise, *Reminiscences*, 149.

82   *the savior would indeed come*: Weisman, *The Chosen Wars*, 104.

82   *"played the hypocrite"*: Sarna, *Jacksonian Jew*, 138.

82   *"a right or a voice"*: Rubinger, "Dismissal in Albany," 164 note 18.

82   *Wise's Albany opponents seized*: See Rubinger, "Dismissal in Albany," passim; Wise, *Reminiscences*, 166.

83   *"the people are young"*: Wise, *Reminiscences*, 234.

84   *a new home in Cincinnati*: Jonathan D. Sarna, "'A Sort of Paradise for the Hebrews': The Lofty Vision of Cincinnati Jews," in *Ethnic Diversity and Civic Identity: Patterns of Conflict and Cohesion in Cincinnati Since 1820*, ed. Henry D. Shapiro and Jonathan D. Sarna (Urbana: University of Illinois Press, 1992), 131–64.

84   *David Einhorn had been raised*: As with Raphall, there is no biography of Einhorn. The most complete account—though by no means impartial—is by his son-in-law, Kaufmann Kohler, appended to a volume collecting some of Einhorn's sermons and writings, published on the centennial of his birth. Kaufmann Kohler, "David Einhorn: The Uncompromising Champion of Reform Judaism," in *David Einhorn Memorial Volume: Selected Sermons and Addresses*, ed. Kaufmann Kohler (New York: Bloch, 1911). See also Bern-

hard N. Cohn, "David Einhorn: Some Aspects of His Thinking," in *Essays in American Jewish History to Commemorate the Tenth Anniversary of the Founding of the American Jewish Archives* (Cincinnati: American Jewish Archives, 1958), 323.

85 *"the first momentous step"*: *Inaugural Sermon Delivered by Dr. David Einhorn Before the Har Sinai Verein, Sept. 29, 1855* (Baltimore: Har Sinai Congregation, 1909), 7.

85 *"axioms of the human spirit"*: The phrase is Aryeh Rubinstein's summation of Einhorn's beliefs. See Rubinstein, "Isaac Mayer Wise: A New Appraisal," 56.

85 *"Judaism in its essence"*: Weisman, *The Chosen Wars*, 135.

86 *"urgent needs of the present day"*: *Inaugural Sermon*, 6.

86 *"like exhaling the breath of life"*: Gershon Greenberg, "The Significance of America in David Einhorn's Conception on History," *American Jewish Historical Quarterly* 63, no. 2 (December 1973): 170.

86 *"insolent and wicked infidel"*: Kohler, "David Einhorn," 422.

86 *Ditching yarmulkes, abolishing circumcision*: Kohler, "David Einhorn," 431–33.

87 *"establishment of a Jewish hierarchy"*: Sarna, *American Judaism*, 87.

87 *a ship across the Atlantic*: Greenberg, "The Significance of America," 161.

88 *abiding belief "in one humanity"*: Greenberg, "The Significance of America," 182.

89 *"The Great Sanhedrin"*: Wise, *Reminiscences*, 133–39.

89 *so many "little republics"*: *The Asmonean*, November 9, 1849.

90 *"perpetual stagnation"*: Weisman, *The Chosen Wars*, 134–35; Fein, *The Making of an American Jewish Community*, 84.

91 *To his rival's slogan*: Kohler, "David Einhorn," 452.

91 *"peace with God"*: Meyer, *Response to Modernity*, 249.

4. Kansas Meshugas

92 *It was the spring of 1856*: August Bondi, letter to American Jewish Historical Society (1903), August Bondi papers, P-178, American Jewish Historical Society. See also Leon Huhner, "Some Jewish Associates of John Brown," *Publications of the American Jewish Historical Society*, no. 23 (1915).

93 *One antislavery lawyer was seized*: Nicole Etcheson, *Bleeding Kansas: Contested Liberty in the Civil War Era* (Lawrence: University Press of Kansas, 2004).

94 *"Shall Kanzas be governed"*: Etcheson, *Bleeding Kansas*, 73.

94 *"the yet virgin soil"*: Doress-Worters, *Mistress of Herself*, 292–93.

94 *"'Yankee Negro thieves'"*: *Autobiography of August Bondi*, 35–45.

95 *The Brown family patriarch*: Etcheson, *Bleeding Kansas*, 109; David S. Reynolds, *John Brown, Abolitionist* (New York: Alfred A. Knopf, 2006), 192.

96 *"that nasty Abolition town"*: Etcheson, *Bleeding Kansas*, 100.

96 *"Let us purge ourselves"*: Allan Nevins, *Ordeal of the Union: Volume II, A House Dividing, 1852–1857* (New York: Charles Scribner's Sons, 1947), 433.

97 *"a great and glorious truth"*: Doress-Worters, *Mistress of Herself*, 189.

97 *her 1847 visit to Charleston*: Doress-Worters, *Mistress of Herself*, 151.

98 *"Where's that sweet Rose?"*: Carol A. Kolmerten, *The American Life of Ernestine L. Rose* (Syracuse, NY: Syracuse University Press, 1999), 67.

98 *She compared American slavery*: Three months after Rose compared the suffering of American slaves with that of Russian serfs, Abraham Lincoln, contemplating a long-shot bid for the United States Senate, would tell a friend that he "should prefer emigrating to some country where they make no pretence of loving liberty—to Russia, for instance, where despotism can be taken pure, and without the base alloy of hypocracy."

98 *"always on the go"*: Anderson, *The Rabbi's Atheist Daughter*, 78.

98 *"She has traveled alone"*: Anderson, *The Rabbi's Atheist Daughter*, 83.

99 *"scoffing Infidel"*: Anderson, *The Rabbi's Atheist Daughter*, 99.

99 *"A good delivery"*: Anderson, *The Rabbi's Atheist Daughter*, 83.

99 *"How very stupid"*: Kolmerten, *The American Life of Ernestine L. Rose*, 129.

99 *"Her eloquence is irresistible"*: Anderson, *The Rabbi's Atheist Daughter*, 2–3.

100 *Her union with William*: Anderson, *The Rabbi's Atheist Daughter*, 78–81.

100 *"remnant of the mighty nation"*: *New York Aurora*, March 28, 1842.

101 *"a first rate lady friend"*: Anderson, *The Rabbi's Atheist Daughter*, 91, 194 note 28.

101 *"I stand before the world"*: Doress-Worters, *Mistress of Herself*, 197–98.

101 *"in a minority of one"*: Anderson, *The Rabbi's Atheist Daughter*, 98.

101 *"ringleted, glove-handed exotic"*: Doress-Worters, *Mistress of Herself*, 166–67.

101 *"We know of no object"*: Anderson, *The Rabbi's Atheist Daughter*, 88.

102 *"the foreigner, who can't speak"*: Anderson, *The Rabbi's Atheist Daughter*, 93.

103 *"There are so few who dare"*: Anderson, *The Rabbi's Atheist Daughter*, 121.

104 *"Whatever the Union might have"*: Doress-Worters, *Mistress of Herself*, 192.

104 *"break that unholy Union"*: Anderson, *The Rabbi's Atheist Daughter*, 116–67.

104 *"Oh how I long to probe"*: Anthony's diary from her Southern trip with Rose is in Doress-Worters, *Mistress of Herself*, 169–75.

105 *"several quite severe attacks"*: Doress-Worters, *Mistress of Herself*, 66.

105 *the Roses left for Europe*: Anderson, *The Rabbi's Atheist Daughter*, 96–97.

106 *"that little Jew from New Orleans"*: Meade, *Judah P. Benjamin*, 112.

106 *"A Hebrew of Hebrews"*: Meade, *Judah P. Benjamin*, 175.

106 *an intense conversation about religion*: Wise's account of the conversation with Webster and Benjamin is in *Reminiscences*, 187–88. For why his account cannot be accurate in every particular, see Bertram W. Korn, "Isaac Mayer Wise on the Civil War," in *Eventful Years and Experiences: Studies in Nineteenth Century American Jewish History* (Cincinnati: American Jewish Archives, 1954), 83–86. For a convincing argument that the conversation did happen in some form, see Heller, *Isaac M. Wise: His Life, Work and Thought*, 208, 723–24 note 15.

107 *During senatorial recesses*: For Benjamin's 1850s legal career, see William C. Gilmore, *The Confederate Jurist: The Legal Life of Judah P. Benjamin* (Edinburgh: Edinburgh University Press, 2023), also Butler, *Judah P. Benjamin*, 113–40; Meade, *Judah P. Benjamin*, 96–98, 111–12, 121–23. Benjamin did not only represent wealthy interests but personally invested in the Tehuantepec railroad project and in Texas lands, as well as other projects.

107 *Benjamin's "acknowledged ability"*: Traub, *Judah Benjamin*, 54.

108 *"bridge the river of bitterness"*: Evans, *Judah P. Benjamin*, 90.

108 *"decidedly Hebrew"*: Traub, *Judah Benjamin*, 55.

108 *"appeals to Sharpe's rifles"*: Meade, *Judah P. Benjamin*, 101.

108 *Benjamin left the splintering Whig*: Butler, *Judah P. Benjamin*, 146.

109 *founder of . . . the Native American Party*: John A. Forman, "Lewis Charles Levin: Portrait of an American Demagogue," *American Jewish Archives* 12 (1960): 150–94.

109 *Benjamin, too, had dabbled*: In 1854, the Know-Nothing Party of New York ran a Jewish candidate for governor, a lawyer named Daniel Ullmann. Ullmann later led Black troops into battle during the Civil War. See Tyler Anbinder, *Nativism and Slavery: The Northern Know Nothings and the Politics of the 1850s* (New York: Oxford University Press, 1992), 77–87; Butler, *Judah P. Benjamin*, 69, 71, 83, 116.

109 *he ridiculed the idea*: Geoffrey David Cunningham, "'You can never convert the free sons of the soil into vassals': Judah P. Benjamin and the Threat of Union, 1852–1861" (MA thesis, Louisiana State University, 2010), 63.

110 *"fast approaching time"*: Butler, *Judah P. Benjamin*, 150.

110 *"last, lamentable catastrophe"*: Cunningham, "'You can never convert the free sons of the soil,'" 45.

110 *"dreadful will be the internecine"*: Butler, *Judah P. Benjamin*, 158.

111 *"big, savage, bloodthirsty Austrian"*: Oswald Garrison Villard, *John Brown, 1800–1859: A Biography After Fifty Years* (Boston: Houghton Mifflin, 1910), 158. Wiener was actually from Posen, in Prussian Poland.

112 *"shot as mad dogs"*: Etcheson, *Bleeding Kansas*, 113.

112 *"midnight attacks"*: Etcheson, *Bleeding Kansas*, 118.

113 *"He showed at all times"*: *Autobiography of August Bondi*, 54.

5. "Israelites with Egyptian Principles"

114 *"There is money to be made"*: Peter Chapman, *The Last of the Imperious Rich* (New York: Portfolio, 2010), 15; Roland Flade, *The Lehmans: From Rimpar to the New World, a Family History* (Würzburg, Germany: Königshausen & Neumann, 1999), 43–45.

115 *"mastering every intricacy"*: Kenneth Libo, ed., *Lots of Lehmans: The Family of Mayer Lehman of Lehman Brothers, Remembered by His Descendants* (New York: Center for Jewish History, 2007), 6.

116 *"quiet and unostentatious"*: Howard N. Rabinowitz, "Nativism, Bigotry, and Anti-Semitism in the South," *American Jewish History* 77, no. 3 (March 1988): 448; Jason Blau, "Paradoxical Toleration: Southern Antisemitism in the Nineteenth Century" (BA thesis, College of William and Mary, 2022), 30, 41–42. ›

116 *traveling peddlers*: Oscar R. Straus, *Under Four Administrations: From Cleveland to Taft* (Boston: Houghton Mifflin, 1922), 5–6; Anton Hieke, *Jewish Identity in the Reconstruction South: Ambivalence and Adaptation* (Berlin: De Gruyter, 2013), 153; Hasia Diner, *Roads Taken: The Great Jewish Migrations to the New World and the Peddlers Who Forged the Way* (New Haven, CT: Yale University Press, 2015), 92, 102–3; Patrick Q. Mason, "Anti-Jewish Violence in the New South," *Southern Jewish History* 8 (2005): 102.

117 *"swarm" of Jewish peddlers*: Frederick Law Olmsted, *A Journey in the Seaboard Slave States* (New York: Dix and Edwards, 1856), 440.

117 *"warn all our brothers"*: Leeser quoted in Whiteman, "Introduction."

117 *ten peddlers were thrown out*: For the expulsion of peddlers from Mississippi, see C. Vann Woodward, *The Burden of Southern History* (Baton Rouge: Louisiana State University Press, 1960), 65; *Anti-Slavery Tracts, Second Series, Nos. 1–25* (New York: American Anti-Slavery Society, 1860–1862), 135.

117 *"something of a Jewish slave-trading dynasty"*: Clive Webb, *Fight Against Fear: Southern Jews and Black Civil Rights* (Athens: University of Georgia Press, 2011), 6; Korn, "Jews and Negro Slavery," 172–74; David W. Blight, *A Slave No More: Two Men Who Escaped to Freedom, Including Their Own Narratives of Emancipation* (Orlando, FL: Harcourt, 2007), 56–61. Hector Davis fathered numerous children with a woman he owned, and in 1860, with war looming, sent them to safety in Philadelphia. When he died in 1863, Davis freed his family in his will.

118 *"going on big scale"*: Hieke, *Jewish Identity in the Reconstruction South*, 167–69.

119 *"not so great a wrong"*: Korn, "Jews and Negro Slavery," 195; Adam D. Mendelsohn, *The Rag Race: How Jews Sewed Their Way to Success in America and the British Empire* (New York: New York University Press, 2015), 68.

119 *In Charleston, South Carolina*: Korn, "Jews and Negro Slavery," 172 note 70; James William Hagy, *This Happy Land: The Jews of Colonial and Antebellum Charleston* (Tuscaloosa: University of Alabama Press, 1993), 97; Mark R. Jones, *Wicked Charleston, Vol. 2: Prostitutes, Politics, and Prohibition* (Charleston, SC: History Press, 2006), 19–23; Sarah Pillman Amundson, "A Woman Lies Bleeding on the Ground: Prostitution and Underground Economy in Nineteenth Century Charleston" (MA thesis, Iowa State University, 2017), 8–11.

120 *"It does not take a prophetic clairvoyance"*: Anton Hieke, "Rabbi Maurice Mayer: German Revolutionary, Charleston Reformer, and Anti-Abolitionist," *Southern Jewish History* 17 (2014): 45–89.

120 *"a harmonizing bond of union"*: Melvin M. Leiman, *Jacob N. Cardozo: Economic Thought in the Antebellum South* (New York: Columbia University Press, 1966).

120 *Uriah P. Levy's stewardship*: Melvin I. Urofsky, "The Levy Family and Monticello," *Virginia Quarterly Review* (Summer 2002): 395–412; Marc Leepson, *The Levy Family's Epic Quest to Rescue the House That Jefferson Built* (New York: Free Press, 2002), 77; Eliza R. L. McGraw, *Two Covenants: Representations of Southern Jewishness* (Baton Rouge: Louisiana State University Press, 2005), 11–32. After the Civil War, Uriah Levy's nephew, Jefferson Levy, purchased Monticello at auction; a three-term New York congressman, he owned it from 1879 to 1923. In all, the Levy family owned Monticello longer than did the Jefferson-Randolph clan.

121 *outnumbered by free-state settlers*: Etcheson, *Bleeding Kansas*, 139–67.

122 *The Lecompton Constitution*: Manisha Sinha, *The Counterrevolution of Slavery: Politics and Ideology in Antebellum South Carolina* (Chapel Hill: University of North Carolina Press, 2000), 192; Kenneth R. Stampp, *America in 1857: A Nation on the Brink* (New York: Oxford University Press, 1992), 279.

122 *"our property, now kept"*: Butler, *Judah P. Benjamin*, 59, 157, 147–48; Traub, *Judah Benjamin*, 57.

123 *a heated exchange in the Senate*: See Evans, *Judah P. Benjamin*, 98–102.

124 *"was merchandise, was property"*: Wiseman, "Judah P. Benjamin and Slavery," 110–11; Rosen, *The Jewish Confederates*, 70.

124 *elaborately veiled yet unmistakable insult*: Some historians have repeated a claim, first published in 1903, that Benjamin sneered in reply to Wade some version of this: "It is true that I am a Jew, and when my ancestors were receiving their Ten Commandments from the immediate hand of Deity, amidst thunderings and lightnings of Mt. Sinai, the ancestors of the distinguished gentleman who is opposed to me were herding swine in the forests of Scandinavia." There is no evidence he actually said it (Benjamin Disraeli said much the same thing to an opponent), and little likelihood he would have, given his reluctance to speak publicly about his Jewishness. See *Saturday Evening Post*, October 3, 1903; Max J. Kohler, *Publications of the American Jewish Historical Society* 12 (1904): 83–84; Butler, *Judah P. Benjamin*, 434.

124 *All three Jewish men*: The three Jews elected to Congress in the 1850s were Henry M. Phillips, son of the president of Philadelphia's Portuguese synagogue; Philip Phillips (no relation), a boyhood friend of Judah Benjamin who won election to Congress from Alabama in 1852 and played a crucial role in the passage of the Kansas-Nebraska Act; and Emanuel Hart, a leader of the Tammany Hall political machine in New York. See Kurt Stone, *The Jews of Capitol Hill: A Compendium of Jewish Congressional Members* (Lanham, MD: Scarecrow Press, 2011), 13–15, 22–23; David T. Morgan, "Philip Phillips, Jurist and Statesman," in *Jews of the South: Selected Essays from the Southern Jewish Historical Society*, ed. Samuel Proctor, Louis Schmier, and Malcolm Stern (Macon, GA: Mercer University Press, 1984), 107–20; Henry Barrett Learned, "The Relation of Philip Phillips to the Repeal of the Missouri Compromise in 1854," *Mississippi Valley Historical Review* 8, no. 4 (March 1922): 303–17; Rock, *Haven of Liberty*, 230.

124 *London-born former umbrella manufacturer*: Rock, *Haven of Liberty*, 231–32; Barbara Straus Reed, "Unity, Not Absorption: Robert Lyon and the *Asmonean*: The Origins of the First English-Language Jewish Weekly in the United States," *American Journalism* 7, no. 2 (1990): 77–95.

126 *"subject one to social ostracism"*: Straus, *Under Four Administrations*, 12–13. Straus does relate that his father purchased the slaves because he thought it was the only way he could help them under the existing system. "If we children spoke to the slaves harshly or disregarded their feelings," he remembered, "we were promptly checked and reprimanded by our parents." See also Webb, *Fight Against Fear*, 7–8.

126 *they met at a boardinghouse*: Korn, "Jews and Negro Slavery," 195; Allan Tarshish, "The Economic Life of the American Jew in the Middle Nineteenth Century," in *Essays in American Jewish History to Commemorate the Tenth Anniversary of the Founding of the American Jewish Archives*, ed. Jacob Rader Marcus (Cincinnati: American Jewish Archives, 1958), 268.

126 *"You may eliminate all suspicious"*: See Randolph G. Adams, *Three Americanists* (Philadelphia: University of Pennsylvania Press, 1939), 1–33; for the controversy over the firing of Harrisse's UNC colleague B. S. Hedrick, see

Richard Hofstadter and Walter P. Metzger, *The Development of Academic Freedom in the United States* (New York: Columbia University Press, 1955), 258 note 127.

127 *"Born and reared at the South"*: Schappes, *A Documentary History of the Jews in the United States*, 293–301, 644 note 5; Albert M. Friedenberg, "Solomon Heydenfeldt: A Jewish Jurist of Alabama and California," *Publications of the American Jewish Historical Society*, no. 10 (1902): 129–40; James Benson Sellers, *Slavery in Alabama* (Tuscaloosa: University of Alabama Press, 1950), 185–90.

128 *"[T]hey have made him a menial"*: Korn, "Jews and Negro Slavery," 198; Emily Bingham, *Mordecai: An American Family* (New York: Hill and Wang, 2003).

129 *"Till this is resolved on"*: Bingham, *Mordecai*, 107–8.

129 *Lazarus lived alone*: Keith Finley, "Dr. Marx Edgeworth Lazarus, the Sand Mountain Hermit," *Valley Leaves* 50, no. 1–2 (2015): 44–47.

129 *"our modern Egyptians"*: Joel S. Baden, *The Book of Exodus: A Biography* (Princeton, NJ: Princeton University Press, 2019), 164. See also David Waldstreicher, *The Odyssey of Phillis Wheatley: A Poet's Journey Through American Slavery and Independence* (New York: Farrar, Straus and Giroux, 2023), 257.

130 *"like the children of Israel"*: Michael Hoberman, "'God Loves the Hebrews': Exodus Typologies, Jewish Slaveholding, and Black Peoplehood in Antebellum America," *American Jewish Archives Journal* 67, no. 2 (2015): 47.

130 *"there breathes a hope"*: W. E. B. Du Bois, *The Souls of Black Folk* (New York: Bantam Books, 2005), 194.

130 *"spared no energy"*: C. L. R. James, *The Black Jacobins: Toussaint L'Ouverture and the San Domingo Revolution* (New York: Vintage Books, 1963), 17; Jonathan Schorsch, *Jews and Blacks in the Early Modern World* (Cambridge, UK: Cambridge University Press, 2004); Bruce D. Haynes, *The Soul of Judaism: Jews of African Descent in America* (New York: New York University Press, 2018), 67–85; Aviva Ben-Ur, *Jewish Autonomy in a Slave Society: Suriname in the Atlantic World, 1651–1825* (Philadelphia: University of Pennsylvania Press, 2020); Wieke Vink, *Creole Jews: Negotiating Community in Colonial Suriname* (Leiden, The Netherlands: KITLV Press, 2010), 256; Laura Arnold Leibman, *Once We Were Slaves: The Extraordinary Journey of a Multiracial Jewish Family* (New York: Oxford University Press, 2021).

131 *at risk of execution*: Jonathan Schorsch, *The Underground World of Secret Jews and Africans: Two Tales of Sex, Magic, and Survival in Colonial Cartagena and Mexico City* (Princeton, NJ: Markus Wiener Publishers, 2021).

131 *more rigid restrictions*: Schorsch, *Jews and Blacks*, 186.

132 *"umbraging the decency of society"*: Joshua D. Rothman, "'Notorious in the Neighborhood': An Interracial Family in Early National and Antebellum Virginia," *Journal of Southern History* 67, no. 1 (February 2001): 73–114.

132 *When an enslaved Black woman*: Whiteman, "Introduction," 22–25, 78–79.

133 *Apparently born in Madagascar*: Ralph Melnick, "Billy Simons: The Black Jew of Charleston," *American Jewish Archives* 32, no. 1 (April 1980): 3–8.

133 *noted in their defense*: Flade, *The Lehmans*, 60–62.

134 *Peter Still recounted*: Peter's real story was different from what he described in the book. He was not kidnapped from his home along the Delaware River.

He was not even born free. He was the son of an enslaved woman in Maryland who, a few years after he was born, escaped from bondage to join her husband, who had previously gained his freedom through self-purchase. She managed to bring her daughters to freedom but had to leave behind her sons. Still knew that if the book mentioned that Peter's mother had escaped from slavery she would be subject to re-enslavement under the Fugitive Slave Law. Still's coauthor was Kate E. R. Pickard, who had taught in a local women's academy in Tuscumbia, Alabama, where Peter sometimes worked. In the early 1850s, she married and moved to upstate New York.

134 *Joseph and Isaac Friedman had moved*: See the introductory note to "The Kidnapped and the Ransomed," *American Jewish Archives* 9, no. 1 (1957): 31 note 8; Spencer R. Crew, "The Saga of Peter Still," *New Jersey History* 125, no. 2 (2010): 62–72.

135 *"Virgin Mary had one son"*: Webb, *Fight Against Fear*, 26.

137 *narrative of his enslavement*: The book was largely ignored on publication, but republished in 1941 with an introduction by the historian Lawrence D. Reddick, who compared the suffering of European Jews under the Nazis with that of Black slaves before the Civil War. As Reddick put it, "the Jewish or political refugee stealing across the border, hunted and haunted, yet finding unexpected, often silent, friends to help him on his way is astonishingly similar to the lone slave following the North Star through thicket and swamp, in his turn, befriended by the agents of the Underground Railroad to freedom." *The Kidnapped and the Ransomed*, xiii.

137 *After a spell at the gold mines*: Joseph is described in California legislative records for 1859 as administrator of the estate of "Isaac S. Friedman, deceased." See Alonzo Phelps, *Contemporary Biography of California's Representative Men, Vol. 1* (San Francisco: A. L. Bancroft, 1881–1882), which wrongly places Tuscumbia in Ohio.

6. On Native Grounds

138 *most Jews had aligned*: Ira N. Forman, "The Politics of Minority Consciousness: The Historical Voting Behavior of American Jews," in *Jews in American Politics*, ed. L. Sandy Maisel (Lanham, MD: Rowman & Littlefield, 2001), 144–47; Andrew Porwancher, *The Jewish World of Alexander Hamilton* (Princeton, NJ: Princeton University Press, 2021), 155; Bennett Muraskin, "Benjamin Nones: Profile of a Jewish Jeffersonian," *American Jewish History* 83, no. 3 (September 1995): 381–85; Morris U. Schappes, "Jews and the Jeffersonians," *Jewish Life*, April 1954, 21–25; Gullotta, "Jews for Jackson," 317.

139 *"fought in the same holy cause"*: Gullotta, "Jews for Jackson," 314.

140 *might not be long before Jews*: Bertram W. Korn, "The Know Nothing Movement and the Jews," in *Eventful Years and Experiences* (Cincinnati: American Jewish Archives, 1954), 58–78.

140 *"aggression of the slave power"*: Morris U. Schappes, "Jews in Lincoln's Third Party, 1854–1860," *Jewish Life*, October 1948, 13–16.

140 *One, Michigan pioneer*: Joan Weil Saltzstein, ed., *Liebman Adler: His Life Through His Letters* (Chicago: privately printed, 1975), 92. Kanter soon returned to the Democrats.

140   *aided fugitives*: Stacie Narlock and Holly Teasdale, "The Underground Railroad: Little Known Jewish Connections," *Michigan Jewish History* 45 (Fall 2005): 51–57; Sharon Luckerman, "Jews on the Underground Railroad," *Detroit Jewish News*, February 27, 2004, 65.

140   *In 1853, a Jewish plumber*: Hannah G. Solomon, *Fabric of My Life* (New York: Bloch, 1946), 18; *Chicago Times-Herald*, June 9, 1895. New York was a hub of Jewish Republican activity. In Brooklyn, a businessman named Joseph Goldmark helped form the Kings County Republican Club. Jonathan Nathan, a celebrated lawyer and member of Shearith Israel, encouraged Hamilton Fish, the state's governor-turned-senator and Nathan's friend from their days at Columbia, to join the new party. Nathan assured Fish that "if Republicanism means abolition I aint there—but if the choice be presented to me of Abolition or Slavery extension and Southern principles and predominance I ask you which must I take." After initially protesting against Nathan's newfound "niggerism," Fish followed his friend into the new party. Schappes, *A Documentary History of the Jews in the United States*, 3rd ed., 349–51; Schappes, "Jews in Lincoln's Third Party," 15.

141   *foreign-born Republicans*: Carl Wittke, *Refugees of Revolution* (Philadelphia: University of Pennsylvania Press, 1952), 203–20.

141   *"Have they read the harrowing history"*: *The Asmonean*, August 8, 1855, 132.

142   *The joys of the "Sabbath peace"*: John J. Weisert, "Lewis N. Dembitz and Onkel Tom's Hutte," *American-German Review* (February 1953): 7–8; Melvin I. Urofsky, *Louis D. Brandeis: A Life* (New York: Schocken Books, 2009), 17–19; Carol A. Eli, "Jewish Community and Synagogues," in *Germans in Louisville: A History*, ed. Victoria A. Ullrich and C. Robert Ullrich (Charleston, SC: History Press, 2015), 78; Josephine Goldmark, *Pilgrims of '48: One Man's Part in the Austrian Revolution of 1848; and a Family Migration to America* (New Haven, CT: Yale University Press, 1930), 230.

143   *He was appalled to find*: Riesser once considered emigrating to America, "had not America disgusted me recently with slavery, the status of the free colored people and all the atrocities which result from these evils." Eleonore Oppenheimer, "A German Jewish Emancipator on the Negro Question," *Negro History Bulletin* 18, no. 1 (November 1954): 11; *New York Tribune*, September 8, 1856, 6; Wittke, *Refugees of Revolution*, 86–87, 207; Jacob Rader Marcus, *United States Jewry, 1776–1985, Vol. III: The Germanic Period, Part 2* (Detroit: Wayne State University Press, 1993), 24; Flade, *The Lehmans*, 38–39.

144   *"very wise and white"*: Wise, *Reminiscences*, 286.

144   *"demons of hatred and destruction"*: "The Secession," *The Israelite*, December 28, 1860; see also Sefton D. Temkin, "Isaac Mayer Wise and the Civil War," in *Jews and the Civil War: A Reader*, ed. Jonathan D. Sarna and Adam Mendelsohn (New York: New York University Press, 2010), 164–65.

144   *unholy alliance between nativists*: Non-Jewish German immigrants also had a difficult time reconciling their liberal politics with the nativist tendencies of antislavery activists. As the editor of the *Springfield (Mass.) Republican* commented: "When you get a German between slavery on one side and Know-Nothingism on the other, you get a stubborn fellow in a very tight place, and

he is quite as apt to let slavery slide for this time in order to make his vote tell against the Know-Nothings." Wittke, *Refugees of Revolution*, 212. See also Dale Baum, "Know-Nothingism and the Republican Majority in Massachusetts: The Political Realignment of the 1850s," *Journal of American History* 64, no. 4 (March 1978): 973–74. .

145   *"act of political injustice"*: "Our Foreign Population," *The Liberator*, April 22, 1859, 62.

145   *The riots marked the end*: See Wittke, *Refugees of Revolution*, 187; "Election Riots in Cincinnati," *New York Times*, April 5, 1855; Bridget Ford, *Bonds of Union: Religion, Race, and Politics in a Civil War Borderland* (Chapel Hill: University of North Carolina Press, 2016), 26–27.

146   *"highly becoming a Christian"*: *The Israelite*, November 14, 1856.

146   *more openly with the Democrats*: Wise sent several letters to Stephen Douglas after he won the Senate race against Lincoln in 1858, offering his journal as a vehicle for organizing Jewish votes behind Douglas in his expected 1860 presidential bid. He attached to one missive a clipping from his newspaper to show Douglas that "I fought with the democracy in favor of your policy in regard to slavery and territories." Douglas never replied. See Heller, *Isaac M. Wise: His Life, Work and Thought*, 318–20.

146   *"it was the Union"*: *Die Deborah*, December 16, 1859; Sefton D. Temkin, "Isaac Mayer Wise: A Biographical Sketch," in *A Guide to the Writings of Isaac Mayer Wise*, ed. Doris C. Sturzenberger (Cincinnati: American Jewish Archives, 1981), 34; Rock, *Haven of Liberty*, 237.

146   *"Does the Negro have less ability"*: Isaac M. Fein, "Baltimore Rabbis During the Civil War," in Sarna and Mendelsohn, *Jews and the Civil War: A Reader*, 188–90.

147   *"A foreigner could only cast"*: Fein, "Baltimore Rabbis," 190; also Fein, *The Making of an American Jewish Community*, 88–89.

147   *"The defeat of the Know Nothing"*: Abraham Lincoln opposed the Massachusetts law as contrary to the spirit of American institutions, and likewise saw his antislavery and his antinativist positions as linked. "I have some little notoriety for commiserating the oppressed condition of the negro; and I should be strangely inconsistent if I could favor any project for curtailing the existing rights of white men, even though born in different lands, and speaking different languages from myself."

148   *Slave ownership among Baltimore Jews*: Eric L. Goldstein and Deborah R. Weiner, *On Middle Ground: A History of the Jews of Baltimore* (Baltimore: Johns Hopkins University Press, 2018), 36; Nicholas B. Fessenden, "'Which Side Are You On?': Baltimore's Immigrants and the Civil War," *Report of the Society for the History of the Germans in Maryland*, vol. 47 (2017); Benjamin Tuska, "Know-Nothingism in Baltimore 1854–1860," *Catholic Historical Review* 11 (July 1925): 217–51.

148   *"never to forget that the Constitution"*: Fein, "Baltimore Rabbis," 181–82; Jayme A. Sokolow, "Revolution and Reform: The Antebellum Jewish Abolitionists," in Sarna and Mendelsohn, *Jews and the Civil War: A Reader*, 137.

148   *Only thirty years*: Edward Eitches, "Maryland's 'Jew Bill,'" *American Jewish Historical Quarterly* 60, no. 3 (March 1971): 258–79.

149   *"gain the proud self-consciousness"*: Marcus, *The Americanization of Isaac Mayer Wise*, 10.

149   *"a light not of this earth"*: Charles Aaron Rubenstein, *History of Har Sinai Congregation of the City of Baltimore* (Baltimore: Kohn & Pollock, 1918).

149   *"the kind of anger"*: Herbert S. Rutman, *Rabbi David Einhorn* (Baltimore: Jewish Historical Society of Maryland, 1979).

150   *"Herr Szold is not able"*: Fein, *The Making of an American Jewish Community*, 190.

151   *"Each society"*: Joseph Buchler, "The Struggle for Unity: Attempts at Union in American Jewish Life: 1654–1868," *American Jewish Archives* 2 (1949): 25.

151   *"plan for establishing religious"*: Sarna, *American Judaism*, 104; see also Zev Eleff, *Who Rules the Synagogue? Religious Authority and the Formation of American Judaism* (New York: Oxford University Press, 2016).

151   *"Slaves and cowards only"*: Marcus, *The Americanization of Isaac Mayer Wise*, 19; Natalie Isser, "Diplomatic Intervention and Human Rights: The Swiss Question, 1852–1864," *Journal of Church and State* 35, no. 3 (Summer 1993): 577–92; Sol M. Stroock, "Switzerland and American Jews," *Publications of the American Jewish Historical Society*, no. 11 (1903): 7–52; Peter Adams, *Politics, Faith, and the Making of American Judaism* (Ann Arbor: University of Michigan Press, 2014), 19.

152   *when police in Bologna*: David I. Kertzer, *The Kidnapping of Edgar Mortara* (New York: Vintage Books, 1998).

152   *"It is not that they love"*: Bertram W. Korn, *The American Reaction to the Mortara Case: 1858–1859* (Cincinnati: American Jewish Archives, 1957), 86.

153   *"glorified it as a moral"*: Fein, *The Making of an American Jewish Community*, 106; Korn, *American Reaction*, 107.

153   *When Northern rabbis*: Korn, *American Reaction*, 45, 92–93.

155   *"did not sanction an increase"*: *Autobiography of August Bondi*, 69.

155   *"insurrection was to be regretted"*: Anderson, *The Rabbi's Atheist Daughter*, 116.

156   *a rabbi was invited*: Bertram W. Korn, "The First Jewish Prayer in Congress," in *Eventful Years and Experiences*, 95–124; Sarna, *American Judaism*, 96; Howard Mortman, *When Rabbis Bless Congress: The Great American Story of Jewish Prayers on Capitol Hill* (Boston: Academic Studies Press, 2020); *Washington Globe*, February 2, 1860; Goldstein, *A Century of Judaism in New York: B'nai Jeshurun*, 121–23.

156   *"The Rabbi did it today"*: Korn, "The First Jewish Prayer," 103–7.

157   *"the Catholicized Slaveocratic Party"*: Korn, *American Reaction*, 84.

158   *"His large, gaunt body"*: Abram J. Dittenhoefer, *How We Elected Lincoln: Personal Recollections* (Philadelphia: University of Pennsylvania Press, 2015), 5, 16.

159   *rail splitter was the friend*: Jonathan D. Sarna and Benjamin Shapell, *Lincoln and the Jews: A History* (New York: Thomas Dunne Books, 2015), 12–14, 56–57; Schappes, "Jews in Lincoln's Third Party," 16; Whiteman, "Introduction," 85; Wittke, *Refugees of Revolution*, 152–53; Isaac Markens, "Lincoln and the Jews," *Publications of the American Jewish Historical Society* 17 (1909): 109–65; Philip S. Foner, *Jews in American History, 1654–1865* (New

York: International Publishers, 1943), 53–54; Max J. Kohler, "Jews in the Anti-Slavery Movement," *Publications of the American Jewish Historical Society* 5 (1897): 152–53; Diane DeBlois and Robert Dalton Harris, "Balancing the Books: Newspapers & the Postal Business of the Confederacy," *Postal History Symposium* (November 2012).

159   *One of Lincoln's closest friends*: Sarna and Shapell, *Lincoln and the Jews: A History*, 14–76. One of Jonas's sons, Edward, recalled attending a political meeting in 1858 where his father was due to speak to the audience of 1,200 people before the Republican Senate candidate took the stage: "While my father was speaking, I suddenly felt a tickling behind my ear. Thinking it a bug or fly I slapped vigorously, but upon its being repeated several times, I became suspicious and turned suddenly and caught the fly. It was Mr. Lincoln with a straw in his hand. He made it all right at once by catching me up with his long arm, drawing me to his side and talking to me very entertainingly until his turn came to address the assemblage."

160   *"land of hypocrisy, guile, and fraud"*: Abram Vossen Goodman, "A Jewish Peddler's Diary 1842–1843," *American Jewish Archives*, no. 4 (1951): 81–111.

161   *"one of the blackest Republicans"*: Schappes, "Jews in Lincoln's Third Party," 15. On the same postelection visit to Chicago when he met Abraham Kohn, Lincoln sat for his second portrait with a Jewish photographer named Samuel G. Altschuler. Taken four weeks after Lincoln had received a letter from an eleven-year-old girl urging him to grow a beard, Altschuler's photograph is the first to show it.

161   *a satin banner*: Markens, "Lincoln and the Jews," 131–33; Simon Wolf, *The American Jew as Patriot, Soldier and Citizen* (Philadelphia: Levytype, 1895), 426–28; Sarna and Shapell, *Lincoln and the Jews: A History*, 72–73.

162   *refuge to runaway slaves*: *Autobiography of August Bondi*, 69–70.

163   *funds to help enslaved people*: Butler, *Judah P. Benjamin*, 195–98.

163   *focused instead on his law practice*: Meade, *Judah P. Benjamin*, 136; Edgar M. Kahn, "Judah Philip Benjamin in California," *California Historical Society Quarterly* 47, no. 2 (June 1968): 157–73.

164   *"look with kindling eye"*: Cunningham, "You can never convert the free sons," 78–80; Meade, *Judah P. Benjamin*, 41.

164   *"wild torrent of passion"*: Benjamin's December 9 letter explaining his support for secession was not published until December 23. Benjamin may even have postdated his letter to make it appear as if he had made up his mind earlier than he had. Meade, *Judah P. Benjamin*, 145.

164   *"the ground giving way"*: Meade, *Judah P. Benjamin*, 151.

165   *"You never can convert"*: *Congressional Globe*, Senate, 36th Congress, 2nd Session, 212–17.

7. Battle of the Rabbis

170   *"pray away the sins"*: "The Secession," *The Israelite*, December 28, 1860, 205.

170   *In Boston, Detroit, and Chicago*: Mitchell Snay, *Gospel of Disunion: Religion and Separatism in the Antebellum South* (New York: Cambridge University Press, 1993), 162–64. For the larger context of mostly Christian debate over

slavery and the Bible in 1860, see Mark A. Noll, *The Civil War as a Theological Crisis* (Chapel Hill: University of North Carolina Press, 2006), 31–50.

170   *"I cannot understand why"*: "Correspondence," *Jewish Messenger*, January 18, 1861, 21.

171   *"a sin before God"*: "State of the Union: Our National Fast Day," *New York Herald*, January 5, 1861), 1; Schappes, *A Documentary History of the Jews in the United States*, 405–18. See also Weisman, *The Chosen Wars*, 159–63.

171   *early proponents of scientific racism*: Nott solicited Raphall's opinion on a pet issue of his: proving that Jews were virtually unchanged as a separate race over thousands of years, no matter where they lived. Raphall affirmed Nott's views. See Josiah C. Nott and George R. Gliddon, *Types of Mankind, Or, Ethnological Researches, Based Upon the Ancient Monuments, Paintings, Sculptures, and Crania of Races, and Upon Their Natural, Geographical, Philological, and Biblical History* (Philadelphia: J. B. Lippincott, 1860), 122; Leonard Rogoff, "Is the Jew White? The Racial Place of the Southern Jew," *American Jewish History* 85, no. 3 (September 1977): 200–201.

172   *the "Curse of Ham"*: For the complex intellectual genealogy of the Ham thesis, see David M. Goldenberg, *The Curse of Ham: Race and Slavery in Early Judaism, Christianity, and Islam* (Princeton, NJ: Princeton University Press, 2003); Jonathan Schorsch points out that as a defense of racial slavery it is primarily a product of medieval Christian interpretation, not Jewish tradition. See Schorsch, *Jews and Blacks in the Early Modern World*, 135–65.

172   *"wrapt in his own affairs"*: Finestein, *Anglo-Jewry in Changing Times*, 191.

173   *Raphall's private affairs*: Sarna, *American Judaism*, 96; Goldstein, *A Century of Judaism in New York: B'nai Jeshurun*, 121.

173   *"no party-man"*: M. J. Raphall, "A.D. Russell, for Recorder," *Jewish Messenger*, October 19, 1860, 115.

173   *"impropriety of any intermeddling"*: Goldstein, *A Century of Judaism in New York: B'nai Jeshurun*, 120; Rock, *Haven of Liberty*, 237–38.

173   *By January 1861, those elites*: Dittenhoefer, *How We Elected Lincoln*, 1; Rock, *Haven of Liberty*, 227–29, 238–39.

175   *argument that scripture sanctioned*: The 1860 Republican Party platform invoked the Old Testament's restrictions on slave ownership as proof that American slavery, by contrast, was "without a peer for its cruelty." See Schappes, *Documentary History*, 405, 687 note 17; Noll, *The Civil War as a Theological Crisis*, 31–74.

176   *thrilled Southern propagandists*: In Richmond, a state representative introduced a bill to allow a rabbi to address the legislature, and cited Raphall in explaining why he thought the city's Jews deserved such an honor: "The Jew as well as the Gentile is equally part of our political system, and affected by our legislation . . . Nor perhaps is it inappropriate to remember here a late powerful and eloquent voice that has been raised by a learned Israelite in New York in vindication of that social institution in which our peace and welfare are vitally involved, and in defence of which we are now engaged in a struggle before (I might almost say against) the world." See *Richmond Daily Dispatch*, January 7 and 29, 1861; Rock, *Haven of Liberty*, 234; Schappes, *Documentary History*, 406; Rosen, *The Jewish Confederates*, 33; Bertram

W. Korn, *American Jewry and the Civil War* (New York: Meridian Books, 1961), 18.

176 *"It is a singular fact"*: *Evening Bulletin* (Charlotte, NC), January 19, 1861.

177 *group of prominent pro-South citizens*: Rock, *Haven of Liberty*, 234–38.

177 *sermon horrified abolitionists*: *Weekly Anglo-African* (January 19, 1861): 4; Jayme A. Sokolow, "Revolution and Reform: The Antebellum Jewish Abolitionists," in Sarna and Mendelsohn, *Jews and the Civil War: A Reader*, 135.

178 *"the sacrilegious words of the Rabbi"*: Heilprin later became a frequent contributor to *The Nation* and a close friend of its second editor, Wendell Phillips Garrison, son of William Lloyd Garrison. In the 1880s, Heilprin helped organize agricultural settlements in the United States for refugees from Russian and East European pogroms. Michael Heilprin, "Slavery and the Hebrew Scriptures: Reply to the Rabbi Raphall," *New-York Daily Tribune*, January 15, 1861, 5; Ferenc Raj and Howard Lupovitch, "Morality, Motherland, and Freedom: The Arduous and Triumphant Journey of Michael Heilprin to America," *Polin: Studies in Polish Jewry* 31 (2019); Ella McKenna Friend Mielziner, *Moses Mielziner, 1828–1903: A Biography with a Bibliography of His Writings* (New York: The Author, 1931), 224–34; Julius Stern, "Michael Heilprin: A Biographical Sketch," *Jewish Exponent*, October 27, 1899; Gustav Pollak, *Michael Heilprin and His Sons* (New York: Dodd, Mead, 1912); Max J. Kohler, "Jews in the Anti-Slavery Movement, II," *Publications of the American Jewish Historical Society*, no. 9 (1901): 49.

178 *"chief city of a slave state"*: Fein, "Baltimore Rabbis," 191; Nicholas B. Fessenden, "Baltimore's Immigrants and the Civil War," *Report of the Society for the History of the Germans in Maryland* 47 (2017): 63–80.

179 *"who can blame"*: Illowy's sermon was so attractive to the Southern position that a congregation in New Orleans invited him to become their new rabbi, an offer he accepted. Fein, "Baltimore Rabbis," 182–84.

179 *"The Jew has special cause"*: *The Rev. Dr. M. J. Raphall's Bible View of Slavery, Reviewed by the Rev. D. Einhorn, D.D.* (New York: Thalmessinger, Cahn & Benedicks, 1861). See also Weisman, *The Chosen Wars*, 165–68; Fein, *The Making of an American Jewish Community*, 97; Friedman, *Jews and the American Slave Trade*, 142–43; Kohler, "David Einhorn," 445–46.

181 *"Such are the Jews!"*: Another powerful response to Raphall's address came from Gustav Gottheil, a rabbi in Manchester, England. "How can we be silent," Gottheil asked, when the Torah is invoked to condone an institution of which it is, in fact, "one grand consistent utterance of condemnation"? See Gustav Gottheil, *Moses Versus Slavery: Being Two Discourses on the Slave Question* (Manchester: John Heywood, 1861).

181 *"one of the greatest blunders"*: Sarna and Shapell, *Lincoln and the Jews: A History*, 66; Temkin, "Isaac Mayer Wise and the Civil War," in Sarna and Mendelsohn, *Jews and the Civil War: A Reader*, 166–67; Marcus, *The Americanization of Isaac Mayer Wise*, 14; Heller, *Isaac M. Wise: His Life, Work and Thought*, 331–49.

182 *"Force will not hold together"*: Marcus, *The Americanization of Isaac Mayer Wise*, 14.

183   *"Pray, Sir? No"*: "The Secession," *The Israelite*, December 28, 1861.

183   *"We have no doubt"*: Sarna and Shapell, *Lincoln and the Jews: A History*, 77–78.

184   *"What can we say now?"*: "Silence, Our Policy," *The Israelite*, April 19, 1861, 334.

185   *a yearslong hiatus*: Yuri Suhl, *Ernestine Rose and the Battle for Human Rights* (New York: Reynal, 1959), 210–13; Kolmerten, *The American Life of Ernestine L. Rose*, 223–27.

187   *"a hindrance to the elevation"*: Kolmerten, *The American Life of Ernestine L. Rose*, 212.

187   *"Look at the present crisis"*: "Speech: 'A Defense of Atheism," in Doress-Worters, *Mistress of Herself*, 295–300.

188   *"no desire to take part"*: "Correspondence," *Jewish Messenger*, January 18, 1861, 21.

188   *agreed with "nearly all"*: Leeser blamed Northern radicals for their "ruthless spirit of intermeddling in matters which concern them not." Yet even he felt compelled to acknowledge later that year that "the Jews in the last 1800 years have certainly not tasted much happiness from the principle that one portion of society has been made for perpetual servitude and another are divinely authorized to oppress them." Lance J. Sussman, *Isaac Leeser and the Making of American Judaism* (Detroit: Wayne State University Press, 1995), 220; Barbara Straus Reed, "Isaac Leeser and *The Occident*: A Jewish Leader's Response to the Civil War," in *The Civil War and the Press*, ed. David B. Sachsman, S. Kittrell Rushing, and Debra Reddin van Tuyll (New Brunswick, NJ: Transaction Publishers, 2000), 235. For the role of Leeser's early years in the South in shaping his views of slavery and the Civil War, see David Weinfeld, "Isaac Leeser and Slavery: A Match Made in Richmond," *American Jewish History* 106, no. 3 (July 2022): 231–54.

188   *Einhorn faced even greater hostility*: Friedman, *Jews and the American Slave Trade*, 143–44, claims that Einhorn "had the courage to say what was in the minds of many of the 7,000 Jews of Maryland, the 2,000 Jews of Virginia, indeed of all 35,000 Jews who resided in the South on the eve of the Civil War." There is no evidence for this.

189   *"completely unheard-of audacity"*: Goldstein and Weiner, *On Middle Ground: A History of the Jews of Baltimore*, 90.

189   *On April 19, 1861*: Nelson D. Lankford, *Cry Havoc! The Crooked Road to Civil War, 1861* (New York: Penguin Books, 2007); George William Brown, *Baltimore and the Nineteenth of April, 1861: A Study of the War* (Baltimore: N. Murray, 1887). Brown was the mayor of Baltimore at the time of the riot.

190   *including Joseph Friedenwald*: "Pratt Street Riots," *Baltimore Sun* (April 16, 1961).

190   *Einhorn hunkered down*: Kohler, "David Einhorn," 445; Kohler, "The Jews and the American Anti-Slavery Movement," 150.

191   *"There is nothing so loathsome"*: Fein, "Baltimore Rabbis," 192. Einhorn's account of his flight from Baltimore and decision to remain in Philadelphia is in Schappes, *A Documentary History of the Jews of the United States*, 444–49, 690 note 1–692 note 12.

8. "No More Pharaohs . . ."

192 *August Bondi had grown used*: *Autobiography of August Bondi*, 71–72.

193 *some six thousand Jewish men*: The first attempt at a comprehensive list of Jewish Civil War soldiers appeared in Simon Wolf's *The American Jew as Patriot, Soldier, and Citizen* (1895), written in response to a critical article in the *North American Review* claiming that Jews had shirked military duty, could never be counted on as loyal citizens, and should therefore be prohibited from entering the United States. But Wolf's list is full of mistakes and omissions. In recent years, the Shapell Foundation has meticulously compiled a more accurate and comprehensive interactive online database with relevant images and documents. See www.shapell.org/roster; Adam D. Mendelsohn, "The Legacies of the Civil War for American Jews," in *Yearning to Breathe Free: Jews in Gilded Age America*, ed. Adam D. Mendelsohn and Jonathan D. Sarna (Princeton, NJ: Princeton University Press, 2022), 30–31.

193 *Civil War has been described*: Bertram W. Korn advances the "Americanization" argument in *American Jewry and the Civil War*; Adam D. Mendelsohn critiques it in "Legacies," 27–54.

194 *"tendency to trumpery"*: Adam D. Mendelsohn, *Jewish Soldiers in the Civil War: The Union Army* (New York: New York University Press, 2022), 224.

195 *"foul stimulants"*: Mendelsohn, *Jewish Soldiers*, 31.

195 *"attack of apoplexy"*: *Jewish Messenger*, April 26, and May 24, 1861; Rock, *Haven of Liberty*, 240; "The Israelites," *New York Times*, August 7, 1863, 1.

195 *a visit to Temple Emanu-El*: *Jewish Messenger*, May 3, 1861, 193.

196 *"Whether native or foreign born"*: *Jewish Messenger*, April 26, 1861, 124.

196 *"black republican paper"*: *Jewish Messenger*, June 7, 1861, 172; Morris U. Schappes, "Jews and the Civil War," *Jewish Life*, June 1954, 24.

196 *"the UNION, which we love"*: *Jewish Messenger*, May 17, 1861, 148.

197 *a businessman named Isidor Bush*: Another influential Jewish Missourian was Meyer Friede, elected just before the war as the first Jew to serve in the state legislature. Apologizing for speaking with an accent, Friede espoused the antislavery politics of his fellow German speakers. "When we left the Fatherland," he said in January 1861, "we were guided by the bright light of liberty burning through this land . . . The hearts of all German citizens beat with gratitude, love and devotion to the Union. They are ever ready to lay down their lives in its defense." See Walter Ehrlich, *Zion in the Valley: The Jewish Community of St. Louis, Vol. 1: 1807–1907* (Columbia: University of Missouri Press, 1997), 151–58; Peter Adams, *Politics, Faith, and the Making of American Judaism* (Ann Arbor: University of Michigan Press, 2014), 28; Wittke, *Refugees of Revolution*, 88; Sokolow, "Revolution and Reform, 129; Schappes, "Jews and the Civil War," 26; Leon Ruzicka, "Isidor Busch," *Judisches Archiv* 1 (1928): 16–21; James A. Wax, "Isidor Busch, American Patriot and Abolitionist," *Historia Judaica* 5 (1943): 183–203.

198 *"not as the Banker"*: Korn, *American Jewry and the Civil War*, 162. See also Michael Kazin, *What It Took to Win: A History of the Democratic Party* (New York: Farrar, Straus and Giroux, 2022), 46–50.

199 *"an earnest effort towards reconciliation"*: Sarna and Shapell, *Lincoln and the Jews: A History*, 88.

199   *Seligmans offered sizable donations*: Joseph Seligman further greased the contracting wheels by gifting the wife of New York's state treasurer a new silk dress. Mendelsohn, *Rag Race*, 167–68.

200   *"keep my hands clear"*: Mendelsohn, *Rag Race*, 184–86; Stephen Birmingham, *Our Crowd* (New York: Berkley Books, 1984), 80–86; Ross L. Muir and Carl J. White, *Over the Long Term . . . : The Story of J. & W. Seligman & Co.* (New York: J. & W. Seligman, 1964), 24–30. I have found no basis for the oft-repeated story that the Seligmans, who briefly spent some time in Selma, Alabama, left the South in protest over slavery.

200   *Nearly as many Jewish men*: Mendelsohn, *Jewish Soldiers*, 25.

200   *veteran of the Prussian army*: Leopold Blumenberg's brother, Rudolph, was convicted and imprisoned in 1861 for helping to organize one of the last illegal voyages of a slave ship out of the port of New York. He served nearly two years at Sing Sing before Lincoln pardoned him in exchange for offering information that helped the federal government suppress the illegal trade. See Ron Soodalter, *Hanging Captain Gordon: The Life and Trial of an American Slave Trader* (New York: Atria Books, 2006), 237–38.

200   *the 82nd Illinois Infantry*: In a speech thanking Chicago Jews for their support, Hecker compared the plight of Jews in Europe with that of Black people in America. His regiment included a company raised and supported by the Jewish community of Chicago, though it was not, as has often been stated, an all-Jewish unit. Of 956 men in the regiment, only 23 were Jews. Mendelsohn, *Jewish Soldiers*, 76.

200   *Salomon helped rescue*: "The Omnibus Riot: Testimony in the Case," *Chicago Daily Tribune*, July 17, 1862; "How the Late Omnibus Riot Occurred," *Chicago Daily Tribune*, July 19, 1862.

201   *Marcus Spiegel had been born*: See Jean Powers Soman and Frank L. Byrne, eds., *A Jewish Colonel in the Civil War: Marcus M. Spiegel of the Ohio Volunteers* (Lincoln: University of Nebraska Press, 1995), 1–19. Additional details about Spiegel's life and death are in the reminiscences of his daughter, excerpted in *American Jewish Archives* (1961), 191–99.

201   *"for the Constitution, the Union"*: Soman and Byrne, *A Jewish Colonel in the Civil War*, 62.

201   *"a nice a litte He nigger"*: Soman and Byrne, *A Jewish Colonel in the Civil War*, 177.

202   *"The poor devils"*: Soman and Byrne, *A Jewish Colonel in the Civil War*, 203–4.

203   *"whole Army is discouraged"*: Soman and Byrne, *A Jewish Colonel in the Civil War*, 230.

203   *"I do not . . . want to fight"*: Soman and Byrne, *A Jewish Colonel in the Civil War*, 226.

203   *letter to his brother-in-law*: Soman and Byrne, *A Jewish Colonel in the Civil War*, 260–61. At Spiegel's request, Greenebaum published the letter in the press.

204   *"see them jump"*: Soman and Byrne, *A Jewish Colonel in the Civil War*, 106.

204   *crossed the Ohio River*: Soman and Byrne, *A Jewish Colonel in the Civil War*, 181.

204   *implored the converted Caroline*: Soman and Byrne, *A Jewish Colonel in the Civil War*, 163.

204 *"a strong abolitionist"*: Soman and Byrne, *A Jewish Colonel in the Civil War*, 320–21.

204 *"such a torrent of shot"*: Soman and Byrne, *A Jewish Colonel in the Civil War*, 336.

205 *"[I]f anything does happen"*: Soman and Byrne, *A Jewish Colonel in the Civil War*, 147.

205 *"No more pharaohs"*: *Autobiography of August Bondi*, 92. The misquotation seems to have first appeared in Yankl Stillman, "August Bondi and the Abolitionist Movement," *Jewish Currents*, March 1, 2004. Simon Schama uses the line ("no more Pharaohs; no more Slaves") to show that Bondi "greeted the news of the emancipation proclamation Jewishly." He cites the excerpt of Bondi's memoir in Morris U. Schappes's *A Documentary History of the Jews of the United States* and recommends the reader explore Bondi's papers at the American Jewish Historical Society for further information. Neither the manuscript of Bondi's memoir at the American Jewish Historical Society nor the excerpt in Schappes features the quote. Schama also says Bondi's wife's father was "a prominent abolitionist," but there is no evidence that was the case. See Schama, *The Story of the Jews, Volume Two: Belonging, 1492–1900* (New York: Ecco, 2017), 520, 742 note 31; also Yvette Alt Miller, "The Jewish Conductor on the Underground Railroad," *Aish*, https://aish.com /jewish-conductor-on-the-underground-railroad/.

206 *The action Bondi saw*: *Autobiography of August Bondi*, 116.

206 *"it would expose them"*: Mendelsohn, *Jewish Soldiers*, 103.

207 *"I encourage all hands"*: *Autobiography of August Bondi*, 91.

207 *Bondi's war ended*: *Autobiography of August Bondi*, 117–22.

9. "A Storm, Vast and Terrible"

209 *a rabbi in Chicago mulled*: Felsenthal's article is translated and published in "The Jews of the Union," ed. Bertram Korn, *American Jewish Archives* 13, no. 2 (November 1961): 161–69. Einhorn reprinted it in his *Sinai* newspaper.

210 *By 1861, Jews could be found*: Rabinowitz, "Nativism, Bigotry, and Anti-Semitism in the South," 437–51.

210 *rate of slave ownership among Jews*: Mark Greenberg, "Becoming Southern: The Jews of Savannah, Georgia, 1830–1870," *American Jewish History* 86, no. 1 (March 1998).

211 *"poor victims of abolition despotism"*: Rosen, *The Jewish Confederates*, 48.

211 *In Savannah, Jewish immigrants*: Rosen, *The Jewish Confederates*, 41. For the influence of the 1848 revolutions on the Confederate rebellion, see Andre M. Fleche, *The Revolution of 1861* (Chapel Hill: University of North Carolina Press, 2012); Ann L. Tucker, *Newest Born of Nations: European Nationalist Movements and the Making of the Confederacy* (Charlottesville: University of Virginia Press, 2020), 93–114.

212 *"one man never has the right"*: Jacob Weil witnessed Jefferson Davis's inauguration on the steps of the Alabama statehouse and confided to his brother that he thought Davis possessed "not the stomach nor the verstandt [the sense] to lead us through the struggle that ensues." Weil also noted that he enlisted in the Confederate Army against the advice of his friend, cotton broker Mayer Lehman. Letter from Leopold Jacob Weil to Josiah Weil,

May 16, 1861, Special Collections of the University of Memphis, MSS0049: American Jewish Archives selected documents, folder 113. See also Friedman, *Jews and the American Slave Trade*, 213; Patricia A. Hoskins, "'The Best Southern Patriots': Jews in Alabama During the Civil War," in *The Yellowhammer War: The Civil War and Reconstruction in Alabama*, ed. Kenneth Noe (Tuscaloosa: University of Alabama Press, 2013), 155.

212 *a Jewish contractor*: Barry Stiefel, "David Lopez Jr.: Builder, Industrialist, and Defender of the Confederacy," *American Jewish Archives Journal* 64, no. 1/2 (2012): 53–81; Johnny Dwayne Littlefield, "*David* and the David-Class of American Civil War Era Torpedo Boats of Charleston, South Carolina" (PhD diss., Texas A&M University, 2020), 87.

213 *donated $10,000*: Barnett A. Elzas, *The Jews of South Carolina* (Philadelphia: J. B. Lippincott, 1905), 221; Rosen, *Jewish Confederates*, 41; *New York Times*, January 4, 1861; Shari Rabin, "The 'Kingdom of Israel' in this town: Jewish Merchants in Antebellum Charleston," *Jewish Historical Society of South Carolina* 22, no. 1 (Spring 2017): 8–11.

213 *Jewish Charlestonian named Charles Moise*: See Hieke, *Jewish Identity in the Reconstruction South*, 113–14.

214 *Manasseh's Gap*: Rosen, *The Jewish Confederates*, 20.

214 *An Arkansas private*: Eli N. Evans, "Overview: The War Between Jewish Brothers in America," in Sarna and Mendelsohn, *Jews and the Civil War: A Reader*, 30.

214 *"it would unfavorably reflect"*: Rosen, *The Jewish Confederates*, 53.

214 *"I found in this country"*: "Isaac Hermann: A Hard-Hitting Private in the War Between the States," in *Memoirs of American Jews: Vol. 3*, ed. Jacob Rader Marcus (Philadelphia: Jewish Publication Society of America, 1956), 238, 260.

215 *ideal commissaries and quartermasters*: Rosen, *The Jewish Confederates*, 123.

215 *Col. Abraham Charles Myers*: Rosen, *The Jewish Confederates*, 13.

216 *Known fondly as the "peach man"*: "Raphael Jacob Moses: A Southern Romantic," in *Memoirs of American Jews, 1775–1865, Vol. 1*, ed. Jacob Rader Marcus (Philadelphia: Jewish Publication Society, 1955), 146–202.

217 *"It is but a very miniature"*: Elliott Ashkenazi, ed., *The Civil War Diary of Clara Solomon: Growing Up in New Orleans, 1861–1862* (Baton Rouge: Louisiana State University Press, 1995), 61.

217 *Alfred Mordecai, a North Carolina native*: Stanley L. Falk, "Divided Loyalties in 1861: The Decision of Major Alfred Mordecai," in Sarna and Mendelsohn, *Jews and the Civil War: A Reader*, 201–25; Bingham, *Mordecai*, 246–51.

218 *"eager demagogues, parsons"*: Rosen, *The Jewish Confederates*, 51.

218 *Friedenwalds of Baltimore*: Fein, *The Making of an American Jewish Community*, 98–99.

219 *"I never fully realized"*: Septima Maria Collis, *A Woman's War Record, 1861–1865* (New York: G. P. Putnam's Sons, 1889), 18, 73.

219 *Julius and Bertha Ochs*: Evans, "Overview," 30; Rosen, *The Jewish Confederates*, 264; Helene Schwartz Kenvin, *This Land of Liberty: A History of America's Jews* (Millburn, NJ: Behrman House, 1980). Adolph Ochs was married to a daughter of Isaac Mayer Wise.

219 *most explosively divided Jewish household*: "Philip Phillips: Southern Union-ist," and "Eugenia Levy Phillips: Defiant Rebel," in Marcus, *Memoirs of American Jews, 1775–1865, Vol. 3*, 133–96; Rosen, *The Jewish Confederates*, 288; David T. Morgan, "Philip Phillips, Jurist and Statesman," and "Eugenia Levy Phillips: The Civil War Experience of a Southern Jewish Woman," in *Jews of the South: Selected Essays from the Southern Jewish Historical Society*, ed. Samuel Proctor, Louis Schmier, and Malcolm Stern (Macon, GA: Mercer University Press, 1984), 95–120.

221 *Chaos engulfed the city*: Ashkenazi, *The Civil War Diary of Clara Solomon*, 343. When the federal troops occupied New Orleans, Solomon's friends at school began wearing black crepe bows on their shoulders to signify their state of mourning. She objected to the practice, for "our *cause* is not *dead*, it is only *sick*. The Yankees are here on a *visit*."

222 *Jews largely felt at home*: In 1861, Rabbi Max Michelbacher of Richmond asked Lee to permit all Jewish soldiers to return home to observe the High Holidays. Lee declined a mass furlough, noting to the rabbi, "I feel assured that neither you or any member of the Jewish Congregation would wish to jeopardize a Cause you have so much at heart." Individual soldiers, however, were permitted to apply to their commanders for leave.

222 *Jews were allowed to serve*: Sarna, *American Judaism*, 118. In 1861, Congress passed a law requiring all Union Army chaplains to be "regularly ordained ministers of some Christian religion," even though at least one congress-man, Clement Vallandigham of Ohio, had pointed out during the debate that it would exclude Jews from serving. The restriction was repealed, af-ter organized Jewish protests, in July 1862. Sarna, *American Judaism*, 116; Rosen, *The Jewish Confederates*, 16, 43; Korn, *American Jewry and the Civil War*, 29.

223 *"the Dictator in Washington"*: Gutheim supported the Confederacy through the war. But in the fall of 1864, he privately rebuked Alabama governor Thomas Hill Watts's reference to "a christian people" in a call for a day of fasting and prayer. Any official message in a state without an established church, Gutheim protested, "should be free from the least tincture of dis-crimination allusions." After the war, Gutheim returned to New Orleans. See William Warren Rogers, "'In Defense of Our Sacred Cause': Rabbi James K. Gutheim in Confederate Montgomery," *Journal of Confederate History* 7 (1991); Weisman, *The Chosen Wars*, 147.

223 *the old Jewish neighborhood*: Of the merger of the Charleston synagogues, Robert Rosen observes, "Secession on one level had ironically led to union on the congregational level." Rosen, *The Jewish Confederates*, 237, 312–13, 337; Korn, *American Jewry and the Civil War*, 52–53.

225 *"All the rest of us"*: Meade, *Judah P. Benjamin*, 165–66.

226 *"without the shedding of blood"*: Meade, *Judah P. Benjamin*, 273–75; Rosen, *The Jewish Confederates*, 70, 251–52. Benjamin's sisters were evicted from their New Orleans house when the Union Army arrived in 1862. At Benja-min's encouragement, they escaped to rural Georgia, where, with assistance from Benjamin, they lived out the rest of the war.

226 *Davis appointed him attorney-general*: Meade, *Judah P. Benjamin*, 168–69.

227 *"unusual and offensive style"*: Evans, *Judah P. Benjamin*, 123–26.

227 *Davis always backed Benjamin*: Meade, *Judah P. Benjamin*, 244–47; Rosen, *The Jewish Confederates*, 77; Traub, *Judah Benjamin*, 84–87. Jewish names *have* appeared on American currency, however. The initials of Victor David Brenner, the Lithuanian-born designer of the Lincoln Penny, can still be found microscopically engraved below the sixteenth president's shoulder, and several Jewish secretaries of the treasury have had their names printed on US dollars, starting with Henry Morgenthau in 1934.

228 *serving as scapegoat*: Evans, *Judah P. Benjamin*, 145–49. One charge against Benjamin was that the Louisianan had maintained his memberships in New York clubs, which was true. An unsuccessful effort to expel Benjamin from Manhattan's Union Club led to the secession of some seventy members and the establishment of the more Republican-leaning Union League Club. Frederick Law Olmsted was among its founders.

229 *Benjamin's European connections*: Evans, *Judah P. Benjamin*, 194–97. When Northern papers criticized Erlanger's loan to the Confederacy as reflecting poorly on all Jews, Isaac Mayer Wise took pains to remind his readers that Erlanger had been baptized and converted to Christianity, thus he was "not one of those common Jews and usurers." See Korn, *American Jewry and the Civil War*, 160.

230 *"fresh and buoyant"*: Traub, *Judah Benjamin*, 84, 97.

230 *experiment ended disastrously*: Traub, *Judah Benjamin*, 64–66; Meade, 123–26.

231 *crackdown on a gambling den*: William H. Russell, the war correspondent for the *London Times*, would write in his memoir that Benjamin's "love of the card-table rendered him a prey to older and cooler hands." See Evans, *Judah P. Benjamin*, 217–28; Meade, *Judah P. Benjamin*, 277–82.

232 *"as elegant a manner"*: Jules St. Martin did briefly serve as a private in the trenches outside Richmond. Meade, *Judah P. Benjamin*, 272.

232 *"The poor fool to try"*: Evans, *Judah P. Benjamin*, 145.

232 *"Why 'sinner'?"* The editor of Chesnut's diary, C. Vann Woodward, merely confirms in a footnote that St. Martin was "indeed Benjamin's brother-in-law and close friend." As Daniel Brook has written, Benjamin's early biographers "present . . . him as an almost farcically stereotypical gay man and yet wear such impervious heteronormative blinders that they themselves know not what they write." James Traub, Benjamin's most recent biographer and the first to explore questions related to his subject's sexuality, concludes that Jules served Benjamin "almost as a stand-in for Natalie." Regardless of whether their relationship was sexual, Benjamin's "infatuation" may have been "a means to indulge an otherwise repressed love of men." See Traub, *Judah Benjamin*, 90–91; C. Vann Woodward, ed., *Mary Chesnut's Civil War* (New Haven, CT: Yale University Press, 1981), 548; Daniel Brook, "The Forgotten Confederate Jew," *Tablet*, July 17, 2012.

233 *"A grander rascal"*: Evans, "Overview," 38.

233 *"'Mr. Davis's pet Jew'"*: Woodward, *Mary Chesnut's Civil War*, 288–89.

10. "You Are Jews"

234 *"oh what may this Book"*: Diary of Edward Rosewater, American Jewish Archives, Rosewater Family Papers, MS-503, box 4, folder 3.

235 *a wholesale invention*: For the story about Rosewater and the Emancipation Proclamation, see Albert A. Woldman, "Clevelander Announces Emancipation Proclamation to World," *Cleveland Plain Dealer*, February 12, 1939. See also Mendelsohn, *Jewish Soldiers*, 258 note 13. The 1957 film *Ready, Mr. Rosewater* can be viewed at https://ajcarchives.org/Portal/Default/en-US /RecordView/Index/1989.

235 *"The crowd was large"*: Not all is lost, however, for those eager to claim a role for Jews in the dissemination of Lincoln's hallowed words. A Washington stationery firm co-owned by Adolphus Simeon Solomons, an observant Jew born in New York, supplied the paper on which Lincoln wrote the final version of the Gettysburg Address. See Rachel Delia Benaim, "Why the Gettysburg Address Was Made to Last," *Tablet*, November 17, 2016, https://www.tabletmag .com/sections/news/articles/why-the-gettysburg-address-was-made-to-last.

236 *"pork-hating descendants"*: *New York Times*, December 25, 1862. "In the crucible of sectional conflict," Frederic Jaher observed, "was forged modern American anti-Semitism." Frederic Cople Jaher, *A Scapegoat in the New Wilderness: The Origins and Rise of Anti-Semitism in America* (Cambridge, MA: Harvard University Press, 1994), 170.

236 *"the Jew banker"*: Rock, *Haven of Liberty*, 246; Korn, *American Jewry and the Civil War*, 160.

237 *New York City draft riots*: Dittenhoefer, *How We Elected Lincoln*, 66–67; *Jewish Messenger*, July 17, 1863, 22; *New York Herald*, July 16, 1863, 1.

237 *"curbstone Jew brokers"*: Adams, *Politics, Faith, and the Making of American Judaism*, 35.

237 *"You are here solely"*: "The Lounger: An Open Letter," *Harper's Weekly*, August 1, 1863, 482; Mendelsohn, *Jewish Soldiers*, 126, 134–35, 285 note 31; Adams, *Politics, Faith, and the Making of American Judaism*, 35, 44.

237 *"the tribe of gold speculators"*: Mendelsohn, *Jewish Soldiers*, 285 note 31.

237 *character of "Mr. Shoddy"*: Mendelsohn, *Rag Race*, 170–72; Gary L. Bunker and John J. Appel, "'Shoddy' Antisemitism and the Civil War," in Sarna and Mendelsohn, *Jews and the Civil War: A Reader*, 311–34.

238 *an Associated Press reporter*: Korn, *American Jewry and the Civil War*, 163.

238 *"now is the time"*: Morton Borden, *Jews, Turks, and Infidels* (Chapel Hill: University of North Carolina Press, 1984), 67.

238 *"a coming storm"*: Sussman, *Isaac Leeser and the Making of American Judaism*, 226.

239 *"a beautiful City"*: Soman and Byrne, *A Jewish Colonel in the Civil War*, 188–89.

239 *"The Israelites have come"*: Jonathan D. Sarna, *When General Grant Expelled the Jews* (New York: Nextbook, 2012), 42–43.

239 *"greedy birds of prey"*: Fein, "Baltimore Rabbis," 188. When the war began, Tuska proclaimed, "The Jews of Memphis are ready, in common with their Christian brethren, to sacrifice their property and their lives in defense of southern rights."

239 *Even Union Army officers*: Adams, *Politics, Faith, and the Making of American Judaism*, 49; Sarna, *When General Grant Expelled the Jews*, 31.

240 *Jews "should receive"*: John Simon, "That Obnoxious Order," in Sarna and Mendelsohn, *Jews and the Civil War: A Reader*, 357–58.

240   *"All Cotton-Speculators, Jews"*: Ulysses S. Grant to General Joseph Dana Webster, November 10, 1862, in *The War of the Rebellion: A Compilation of the Official Records of the Union and Confederate Armies*, series 1, vol. 17, pt. 2, 337; Adams, *Politics, Faith, and the Making of American Judaism*, 54. Even before the war, Grant already had something of a nativist streak. Once, after losing a local election in St. Louis to a German immigrant, he had attended a meeting of the Know-Nothing Party. See Tyler Anbinder, "Ulysses S. Grant, Nativist," *Civil War History* 43, no. 2 (June 1997): 119–41.

240   *Henry Mack, a Bavarian-born*: Michael Rich, "Henry Mack: An Important Figure in Nineteenth-Century American Jewish History," *Stammbaum* 23 (2003): 1–10.

240   *struck an agreement*: Sarna, *When General Grant Expelled the Jews*, 47–48.

241   *"You are Jews"*: Sarna, *When General Grant Expelled the Jews*, 18.

241   *"no longer bear the taunts"*: It is worth noting that Philip Trounstine, the Jewish captain who resigned his commission, had been charged months earlier with mutiny and sedition for signing a petition "disrespectful" of a superior officer. Had he stayed in the army he would have faced a court-martial. See Sarna, *When General Grant Expelled the Jews*, 30; Mendelsohn, *Jewish Soldiers*, 129, 132.

241   *"So the children of Israel"*: Sarna and Shapell, *Lincoln and the Jews: A History*, 118.

242   *"the wisest order yet made"*: The exiled Jews from Paducah were not without their supporters. The *New York Times* regretted that the "freest nation on earth" had seen "a momentary revival of the spirit of the medieval ages." "Gen. Grant and the Jews," *New York Times*, January 18, 1863, 4; Adams, *Politics, Faith, and the Making of American Judaism*, 51.

242   *"darkest days of superstition"*: Adams, *Politics, Faith, and the Making of American Judaism*, 33.

242   *"the slightest apology"*: *Jewish Messenger*, January 16, 1863, 20.

243   *"We are still in bondage"*: Sarna, *When General Grant Expelled the Jews*, 28. In the spring of 1861, Leeser had criticized a pro-Union speech given by the Philadelphia businessman Moses Dropsie. "You better take care of what you say," Dropsie warned Leeser in a letter; "you are already on the suspected list, and you may be compelled to quit the city before long." Leeser wrote to the mayor of Philadelphia asking whether there was indeed such a list, "so that I may make in time the necessary preparations" to return to Germany, the land from which he had emigrated nearly forty years earlier. The mayor assured him there was no such list, and that "your loyalty has never been impugned, so far as I am aware." Korn, *American Jewry and the Civil War*, 46.

243   *printed the two texts*: *Memphis Daily Bulletin*, January 6, 1863.

243   *the birth of American Jewish politics*: See Adams, *Politics, Faith, and the Making of American Judaism*. Sarna explores the contrasts that American Jews perceived between their own treatment during the war and the advances made by African Americans in *When General Grant Expelled the Jews*, 35–36.

243   *"Are Israelites slaves?"*: *The Occident*, February 1, 1863.

244   *"insult the choice of God"*: *Jewish Record*, January 23, 1863.

244   *"knows of no distinction"*: Sarna, *When General Grant Expelled the Jews*, 14, 23.

245 *"If so many Negroes"*: Heller, *Isaac M. Wise: His Life, Work and Thought*, 344; Sarna, *When General Grant Expelled the Jews*, 36.

245 *"politely, but most emphatically"*: See Temkin, "Isaac Mayer Wise and the Civil War," in Sarna and Mendelsohn, *Jews and the Civil War: A Reader*, 173; and Bertram D. Korn, "Isaac Mayer Wise on the Civil War," in *Eventful Years and Experiences*, 125–50, and Korn, *American Jewry and the Civil War*, 42–43.

246 *"tended to the blessing"*: Heller, *Isaac M. Wise: His Life, Work and Thought*, 338, 346.

246 *"men of the pseudopeace"*: "A Farewell to Baltimore," in *American Jewish Archives: Civil War Centennial Northern* 13, no. 2 (November 1961): 156–61.

247 *"It would be petty selfishness"*: Korn, "The Jews of the Union," 159.

248 *"Bless Israel"*: David Einhorn, "A Sermon Delivered on Thanksgiving Day, 26 November 1863," in *Jewish Preaching in Times of War, 1800–2001*, ed. Mark Sapirstein (Oxford: Littman Library of Jewish Civilization, 2008), 199–210.

249 *"Agitate! agitate!"*: Anderson, *The Rabbi's Atheist Daughter*, 78.

250 Proclamation was a *"mockery"*: Rock, *Haven of Liberty*, 237.

250 *"If the President cannot move"*: Anderson, *The Rabbi's Atheist Daughter*, 121–53.

251 *"sight of thy soul-lit"*: Anderson, *The Rabbi's Atheist Daughter*, 121–22.

252 *"a lady of fine abilities"*: Kolmerten, *The American Life of Ernestine Rose*, 211.

252 *"ridiculous customs"*: Doress-Worters, *Mistress of Herself*, 311–33; Anderson, *The Rabbi's Atheist Daughter*, 126–32.

253 contact with American Jews: Sarna and Shapell, *Lincoln and the Jews: A History*, esp. 159–70.

254 Lincoln met Issachar Zacharie: E. Lawrence Abel, *Lincoln's Jewish Spy: The Life and Times of Issachar Zacharie* (Jefferson, NC: McFarland, 2020); Sarna and Shapell, *Lincoln and the Jews: A History*, 124–45, 178–82; Korn, *American Jewry and the Civil War*, 194–202. During a brief sojourn in Gold Rush–era California, where he made a fortune supplying miners from his store in Stockton, Zacharie performed what his biographer describes as "the first *bris* . . . on the Pacific coast." The podiatrist was "the only Jew in San Francisco with any skill with a knife." Abel, *Lincoln's Jewish Spy*, 39.

254 other perceived insults and abuses: Gen. Benjamin Butler, the Union general in New Orleans who had Eugenia Levy Phillips arrested, was known for expressing anti-Jewish sentiments. In an October 1862 letter about captured rebel smugglers, Butler wrote, "They are Jews who betrayed their Savior; & also have betrayed us." Mendelsohn, *Jewish Soldiers*, 116.

254 *"excepting his case"*: This note of Lincoln's would seem to undermine the usual triumphalist account that emphasizes how Lincoln overturned Grant's discriminatory Order No. 11 banning Jews from the district entirely. He did, but he had also known about the earlier ban on Jewish railroad travel, and he did nothing. See Abel, *Lincoln's Jewish Spy*, 85.

255 *"never regret the interview"*: Zacharie's morning-after words to Benjamin could be, as James Traub notes, "a reference to a homosexual tryst," or simply its author's usual fawning over his encounters with powerful men. Unfortunately, Zacharie's biographer, E. Lawrence Abel, confuses things by

misprinting the quote as "the intercourse we had last night." The fan fiction evidently writes itself. See Abel, *Lincoln's Jewish Spy*, 129; Traub, *Judah Benjamin*, 110; Sarna and Shapell, *Lincoln and the Jews: A History*, 142. The letter is printed in Gary Phillip Zola, ed., *We Called Him Rabbi Abraham: Lincoln and American Jewry, a Documentary History* (Carbondale: Southern Illinois University Press, 2014), 59–60.

255   *foot doctor's peace plan*: Zacharie may have imagined that Lincoln would elevate him to high office. "[I]n this republican and enlightened country," Zacharie once mused, "where we know not how soon it may fall to the lot of any man to be elevated to a high position in the government, why may it not fall to the lot of an Israelite as well as any other?" Bertram Korn suggested Zacharie might have seen himself as potentially filling a similar role for Lincoln as Benjamin did for Jefferson Davis: a court Jew and diplomatic jack-of-all-trades. But he soon grew frustrated with Lincoln's delays: "He has it in his powers to stop all fighting in 24 hours if he would follow out my program." Zacharie believed that Lincoln and secretary of state William Seward were trying to take the credit for Zacharie's initiative as a way of blocking the bid that Zacharie's boss, General Nathaniel P. Banks, appeared to be making to replace Lincoln as the Republican presidential nominee in 1864.

256   *"the Jews, as a body"*: Sarna and Shapell, *Lincoln and the Jews: A History*, 181.

256   *Zacharie's final mission*: Zacharie continued to organize for Lincoln's election even after being shot in the face by an estranged business partner six weeks before the election. Abel, *Lincoln's Jewish Spy*, 146–49.

256   *Nearly 15 percent*: Mendelsohn, *Jewish Soldiers*, 26–27.

257   *conflict was largely absent*: As Adam Mendelsohn writes, those leaders' "conspicuous silences spoke as loudly as words." Mendelsohn, *Jewish Soldiers*, 30.

257   *"deprived millions of others"*: Mendelsohn, *Jewish Soldiers*, 196.

257   *"demagogues, fanatics"*: *New York Times*, May 1, 1863.

258   *more comfortable and prosperous existence*: Quite a different hypothetical scenario is entertained in Kevin Willmott's 2004 mockumentary *C.S.A.* The film envisions an alternate timeline in which a Confederate victory at Gettysburg (aided by French and British troops) leads to the takeover of Washington, DC; the capture, imprisonment, and exile of Abraham Lincoln; and the extension of the Confederacy—and slavery—across the whole of the former United States. In 1895, the Confederate Congress passes a bill banning all non-Christian religions. From his deathbed, Jefferson Davis opposes the bill, urging his compatriots to remember the services rendered to the Southern cause by Judah Benjamin and other Jewish Confederates. After the bill's passage, thousands of Jews flee to Canada, except for a select few who, thanks to Davis's lobbying, are permitted to remain on a Long Island reservation.

11. "This Otherwise Blessed Land"

259   *"vast bewildered chaos"*: Thomas Wentworth Higginson, *Army Life in a Black Regiment* (New York: W. W. Norton, 1984), 49.

259   *"magnificent trumpet tones"*: W. E. B. Du Bois, *Black Reconstruction in America, 1860–1880* (New York: The Free Press, 1998), 124.

260   *"Sound the loud timbrel"*: David W. Kling, *The Bible in History: How the Texts Have Shaped the Times* (New York: Oxford University Press, 2004), 218, though

it is misprinted as "land timbrel." Albert J. Raboteau wrote, "The slaves' identification with the children of Israel took on an immediacy and intensity which would be difficult to exaggerate . . . In identifying with the Exodus, they created meaning and purpose out of the chaotic and senseless experience of slavery." Quoted in Jacob Morrow-Spitzer, "The 'Theoretical Jew' Versus the 'Southern Jew': Black Perceptions of Jewish Whiteness in the Nineteenth-Century American South," *American Jewish History* 106, no. 1 (January 2022): 35.

260   *themes and images of Exodus*: See Eran Shalev, *American Zion: The Old Testament as a Political Text from the Revolution to the Civil War* (New Haven, CT: Yale University Press, 2013).

261   *"culture with Jews on the mind"*: Mendelsohn, *Jewish Soldiers*, 12.

261   *"God of Abraham"*: Rogoff, "Is the Jew White?" 33.

261   *"Prayer for Peace"*: Sarna, *American Judaism*, 117–18.

261   *"As Israelites"*: Rosen, *Jewish Confederates*, 333.

262   *"peculiar, chosen people"*: Herman Melville, *White-Jacket; or, the World in a Man-of-War* (Boston: C. H. Simonds, 1892), 144.

262   *"To Canaan, to Canaan"*: Oliver Wendell Holmes, "To Canaan," in *Proclaim Liberty Throughout the Land: The Hebrew Bible in the United States: A Sourcebook*, ed. Meir Y. Soloveichik, Matthew Holbreich, Jonathan Silver, and Stuart W. Halpern (New Milford, CT: Toby Press, 2019), 331–33.

262   *Union's theologian-in-chief*: Lincoln cited the Old Testament "about a third more times than he did the New." Sarna and Shapell, *Lincoln and the Jews: A History*, 2.

262   *"He, from Whom all"*: Sarna and Shapell, *Lincoln and the Jews: A History*, 206.

262   *"'judgments of the Lord'"*: Years later, Myer Isaacs, the editor of the *Jewish Messenger*, who had met the sixteenth president, reflected that Lincoln's "idea of atonement was the Jewish inspiration, 'let the oppressed go free.'" Adam Mendelsohn, "Before Korn: A Century of Jewish Historical Writing About the Civil War," in Sarna and Mendelsohn, *Jews and the Civil War: A Reader*, 11. For a contrary view that sees Lincoln's "political theology" as increasingly tinged by Christianity, see Noah Feldman, *The Broken Constitution: Lincoln, Slavery, and the Refounding of America* (New York: Farrar, Straus and Giroux, 2021), 312–18.

262   *wished to see Jerusalem*: Sarna and Shapell, *Lincoln and the Jews*, 214.

263   *notions of far-off Jews*: Jonathan D. Sarna, "The 'Mythical Jew' and the 'Jew Next Door' in Nineteenth-Century America," in *Anti-Semitism in American History*, ed. David A. Gerber (Urbana: University of Illinois Press, 1986).

263   *"worthy of the dark ages"*: *Richmond Dispatch*, January 16, 1863, quoted in Blau, "Paradoxical Toleration." 27.

263   *rabble of young men*: See Hieke, *Jewish Identity in the Reconstruction South*, 141–42; Patrick Q. Mason, "Sinners in the Hands of an Angry Mob: Violence Against Religious Outsiders in the U.S. South, 1865–1910" (PhD diss., University of Notre Dame, 2005), 211–12.

264   *Dodging the bullets*: "Heyman Herzberg: Civil War Adventures of a Georgia Merchant," in Marcus, *Memoirs of American Jews: 1775–1865, Vol. 3*, 115–32; see also Steven Herzberg, *Strangers Within the Gate City: The Jews of Atlanta, 1845–1915* (Philadelphia: Jewish Publication Society of America, 1978), 26–27.

264 *certain merchants*: Hieke, *Jewish Identity in the Reconstruction South*, 140.

264 *"un-Southern"*: Evans, "Overview," 28.

264 *"instead of being vassals"*: John Beauchamp Jones, *A Rebel War Clerk's Diary* (Philadelphia: J. B. Lippincott, 1866), 164, 221; Korn, *American Jewry and the Civil War*, 179; *Richmond Examiner*, December 20, 1862.

265 *Talbotton grand jury*: Hieke, *Jewish Identity in the Reconstruction South*, 142–5; Louis Schmier, "Notes and Documents on the 1862 Expulsion of Jews from Thomasville, Georgia," *American Jewish Archives* 32 (April 1980): 9–22.

266 *first Jewish student*: Of his first glimpse of war, Cohen wrote in his diary: "Last winter was indeed a little romance of excitement, of much pleasure, but its recollection is mingled with so much pain and can never be recalled without a sigh. Louis. Your name has stamped its self on my Life. In the doctrine of Counterparts my poor ebony Idol, you were mine and every event of that bright little life of mine last winter had entwined you with it." See Richard Kreitner, "A Savannah Poet," *Jewish Review of Books* (Summer 2024); Jason K. Friedman, *Liberty Street: A Savannah Family, Its Golden Boy, and the Civil War* (Columbia: University of South Carolina Press, 2024); Korn, *American Jewry and the Civil War*, 143; Rosen, *Jewish Confederates*, xii.

266 *"this peculiar race"*: See Korn, "The Jews of the Union," 139–43.

266 *"foul and wicked plot"*: Korn, *American Jewry and the Civil War*, 159, 168; Rosen, *Jewish Confederates*, 35, 70.

267 *"little Jew"*: Rosen, *Jewish Confederates*, 47; Korn, *American Jewry and the Civil War*, 167.

267 *move to ban Jews*: Korn, *American Jewry and the Civil War*, 178; Schappes, "Jews and the Civil War," 25.

268 *"fierce and passionate dissensions"*: Traub, *Judah Benjamin*, 116–19.

268 *"strictly legitimate"*: Meade, *Judah P. Benjamin*, 301; Rosen, *Jewish Confederates*, 80–81.

269 *"food for thought"*: Meade, *Judah P. Benjamin*, 290.

269 *"sincere conviction"*: Traub, *Judah Benjamin*, 115.

270 *Alone among top Confederates*: Meade, *Judah P. Benjamin*, 289–91.

270 *"slaves are in their proper sphere"*: Rosen, *Jewish Confederates*, 38, 322; Traub, *Judah Benjamin*, 121.

271 *broke his four-year public silence*: Evans, *Judah P. Benjamin*, 276–91; Rosen, *Jewish Confederates*, 83–85.

271 *"Are they in this country?"*: *New York Times*, February 13, 1865.

273 *ring of conspirators*: After the war, Thomas Conrad, a Virginia cavalry officer, claimed that Benjamin had paid him $400 in gold from the Confederate treasury to kidnap—though not assassinate—Abraham Lincoln. Records unearthed only twenty years ago confirmed the timing and the amount of the withdrawal that Conrad disclosed in his 1892 memoir. Benjamin may also have been aware of a plot to lay land mines outside the White House. That plot was only foiled when some Union cavalry troops stopped the conspirator and took him prisoner. A week later, Booth shot Lincoln. See Traub, *Judah P. Benjamin*, 132–33.

274 *"simply a measure of prudence"*: Warren F. Spencer, "A French View of the Fall of Richmond: Alfred Paul's Report to Drouyn De Lhuys, April 11,

1865," *Virginia Magazine of History and Biography* 73, no. 2 (April 1965): 178–88; Traub, *Judah Benjamin*, 126–27.

274   *"In one night"*: "Eleanor H. Cohen: Champion of the Lost Cause," in Marcus, *Memoirs of American Jews, 1775–1865, Vol. 3*, 362, 367.

275   *"We are fighting"*: "Emma Mordecai: The End of the Old South," in Marcus, *Memoirs of American Jews, 1775–1865, Vol. 3*, 324–48.

276   *"the great Disposer"*: Bingham, *Mordecai*, 259.

277   *"As the forefathers"*: Sarna and Shapell, *Lincoln and the Jews: A History*, 205.

277   *"Slavery was a disaster"*: Saltzstein, *Liebman Adler: His Life Through His Letters*, 92.

278   *"twice anointed high priest"*: Zola, *We Called Him Rabbi Abraham*, 146–48.

278   *"Messiah of his people"*: Fein, "Baltimore Rabbis," 193; Zola, *We Called Him Rabbi Abraham*, 157.

279   *"a son of Israel"*: Zola, *We Called Him Rabbi Abraham*, 142.

279   *"greatest man that ever sprung"*: Sarna and Shapell, *Lincoln and the Jews: A History*, 218; Zola, *We Called Him Rabbi Abraham*, 160–65.

279   *Morris Raphall praised*: Emmanuel Hertz, ed., *Abraham Lincoln: The Tribute of the Synagogue* (New York: Bloch, 1927), 169–72.

280   *"Right must be right"*: "The Flag and the Union," in Philipson, *Max Lilienthal, American Rabbi: Life and Writings*, 398–414.

280   *"Let us carry into effect"*: Zola, *We Called Him Rabbi Abraham*, 164.

280   *"die the most disgraceful"*: *New York Times*, May 1, 1865.

280   *believed that Benjamin alone*: Rosen, *Jewish Confederates*, 320–21.

281   *not receive a fair trial*: Evans, *Judah P. Benjamin*, 303–7.

281   *"his pleasant smile"*: Traub, *Judah Benjamin*, 128–29.

281   *"Let us bury"*: Meade, *Judah P. Benjamin*, 316; Alfred Lord Tennyson, "Ode on the Death of the Duke of Wellington," in *Selected Poems* (London: Penguin Books, 2003), 278.

282   *"the farthest place"*: Traub, *Judah Benjamin*, 138.

282   *Once in Florida*: See Rodney H. Kite-Powell II, "The Escape of Judah P. Benjamin," *Sunland Tribune: Journal of the Tampa Historical Society* 22 (1996): 63–67; Meade, *Judah P. Benjamin*, 318–25; Evans, *Judah P. Benjamin*, 319.

284   *"exposed to the tropical sun"*: Traub, *Judah Benjamin*, 142.

12. "Into the Light"

286   *"how thin the floor"*: See Cohen, *Encounter with Emancipation*, 149; Sarna, *When General Grant Expelled the Jews*.

286   *"keeps up the feelings"*: Mendelsohn, *Jewish Soldiers*, 189.

287   *"an inhuman institution"*: "Theological Department," *The Israelite*, July 3, 1868, 4; Goldstein, *A Century of Judaism in New York: B'nai Jeshurun*, 147–53.

287   *"not only worship"*: Greenberg, "The Significance of America," 163.

288   *"Barnum of the Jewish pulpit"*: Adams, *Politics, Faith, and the Making of American Judaism*, 118.

288   *"As proud as I am"*: Meyer, *Response to Modernity*, 248; Abraham Shusterman, *The Legacy of a Liberal* (Baltimore: Har Sinai Congregation, 1967), 23.

289   *"Here in America"*: Greenberg, "The Significance of America," 162.

290   *"I, who believe"*: "Eleanor H. Cohen: Champion of the Lost Cause," in Marcus, *Memoirs of American Jews, 1775–1865, Vol. 3,* 368.

290   *"The owner of two hundred"*: Korn, "Jews and Negro Slavery," 193–95.

290   *a woman once enslaved*: Libo, *Lots of Lehmans,* 6; Chapman, *The Last of the Imperious Rich,* 31; Sarah Churchwell, "'The Lehman Trilogy' and Wall Street's Debt to Slavery," *New York Review of Books,* June 11, 2019, https://www.nybooks.com/online/2019/06/11/the-lehman-trilogy-and-wall-streets-debt-to-slavery/.

291   *"Old London"*: Friedman, *Jews and the American Slave Trade,* 170.

291   *"Our grandfather bought"*: "The next day," the letter continues, "her husband came, demanding that she go back with him. She refused to, telling him that this was her home and her folks. The children all armed themselves with brooms and came and threatened him if he would take her." Herb Kaufmann, email message to author, June 24, 2023.

292   *the idea of a nation subjugated*: In 1893, the Richmond-based *Jewish South* newspaper compared the rebels' fate to that of the Jews: "they were crushed by irresistible odds, but the cause is still alive . . . its sacredness will be inviolable so long as the sun shines in this fair land of ours." Quoted in Webb, *Fight Against Fear,* 15.

292   *Moses Ezekiel*: See Lara Moehlman, "The Not-So-Lost Cause of Moses Ezekiel," *Moment Magazine,* September–October 2018; Clint Smith, "Arlington's Civil War Legacy Is Finally Laid to Rest," *The Atlantic,* December 23, 2023, https://www.theatlantic.com/ideas/archive/2023/12/arlington-cemetery-confederate-monument/676965/.

292   *"in defense of this glorious cause"*: Sarna, *American Judaism,* 123.

293   *"nasty voices"*: Hieke, *Jewish Identity in the Reconstruction South,* 149.

293   *"our Jewish friends"*: Hieke, *Jewish Identity in the Reconstruction South,* 121.

293   *"scattered nation"*: Vance had both personal and political motives for giving the speech. When Vance was arrested at war's end, in 1865, federal troops wanted to humiliate the corpulent governor by making him ride a weary mule thirty-five miles to the train waiting to take him north to prison. Seeing this, a Prussian-born Jewish hat manufacturer lent Vance a carriage. A few years later, Vance composed his speech, "The Scattered Nation," out of gratitude for the assistance and perhaps in a bid to court the votes, as one scholar has put it, "of a somewhat white minority in the struggle for southern white self-determination." Vance was among those who saw white Southerners as modern-day Israelites. In 1864 he referred to the people of North Carolina as "this suffering and much oppressed Israel." Returned to the governorship in 1876, Vance vowed to deliver the state "from the bonds of oppression and from the Egypt of reconstruction." A monument to Vance stood in a prominent public square in Asheville, North Carolina, until its removal in 2021. Until the early 2000s, the local chapter of B'nai B'rith had gathered around it every year, along with the United Daughters of the Confederacy, to commemorate Vance's support for American Jews. Selig Adler, "Zebulon B. Vance and the 'Scattered Nation,'" *Journal of Southern History* 7, no. 3 (August 1941): 357–77; Hieke, *Jewish Identity in the Reconstruction South,* 163.

294   *Confederate veteran Edwin Moise*: Rosen, *Jewish Confederates,* 346–49.

294 *"heroic band fighting"*: Bernard Baruch, *My Own Story* (New York: Henry Holt, 1957), 289. Some early accounts of the group's name even ascribe it a Hebraic origin. A newspaper in Savannah, Georgia, claimed in 1868 that "'Cu Clux Clan' . . . is interpreted in the English language, the 'Straw Club,' which is supposed to allude to the fact that Pharaoh required [the Jews] to furnish their own straw." Hieke, *Jewish Identity in the Reconstruction South*, 126, 179; Webb, *Fight Against Fear*, 18.

295 *By 1880, Jewish merchants*: Elliott Ashkenazi, *The Business of Jews in Louisiana, 1840–1875* (Tuscaloosa: University of Alabama Press, 1988), 28–29; Michael R. Cohen, *Cotton Capitalists: American Jewish Entrepreneurship in the Reconstruction Era* (New York: New York University Press, 2017), 414; Webb, *Fight Against Fear*, 13.

296 *Jews had less of a problem*: Commercial ties between Blacks and Jews did not always foster solidarity between the two groups. Jewish traders were just as willing to claim deeds to properties owned by Blacks as those owned by whites. Black Southerners who admired Jews as the model of a self-liberated people increasingly saw those actually living in their midst as exploiters who had betrayed them in order to enjoy the benefits of white supremacy. "The Jews have a grip upon the South of amazing strength," one Black journalist raged in 1884, "that makes masses of the ex-slaves worse off than ever, from the cruel 'grind' and extortion under which they live." For some Southern Jews' liberal attitudes toward Black people in the late nineteenth century, see Eric L. Goldstein, *The Price of Whiteness: Jews, Race, and American Identity* (Princeton, NJ: Princeton University Press, 2006), 59–61, 77. Still, Goldstein notes that Southern rabbis of the period "never challenged the basic structure of race relations in the South or advocated meaningful social equality for blacks. None argued for an end to segregation, or even for the protection of African Americans' right to vote and hold office."

296 *"America's first black-Jewish"*: Benjamin Ginsberg makes the case that Moses's notorious corruption—he remains known among South Carolinians as the "Robber Governor," ranked as the worst chief executive in state history—was overstated and that he had really earned enmity by defending Black civil rights. See Ginsberg, *Moses of South Carolina: A Jewish Scalawag During Reconstruction* (Baltimore: Johns Hopkins University Press, 2010).

298 *"identified himself with the Radical"*: Daniel R. Weinfeld, "Samuel Fleishman: Tragedy in Reconstruction-Era Florida," *Southern Jewish History* 8 (2005): 31–76; Patrick Q. Mason, "Anti-Jewish Violence in the New South," *Southern Jewish History* 8 (2005): 92; "The Murdered Peddler," *Jewish Messenger*, April 29, 1870, 5; Schappes, *A Documentary History of the Jews of the United States*, 515–17.

298 *In 1892, self-styled Whitecappers*: William F. Holmes, "Whitecapping: Anti-Semitism in the Populist Era," *American Jewish Historical Quarterly* 63, no. 3 (March 1974): 244–61.

299 *most Southern whites opposed*: As Patrick Mason writes, "elites advocated social violence as a surgical instrument to be used in certain situations"—i.e., when a Black man looked at a white woman—"rather than a blunt weapon to be applied indiscriminately. They therefore encouraged some forms of vigilantism as necessary and good while condemning others as excessive and

dangerous." Mason, "Anti-Jewish Violence in the New South," 99; Holmes, "Whitecapping," 251.

299 *1893 eviction*: "More Intolerance," *Jewish South*, September 9, 1893.

300 *"The lowest, cheapest thing"*: Faulkner quoted in Rogoff, "Is the Jew White?" 216.

300 *"the aberration that proves"*: Mark K. Bauman, "A Century of Southern Jewish Historiography," *American Jewish Archives Journal* 59, nos. 1/2 (2008): 24.

301 *"trample mistaken Judaism"*: Anderson, *The Rabbi's Atheist Daughter*, 124, 136–38.

302 *"an ardent adherent"*: *Hebrew Leader*, May 21, 1869, 1.

302 *The Roses set sail*: Anderson, *The Rabbi's Atheist Daughter*, 141–46.

303 *"As her long avowed"*: Anderson, *The Rabbi's Atheist Daughter*, 162–68. Rose would have been eighty-two at her death, according to the date of birth she gave a journalist in the 1850s: January 13, 1810. Yet her Berlin conversion record dug up by Susan Higginbotham gives an earlier date, February 18, 1806.

304 *"series of alternative communities"*: Ellen Carol DuBois, "Foreword," in Doress-Worters, *Mistress of Herself*, xviii.

304 *her Jewish relatives*: Once again, Susan Higginbotham's research clarifies who the beneficiaries of Rose's will were: not the daughters of her half-sister through her father's second marriage, as previously believed, but the daughters of her own older sister, Sophie, who apparently lived in Berlin at the time Rose took refuge there to escape the engagement her father had arranged against her will. Higginbotham speculates that Rose may have listed her nieces as beneficiaries because "she wanted to reward Sophie's children for their mother's discretion concerning an episode she would not have wanted to make public": Rose's secret marriage and conversion in Berlin, nearly seventy years earlier. Susan Higginbotham, "The Early Life and Family of Feminist Ernestine Rose: New Findings and an Old Secret," *Journal of Genealogy and Family History* 7, no. 1 (2023): 3–7.

304 *"had been less honest"*: Sara Underwood, *Heroines of Free Thought* (New York: Charles P. Somerby, 1876), 267.

304 *"is not a Christian"*: Anderson, *The Rabbi's Atheist Daughter*, 151.

304 *"I doubt whether one"*: Anderson, *The Rabbi's Atheist Daughter*, 169. American Jews were ambivalent about embracing Rose on account of both her atheism and her non-Jewish husband. One twentieth-century chronicler who wrote a short sketch about Rose for young readers in a publication sponsored by the Jewish Education Committee confided to the historian Morris U. Schappes, whom she asked to fact-check her piece, that she had been told it would only be published on the condition that she left out those two embarrassing aspects of Rose's life. Letter from Isabelle A. Roth to Schappes, Morris U. Schappes Papers, American Jewish Historical Society, box 95, folder 8.

304 *"To enlighten and free"*: Underwood, *Heroines of Free Thought*, 268.

305 *"much prefer that no 'Life'"*: Traub, *Judah Benjamin*, 4.

306 *"a Political Exile"*: Gilmore, *The Confederate Jurist*, 81.

306 *"I am as much interested"*: Evans, *Judah P. Benjamin*, 342.

306 *"to have no harassing anxieties"*: Traub, *Judah Benjamin*, 148–51.

307 *"turned out to be an Englishman"*: Wigfall suspected that Benjamin and other Confederates in Europe had "divided among themselves all that is left of

Confederate funds." Traub, *Judah Benjamin*, 152; Hudson Strode, "Judah P. Benjamin's Loyalty to Jefferson Davis," *Georgia Review* 20, no. 3 (Fall 1966): 251–60.

307 *"if external influences"*: Evans, *Judah P. Benjamin*, 346.

307 *Benjamin reportedly borrowed money*: See the letter from Morris U. Schappes, commenting on David Brion Davis's review of Eli Evans's biography, in "Communications," *American Jewish History* 78, no. 4 (June 1989): 591–96, citing a self-published work by Klan defender Susan Lawrence Davis, *Authentic History: Ku Klux Klan, 1865–1877* (1924), 45–46. In his own reply to Schappes, David Brion Davis contests the accuracy of the story.

308 *"In speaking of his grief"*: Traub, *Judah Benjamin*, 154–57.

308 *"a necessity against which"*: Catherine MacMillan, "Judah Benjamin: Marginalized Outsider or Admitted Insider?" *Journal of Law and Society* 42, no. 1 (March 2015): 150–72.

309 *into the grave*: In 1924, a group called the Judah P. Benjamin Memorial Association purchased Benjamin's former plantation, Bellechasse, which they planned to turn into "the Mount Vernon of the South," a "Confederate shrine and a museum and a headquarters for . . . organizations of the Confederacy." At the dedication, Rabbi Max Heller of New Orleans proclaimed, "We consecrate this old mansion, this historic house . . . to be a place to spur the impulse of patriotism." When the Mississippi River flooded the grounds, as it had in Benjamin's day, the group tried to move the mansion a few hundred feet inland, but the effort damaged the structure. Eventually the house was taken over by squatters and left to rot. It was demolished in 1960. All that remains is the old plantation bell, which stands in front of the local library on Belle Chasse Highway, part of a monument sponsored by the United Daughters of the Confederacy in 1968. See Richard Campanella, "The Multiple Narratives of the Belle Chasse Plantation House," *Preservation in Print* (December 2019); Traub, *Judah Benjamin*, 162; Evans, *Judah P. Benjamin*, 108.

309 *victims of their own success*: John Higham, "Anti-Semitism in the Gilded Age," *Mississippi Valley Historical Review* 43, no. 4 (1957): 567; "Roundtable on Anti-Semitism in the Gilded Age and Progressive Era," ed. David S. Koffman, *Journal of the Gilded Age and Progressive Era* 19 (2020): 473–505.

310 *"respectable Jews"*: Benjamin Nathan—uncle and namesake of the future Supreme Court justice Benjamin N. Cardozo—was brutally murdered in his Manhattan townhome in 1870, a crime that was never solved. See *New York Times*, July 30, 1870. For the insurance controversy, see Jeffrey A. Marx, "Moral Hazard: The 'Jew Risks' Affair of 1867," *American Jewish History* 106, no. 3 (July 2022): 255–81; Cohen, *Encounter with Emancipation*, 25–27; Schappes, *A Documentary History of the Jews in the United States*, 510–14.

310 *new wave of persecution*: Adams, *Politics, Faith, and the Making of American Judaism*, 3, 102; Naomi W. Cohen, "Antisemitism in the Gilded Age: The Jewish View," *Jewish Social Studies* 41, no. 3/4 (Summer/Autumn 1979): 188–89.

312 *"the black man, like the Jew"*: Like other Black leaders at the turn of the twentieth century who praised the Jews' business acumen and cultural malleability, Washington believed Black Americans should model themselves on

the tenacity and collective self-dependence of Jews: "There is, perhaps, no race that has suffered so much, not so much in America as in some of the countries in Europe. But these people have clung together . . . Unless the Negro learns more and more to imitate the Jew in these matters, to have faith in himself, he cannot expect to have any high degree of success." Washington quoted in Morrow-Spitzer, "The 'Theoretical Jew' Versus the 'Southern Jew,'" 37–38. See also Rogoff, "'Is the Jew White?'" 220; Goldstein, *Price of Whiteness*, 18; Blau, "Paradoxical Toleration," 48. Clive Webb notes that Washington's praise may not have been entirely sincere, as he relied on Jewish donations to keep his Tuskegee Institute running. See Webb, *Fight Against Fear*, 32. See also Arnold Shankman, "Friend or Foe? Southern Blacks View the Jew, 1880–1935," in *Turn to the South: Essays on Southern Jewry*, ed. Nathan M. Kaganoff and Melvin I. Urofsky (Charlottesville: University Press of Virginia, 1979), 105–23.

312 *"All Jewish Americans are Caucasians"*: American Jews of the time were themselves uncertain as to whether they comprised a race, a religion, a people, or a nation, and they often used the words interchangeably. Isaac Mayer Wise, for example, could be wildly inconsistent, as Eric Goldstein writes, "often allowing spur-of-the-moment political motivations to override any concern for intellectual coherence." See Goldstein, *The Price of Whiteness*, 29–31, 57.

312 *"The white man will rule"*: In his book *Fight Against Fear*, the historian Clive Webb includes an astonishing anecdote about a Jewish Alabaman, Karl Friedman, recalling that for his 1937 bar mitzvah his family invited guests "to view a Saturday night lynching in downtown Birmingham." Webb, *Fight Against Fear*, 20.

312 *"It seems strange"*: *Weekly Louisianan*, October 4, 1879, quoted in Morrow-Spitzer, "The 'Theoretical Jew' Versus the 'Southern Jew,'" 52.

313 *"What right has the United States"*: See Webb, *Fight Against Fear*, 36.

313 *frenzy of institution building*: See Joseph Buchler, "The Struggle for Unity: Attempts at Union in American Jewish Life: 1654–1868," *American Jewish Archives* 2 (1949): 21–46.

313 *"This is no time"*: Rosen, *Jewish Confederates*, 278; Korn, *American Jewry and the Civil War*, 112.

313 *"the ruin and misery"*: Webb, *Fight Against Fear*, 12.

314 *increasing sense of difference*: See Mendelsohn, *Jewish Soldiers*, 217–18.

314 *"reconstruction with a vengeance"*: *The Israelite*, January 14, 1870, 8; February 21, 1873, 4.

315 *"grandest scenery imagination"*: Temkin, *Isaac Mayer Wise*, 188–89. In 1876, Wise remarried, to Selma Bondi, a distant cousin of August Bondi.

315 *daughter Helen eloped*: Reports of Helen Wise's scandalous marriage were reprinted as far away as Sydney, Australia. See *Evening News* (Sydney), September 25, 1878, 2.

315 *"half-civilized"*: Heller, *Isaac M. Wise, His Life, Work and Thought*, 586.

315 *more radical ideas*: Kauffman Kohler, David Einhorn's son-in-law and successor at Temple Emanu-El in New York, took over the helm of Wise's Hebrew Union College in 1903, three years after the founder's death.

315 *"nearest the Mosaic state"*: *American Israelite*, December 29, 1898, 4.

316 *"for most 15 years"*: *Autobiography of August Bondi*, 133; August Bondi, "Supplementary to My Reminiscences," August Bondi collection, American Jewish Historical Society, P-178, folder 1.

318 *"that Jehudim were active"*: August Bondi collection, American Jewish Historical Society, P-178, folder 7.

318 *"I do not regret a single step"*: *Autobiography of August Bondi*, 133.

Conclusion

319 *"Many men and women"*: In a critical "Canaanite reading" of Walzer's book, Edward Said argued that there is nothing especially progressive about the "irreducibly sectarian premises" of the Exodus narrative or the latter-day celebration of it as a prototypical revolution. Given that the Hebrews' liberation is followed by the violent conquest of Canaan, including the ruthless slaughter of men, women, and children, and the enslavement of the few allowed to survive, it is morally and intellectually wrong, Said wrote, to ignore the darker parts of the narrative and only celebrate the journey from bondage to freedom. Indeed, for Said, Walzer's celebration of the Exodus reflected the latter's unwillingness, shared by many liberal American Jews, to confront modern Israel's oppression of those latter-day Canaanites, the Palestinians. See Michael Walzer, *Exodus and Revolution* (New York: Basic Books, 1985), 10; Edward W. Said, "Michael Walzer's 'Exodus and Revolution': A Canaanite Reading," *Grand Street* 5, no. 2 (Winter 1986): 93. A subsequent round of salvo and countersalvo is in "An Exchange: 'Exodus and Revolution,'" *Grand Street* 5, no. 4 (Summer 1986): 246–59.

321 *once again hotly debated*: Brandeis University Press refused to publish Marc Dollinger's preface to a new printing of his book *Black Power, Jewish Politics*, because it argued that American Jews had benefited from "white supremacy." Ari Feldman, "Brandeis U. Press and a Historian Split over How to Talk About Jews and White Supremacy," *The Forward*, December 20, 2020, https://forward.com/news/460600/jews-white-supremacy-brandeis-black-lives-matter/; Ari Y. Kelman et al., "Open Letter: Brandeis University Press Is Silencing Debate," *The Forward*, December 23, 2020, Rogoff, https://forward.com/opinion/460889/open-letter-brandeis-university-press-is-silencing-debate/; Rogoff, "Is the Jew White?"

321 *others reject the term*: See Kylie Unell, "My Mom Is White and My Dad Is Black. Don't Call Me a 'Jew of Color,'" Jewish Telegraphic Agency, June 16, 2020, https://www.jta.org/2020/06/16/ideas/my-mom-is-white-and-my-dad-is-black-dont-call-me-a-jew-of-color.

323 *"I'm so sorry"*: *Finding Your Roots*, season 4, episode 1.

323 *turn of the twentieth century*: Having long defined themselves against the majority Christian world, there were "serious emotional liabilities," the historian Eric Goldstein has written, for Jews identifying themselves wholeheartedly with it. Eric L. Goldstein, "Introduction," in *"Jewishness" and the World of "Difference" in the United States*, ed. Marc Lee Raphael (Williamsburg, VA: Dept. of Religion, College of William and Mary, 2001), 3.

324 *"Alabama justice cannot be bought"*: Stephen J. Whitfield, "The Braided Identity of Southern Jewry," *American Jewish History* 77, no. 3 (March 1988):

379; Hasia Diner, *In the Almost Promised Land: American Jews and Blacks, 1915–1935* (Baltimore: Johns Hopkins University Press, 1977).

324   *"Seen in the light"*: Eric J. Sundquist, *Strangers in the Land: Blacks, Jews, Post-Holocaust America* (Cambridge, MA: Harvard University Press, 2005), 32.

325   *"the most urgent"*: Sarna, *American Judaism*, 310.

325   *"[I]n most Southern towns"*: Rabinowitz, "Nativism, Bigotry, and Anti-Semitism in the South," 447.

325   *Jewish pawnshop owner*: Webb, *Fight Against Fear*, 18.

326   *"walk humbly before God"*: Webb, *Fight Against Fear*, 129–38.

326   *"Sure, I felt sorry"*: Eli N. Evans, *The Provincials: A Personal History of Jews in the South* (New York: Atheneum, 1973), 326.

326   *"There would be no Negro problem"*: Webb, *Fight Against Fear*, 52.

326   *"found the $3 or $5"*: Webb, *Fight Against Fear*, 47.

326   *rabbis and other community leaders*: When they asked their meddlesome Northern counterparts not to get involved in the effort to desegregate the South, Southern Jews pointed to the racial inequalities of Northern cities, which, though it was not enforced by law, were segregated all the same. One Southern Jewish publisher criticized those who wanted Southerners "to fight and die for liberal causes, while in the North the same liberals move out when Negroes buy homes in their neighborhood." Webb, *Fight Against Fear*, 74.

326   *nineteen rabbis traveled*: "Bearing Witness: A Controversial 1963 Trip to Birmingham by 19 Rabbis," *Southern Jewish Life*, May 3, 2013, https://sjlmag.com /2013/05/03/bearing-witness-a-controversial-1963-trip-to-birmingham -by-19-rabbis/.

327   *"We have to play ball"*: Rabinowitz, "Nativism, Bigotry, and Anti-Semitism in the South," 450.

327   *When a Jewish grocer*: Emily Tamkin, *Bad Jews: A History of American Jewish Politics and Identities* (New York: HarperCollins, 2022), 102.

327   *History seemed to repeat*: Oral history interview with Burton Padoll, Jewish Heritage Collection (MSS 1035–224), College of Charleston Libraries; Allen P. Krause, "Charleston Jewry, Black Civil Rights, and Rabbi Burton Padoll," *Southern Jewish History* 11 (2008): 65–122; Bradley G. Levenberg, "Applying the Present to the Past: The Experiences of Five Civil Rights Rabbis in Context of Contemporary Leadership Theory" (PhD diss., Antioch University, 2021), 133–46.

328   *"How can we condemn"*: Whitfield, "Braided Identity," 377; Webb, *Fight Against Fear*, 63, 65; Janice Rothschild Blumberg, *One Voice: Rabbi Jacob M. Rothschild and the Troubled South* (Macon, GA: Mercer University Press, 1985), 75–78; P. Allen Krause, *To Stand Aside or Stand Alone: Southern Reform Rabbis and the Civil Rights Movement*, ed. Mark K. Bauman and Stephen Krause (Tuscaloosa: University of Alabama Press, 2016), 92–116.

329   *monthlong teachers' strike*: Jerald E. Podair, *The Strike That Changed New York: Blacks, Whites, and the Ocean Hill-Brownsville Crisis* (New Haven, CT: Yale University Press, 2004).

330   *Forman interrupted services*: Marc Dollinger, *Black Power, Jewish Politics: Reinventing the Alliance in the 1960s* (Waltham, MA: Brandeis University

Press, 2018), 149; "Black Manifesto," *New York Review of Books*, July 10, 1969.

330   *"almost all of his best friends"*: David Levine, *Bayard Rustin and the Civil Rights Movement* (New Brunswick, NJ: Rutgers University Press, 2000), 227; Bayard Rustin, "When Yesterday Becomes Tomorrow," in *When Yesterday Becomes Tomorrow: 125th Anniversary Celebration, Congregation Emanu-El of the City of New York, 1845–1970* (New York: Congregation Emanu-El of the City of New York, 1971), 45–46.

Acknowledgments

Many debts were incurred in the manufacture of this book—debts so staggering that, were this a few thousand years ago, I might have to forfeit my liberty to repay them. It is a relief to instead have the chance to acknowledge them in print. The oldest debt, itself nearly ancient at this point, is to Professor Eugene Orenstein, whose seminar set me on the long and winding course to writing this book. His marginal notes on my original paper were a spur to further and better research, while his encyclopedic grasp of American and Jewish history and infectious enthusiasm for both sparked a flame that remains lit all these years later. Zev Moses, founder and director of the Museum of Jewish Montreal, allowed me to immerse myself in the process of doing real-world history work and inspired me to dream of likewise creating something useful and lasting. (In the meantime, I write books.)

There were others over the years who, in some cases unbeknownst to them, clapped the idea for this project on the back and urged it on its way. Early in my tenure at *The Nation*, Peter Rothberg handed me his copy of *The Jewish Confederates* and suggested there might be more to be said on the matter. On long lockdown-era walks around Prospect Park, my newborn son in the stroller, Hamilton Cain encouraged me to pursue this topic rather than another, seeing it had grabbed me by the soul. Ian Becker, Sam Appel, and Matthew McKnight read early snippets and shared their thoughts. My thanks to Emily Bingham for taking the time to talk about the Mordecai family, and to Mandy Berman and Herb Kaufmann for sharing the family letter cited in chapter 12. Eran Bellin and Yitz Landes also directed me to useful material. I am grateful to the staff at the following institutions for their assistance: New York Public Library, Kansas Historical Society, American Jewish Archives, Cleveland Public Library, Jewish Museum of Maryland, Historical Society of Pennsylvania, Jewish Theological Seminary, University of Memphis, Mercer Museum (Doylestown, PA), Temple Beth El (Detroit), Jewish Historical Society of Michigan, and, of course, Center for Jewish History in New York.

I owe one of my greatest debts to my agent, Elias Altman, for whom I would gladly become hewer of wood and drawer of water. Early on he pushed me to think bigger about the topic, more empathetically and, ultimately, more historically, and he has remained engaged and encouraging along the way. Would that every writer had an Elias of their own.

Ever since he visited my cohort of wide-eyed *Nation* interns and talked about the practice of literary journalism and the art of writing (and publishing) serious narrative history for a general audience, I had hoped to someday have the chance to work with Alex Star. Getting to do so—and getting to know him—has been a joy. He has known at every step just what this book should be and what it needed. It is a great honor, especially as a mere colt, to lodge in such a champion stable. Thank you, also, to Ian Van Wye, Eliza Rudalevige, Stephen Weil, Rima Weinberg, Janine Barlow, and everyone else at Farrar, Straus and Giroux for turning my keystrokes into physical form and figuring out how to present them to the world.

When Isaac Mayer Wise sailed up the Hudson River in 1846 and admired the sun-speckled farmland on the banks of a broad bay, he glimpsed the promise and possibility of America. Had he, at that moment, glanced off to starboard and a little way up the slope of the highest hill, he'd have seen the spot where I live and where I wrote this book. Moving to Beacon and finding such a warm and lively community has been another dream come true. My thanks to everyone here for the hearty welcome, friendship, and encouragement. Also to the editors of *Hudson Valley* magazine for giving me a forum to explore my burgeoning interest in the region's endlessly fascinating history. I am deeply appreciative of my parents, Robin and Al Kreitner, and in-laws, Florence Berkowitz and Alan Siegelberg, for their support, encouragement, and enthusiasm for babysitting.

My wife, Brahna, has been unflaggingly devoted to this project and ensured I had the time and space to see it through to completion. Our fifteen-year conversation about Jewishness, America, and (occasionally) other topics nurtured my interest in this story at the beginning and has sustained it every step of the way. Her love is the secret sturdy backing against which everything I write is staked; it keeps the letters and lines pinned to the page rather than plummeting down through the bottom margin into nothingness. I have no words to express the depth and breadth of my gratitude. Only these: I love you. Thank you.

Finally, this book is dedicated to my grandparents, three of whom I was given the chance to know but all of whom have shaped my life in profound and persistent ways, even if only in passed-down memories. With immense love and admiration for her poise, presence of mind, and fortitude in the face of adversity, I dedicate it, in particular, to my dear bubbe, Muriel Lesonsky.

Index

A Note About the Author

Richard Kreitner is the author of *Break It Up: Secession, Division, and the Secret History of America's Imperfect Union* and *Booked: A Traveler's Guide to Literary Locations Around the World*. He has written for *The New York Times, The Washington Post, The Boston Globe, The Nation, Slate, Raritan, The Baffler, Jewish Currents,* and other publications. He lives in Beacon, New York.